Looking after
Antiques

Looking after
Antiques

Frances Halahan & Anna Plowden

THE NATIONAL TRUST

New edition published in 2003 by National Trust Enterprises Ltd,
36 Queen Anne's Gate, London SW1H 9AS
www.nationaltrust.org.uk

First published in Great Britain in 1987 by Pan Books Ltd.

Text © Anna Plowden and Frances Halahan 1987
Revised text © Frances Halahan 2003

No liability shall attach to any author, editor or publisher of this book for
action taken or refrained from as a result of any of the contents of this book.
That content is not, and is not intended to be taken as, advice specific to
individual antiques or goods. If an item is valuable or fragile, expert advice
should be taken before undertaking any treatment which is capable of
damaging it or affecting its value.

No part of this publication may be reproduced in any material form,
whether by photocopying or storing in any medium by electronic means,
whether or not transiently or incidentally to some other use for this
publication without the prior written consent of the copyright owner,
except in accordance with the provisions of the Copyright, Designs &
Patent Act 1988, or under the terms of the licence issued by the Copyright
Licensing Agency Limited of 33-4 Alfred Place, London WC1.

British Library Cataloguing in Publication Data
A catalogue record for this book is available from the British Library

ISBN 0 7078 0286 5

Line illustrations by James Robins

Picture research by Margaret Willes

Designed by the Newton Engert Partnership

Production management by Bob Towell

Phototypeset in Minion by SPAN Graphics Limited, Crawley, West Sussex

Printed and bound in China
Phoenix Offset

HALF TITLE: *Shoes belonging to William and Walter Straw, in the Sitting
Room of Mr Straw's House in Worksop, Nottinghamshire. The Straws looked
after their shoes by stuffing them with old paper: now acid-free paper would
be recommended for precious items.*

FRONTISPIECE: *Woodworm are no respecters of persons. Here they have
attacked a seventeenth-century masterpiece by Grinling Gibbons in the Carved
Room at Petworth House in Sussex. The lime of the carving has been attacked
to a greater extent than the oak backing, but the latter may well be more
modern. The National Trust has recently undertaken a major conservation
and restoration programme of the Carved Room.*

CONTENTS

OBJECTS

Acknowledgements

The basis of this book was created in 1987 when Pan published an edition written by the late Anna Plowden and myself. The original version could never have existed without Anna's drive and determination, and I am grateful to her family, especially Penelope Martin and William Plowden, for their support throughout this recent project. My own family and friends have also been exceedingly tolerant of the time needed to compile and write this book.

It would be impossible to complete such a comprehensive book without the advice and knowledge of friends and colleagues. In particular I would like to thank Foekje Boersma, Sophie Budden, Shona Broughton, Susie Clark, Jennifer Dinsmore, Patricia Jackson, Lindsey Morgan, Valentine Walsh and Amber Xavier Rowe.

I am very grateful to the conservators and advisers of the National Trust who had the laborious task of checking the text and helping to maintain the quality of information throughout the book: Nigel Seeley, Sarah Staniforth, Helen Lloyd, Christine Sitwell, Katy Lithgow, Chris Calnan, Jonathan Betts, Caroline Bendix, Anita Bools, Andrew Busy, Bob Child, Caroline Cotgrove, Christine Daintith, Ann French, Andrew Garrett, Brian Godwin, Rupert Harris, John Hartley, Kysnia Marko, Simon Moore, Christopher Nicholson, Trevor Proudfoot, Hugh Routh. Ultimately, however, I must take responsibility for any errors that I may have made.

Putting the book together has proved an enormous task. I am grateful to Helen Fewster, my editor, and Margaret Willes, my publisher, for firmly and patiently guiding me through the project, encouraging me when necessary, gently cajoling when I was dragging my feet, and for understanding what I was aiming to achieve. Thanks also must go to Margaret for researching the photographs, the illustrator James Robins who has skilfully interpreted my sketches and notes, and to the book's designers, Gail Engert and Martin Newton.

FRANCES HALAHAN, July 2002

Photographs: All the photographs are from the National Trust Photographic Library, with the exception of p.110, Christina Gascoigne, and p.125, Graham Wilson.

NTPL photographers: Bill Batten, pp.167, 214; Andrew Butler, pp.36, 88; Michael Caldwell, pp.102, 170; Nick Carter, pp.30 (RIGHT), 90, 134; Eric Crichton, p.127; Derek Croucher, p.135; Andreas von Einsiedel, pp.10, 13, 25, 29, 32, 41, 49, 53, 55, 58, 61, 69, 71, 76, 83, 85 (BELOW), 89, 93, 99, 118, 121, 122, 128, 133, 139, 141, 148, 159, 160, 173, 181, 182, 185, 195, 196, 202, 205, 209, 212, 217, 221, 223, 224, 230, 240, 243 (ABOVE & BELOW), Roy Fox pp.28, 113; Geoffrey Frosh, pp.1, 42, 65, 235, Jonathon Gibson, p.74; Dennis Gilbert, p.45; Fay Godwin, p.46; Ray Hallett, p. 204; John Hammond, pp.37, 50, 51, 52, 57, 67, 80, 84, 105, 114, 116, 138, 149, 161, 169, 178, 192, 207, 225, 226, 232, 234, 238, 242; Derek Harris, p.123; Angelo Hornak, pp.162, 165; Chris King, p.24; Nadia Mackenzie, pp.26, 44, 54, 68, 91 (ABOVE & BELOW), 103, 119, 126, 193; Rob Matheson, pp.2, 16, 17, 95, 106, 171, 190, 219; James Mortimer, pp.31, 199, 215; Ian Shaw, pp.59, 72, 144, 151, 158, 172, 179; Rupert Truman, p.78; Mike Williams, pp.85 (ABOVE), 187; Derrick E. Witty, pp.137, 208, 231

The photograph on p.37 is copyright the Estate of Edward Bawden.

The table on p.15 is reproduced by courtesy of Resource: The Council for Museums, Archives and Libraries.

FOREWORD

Dr Nigel Seeley, Head of Conservation, The National Trust

Even with proper care, all man-made objects deteriorate to some extent with the passage of time. Sometimes this deterioration is seen as enhancing their appeal – the patina of age. More often, however, it is viewed as merely disfiguring, or as a threat to their survival. In such cases the natural instinct is to look for a remedy, and to invoke conservation. Conservation is popularly seen as resetting the clock, and giving damaged or deteriorated objects a fresh start in life, but sadly this is not really the case. However clever we are, we cannot reverse deterioration – and we will never be able to do so – we can merely make cosmetic or structural improvements which are, hopefully, in sympathy with the original form of an object. Quite apart from any visual changes which may have occurred, deterioration inevitably results in a permanent loss of material evidence about objects, and generally also a loss of value. While some of this lost value may be regained by good conservation work, the lost evidence is gone for ever. Sometimes, it is true, the conservation process reveals information about an object which might otherwise have remained undiscovered – but not without cost in other respects.

There are many parallels between conservation and medicine – diagnosis, prevention, treatment, and repair. The dual approaches taken in this book may perhaps best be described as first aid and risk management, and the same rules essentially apply. As with human beings, no two objects are usually exactly alike, so there are no simple universal rules governing deterioration and conservation which can be passed on for all to employ. A detailed knowledge of the processes involved, and as much relevant experience as possible, together form a sound basis for getting things right.

Nor do we have all the answers – today we often find that work carried out by professional conservators some years ago is not as satisfactory or long-lasting as had been expected. There are always further improvements in materials and techniques on the horizon, and procrastination in conservation has often had real benefits for the objects concerned.

Collectors and other private owners frequently find themselves in a situation where they wish to have relatively modest objects cleaned or repaired, and the cost of having this done professionally is prohibitive. The temptation is then to 'have a go' themselves, usually employing common DIY materials which may be to hand, and the result – while often appearing to be an improvement visually – is more frequently than not detrimental to the long-term interests of the objects. The purpose of this book is not to provide collectors with a training in conservation. Rather, it sets out to explain some of the procedures which may be attempted by the non-specialist exercising due caution.

In the museum and gallery world today remedial conservation is increasingly being seen as a last resort, if not actually an admission of defeat. Ever more effort is being put into preventive conservation, designed to minimise the rate of deterioration in the first place, rather than to 'correct' it once it has taken place. This approach is less interventive, more cost-effective, and ethically preferable. The private owner can also take advantage of these developments to safeguard treasured objects by handling them in the right way, and by keeping them in an environment in which damage by light, heat, moisture, pollutants and living organisms is minimised or eliminated. Guidance on the routine care of historic objects is an important aspect of this book.

Professional conservators have usually been reluctant to write books aimed at the private owner or collector – they see this as being on a par with encouraging DIY surgery or dentistry. The reasoning behind this is understandable, but it does not wholly accord with the economics and practicalities of the real world. This book is based on the assumption that owners and collectors will always attempt to repair objects, and that some guidance is better than none at all. Conservators usually go through a period of at least three years' training, often devoted to a single category of object or material, and even then they require further working experience before they can be considered qualified to practise without guidance. Even then, no conservator claims to know all the answers, or is completely immune from making mistakes. While it follows, therefore, that the private owner or collector is ill-advised to try out complicated procedures or work on valuable objects, and will probably not be familiar with the ways in which decisions to carry out work in a particular manner are arrived at, it is also recognised that they will frequently try to 'improve' a deteriorated or broken object, often with detrimental results if no guidance whatsoever is available.

The purpose of conservation is not just (or even) to make an object look as if it is new. The approach to optimising its physical state and aesthetic value requires great experience, and these vary with individual circumstances. Once the desired result has been decided upon, an appropriate combination of the four principal conservation processes – cleaning, stabilisation, repair, and restoration – can be considered.

The aim of this book is to try to show how some conservation work can be done as safely as possible by owners of objects who are not themselves trained conservators. The bottom line is not to do more to an object than is absolutely essential. It should never be forgotten that many objects are becoming more desirable in their original state than when restored, nor that it is unwise to work on objects known or suspected to be rare or valuable, even if the processes seem simple. Finally – the outcome is likely to be better the more that is known about the objects concerned and, in case of doubt, professional advice is invaluable.

INTRODUCTION

Many people have possessions that they want to look after, be they inherited or bought on the spur of the moment at a market. The aim of this book is to help you to look after your collections. Rather than repairing things when they are broken, this is advice on reducing the risk of breakage and accidents, and slowing down inevitable decay. Museums, galleries and many historic houses have studied the causes of deterioration, and how best to protect objects. As a result, good housekeeping has regained its importance, and housekeepers are beginning to exert the sort of influence they had in the past. It is no coincidence that we have quoted the eighteenth-century manual of Susannah Whatman on the jacket of this book.

In order to look after our possessions, we need to have some understanding of the way they deteriorate, and the effect of our interaction with them. The more you know about objects and what happens to them, the easier it is for you to recognise problems and assess their condition. Once signs of deterioration and possible treatments are identified, you may be able to decide whether changing the conditions in which the object is kept will help, or whether you need to call in conservation advice. For example, if you want to clean a piece of sculpture without harming it, you will need to know what it is made from, its condition, the type of dirt that is to be removed, and whether or not a cleaning process is likely to cause damage.

You have, therefore, to think first of objects in terms of the materials from which they are made, rather than their function or cultural and aesthethic significance. For example, a gun, of wood and metal, may need the same kind of treatment and conditions as a clock made from the same combination of materials. You also, of course, have to consider the use of the object: it is likely that you will want the clock to run, but it may be neither necessary nor desirable to fire an antique gun.

The main part of this book is organised alphabetically by the most common materials, from amber through the various different types of metal (which behave differently from each other) to wood. Care of the most common objects made entirely or predominantly from these materials are discussed at the end of each section, for example, glass bottles in GLASS. However, some objects such as clocks, books and paintings are complex in their construction or have such special requirements that they have been given a section of their own, with frequent cross references to the relevant material section. Words or phrases in bold refer to the glossary, where special terms are defined, and which also provides more general information about the tools or treatment suggested.

LEFT: *The National Trust puts its properties 'to bed' each year at the end of the visitor season. This photograph shows the Boudoir at Berrington Hall in Hereford & Worcester, with objects wrapped in acid-free tissue to protect them from dust and light. The rug and its underlay have been rolled up, and furniture covered in loose covers.*

Conservation and Restoration

In English-speaking countries, conservation and restoration refer to two distinct processes, although both are concerned with the care of objects. The purpose of conservation is to slow down the rate that materials and objects deteriorate. This is done by taking preventive measures to limit the factors that cause decay and reduce the risk of damage. Good general housekeeping has an important part to play in such 'preventive conservation', as damage can then be noticed before it becomes a problem. In addition, threats like insects can be controlled, and the collection can be kept looking good.

Sometimes preventive conservation is not enough and the object may require treatment, known as 'remedial conservation'. This might be limited to stabilising the object so that the rate of its deterioration is slowed – 'minimum intervention', such as consolidating flaking paint – but it can also involve restoration. The latter might result in significant change to the appearance of the object, like the removal of discoloured surface accretions such as old varnish, or the replacement of missing parts – remodelling a finger or retouching an area of paint. Restoration is often undertaken for aesthetic reasons. For example, if the veneer is lifting from a piece of furniture, it must be re-adhered, otherwise it will continue to come off. However, if there are areas of lost veneer, it is not essential to replace them for the preservation of the furniture, although it may be desirable to do so to improve the appearance of the piece.

The degree to which objects are cleaned or restored is the subject of much debate, often influenced by fashion as much as by philosophical and ethical principles. Curators of collections on public view have different expectations from a private owner. They do not expect the pieces in their care to be used, and thus a chair need only be strong enough to remain upright, but must retain as much of the original finish as possible. The private owner, on the other hand, often does expect that chair to be able to withstand use. It may not be possible to make a clock run to time without significantly restoring the movement; for a collector this may be out of the question as the original mechanism is valuable, but a private owner may decide that having an accurate, working clock is more important than the state of the movement.

What can go wrong

The factors that work towards the disintegration of materials can be divided into two groups. The first – fire, flood and theft – are potentially disastrous. The second is more insidious, causing cumulative damage that can become critical if not checked.

DISASTERS

Fire, flood, storms, earthquake, vandalism, theft, accidents, terrorism, war: this list sounds terrifying, but all are possible. Museums, galleries and historic houses have experienced one or other of these – in recent years, major fires have broken out at Hampton Court Palace, Windsor Castle and Uppark in Sussex. Collectors and curators have therefore developed plans to avoid disasters, and to cope with them when they happen.

Fire and Flood

• Keep the building in good repair so that the risk of flood from the roof, blocked gutters, and plumbing is reduced.

• Check electrical wiring and portable appliances regularly to reduce the risk of fire.

• When maintenance or construction work is carried out, keep the building weatherproof, protect contents and take particular care in respect of flood or fire.

• Install smoke alarms and get advice on fire prevention from your local authority, fire service, etc.

• In the event of a flood or fire, seek conservation advice immediately on how best to salvage your collection. Correct handling and temporary storage can minimise the damage. Insurance cover might be affected if the objects are mishandled in the crisis.

• Avoid touching the surface of any object when it is wet, as wet surfaces easily mark. Once salvaged, allow objects to dry naturally and increase the ventilation, using a cool fan if necessary. Do not use heat. Items made of paper will require specialist drying facilities.

• Objects packed in black plastic or rubbish disposal bags may be mistaken for rubbish, so if you need to store objects temporarily in a bag, use one of another colour. Don't store wet objects in plastic bags or other airtight containers, otherwise mould outbreaks are likely.

THEFT

The local police will give advice on the most effective way of securing your home.

The following will assist police in recovering your objects:

• Make a list, giving a good description of each item, including any identifying features such as chips, cracks, or dents. Leave a copy of the list with a relative or solicitor for safekeeping.

• Take clear photographs of each object – front, back and underneath if there are any identifying marks such as the factory on ceramics, hallmarks on silver, or areas of damage. Where appropriate, mark the objects.

• When moving house, it is wise to pack and transport small objects such as watches and jewellery boxes yourself.

• Inform your insurance company if you take an object out of the house for any purpose.

Physical Damage

Physical damage, such as chips, breaks, creases, cracks, folds, tears and dents can occur to an object from handling, moving, or even an earthquake. Earthquakes and collapsing buildings are disastrous but unusual in many parts of the world. Day-to-day wear and tear is more common and can often be avoided by simple measures, such as not putting furniture in front of fragile paintings. Inappropriate repairs, vigorous cleaning, unecessary or incorrect handling and accidents during building work can all cause damage. Protecting objects against physical damage is usually a matter of common sense and thinking ahead.

Although vibrations are not the most likely cause of damage to most collections, the effects should still be considered. The most vulnerable materials are usually inorganic – glass and fine ceramics, which can shatter in extreme circumstances. Pastel drawings and objects decorated with powdery paint, such as ethnographic sculpture, are also at risk as the paint can drop off. Typical sources of vibrations include building work, road traffic, trains, or loud music. Even walking across a wooden floor may make the boards vibrate. As a result, objects standing on shiny or glass shelves can work their way to the front and eventually fall off.

You can guard against this by:
• Checking objects on shelves regularly.
• Keeping glass, ceramics and precious stones away from the source of the vibrations.
• Packing objects with cushioning materials when transporting them or while in store.
• Removing objects during construction work. Ideally they should be packed away until the work is complete.

HANDLING

• Handle objects as infrequently as possible.

• If you have to move an object, prepare a space to receive it. Ensure that your route is clear, free of electrical flexes or other obstacles, and have another person to open doors for you.

• Make sure your hands are clean before you touch any objects.

• Always wear clean **gloves** when handling metals, gilded frames and furniture, and with other objects unless you think they will reduce your grip. Gloves will protect the objects from the skin's salts and oils: this deposit can cause materials to mark or corrode, particularly metals and lacquer and other surface finishes. Fingerprints will gather dirt, and leave marks. Avoid using textured washing-up gloves, as they can leave marks that are difficult to remove.

• Remove rings, bracelets, long necklaces and chains which may catch on, or scratch objects. Buttons, belts and buckles should be covered up when lifting large objects to prevent damage to anything held against the body. Loose clothing such as scarves, skirts and open cardigans might also catch on objects: a protective overall is the ideal solution.

• Before picking the object up, check carefully for weaknesses such as cracks, old repairs, vulnerable parts, and remove anything detachable, such as lids. Use caution when lifting an object with a base, in case the base is loose and might fall off.

• Carry one object at a time and support as much of the weight as possible from underneath. Do not carry anything by its protruding parts, such as handles or arms.

• For smaller objects, place one hand underneath, and use the other to steady it. Small objects can be carried in shallow plastic trays or boxes lined with **acid-free** tissue paper. Wrap each piece in tissue paper or padding to prevent them knocking against each other. Padding can be made from rolls of scrunched-up tissue paper. Do not stack boxes on top of each other, or the lower ones may be squashed.

• Do not put so many items in a box that it becomes too heavy to carry safely.

• Make sure that objects do not protrude above the top of the box in case somebody tries to put something else on top.

• Do not stick labels or self-adhesive tape on the surface of an object. Use tie-on labels where possible. Identification numbers are often written on objects in large collections, but the method for doing this will vary with the materials. Your local museum will be able to advise you.

• Move large objects on a well-padded trolley. There should always be two people to hold it steady. Large, flat objects such as table-tops should be kept vertical.

• When using a ladder in a room, remove valuables to a safe place in case of accident. Use two people to move any but the smallest ladder.

If an object gets broken, pick up all the pieces, wrap them in tissue paper or put them in a good quality envelope and store them together until you can contact a conservator. Do not throw any of the pieces away thinking they are too small, as the conservator may be able to use them all. It is not advisable to attempt to make repairs yourself at the time of the accident.

Objects on display

• Position objects where they will not get damaged, so avoid putting breakable objects in risky places, such as immediately behind a door, or near flapping curtains. Make sure there is enough room for people to pass between furniture and a picture. Do not rest furniture against a wall hanging, or picture frame.

BELOW: *Glass domes have always provided attractive, excellent protection for objects on display. These domes, covering stuffed birds and ceramics, stand on the mantelpiece of the Dining Room at Calke Abbey in Derbyshire.*

- Make sure that pictures or other objects hanging on walls are securely fixed. If they fall, not only would they be damaged, but so would anything displayed underneath them.

- Cats and small children can knock objects from tables, window sills or mantelpieces. It is difficult to recommend any particular action for this, other than to chose your display area carefully, or to keep the potential perpetrators out of the room.

- Flowers and plant displays can mark the surface on which they are standing through water drips, pollen stains and scratches from the container, so avoid placing plants on rare or valuable furniture. If you do, place glass discs underneath that are appreciably larger than the bottom of the container. If the container is not too heavy, move it in order to water plants.

- Raise sculpture and other heavy objects a few centimetres/inches above the floor by placing them on battens or a plinth. This will make it easier to clean the floor, and to move the objects.

- Remove valuables from rooms in which building work or redecoration is taking place. Cover furniture and carpets with **dust-sheets**. Where possible, move furniture to the centre of the room.

Storage

- Cover objects in store with **acid-free** or **archival tissue** paper, a clean **dustsheet**, **washed calico** or **Tyvek**. Alternatively, pack them in archival-quality boxes with acid-free tissue padding to protect them from dust, pollution and physical damage.

- Do not pack objects in bubble wrap or polyethylene sheet for more than a few days, as problems, such as mould or corrosion, can occur from the lack of air circulation; also, dirt can be attracted by static electricity.

- Label clearly the contents of the box.

- Do not put heavy or large objects on high shelves. They will be safer kept on lower shelves.

- **Polyethylene foam** can be cut with a sharp knife or a scalpel to make shapes and indents that cradle and support the weight of an object more evenly. This is preferable to having all the weight resting on a rim or handle.

- Raise boxes or objects off the floor, on battens or wooden pallets to prevent them being kicked and to ensure some protection if there is a flood from a leaking pipe. This will also make them easier to move.

- Do not stack furniture or objects on highly polished furniture, as the surface is easily scratched.

Pests

Insects, birds, rodents and other vertebrates can severely damage or destroy objects by eating or shredding them to make a nest, or by staining them with urine and faeces. The nests of rodents and birds also harbour insects that can move into your collection.

The table on the opposite page lists the insects most commonly found in Northern Europe. However, it is important to remember that unusual and exotic insects can be imported with the objects. Collectors in tropical countries or locations with voracious insects must seek advice on pest control from their local museums.

Although the adults are what we usually see, it is the insect larvae that cause the damage. Eggs are laid in or near an object, and the larvae develop there and feed off it. The larvae of wood-boring insects can tunnel through the wood for up to 5 years, while a clothes-moth has a life cycle of about 6 months to 1 year. Once the adult emerges from the object, it will soon lay eggs and perpetuate the cycle unless it is terminated.

Guidance on recognising the signs of insect infestations and distinguishing between active and old infestations is given in the sections on relevant materials. If you think an object has an insect problem, immediately separate it from the rest the collection, and wrap it in polyethylene until you can arrange for treatment. Try to do this immediately; don't leave it for more than a month.

Good housekeeping is fundamental to controlling pests and inhibiting infestation. Crumbs of food, general dust and fluff are all that insects require to live off. Therefore it is important to keep the house, including attics and cellars, clean and to give a deep clean from time to time (*see* p.20). Before storing, clean or have cleaned dirty textiles, or costumes that have been worn. Check your collections regularly, particularly in spring and early summer.

Museums, galleries and historic houses often use **insect traps** to monitor insects as part of their **integrated pest management**. This degree of observation may not be necessary for most people, but if you have a collection of costume, or of objects particularly vulnerable to insects, it may be worth considering.

At certain stages in their lives, some insects need high humidity, so keeping the building reasonably dry helps to slow down their development. Make sure there are no missing tiles or leaky pipes. Check that drains and ventilation grills are not damaged and, if necessary, cover them with netting. Windows should be well fitting. Use netting and anti-perching products to prevent birds and squirrels nesting in chimneys and roofs.

When acquiring a new object, inspect it carefully before integrating into the collection. If in doubt, keep wrapped in polyethylene over the summer to see if any adult insects emerge.

Problems with rodents or squirrels are best dealt with by a pest control officer. If possible, use traps to eradicate vertebrates, rather than poison so that their corpses can be disposed of. When poison is used, the animals may die in an inaccessible area within the house, and provide food for insects.

Insecticidal dust and sprays can be effective. Museums, galleries and historic houses often use **desiccated insect powders** in dead spaces, ducts and storage areas. Some liquid insecticides based on permethrin have been specifically developed for historic collections. The solution can be sprayed onto shelves, floors and storage materials, but not directly on precious objects.

There is some evidence that high doses of lavender and cedar-wood oil act as insect repellents, and there are now some commercially available in **sachets**. A traditional pot pourri recipe of aromatic herbs may discourage insects, but as yet there is no scientific evidence for this.

In the past, insect problems were dealt with using chemical insecticides, either as a gas or liquid. This is less common now because of toxicity. Instead, the methods most commonly used are freezing, increased temperature, carbon dioxide, and oxygen depletion using nitrogen. All these methods are successful, but there are occasions when treatment has to be undertaken more than once to eradicate completely an infestation.

Freezing is most commonly used to kill larvae and eggs in textiles, books, natural history specimens and paper. It can be carried out in a domestic freezer, and so can be done at home. However,

Summary of the Most Common Insect Pests and Damage

PEST	TYPE OF DAMAGE	MATERIALS DAMAGED
Woodworm/Furniture beetle *Anobium punctatum*	Small 2 mm/¹⁄₁₆ in round exit holes, gritty frass in tunnels	Sapwood of hardwoods, ply animal glue, some composite cellulose materials and books
Death-watch beetle *Xestobium rufovillosum*	Large 3 mm/¹⁄₈ in exit holes, rounded frass in tunnels	Structural hardwoods, particularly when in contact with damp walls
Powderpost beetle *Lyctus brunneus*	Small 2 mm/¹⁄₁₆ in round exit holes, fine talc-like frass in tunnels	Starchy wood
Wood weevil *Euophryum confine*	Surface damage and holes on damp wood	Damp wood, paper and books
Carpet beetle *Anthrenus sp.*	Irregular holes in textiles, loose fur, short hairy cast skins of larvae	Bird and mammal skins, insect specimens, wool textiles
Carpet/Fur beetle *Attagenus sp.*	Irregular holes in textiles, loose fur, long banded cast skins of larvae	Bird and mammal skins, insect specimens, wool textiles
Webbing clothes moth *Tineola bisselliella*	Large irregular holes with quantities of silk webbing tubes and gritty frass	Wool, fur and feather textiles, bird and mammal skins
Case-bearing clothes moth *Tinea pellionella*	Irregular holes and grazed fabric with loose silk bags	Wool, fur and feather textiles, bird and mammal skins
Biscuit beetle *Stegobium paniceum*	Round exit holes and gritty dust	Dried food and spices, starchy plant specimens and seed heads, papier mâché, freeze-dried animal specimens
Cigarette beetle *Lasioderma serricorne*	Round exit holes and gritty dust	Dried food and tobacco, starchy plant specimens and seed heads, freeze-dried animal specimens
Spider beetle *Ptinus sp.*	Some holes or cavities, spherical silk pupal bags	Starchy dried plant specimens and seed heads, animal specimens
Booklouse *Liposcelis sp.*	Scratched and eroded surface of materials	Starchy paper and glues
Silverfish *Lepisma sp.*	Irregular scratched and eroded surface of materials	Damp paper and textiles, animal glue, Silverfish are very partial to paper labels on objects

Frass is the fine powdery debris left by insects and is mostly excrement, with fragments of the material it is boring through and eating

very fragile, old and valuable objects should be assessed and treated by a conservator. Problems can occur: an object may break, or staining may develop from condensation. Use a freezer thermometer to check that your freezer can reach -18°C or colder (most domestic models can do this). Wrap each object individually in plenty of **acid-free** tissue paper and place in closed polyethylene bags. Place in a freezer for 3 days at -30°C, or at least 7 days for -18°C. Remove the packets and allow them slowly to reach room temperature before unwrapping. If the packet is small enough, you can defrost in the fridge. Alternatively, find a cool spot – not a hot kitchen – for the defrosting process. Handle each bundle carefully when you remove it from the freezer, as it may be very brittle. Once at room temperature, clean the objects with a vacuum cleaner to remove eggs, insects, etc. The freezing can be repeated if it has not been completely successful. It should be remembered that this treatment will not prevent a reinfestation.

The heat treatment is a commercial method, used mostly for furniture, vehicles, farm instruments and larger items. The objects are gradually heated in a humidity-controlled chamber. The carbon dioxide and nitrogen oxygen depletion treatments can be used on any type of object. The items are placed in a humidity-controlled closed environment and exposed to high concentrations of the gas for a prolonged period. These are available either commercially or through a conservator.

Biodeterioration

Occasionally you will find mould or fungi, algae or lichen on objects. Algae, lichen and moss can grow on stone, wood, metal and other materials displayed outside. Mould will grow on any damp **organic material** and on some **inorganic materials** if there is enough dust and dirt for them to thrive.

Mould and fungi will eventually break down the material on which they are growing, causing it to weaken; wood rot is an example of the damage that micro-organisms can cause. In temperate as opposed to tropical climates, it is seldom that the conditions within a building cause such severe deterioration. The problem mostly associated with mould is staining. Mould appears as brown, orange, blue, white or black dots on the surface, and sometimes as long hairs.

If mould develops on an object, the first thing to do is to improve the conditions. Either move the object to a drier room, or improve matters within the room, for instance, the air circulation. Mould can probably be washed off stone and ceramic objects (*see* appropriate sections) but organic objects must be treated more carefully. Once the object is dry, take it outside on a sunny day and carefully brush the mould off the surface with a ponyhair or hogshair **brush**. By performing this outside, you prevent the spores from spreading to other parts of your collection. Protect yourself from the dust with a face-mask. Then clean the object as described in the appropriate section. Wash your cleaning brush thoroughly so that you do not spread the spores next time you use it.

It is difficult to remove any staining that does not come off with cleaning, especially from paper and textiles. For these, you must seek advice from a conservator. Likewise seek specialist help for treatment of cases of wood rot or dry rot.

In tropical climates, controlling mould is more difficult. Desiccating agents, such as **silica gel**, are often used in closed containers. Fungicides are not recommended as these may have a detrimental effect on the object.

Algae, lichen and moss can damage stone, brick and terracotta by their roots penetrating the surface and weakening it. In addition, some species produce small amounts of acid. These plants also attract water, encouraging metal corrosion. The safest method of removal is an annual light brushing and cleaning. Proprietary products are available but are not recommended for use on works of art. If the lichen, moss or algae are well established, removing them can damage the material on which they are growing. Objects placed under trees and in sheltered spots are particularly vulnerable, so these areas should be avoided if you want to keep your sculpture clean.

Light

Most people are aware of how light can change the colour of some materials, but it is not always understood how destructive light exposure can be. **Organic materials**, particularly textiles and paper, are badly damaged by light: it causes colour change and eventually makes the material itself break up. This can often be seen on the backs of curtains, or the tops of upholstered chairs by a window where the material disintegrates into ribbons. Newspapers turn yellow and become brittle if left in light for a few days. Light damage is cumulative and can be caused by artificial as well as day light. Direct sunlight is the most damaging.

There are a number of things that can be done to reduce the effects of light:

• Roller blinds and/or curtains can cut out direct sunlight and some daylight. There are blinds available that cut out most light, or you can use calico or similar material that lets in diffused light. Draw the blinds or curtains whenever a room is not being used.

• Rotate light-sensitive objects so that they are not on display all the time, and can be stored away in the dark. The pages of an open book may be turned, different covers used on a bed, watercolours and photographs substituted by others from store.

• Make loose covers for upholstered furniture.

• Place light-sensitive objects in darker parts of a room. Corridors and halls often have dimmer lighting, so can be better than living rooms for displaying textiles. Window walls can be quite dark, but check they are dry; often outside walls are slightly damp.

• Think about the interior decoration of your room. In a room painted in pale colours, there is often less need for stronger artificial lighting than darker schemes.

• Protect objects on display by using a curtain on the case or over a picture that can be drawn back for viewing.

BELOW: *The effects of light can be clearly seen in this detail of damask wallpaper at Uppark in Sussex.*

Ultraviolet light is not visible to the human eye, but is very destructive. Ultraviolet-absorbing filters cut down the total light damage by about half for a given level of illumination; the other half derives from the damaging components of visible light. The filters can be placed over windows or light sources (fluorescent tube or light bulb), or on a display case or picture glass. UV filters should not be adhered directly to historic or stained glass, and should be applied to windows by the supplier. Ready-made filters can be bought for fluorescent tubes. The filters usually last between 5 and 10 years, after which they lose their effectiveness. This effectiveness can be assessed by measuring with an UV light meter.

LIGHT

Visible light is measured in units of lux.

The recommended light intensity for very sensitive objects (watercolours, textiles) is about 50 lux.

Less sensitive objects are exposed at 100–200 lux.

The recommended maximum annual exposure for objects is in the region of 150,000 lux hours, i.e. 1500 hours at 100 lux, 750 hours at 200 lux per annum. This level of exposure applies to museums and galleries; private owners should be able to achieve much lower exposures, to the benefit of the objects.

Ultraviolet light is commonly measured in microwatts per lumen, the lumen equalling lux per square metre. UV light should be reduced to levels below 75 microwatts/lumen.

Materials and objects most sensitive to light include: watercolours, photographs, miniatures, embroidered fabrics, any dyed material, wood and other organic materials.

Humidity

The air contains water vapour – the precise amount varies from day to day, place to place. It is influenced by the weather, the state of a building (leaks, rising damp), heating systems, ventilation, and activities such as floor washing and drying clothes. People too give off water vapour, a crowd in a room will increase the humidity.

Effects
• high humidity can cause metals to corrode, mould to form, wood and other **organic materials** to swell, animal glues to soften – causing veneers to lift – and provides the preferred environment for insects.

• low humidity will make organic materials shrink and split because they contain water which will leave the materials in a dry environment. Textiles, paper and adhesive may become brittle, and furniture joints loosen. Again, veneers may lift.

• fluctuating humidity, for instance produced when central heating goes on and off, causes organic materials to change dimension. This is particularly problematic with objects made up of more than one material, as the different materials will swell and contract at different rates. For example, the wooden substrate of a painted wood sculpture may swell and contract with changing humidity, while the paint may not move to the same degree. Eventually they separate along the join and the paint begins to flake.

Certain objects and materials survive better at particular humidities. For example, wooden vehicles, carriage wheels, barrels and some machinery must be kept at quite high humidity levels, or the wood will shrink. Archaeological metal, on the other hand, has usually to be kept very dry or it will corrode. However, a painting in a house may have acclimatised itself to a fairly damp environment and may be damaged by moving it to the more controlled environment of a gallery.

Humidity is measured as **relative humidity**, which is altered by temperature changes in a room. When cold air is heated, the relative humidity will drop and become lower than the air outside. The central heating going on and off during the day causes the relative humidity to rise and fall. Relative humidity over and near a radiator is usually low and not the place for furniture and paintings.

Relative humidity is measured with a hygrometer. Museums, galleries and historic houses usually maintain a continuous record and monitor to keep objects within the environment that suits them best. The aim is to keep the relative humidity as steady as possible, within a range that is neither too high nor too low. It would be difficult to replicate this at home because the temperature would fluctuate unacceptably, but if you think it would be appropriate for your collection, a conservator would be able to advise.

A room with organic materials – a wood floor, a wool carpet, natural fibre curtains and wooden shelves – is likely to maintain a more stable relative humidity than a room with a stone floor,

A wardrobe at Dunham Massey in Cheshire, showing how wood can crack under changing humidity. Veneer is very thin by nature, and the wood has torn where two pieces have been attached to each other.

chrome and glass furniture and large, curtainless windows because these organic materials act as a buffer. Objects stored in an **acid-free** cardboard box with tissue paper will be more protected from changes than those stored in a plastic or tin box.

A number of practical measures can be undertaken to try to limit the effects of humidity without having to resort to full air-conditioning.

- Ensure the building is well maintained: the roof does not leak, the ventilation is good, the damp-proof course is not bridged or broken, windows fit well, there is good insulation.

- Use double or secondary glazing where possible to keep the temperature as steady as possible, as it reduces heat loss and solar gain.

- Place objects needing a steady environment out of any draughts.

- Avoid displaying objects sensitive to changes of humidity near radiators, fireplaces, hot or cold water pipes, or in hallways.

- Wet wash floors only when necessary, rather than as a matter of course.

- Do not keep objects in attics, where the temperature and thus relative humidity fluctuate, unless the attic is insulated.

- Use a cellar for storage only if it is dry and not in danger of flooding.

- Do not keep organic materials in very dry conditions.

- Use **archival quality** cardboard boxes and acid-free tissue paper for packing objects, rather than polyethylene boxes or metal tins (unless specifically recommended in the appropriate sections of this book).

- Avoid using spotlights, which throw out heat and dry objects out.

- Ensure there is good ventilation behind objects hanging on, or standing against an outside wall. Apply a moisture barrier, such as aluminium foil or **clear polyester film**, to the back of pieces of furniture, framed pictures, etc.

- Raise objects off stone, brick and tile floors. Stand them on a pallet tray or battens. If the floor shows signs of damp, the supports should be insulated with a moisture barrier such as thick polyethylene sheet.

- Use a heater attached to a humidistat in the winter to raise the temperature in a store enough to lower the RH to acceptable levels (*see* table below). A humidistat is the equivalent of a thermostat, but reacts to humidity and turns the heating on and off according to RH levels.

- If the conditions are severe and the collection very vulnerable, install a humidifier or dehumidifier. Consult a conservator who will advise on this.

Where there are only a few sensitive objects in a room, museums, galleries and historic houses try to control the micro-environment around the object. A picture may have a particular frame designed for it that enclose it with a buffer, such as **silica gel**, thus controlling the environment immediately around the picture. Archaeological metalwork is stored in sealed boxes with dry silica gel. Display cases are designed to hold a buffering material and maintain a certain relative humidity. The silica gel can be hidden underneath a plinth or in drawers that are perforated to allow for air circulation within the case. All these types of provision can be made with advice from a conservator.

RELATIVE HUMIDITY

Mould growth is not often encountered at humidities less than 65%RH.

Embrittlement and shrinkage usually become evident below 35%RH, although it depends on the level to which the collection is acclimatised.

Metals and alloys corrode at different RHs, but generally will not corrode below 45%, although archaeological metal may corrode even as low as 20%RH.

Most collections aim for a range of 50–65%RH with fluctuations of humidity in organic collections limited to less than 10% in 24 hours.

The ideal RH for humidity-sensitive collections is 50–60%.

Human comfort is from 30–70%RH.

The RH in a bathroom after a shower is *c.*90%.

The objects most sensitive to humidity fluctuations are miniatures, particularly on ivory, panel paintings, illuminated parchment or vellum manuscripts.

Good ventilation helps to reduce the risks of problems from high relative humidities.

Temperature

Some materials will not tolerate certain temperatures. For instance, wax melts at quite a low temperature, and a brief spell in sunlight can destroy a wax figure. Temperature affects the relative humidity (*see* above), and it is important to keep organic objects away from any source of heat as they may dry out.

Frost and freezing temperatures can damage stone, terracotta, and other porous materials if they are wet before becoming frozen. The damage is most commonly seen on flowerpots wintering outside. Very cold temperatures can make some materials, such as metals, brittle.

As the temperature rises, so does the likelihood of chemical reaction, speeding up the process of deterioration. Ideally objects should be kept at low temperatures, but in a house this cannot be incompatible with human comfort (*see* below).

Heat sources include artificial lights. It is important not to shine spotlights on objects. Fibre optics in display cases allow the objects to be illuminated without generating heat.

TEMPERATURE

The general recommendations, based on human comfort, are for an ambient temperature of 16–20°C/61–68°F. Usually the temperature is maintained lower in winter and higher in summer to reduce the contrast with exterior temperatures. Storage areas can be kept cooler, but no less than 5°C/41°F.

Photographic material benefits from being stored at as low a temperature as possible. It is often stored at 5–10°C/41–50°F.

Pollution and Chemical Damage

Gases, dust and dirt are all forms of pollution that can damage or disfigure.

The gases most detrimental to objects are the oxides of sulphur and nitrogen produced by combustion and motor vehicles, hydrogen sulphide produced by putrefaction, and ozone, which is often generated by electrical equipment or by the action of sunlight. Organic acids are released from various timbers, and formaldehyde from some grades of fibre board. Many adhesives, paints and dyestuffs, which might unwittingly be used for display purposes, are also the source of pollutants. Even we give off sulphur-containing compounds in our breath.

The effects of acidic vapours are to weaken materials containing cellulose, including linen, wool, silk, cotton and paper. Most metals will corrode in an acid environment, particularly if the humidity is high. Red rot, a problem found in leather bookbindings and other leather items, is caused by a combination of poor tanning methods and air pollution. The surface of stones based on calcium carbonate, such as marble and limestone, will be etched by acid rain and dirt, which results eventually in severe damage. Many compounds containing sulphur will tarnish silver, silver alloys, silver gilt, copper and its alloys, and alter some paints. Photographic material is particularly vulnerable to sulphur compounds and acidic gases. The rate of damage is exacerbated if the object is in close contact with the source of the gases, or is enclosed with them in an airtight container.

Occasionally materials used in the construction of an object can produce acid gases, such as for example, cellulose nitrate which was used to make beads and imitation tortoiseshell and ivory. Thus metal beads strung with beads of cellulose nitrate may suffer problems of corrosion.

Little can be done about pollution produced externally, which is often absorbed by the building and curtains before it has the chance to penetrate too far into the collection. But there are plenty of things that you can do to protect the objects within your home. Throughout this book you will see recommendations to use **acid-free** or **archival quality** materials, because they cause less damage than the more usual storage or display products such as mounting board, cardboard, newsprint or PVC that may give off acids. Proprietary cleaning materials are seldom recommended here because many of them contain ammonia or vinegar, or other potentially damaging products.

Particulate pollution or dust is another problem. The main sources are carpets, concrete floors, unsealed walls and other construction work, pets and even people who shed skin, hair and fibres. Dust and dirt on objects looks unpleasant, but the more the object is cleaned, the more we may wear away the surface. Good storage will avoid having to keep cleaning, so cover and pack objects when they are not being used. Well-fitting windows and doors will keep out sources of pollution, and display cases and glazed framing will protect, though these are not always possible or desirable.

Deterioration

The manufacturing process of some objects, or materials used in objects, can leave them inherently unstable and prone to deterioration. Cellulose nitrate has already been mentioned (*see* above), but there are many other examples. The standard mixture of raw materials to make glass has been altered to enable very ornate pieces to be made. As a result, some glass remains unstable: little can be done about this, except to keep the object in a stable environment. The production process for cheap paper uses wood pulp which eventually produces acids, thus destroying the paper. This is impossible to stop and again the best remedy is to keep paper in the best possible conditions.

Methods of construction also play their part in durability. Bone knife handles are usually stuck onto a metal tang of the blade and held by a ring or ferrule, often silver. If the bone is also pinned onto the tang, it is much more likely to split because of the restriction to its movement.

Many objects are made from a combination of materials, such as a lamp made of metal, wood and textile, or a tortoiseshell box with a felt lining, a wood carcass, tortoiseshell exterior with ivory inlay, and lock plates and hinges of metal. Ethnographic objects are often a combination of many materials including wood, skin, feather, shell and metal. The humidity level at which these objects are kept has to be very carefully monitored. Light levels also need to be controlled, especially for objects with organic materials. The more delicate the object, the more prone it will be to physical and environmental damage.

Even with serious cases of deterioration, it is not usually appropriate to dismantle the object to separate the incompatible elements, as this is ultimately even more destructive.

GENERAL ASSESSMENT

Inspect objects from time to time to make sure they are not deteriorating. Examine them carefully before cleaning to ensure this will not be damaging.

- Dust and dirt – are the objects being cleaned too much, is the dirt loosely attached or firmly stuck on? Are there already signs of damage from over-cleaning?

- Insects – these like dark and undisturbed places, such as pockets and folds of clothes and hangings, the backs of furniture. Are there signs of infestations, such as frass, larvae skins, clothes-moth webbing, holes, chewed areas, or even insects, dead or alive?

- Deterioration – look for colours fading or changing, mould or damp stains, flaking or lifting paint, cracks in wood, lifting veneers, corrosion or tarnish on metals, unravelling fringes on upholstery, finger marks, scratches and dents.

- Decoration – look for any form of decoration that could be damaged by treatment, such as paint, applied gems and niello.

Cleaning

There are two levels of cleaning a collection. The first is routine general housekeeping, maintaining the appearance of an object. The second is carried out less regularly, and is more likely to improve significantly the appearance of the object. Typically, an object would undergo the second level when newly acquired, or if it has been on display for a long time and has become rather grimy.

FIRST LEVEL

The best way to remove dust from objects is by flicking it off with a suitable **brush**, of ponyhair or hogshair, into the nozzle of the vacuum cleaner. Holding the vacuum cleaner nozzle in one hand and the brush in the other, you can dislodge and remove the dust from all the nooks and crannies more effectively, and prevent the dust being rubbed into the surface, or moving from one object to another. Brushes are now available especially for this purpose. Swap the brush for a clean one when it is dirty, and make sure that the metal ferrule does not scratch the surface – you can bind it with self-adhesive tape to cushion it. Once you get accustomed to this method of cleaning, it becomes very quick and extremely thorough. Do not use the brush attachment of the vacuum cleaner directly on the object: the strong suction is damaging, and the nozzle can knock the object. If the object is unstable, you may need someone to hold it steady.

Nylon net is usually placed over the nozzle for cleaning textiles, fragile painted surfaces and upholstered furniture. This prevents threads or paint flakes, tassels or other loose pieces being sucked into the cleaner. Upholstery and hanging textiles can be cleaned by using the smooth nozzle of the vacuum cleaner through a net frame.

A photographic **compressed air can**, readily available from camera shops, is very useful for blowing away dust from cracks and crevices on small objects and inside hollow ones.

Dusters and **microfibre cloths** are used for polishing flat surfaces. Hemmed dusters are preferable to ones with oversewn edges, as threads are less likely to come loose and catch on edges. A banister brush, available from good hardware and specialist shops, is useful for carved furniture. Avoid using feather dusters as the feathers can break and scratch surfaces. Dusters impregnated with cleaning materials are not recommended as they leave deposits on the surface that may be damaging.

If pieces of the object (eg. flakes of paint or pieces of veneer) come off during cleaning, keep them in a marked envelope until you can re-fix them or get help from a conservator.

Start at the top of an object or room so that any dust knocked down will be cleaned up later.

Spring clean once each year to help protect against insect infestation. This involves a thorough clean to remove accumulated dust from dark corners and high shelves. Clean behind objects, shelves, ducting, pipework, at the top of curtains, in upholstery. Vacuum under furniture, carpets, radiators, in drawers, the top of cupboards and shelves. Clean attics and cellars as well.

SECOND LEVEL

This should only be done occasionally. Before starting to clean an object, assess what it is made from and its condition. If you are in any doubt about what can be done, leave the object alone until you get advice from a conservator: there is always a danger of causing damage during cleaning. Conservation cleaning of objects can be slow and you do not always get spectacular results, but it can also be very rewarding.

Make sure you have all the equipment and material you need before you start. Make yourself comfortable in a clean, well-lit room with plenty of clear working space. It is important to be able to see well, and there are a number of magnifying devices on the market. If you are working on the object *in situ*, protect other objects nearby in case of an accident, and ensure you have good lighting.

Always test a cleaning method or solution in an inconspicuous corner before you start. Once you have begun a cleaning operation, keep an eye on the cotton wool buds or whatever you are using, to make sure you are not removing part of the object. If you think you might be removing more than you want, stop, leave the object alone and ask for conservation advice.

Very often the surface of an object does not clean evenly, so you can end up with a patchy appearance. This is particularly noticeable with stone, plaster, terracotta and similar materials. Under these circumstances, it is safer to clean lightly first, then to go back over the object if you think you can remove more dirt evenly. There are many instances when you have to accept that it is simply not possible to remove all the dirt.

The quality of dirt and method of its removal from a surface vary. The cleaning technique for one object may be quite different from another, because the materials used in their construction can react to different substances, and the dirt you are trying to remove may not be the same. To make it more complicated, you can find that a successful method of cleaning one object may not work as well on something that appears identical.

There are four types of cleaning: dry or mechanical, water, organic solvents, reagents.

Begin by removing all dust and dirt with a brush and vacuum cleaner, as mentioned above. Try to find out what is the best method of cleaning to use, starting with the dry method. If that is not successful, you can try the other three, with reference to the material sections in this book.

DRY OR MECHANICAL

Not to be confused with dry cleaning associated with textiles, dry or mechanical cleaning physically removes the dirt using an eraser, scalpel, fine wire wool, wire brush or other appropriate tool. If the right equipment is chosen, this can be a very successful cleaning method. It is easy to control and does not introduce chemicals, so is safe when used with care. But if used clumsily, or with the wrong equipment, a lot of physical damage can ensue. The object surface must be sound and in good condition, and the person cleaning it should have good eyesight and/or suitable magnification and lighting.

Soft **pencil erasers** are very useful for removing surface dirt from many materials other than paper: they will even take light tarnish off silver without scratching. Always use a soft plastic eraser or a putty type, rather than the more old-fashioned erasers with abrasive which can be damaging.

The **chemical sponge** mentioned in appropriate sections is made of latex, and is effective in picking up and removing dirt from all sorts of surfaces.

Microfibre cloths are fairly new on the market. Originally they were sold for cleaning camera lenses and spectacles, but now are also sold as household dusters as they pick up general dust, grime and greasy finger marks very effectively.

If you want to pick or scrape dirt off the surface, it is best to use as soft a tool as possible. **Bamboo sticks** are particularly useful for this. They are quite strong but will not usually scratch metal or hard stone, although they can inflict a lot of damage on soft limestones, alabaster and other softer stones and surfaces. If bamboo sticks appear to be scratching the surface, use **softwood** cocktail sticks instead. Bone knife handles, which you can sometimes pick up cheaply, can be removed from the knife and cut and shaped to form useful scrapers.

Wire wool is recommended in the section on metalwork for iron and steel, but is too abrasive to use on most surfaces. Wire wool is available in grades from very fine (grade 0000) to coarse (grade 3). For antiques, you must use only grade 0000, which you can obtain from specialist suppliers or well-stocked hardware shops.

Conservators often use a scalpel for gently removing layers of corrosion or dirt. It is an efficient tool, but can cause a lot of damage if not used carefully. A number 3 handle is mostly used with number 10 or 15 blades. When the blades are first removed from their packing, they are often slightly burred. This can scratch any surface badly, so just rub the blade gently on a fine sharpening stone. Take care as well not to cut yourself. Usually the scalpel is held almost parallel to the surface to scrape the corrosion or dirt off gently. It takes a lot of practice to use a scalpel successfully.

Mechanical cleaning is very important for certain specialist areas of conservation, such as removing corrosion or concretions from archaeological material. This type of work should always be carried out by a conservator.

WATER

Very often dirt can be removed by 'washing' an object. But before this is undertaken, it is essential to test that the surface will not be stained or damaged. Water may remove or damage paints, dyes and varnishes or other surface finishes, so it is always imperative that you test a small area before starting to clean.

Washing is seldom done by actually immersing an object in water, as too much damage can be caused and the dirt may be pushed further into the surface. The surface is washed using a dampened cotton wool swap or **cotton bud**. Roll the buds over the surface rather than rub, and change the cotton wool as soon as it is dirty. It is easy enough to buy cotton buds, but **bamboo sticks** with some strands of cotton wool wrapped round the end can be more efficient. Once you master the art of making these swabs, they are slightly more resilient and easier to use than the commercial ones. You can also make very small ones that are useful for getting into corners or detail of decoration. A practical way of removing the swab from the stick is to make a small hole in the metal lid of a jam jar (about 0·5–1cm/¼–½in wide). Then push the swab end of the stick into the jar and pull it out, scraping the stick against the side of the hole so that the bud is pushed off. Your dirty buds will be collected in the jar.

Throughout the book there is a distinction between tap water and other water, referred to as de-ionised, purified or distilled. Tap water contains a number of chemicals, espcially in hard water areas, so it is advisable to use purer water. Garages, chemist and pharmacies sell purified water, but larger quantities can be bought from specialist suppliers.

Water on its own is seldom effective in removing most dirt, so a detergent is usually added. Most commercial detergents contain colour, perfume, brighteners and other ingredients that are not needed for care of the object, and may be damaging. For this reason, a purer detergent, **conservation-grade detergent**, is recommended. Only a few drops are necessary. Make up a mixture in a jam jar or glass beaker so it is near where you are working. Do not have too large a quantity near you in case it gets knocked over.

Wherever possible, 'rinse' the surface when you have finished with the detergent mixture, going through the same process as using clean cotton buds and purified water (see above). It is often easiest to clean one area of the surface, then rinse it before going on to the next area.

Saliva is a very useful cleaning agent for surfaces that are suitable for wetting, though not everybody relishes the idea. It sometimes removes more than water because the enzymes in the saliva help to break down the dirt. Roll the cotton bud on your tongue and rinse the surface of the object with clean water afterwards.

ORGANIC SOLVENTS

A lot of dirt cannot be removed by water and detergent because the dirt does not dissolve in the water. In this case, other liquids are used, which may be more successful. The liquids are **organic solvents**, including **white spirit**, **alcohol** and **acetone**. They are slightly different from each other and dissolve different things. White spirit removes oils and waxes, alcohol and acetone are useful for resins and paints. They are not interchangeable. When using organic solvents, take care not to get them on the surface of furniture, varnished or painted objects or floors. Use them in a well-ventilated room and do not smoke. Read the health and safety information provided by the supplier.

Alcohol comes in a number of forms. In many countries it is possible to buy ethanol or absolute alcohol, but in others, such as the United Kingdom, the sale is restricted. Instead, you can buy isopropanol (propan-2-ol), which is almost as good as ethanol for cleaning. Purple methylated spirit (meths) is easy to find, but the colouring and other additives used to denature it can stain the object.

Occasionally, a mixture of organic solvents, or a mixture of water and an organic solvent is used (see **solvent mixtures**). One very useful mixture for cleaning painted surfaces and stone is sometimes referred to as the V&A mixture. Put 300ml/10fl oz of purified water with 300ml/10fl oz of white spirit and a small teaspoon of **conservation-grade detergent** in a screw-top jar. Close the jar and shake the mixture. A white emulsion will be formed. The mixture will gradually separate out, leaving the white emulsion on top and clear liquid below. Use the white emulsion for cleaning. Another useful mixture is either acetone or alcohol with purified water in a 1:1 mixture. A small drop of detergent may also be added.

Apply the organic solvents in the same way as described for water (see above).

Dichloromethane-based paint remover breaks down paint, waxes and oils and can be used on some objects (see appropriate sections). It must be washed off well with cold water or white spirit, and used according to the instructions. Do not heat it up as it can break down to produce an unpleasant gas.

REAGENTS

There are other chemicals mentioned in this book that are used for cleaning or treating an object by reacting with the material being removed. These are discussed in the appropriate sections, but it must be noted that they can also damage the objects and should be used with care and caution. They must also be rinsed off the object.

Polishing

Wax is often applied to objects as protection against dirt and staining, and sometimes to improve the appearance.

Beeswax polish is usually used on furniture because it gives a good, soft shine. Only a little is used, applied with a brush or cloth, and polished off.

On other objects, a **microcrystalline wax** is more widely recommended. It is harder and less likely to attract dust. Again, only a very little is needed and it should be polished before it dries, as it is hard to polish to a shine once it has hardened. It is also applied with a brush or cloth, as recommended in the appropriate sections.

Repairs

Repairing objects, particularly furniture, can be complicated and difficult as it requires a thorough understanding of the construction and nature of the object, and bad repairs can be both destructive and unsightly. Therefore only simple repairs have been discussed in this book. It is advisable to get conservation help if you need to repair valuable, fragile or very special objects.

There is a variety of methods for joining two pieces together. They can be mechanically joined using nails, screws, rivets, thread, etc. Some materials, such as metal or plastic, can be heated and welded or soldered. Some can be stuck with an adhesive. A combination of these techniques can also be used. **Adhesives** include inorganic cements and mortars, but are generally thought of as sticky materials which become solid. In the past, natural bitumen, waxes, gums, resins from plants and animal glues have been used for making and repairing objects. More recently, since the mid-twentieth century, a vast range of synthetic materials have become available and are used as adhesives. The production of adhesives is now a giant industry, with a wide range of objects – shoes, buildings, planes – constructed using them.

Although mechanical methods are sometimes used, especially for textiles, adhesives are usually preferred on other objects as they are less invasive and should not, if used correctly, damage or alter the object. Conservators select an adhesive that is known to last, sticks well to the material being repaired, is compatible with it and can be removed. The adhesive must not become brittle or discolour with time. If it is stronger than the material, it can cause the object to break or crack in another place. If it is too weak, the object may fall apart. For these and other reasons, the use of tough resins, such as **epoxy** and **polyester resins** and **cyanoacrylates**, is not recommended except under exceptional circumstances. Some adhesives, such as **PVAC (polyvinyl acetate) emulsion adhesive**, or 'PVA white glue' often used as wood adhesive, become insoluble and very difficult to remove after a few years, so they are no longer recommended. In the section on wood, **Scotch glue** is recommended because it holds wood together well, is flexible enough, is very durable and can be removed if necessary. It may appear a little old-fashioned and is slightly complicated to use because it needs warming, but it is successful.

Easily reversible adhesives are recommended in the book. These can be removed with a solvent, are known to be long lasting and are strong enough to hold many objects together. The ingredients are known, which is not always the case with commercial adhesives. Reversible adhesives are used as they have been found to be stable and they can be removed in the future if problems occur, or it becomes necessary to take the object apart.

A repair will only look good if the surfaces are well prepared and you have checked that the pieces join tightly. Otherwise, there will be an unpleasant gap along the break. Therefore, before sticking anything together, all the surfaces to be joined must be clean and old adhesive removed. Methods for removing old adhesives will vary depending on the adhesive and the material it is applied to. Sometimes it is easy to pick or scrape the old adhesive off, but very often a solvent has to be applied to soften it.

Remove as much of the old adhesive as possible mechanically, using a **bamboo stick** and scalpel, but make sure you do not damage the surface of the join by doing this. Test the solvents first and check the appropriate section of this book to assess whether the solvent is likely to damage the object. Apply a little of the solvent with a brush or on a cotton wool pad, and leave it for a few minutes to soften the adhesive. Remove what you can mechanically, or by wiping with more solvent.

IDENTIFYING ADHESIVES AND REMOVAL

• Scotch glue and gum arabic are brown to honey-coloured, and quite brittle. They will soften with water. Remove as much as possible by picking with a bamboo stick or scalpel. Soften the rest by painting a little warm water on the adhesive and scraping it off when it is soft. Some objects, such as ceramics, can be soaked.

• PVAC polyvinyl acetate emulsion adhesive (white wood glue) may be slightly opaque but is colourless and quite soft and flexible. It may go white and soften with water. It may be soluble in acetone.

• Shellac, used in the past as an adhesive and often found on ceramics, is dark brown and quite brittle. It may soften with alcohol. Remove as much as possible mechnically. Unfortunately it is not always easy to remove, and may stain the material it is used on. If it cannot be removed mechanically and with alcohol, try a little **dichloromethane-based paint remover** to soften the shellac. This may produce a purple dye that can stain the ceramic or other material.

• Solvent-based adhesives are commonly used for repairing objects, and are usually colourless in the tube. On an object, they may still be colourless, and often produce visible air bubbles. Should soften with acetone. Remove mechanically as much as possible first.

• Epoxy resins often look yellow and translucent. They are very hard, and will not soften in any solvent. Remove as much possible mechanically and then use a little dichloromethane-based paint remover. Paint it on the adhesive and scrape off the softened adhesive. Repeat until it has all gone. Wash well in cool water.

• Rubber adhesives are usually yellow/brown and very flexible. These are difficult to remove as they are not easily soluble. Remove mechanically.

• Plaster of Paris (gypsum plaster) is an opaque soft white material. Remove mechanically.

REPAIRING AN OBJECT

Occasionally there are a number of broken pieces; in this case, you will need to work out the order in which the pieces go together so that, in the process of reassembling, one section will not be locked out.

When joining two pieces together, apply enough adhesive to cover the surfaces of one of the joins, but not too much, otherwise the excess will dribble down the object. If there is a little excess adhesive pushing out of the sides of the join, let it dry, then cut it off carefully with a scalpel. If there is a lot of excess, remove it with a clean tissue before it sets. Try not to 'wash' it off with solvent, as this may weaken the join or may wash the adhesive into the body of the object, thereby discolouring it. Make sure that the join is well aligned and that the pieces are as close together as possible.

It is usually safest to stick two pieces together and let the adhesive set before sticking more pieces. You will need to hold the pieces in place until the adhesive has set. This can be done by just holding the piece, but often it helps to use some form of clamp. The clamping must not damage the object surface, and the holding method must be prepared before applying the adhesive. Small **carbon fibre clamps**, available from hobby shops, are very useful for this.

Rubber bands or cut-up bicycle inner tubes are another possibility. Self-adhesive tape can be used on ceramics and glass with a hard, sound surface. You may need to place some **silicone release paper** between the clamp and the adhesive to prevent them sticking together. Some padding, such as card, may protect the surface from being marked. Small objects, or pieces being repaired, can be propped up to hold them in place in a bowl of rice or lentils. Bowls of sand have often been used for this purpose, but the sand always seems to get stuck in the joins.

REMOVING SELF-ADHESIVE LABELS

Self-adhesive labels or tape can be very harmful: they can pull off the surface to which they are stuck when they are removed, or as they deteriorate. The adhesive can also corrode or discolour many materials. This is often very obvious on paper that has been repaired with self-adhesive tape.

If the surface is sound enough, try warming the label gently with a hair dryer, and carefully lifting it off with your fingernails. Sometimes you can use a solvent to soften the adhesive, and ease the label or tape up with an artist's paintbrush, but take care that the solvent does not damage the object.

Health & Safety

For your own well-being, make sure you obtain and read the health and safety advice for all the products you use. All chemicals, equipment and machinery should be treated with respect.

Manufacturers and suppliers should be able to supply on request a materials safety data sheet which includes all necessary precautions for the use, handling and storage of their product. In some countries it is mandatory to provide this information on request. Unfortunately the information is often difficult to interpret, but a pharmacy should be able to help. The packaging of most proprietary adhesives and cleaning materials contain an address or telephone number to contact for a data sheet.

- Suitable lifting and carrying equipment must be used for heavy objects, as damage can occur to backs, fingers and feet if lifting is not carried out correctly.

- When lifting a heavy object, bend your knees and keep your back straight as you pick it up and when you set it down.

- Wear steel-capped boots if you are moving heavy objects.

- Wear an appropriate mask or respirator, particularly when using paint remover or producing dust, or dusting off mould.

- Always work in a really well-ventilated room. If using chemicals, work outside if possible.

- Do not eat or drink near chemicals. Do not mix chemicals in eating or cooking pots, or with cutlery.

- Always wash your hands after handling chemicals and objects, especially before preparing food or applying make-up.

- Never smoke when using chemicals, particularly solvents. Not only are they flammable, but some of their fumes form very toxic mixtures if inhaled through a cigarette.

- If you are using solvents, adhesives or paint stripper and begin to feel peculiar or develop a headache, stop, go outside, take some deep breaths of air, and do not continue to work until you have improved the conditions. Put used cotton wool swabs in a lidded container and then put them outside to dry, to prevent the solvent on the swabs continuing to evaporate into the room.

- Do not sleep or sit in a room where you have recently used solvents or insecticide.

- If you get paint or adhesive on your hands, do not 'wash' them with solvents. Use a cream or gel hand cleaner, then wash them in soap and water.

- Solvents and detergents remove oils from you skin and dermatitis can develop. Most domestic rubber gloves will soften in solvents other than alcohol, so if you are planning to use any quantity of solvents, obtain neoprene **gloves** for acetone and nitrile **gloves** for white spirit and dichloromethane.

- Wear goggles to protect your eyes from splashes or dust. If you get any chemical in your eyes, wash them in copious amounts of water.

COMMON SOLVENTS & CHEMICALS

Acetone. Flammable, may cause headaches and/or sleepiness with over-exposure. Use in a well-ventilated area. Acetone removes the skin's natural oils. Use neoprene gloves.

Alcohol. Flammable, may cause headaches and/or sleepiness with over-exposure. Can produce a build-up of toxins over prolonged exposures. Use in a well-ventilated area. Dehydrating agent in contact with skin. Use nitrile gloves.

White spirit/Stoddard solvent/Turpentine substitute. Flammable. Use in a well-ventilated area. Tends to extract skin oils and dry out the skin. Use nitrile gloves.

Formaldehyde. This is sometimes found in wet natural history collections. Refer to health and safety sheets from the supplier. Combustible. Possible carcinogen and can cause skin sensitisation upon contact. Vapours aggravate mucous membranes and cause toxic headaches. Possible long-term cumulative effect. Use neoprene gloves.

Conservators

Throughout this book, the term conservator has been used to describe a professional who conserves and restores objects, although these professionals may refer to themselves as 'restorers'. You are recommended to seek specialist advice if your collection or individual objects are very rare and fragile, or of sentimental value to you. Many of the repairs suggested require high levels of dexterity – one slip of the scalpel or spillage of chemicals can damage irrevocably. So, if you are in any doubt as to how to clean or repair an object, seek specialist advice.

Conservators often work in a specialist field, and few individuals now work on all materials. Conservation companies may employ a range of specialist conservators to offer a broad service.

But how do you find a conservator? The conservation bodies listed at the back of the book may be able to provide information on professionals locally, but it should be noted that is not necessarily a recommendation. Similarly, if a conservator is not listed, it does not mean their work is not of a good standard. You can also enquire at your local or national museums or galleries. Although they too may be reluctant to make a recommendation, they should be able to supply you with a list of those working in your area. A reputable antique shop may also be able to help.

Once a conservator has been identified, you will have to evaluate their standard of work. If you are not familiar with conservation, this is difficult, but consider the following points.

• A reputable conservator is likely to be a member of at least one professional body.

• Ask details of their training and experience. Lack of formal training does not necessarily preclude somebody from being a good conservator, but lack of experience might.

• Request references from clients who would be prepared to vouch for their work.

• Ask to see reports and photographs taken before and after similar work they have done.

• Discuss in detail with them the methods they would consider using for the conservation of your object. A conservator should advise you on the options available, what work can be done, what cannot, and the cost of each stage.

• Discuss the final appearance of the object, so that you are both clear about what is expected.

• Obtain an approximate date of when the work will be finished. Don't expect either this, or the estimate of costs, on the spot. It will be necessary for the conservator to take time to examine the object and evaluate the work necessary.

• Your conservator should be prepared to give a written report at the end of the work, though you may have to pay extra for it.

• Ensure the workshop or studio are orderly and clean.

• Check security and insurance arrangements. Be prepared to organise the insurance cover for your object on their premises, or for them to arrange it, with the costs transferred to you.

• Agree transport arrangements with the conservator, and check that the object is covered for insurance in transit.

Conservation is a skilled and time-consuming business. A reputable conservator is likely to be busy with a waiting list. Most conservators charge for their work by the hour, so that the cost of conservation will not reflect the worth of the object – it takes as long to put together a broken cheap vase as a priceless one.

Traditionally conservators have been reluctant to advise the public on how much a non-specialist can do, but professionals are becoming more willing to explain what can and cannot be done to an object, and how it should be looked after. However, many of the tasks undertaken by conservators involve considerable manual skill, which a lay person may find difficult to carry out. You should regard your conservator rather like your solicitor or private doctor, and expect to pay for their advice and professional opinion. As with a solicitor or doctor, you should develop a working relationship and a good understanding.

A professional conservator cleaning a painting. He is using cotton swabs on bamboo sticks to remove atmospheric grime and discoloured layers of old varnish. He has a range of solvents that he would have tested before beginning work.

MATERIALS

Travelling case that belonged to Thomas Agar Robartes, heir to the Cornish estate of Lanhydrock, who was killed in the First World War. The case and contents provide a good example of a mixture of materials, all requiring different conditions and treatment: the case itself is of crocodile skin, the fittings are metal, the bottles are glass with silver tops, the brushes of bone or ivory, the visiting cards of paper.

Amber

Amber is a fossilised plant resin from conifer trees. Fossilisation means that the age of the resin is measured in geological terms, in millions rather than in thousands of years. The best known amber is found in a geological stratum on the Baltic coast and, as the result of a flourishing trade dating back to the Bronze Age, Baltic amber has reached many parts of the world. There are other fossil resins known as amber from different parts of the world and not all originate from conifers.

Amber can be translucent or opaque and ranges in colour from pale yellow to dark red; occasionally, pieces are found with insects or plant seeds trapped inside. It is used mostly in jewellery, but also to decorate furniture and to make small objects such as vases.

There are many false ambers made from glass, synthetic materials and non-fossilised plant resins. It is often difficult to distinguish between the genuine amber and copies without analytical equipment. However, genuine amber is warm to the touch and, if you rub it on a piece of wool, it may give off a faint smell of pine.

Problems

Amber is brittle and will crack and chip if it gets knocked. Bright light, sunlight and heat can speed up deterioration, make the amber brittle and change its appearance. **Organic solvents**, such as **alcohol** or **white spirit**, may dissolve the surface and leave it matt or crazed, so they should not used for cleaning amber, and products such as wax paste or fine abrasive cleaners containing organic solvents are not recommended. Perfume, hairspray and similar products also contain organic solvents and should not be used near amber jewellery. Do not soak amber in water to clean it, as this may make the surface cloudy.

Ancient and archaeological amber is very delicate and a conservator should be consulted about its handling, cleaning, display and storage.

RIGHT: *Amber elephant, now displayed in the White Drawing Room at Arlington Court, Devon. Most amber pieces are from the Baltic coast and brown in colour, but this is a much rarer piece, in red, brought back by Miss Chichester from her travels in China. It stands 15·25cm (6in) high.*

Handling

Amber objects are very delicate and should be handled as GLASS and CERAMICS.

Display

Amber objects must always be kept out of direct sunlight and placed away from radiators, open fires and other direct heat sources (*see* pp.17–18). Cleaning amber objects exposes them to potential harm so, if possible, keep them in a glass-fronted cabinet, where they will be protected from dust and dirt.

Storage

Wrap pieces of amber individually in **acid-free** tissue and store them in a cool, dry area. For extra protection, amber objects should be stored in boxes and amber jewellery in a jewellery box or a cotton or linen roll. Roll necklaces diagonally across the sheet of acid-free tissue and keep them as straight as possible to minimise the strain on the thread.

Housekeeping and Maintenance

Remove dust from objects with a soft brush.

Cleaning

If the amber is dirty, use a dry chamois leather or dry **microfibre cloth** to remove the dirt. If this is unsuccessful, wipe the surface with **cotton buds** dampened with a solution of warm water containing a few drops of **conservation-grade detergent** or a cotton bud moistened with saliva. Rinse with cotton buds dipped in clean water and dry immediately with a soft, clean cloth. Polish the amber with a soft chamois leather to restore the sheen.

If the amber is very scratched and the surface has turned matt, there is very little that can safely be done about it, but you could try gently buffing it with a dry chamois leather.

Repair

Rare, old or precious objects or jewellery should be repaired by a conservator. Minor repairs to modern amber can be carried out using a neutral pH emulsion **adhesive**. Do not use epoxy resin adhesive, as it is too hard and strong for amber.

A very brittle and friable piece of amber should be treated with particular care, and advice should be sought from a specialist conservator regarding strengthening or consolidating it.

Antler

Antler is a modified form of bone. It is an extra growth on the skulls of stags, reindeer, elk or moose and other even-toed ungulates. The outer layer of the antler is usually dark and somewhat rough. If antlers are mounted, they are usually backed on to boards using part of the deer's frontal bone or complete with the head or skull and possibly part of the neck. Antler has been used for making decorative items such as buttons and knife handles and, more recently, ashtrays and spoons. The Victorians used antler for making chairs, chandeliers and coat stands.

Problems

Antler is quite strong and durable. In very damp conditions, it can support mould growth. If the humidity fluctuates widely, antler can split, although it is mostly thin pieces of worked antler that are vulnerable.

Handling

Mounted antlers on heads should be handled as little as possible to prevent damage to the fur and skin. Where there is 'velvet' remaining on an antler, it should be handled carefully so that it is preserved. *See* NATURAL HISTORY.

Objects made from antler should be handled as described in the Introduction (*see* p.12).

Display

Display antlers where the **relative humidity** and temperature remain fairly stable (*see* pp.17–18). Avoid hanging antlers in direct sunlight or directly above radiators, open fires or other heat sources, as heat can damage antler and rising dust will settle on the head or antlers (*see* p.18). Do not hang antlers on a damp outside wall. Although antler is not as sensitive as IVORY and BONE, it still needs care.

Storage

Store antler objects in a cool, dark area free from damp (below *c*.65% RH). If the antler is attached to a head and it is going to be stored for a long time, you will need to protect it against insect attack (*see* pp.14–15). Objects made from antler should be examined periodically for insects and mould.

Wrap small objects in **acid-free** tissue. To protect large objects from dust, cover them with a clean **dustsheet** or drape acid-free tissue over them. *See* NATURAL HISTORY.

Housekeeping and Maintenance

Smooth antlers or objects made from antler can be dusted with a soft, clean duster or **microfibre cloth**, but antler with a rough surface should be gently dusted with a brush and vacuumed (*see* pp.19–20).

Smooth antler can be very lightly waxed with **microcrystalline wax** to improve its appearance.

Cleaning

If the antler is very dirty, wipe the surface with a soft, clean cloth or cotton wool swabs or buds dampened with warm water containing a few drops of a **conservation-grade detergent**. Do not use a household detergent. Rinse with a clean cloth or swab and clean water. Clean and dry a small area at a time and do not allow the surface to remain damp for long.

Knives with antler handles should not be immersed in hot water or placed in a dishwasher, because the heat, water and chemicals will attack the antler.

Repair

Small repairs to antler can be made using a neutral pH emulsion **adhesive** or an easily reversible adhesive.

Basketry

Basketry is one of the oldest of all the crafts: objects were made in basketry before they were made in pottery or textiles. Baskets have been made since about 5000BC and, in Europe, since about 2500BC. The materials used for basketry include grass, rushes, leaves, cane, young wood stems and a wide range of natural fibres. Baskets are usually woven in a similar fashion to TEXTILES, but matting and some baskets are made by coiling a length of fibrous material and joining the coil together by sewing or wrapping. Basketry is used to make mats, hats, shoes and other items, as well as containers.

Problems

Basketry is sensitive to extremes of humidity: mould will grow in damp conditions and the materials will become brittle in dry conditions. If the humidity fluctuates, damage is caused by the expansion and contraction of the basketry. This weakens the fibres and any applied paint or other surface decoration may become loose.

Dyes will fade in bright light; light also weakens the basketry materials.

Look for unravelling or protruding pieces of fibre. Check carefully for woodworm (*see* p.15).

Basketry is easily damaged if it gets wet. The dyes may run, and the structural materials – particularly of coiled basketry – can disintegrate when drying.

Handling

With time, basketry will become brittle, and it is easily damaged by improper handling and storage. Never lift baskets by their rims or handles. Use both hands to carry an object and support it under its base.

Display

Basketry should be displayed out of direct sunlight, away from spotlights and in a room where the **relative humidity** remains stable. Avoid placing basketry near fireplaces in use and other direct heat sources, otherwise they will become dry and dusty. Soft baskets or hats should be supported by padding them with an inert material, such as crumpled **acid-free** tissue or **polyethylene foam**.

Storage

Store basketry in a cool, dry, dark, clean area. Do not place basketry directly on a stone, brick or concrete floor. To protect objects from rising damp, raise them about 5cm (2in) above the floor by placing them on wooden slats, cork or polyethylene foam. Baskets should be padded to maintain their shape (*see* Display). Try not to stack baskets inside each other, but, if it is absolutely necessary, separate each one with layers of acid-free tissue. Protect basketry from dust with clean **dustsheets** (*see* p.14) or drape acid-free tissue over them. Protect against and check for insect attack (*see* pp.14–15).

Housekeeping and Maintenance

Dust not only looks unpleasant, but is abrasive and encourages mould and insects. Basketry should be kept clean.

If the basket is in good condition, dust can be removed by lightly brushing the surface with a hogshair brush. If the object is very dusty, use the vacuum cleaner as well (*see* pp.19–20). Cover the vacuum nozzle with some **nylon net** to prevent any bits from being sucked up. However, if there is loose or flaking paint or decoration, very gently brush only the sound areas and leave the painted areas until you can get conservation advice.

Cleaning

Old and ethnographic baskets are often stained or contain evidence of their previous use. These stains should not be removed if you are interested in the object's history. Think twice before cleaning off the stains.

It may be possible to remove ingrained dirt by wiping the surface of the basketry with a **cotton bud** moistened with water containing a few drops of a **conservation-grade detergent** or saliva. Do not use a household detergent. If the basketry is coloured, test all the colours in an inconspicuous area to make sure that they will not come off with the water. Rinse with a clean swab dampened with clean water. Do not get the basketry too wet or it may expand or shrink depending on the materials used. Never immerse a basket in water, as this can damage the structure of the object and may push the dirt further into the fibres, making it harder to remove; the dirt may also abrade the fibres.

Repair

Any loose or unravelling pieces can be secured by tying them down with a neutral coloured cotton thread. **Dental tape** is quite useful for this. You may need to use a needle to pass the tape between the rods or fibre bundles, but make sure that it does not split the fibres. Do not tie the tape too tightly, as it will cut the fibres. Nylon thread or fishing line will also cut the fibres and should not be used.

Consult an ethnography conservator for advice on preserving wet basketry and the repair of more complex pieces.

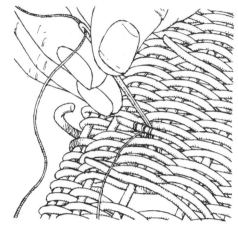

Securing unravelling pieces of basketry by threading tape between the rods/fibre bundles.

Ceramics

Ceramics are made by forming a mixture of wet clay, tempers and/or fluxes into the required shape, allowing it to dry and then firing it in a kiln. The heat alters the structure of the clay and changes it to a hard, sometimes glassy substance. Higher firing temperatures (up to 1450°C/2642°F) produce ceramics that are hard, impact-resistant, vitrified and have low porosity, such as stoneware and porcelain. A lower temperature (up to 800°C/1472°F) produces soft, more porous earthenware and terracotta.

The ceramic body may be decorated in a number of ways and can involve firing the piece more than once. Some glazes and decorative detail, such as applied relief, contrasting clay colour (often called a slip), or sgraffito (incised lines), may be added before the first firing. Other glazes, gilding or lustre may be added before subsequent firings.

Glaze is a thin glassy layer on the surface of the ceramic applied as a decoration to make it less porous and for strength. Glazes can be translucent, opaque, coloured or clear. A painted design with a glaze applied over it is called under-glaze decoration. This technique employs colours that can be fired at high temperatures: cobalt blue, copper red and iron green. On-glaze or over-glaze decoration is where the surface of the glaze is decorated with colours that are fired on to it at a low temperature. These colours are sometimes referred to as enamel colours. Often the basic design is a blue under-glaze with details added as on-glaze decoration.

From an early date gilding was either applied cold as gold leaf, or it was ground into a powder, applied like a paint, and fired on to the glaze at a low temperature. After 1780 an amalgam of gold powder and mercury was painted on and fired until the mercury vaporised.

Lustre is a form of on-glaze decoration where certain metal salts are applied to the surface of the glaze and fired to produce a thin, subtle **iridescence** or a thicker metallic coating.

Most decoration is fixed on to the ceramic surface by firing in the kiln, but there are occasions when unfired paint is used. It is most commonly found on ethnographic pottery and early earthenware, and on some late seventeenth- to mid-eighteenth-century white porcelain.

There are four main types of ceramic: earthenware, stoneware, hard-paste porcelain and soft-paste or artificial porcelain.

- Earthenware, often known as pottery, is soft and porous and is often, but not always, glazed. Unglazed earthenware is porous and may have a coarse texture. It is fired at a relatively low temperature and the body may be very soft. It is usually the colour of earth pigments – browns, reds and greys. Some unglazed earthenware,

Ruby lustreware vase by William De Morgan, made in the 1880s, in the Hall at Standen in Sussex. It is 30 cm (12 in) in height. The left-hand handle shows an old repair: it is important to avoid picking up jugs, teapots, etc. by their handles.

Blue and white Delftware, tin-glazed earthenware, in the Diogenes Room at Dyrham Park, Gloucestershire. These pieces were acquired by the builder of Dyrham, William Blathwayt, during his travels in Holland c.1700, and are in pristine condition as they have remained in the house ever since. The glaze on Delftware is prone to chip off, especially around the base, rim and edges (see page 31). Flower pyramids flank the table, on which are displayed two baluster vases, a condiment set and a tray for sweetmeats.

such as terracotta and black and red Greek and Roman ceramics, have a very fine texture and are quite hard. Many archaeological and ethnographic ceramics are unglazed earthenware.

White tin-glazed earthenware is known in Europe as Hispano-Moresque, maiolica, faience, Delftware or English Delftware, according to the country of origin. It also includes some Islamic ceramics and was known to the Assyrians c.1000BC. (The term **faience** is also used in archaeology to refer to Egyptian objects made from glazed powdered quartz, often coloured turquoise, but also made in white, red, green and other colours.)

There were many European efforts to imitate the much-prized porcelain imported from China. By the mid-eighteenth century, glazed earthenware from Staffordshire became highly refined and was called creamware.

● Stoneware is fired to a higher temperature until it becomes vitrified and no longer porous. It includes celadons from China, European salt-glaze stoneware and jasperware, pioneered by Wedgwood. It is often used to produce utilitarian objects such as cooking and preserving vessels, sanitary ware and drainpipes.

● Hard-paste porcelain is produced from a particular clay – kaolin – and temper, a feldspathic rock known as chinastone or petuntse. When this is fired at a high temperature, it fuses to a non-porous glassy matrix, which is whitish, often with a blue or greyish tone. It was first made in China in about AD 900, then copied by the Japanese. In 1708 the secret of its manufacture was discovered at Meissen near Dresden. From there it spread to Vienna and the rest of mainland Europe, thence to England, where the principal factories were in Plymouth, Bristol and New Hall.

● Soft-paste or artificial porcelain is made from white clay and various materials, including ground glass, in an attempt to copy true porcelain. It is almost non-porous and is usually white. The technique was developed in Florence at the end of the sixteenth century and in France in the seventeenth. The eighteenth-century English factories which produced soft-paste porcelain included Chelsea, Bow, Worcester and Derby. From the mid-eighteenth century they added large quantities of bone ash to help stabilise the material.

Bone china is also porcelain; it was made from the nineteenth century from a hybrid

Minerva and attendant putti in terracotta, dating from the Louis XVI period, in the South Drawing Room at Hinton Ampner, Hampshire. Minerva shows signs of old repairs as well as fairly recent damage on her hand. At one stage this piece has been coated, so the earlier retouching no longer matches the colour. It is dirtiest where it has been handled, especially around the putti.

A statuette of Florence Nightingale after the original sculpture by Hilary Bonham-Carter, 1863. Although this looks like a bronze figure, it is in fact Parian ware, made in the Copeland ceramic factory; most Parian ware is white, to resemble marble. The statuette, 43cm (17in) in height, stands in an alcove of the Library at Claydon House in Oxfordshire, home of Florence's sister, Parthenope.

paste which included bone ash. It is white and fired at a lower temperature than true porcelain, making it cheaper to produce than soft-paste porcelain but with the advantage of durability. Bone china was mainly produced in England.

Both biscuit porcelain and Parian ware were originally unglazed soft-paste porcelain, later imitated in hard-paste. They are white, with a texture similar to marble. Biscuit ware was used widely to make statuettes and, in the mid-eighteenth century, to imitate antique sculpture. Parian ware was introduced in the nineteenth century; it was cheaper to make than biscuit ware. From about 1844 it was also used for dishes, shirt studs and jewellery.

Problems

Generally, the chemical degradation of ceramics is extremely slow and most wares are very durable.

The problems most commonly associated with ceramics are:

• Cracks, breaks and other physical damage. Look for hairline cracks by holding the object up to the light or by tapping it gently with your fingernail. If it gives a good, clear ringing sound, it is probably not cracked, although well-repaired pieces can also ring. The surface of glazed and unglazed ceramics can become scratched and worn.
• The on-glaze decoration may not be firmly attached. Check to see whether the glaze is crazed or flaking. The glaze on Staffordshire figures is particularly prone to flaking and you can often see rough areas on the surface where the on-glaze colour is missing, very often in the black areas.
• Tin-glazed earthenwares tend to chip easily and the glaze may flake off. In some instances, the glaze is not well adhered to the body and may peel off.
• A glaze may craze, which may indicate a

loss of strength and will increase the porosity and risk of staining or damage from soluble salts (*see* below).
• On some ceramics, the glaze can deteriorate and may even flake off. This is particularly common on Islamic ceramics, but can also be seen on **archaeological** ceramics. Some glazes deteriorate either because of the composition of the glaze or from the burial conditions that the object was exposed to. At first they become cloudy on the surface but, as the deterioration gets worse, thin layers like onion skins are formed. These layers of deteriorated glaze are usually iridescent and whitish. Very often the iridescence is attractive, but sometimes it obscures the original design.
• Soluble salts (*see* Salt Removal, p.35) are white, powdery or needle-like crystals that form on the surface or along the cracks in the glaze. They can appear on glazed and unglazed objects and make the body more friable. The salts are the result of the ceramic absorbing chemicals that are soluble in water; when the object is dry and the humidity low, the salts crystallise out, forming white deposits. When the humidity is high, the salts return to a solution. Gradually this

repeated cycle of crystallisation causes the surface of the ceramic to break up and become powdery, or pushes off the glaze.

The chemicals may enter the body of archaeological ware during burial. Other affected ceramics are vases or plant containers which have absorbed chemicals from water and soil, or containers used for food, particularly for preserving food. Inappropriate cleaning with chlorine-containing bleaches frequently causes this problem, and for this reason domestic bleach is not recommended for cleaning ceramic objects. Soluble salts are often found in earthenware teapots that have been bleached with domestic bleach.

These soluble salts should not be confused with the more solid-looking deposits formed on a ceramic surface exposed to

hard water. These deposits may be unsightly but are harmless.

• Paint on earthenware can be poorly adhered to the surface and the little remaining is likely to come off on your fingers.

• Old adhesives and overpainting from previous repairs may have discoloured to yellow or brown and become brittle or corroded. Look for metal rivets that may have loosened. Recent restoration is often difficult to detect, but look for a change in the translucency or colour of the glaze or hold the object at an angle to the light to catch any imperfections on the surface. A repaired area may have a different texture from the original surface. Another test is to stroke the tip of your finger over the surface, because overpaint often feels slightly warmer and softer than the glaze. Antique

ABOVE: *Lambeth Delftware dish in the style of Bernard Palissy, dating from the mid-seventeenth century, now displayed in the Dining Parlour at The Vyne, Hampshire. Unlike the blue-and-white ware from Dyrham (see page 29), this piece shows wear and tear that typically affects Delftware, particularly on the rim and on noses and other raised areas.*

dealers often run a pin over the surface to detect an area of overpainting, but this is not recommended as it may damage the repair and possibly the glaze.

• Ceramics can on occasions become stained. The body under the glaze of earthenware can become discoloured. This usually results from use and frequently from food or drink, although reddish iron staining can develop in archaeological ceramics. Cracks in all ceramics can gather dirt. Occasionally, the glaze itself discolours, but this is not common and is found mostly in archaeological wares. Rivets and other metal attachments can stain the body green if they are brass or copper or rust-coloured if they are iron.

Handling

Most ceramics are very durable provided they are left untouched. The problem with ceramics is that they break easily when mishandled. The risk of damage is high each time a ceramic object is picked up or moved, and where there are small children or pets in the house.

Always have clean hands, particularly when handling unglazed objects, which pick up dirt easily and are difficult to clean. **Gloves** are not necessary when handling ceramics, as they sometimes make it harder to get a secure grip. If you prefer to wear them, use thin latex or vinyl gloves, as they are not too slippery and only slightly dull the sensitivity of touch.

Take care that long necklaces, security badges and other objects hung around the neck, such as spectacles and pens, do not catch the object.

Be particularly aware of crazed or flaking glaze, paint on an unglazed object, gilding, especially unfired gilding, and **bocage**. The bocage and other protruding pieces are easily snapped off. You need to ensure that your fingers or the packing materials do not rub off the glaze, paint or gilding.

Before picking anything up, check for old or loose repairs or for parts that could easily be knocked off. Never pick up objects

A Meissen porcelain cat modelled by J. J. Kaendler, c.1745, in the Mirror Room at Saltram House in Devon. It stands 18cm (7in) high. It has sustained a crack to its haunch. Surprisingly the saluting paw, which is the most vulnerable part, is not damaged. Decorative ceramic pieces should not be picked up by their vulnerable parts.

Carrying ceramics, with one hand underneath and the other supporting the piece.

by their handles, knobs or rims, as they may be weak, or the adhesive or rivets in an earlier repair may fail. Where possible, remove lids and loose pieces before turning an object upside-down. If you cannot take the lid off, always support it with one hand.

Use both hands to carry each piece. Place one hand under the base and use the other to support the object about two-thirds of the way up. Support large plates underneath the centre, not the rim. Always put an object down carefully, because if it has a hairline crack, it could break if it is set down suddenly.

Never carry more than one object at a time. If you need to move several objects at once, pack them carefully in a padded box or high-sided tray, making sure they will

not knock against each other. It is better to make several journeys rather than risk damaging pieces by cramming too many into a box at once.

Unpack ceramic objects on a table you have first covered with a thick cloth, bubble wrap or **polyethylene foam**.

Unglazed earthenware is often more fragile than other ceramics, so pay particular attention when moving it. If there is a friable surface or loose paint, avoid touching it with your fingers, handle it as little as possible and carry it by holding the base and the rim. Do not allow oil, grease or wax to get on the surface. Protect earthenware objects from dust if possible.

People often wet deteriorated iridescent glaze to show off the underlying colour, but repeated wetting and drying can make the situation worse. If the layer is very flaky, handle the object as little as possible and wear vinyl or latex gloves. Never wrap objects with deteriorated glazes in cotton wool, as the fibres may stick and pull off the flaking layers; use **acid-free** tissue paper.

Display

Ceramic objects are not usually harmed by light, so they can be placed in sunlight. However, repaired objects should be kept out of direct sunlight, otherwise the adhesives may become brittle and the painting may discolour. Sunlight will also exacerbate existing problems from soluble salts (see above). Avoid putting objects in a position where they will get dirty quickly, such as on mantelpieces or radiators and other heat sources. Dust and dirt rise with heat and are deposited on the objects.

Make sure that ceramic objects cannot be knocked by passing people. Some floors are quite springy and, when walked on, the furniture vibrates slightly, causing objects on tables or in display cabinets to move around and rub against each other. In the worst case scenario objects may work their way to the edge of a shelf or table and fall off. One way to stop them moving is to fix a piece of chamois leather underneath the object with a little easily reversible **adhesive**.

The bases of many ceramic objects are rough and can easily scratch wooden and marble surfaces. To prevent this, make some pads from chamois leather, cork, felt or **polyethylene foam** cut to size and, if necessary, stick the pads on to the base with an easily reversible adhesive. Choose a colour that will blend with the furniture. Flower vases should always be put on water-proof mats in case water spills or seeps out (see p.14).

Plates and tiles in good condition can be hung on the wall using plastic-coated metal hangers, but make sure the hanger is the correct size. If it is too small, the plate will chip and possibly break from strain, and if it is too large, the plate can easily drop out. If the plate has a hairline or travelling crack, it is not safe to display it in this way, as it could break under the stresses. If you cannot obtain plastic-coated hangers and have to use uncoated metal, cover the metal of the hanger with a soft material which will not chip or scratch the plate. You can wrap some chamois leather or polyethylene foam around the hooks, or slide some soft plastic tubing over them. Alternatively,

the hooks can be dipped in silicone bath sealant and allowed to harden. Metal hangers usually incorporate a spring, which helps to keep the hanger in place, and make it easier and safer to take on and off. However, the spring can catch on the foot rim and chip or scratch it. Slip a sheet of thin card behind the plate to avoid this.

Glass-fronted cabinets are good places to display ceramics. Plates can be propped up at the back of the shelf. There should be a groove or ridge in the shelf to stop the plates from sliding forward. Wood or plastic plate stands are available from stores or antique shops; choose the correct shape and size to fit. Avoid using hinged wooden stands as they can be unstable. Metal stands are also not recommended.

It is not advisable to hang cups by their handles for display, but, if you insist, make sure that each handle is not cracked or repaired.

Do not put houseplants directly into tin-glazed earthenware containers; use an inner plastic liner (see Problems and Removing Soluble Salts). It is advisable to use a liner in any ceramic container, but essential for tin-glazed earthenware.

Biscuit and Parian ware are difficult to clean, as dirt seems to cling to them. It is particularly important not to allow the surface of these wares to become dusty or dirty from handling. Try to display them in a glass-fronted cupboard or under glass domes, and keep covered when in store.

Storage

Keep ceramic objects in a clean, dry area. Objects with soluble salts or with deteriorating glaze should be stored in a stable **relative humidity**. Ceramics, particularly earthenware, may be stained by mould growth if they are kept in damp conditions for too long.

Try to keep the dust off objects (see p.14). Cover them with **acid-free** tissue paper hats. Wrap smaller objects in acid-free tissue and keep them together in a labelled box; avoid using cotton wool or other fibrous materials. Dry objects well before putting them away. Metal hangers or any other attachments should be removed from the objects before they are stored.

It is better to store ceramics on closely spaced, fairly narrow shelves rather than wide shelves. In this way, the objects only stand one or two deep and you do not have to reach over many to retrieve something from the back. Do not put too many objects

on one shelf and keep the smaller ones at the front. A bar running across the front of the shelf will prevent any objects from falling off or being knocked off inadvertently. Do not place pieces so that they are jutting over the edge of the shelf. If they are being stored in a cupboard, make sure that the door can close without causing damage.

If you only have a few deep shelves, you can increase the space by using plastic-covered wire shelves that stand on, or hang from, the existing shelves. Make sure that they are stable and only store objects with a broad base, such as plates, on these shelves.

Try to avoid stacking cups and bowls, because they can break from the accumulated weight. They can also stick together and become difficult to separate. Do not stack too many plates in one pile; keep the same size and shape in each pile and never stack larger plates on top of smaller ones. Avoid stacking cracked or repaired ceramics, as they may break, although you could place a single damaged object at the top of a stack. Put acid-free tissue folded at least double or sheets of white kitchen roll between each plate or bowl to stop the pattern or glaze from being worn or scratched by the foot rim of the plate above.

If an object has ormolu mounts, it should be stored in dry conditions (see ORMOLU).

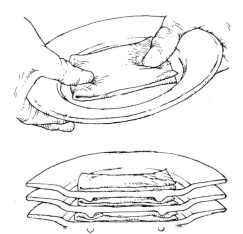

Stacking plates interleaved with folded acid-free tissue.

Housekeeping and Maintenance

Provided the surface is not flaking or very fragile, remove dust using a soft brush. Hold the object steady with one hand. Take care not to brush dirt into any cracks or it could become trapped.

Cleaning

Do not clean rare, old, fragile or precious ceramics; they should be cleaned by a conservator or following conservation advice.

Occasionally, ceramics need a more thorough clean. Always remove as much loose dust as possible with a brush first. Some ceramics may be washed, but not all. Many can be damaged by immersing them in water. Porcelain and stoneware in good condition and which have not been repaired can be washed.

Unglazed earthenware and terracotta, glazed earthenware such as creamware, tin-glazed earthenware, objects with deteriorated glazes or flaking over-glaze, gilded objects, objects with metal or ormolu mounts or objects which have been repaired should not be washed. Enamel or on-glaze decoration may come off. Old adhesives in previous repairs can come apart and overpainting may be damaged. Metal and ormolu mounts can corrode if they get wet. Unglazed earthenware and terracotta may be softened by water and can also become stained.

If glazed earthenware gets very wet, dirt can be carried into the body through tiny cracks in the glaze, causing further staining. Impurities in the clay body, such as iron, may cause discoloration once they are wet, but the staining may not show until the object dries.

Never wash old ceramics or any ceramics decorated with gilding in a dishwasher. Heat and chemicals used in the washing process will bleach some glaze colours, may remove the gold and can damage the glaze.

Washing porcelain or stoneware
(a) *Place a folded towel or foam rubber in bottom of bowl, and add water* (b) *Use a hogshair brush to remove dirt from crevices* (c) *Remove piece before throwing away the water* (d) *Mop up surplus water with paper towels.*

● **WASHING PORCELAIN AND STONEWARE**
Only wash one object at a time. It is safer not to wash objects directly in the sink but to use a plastic bowl large enough to hold the whole object. If you are unable to find a bowl of the right size and have to use the sink, wrap the taps with cloth or foam plastic to prevent the object from being chipped.

Place a folded towel or some foam rubber at the bottom of the bowl or sink. Fill the bowl with warm, not hot, water and a few drops of a **conservation-grade detergent** or a mild household detergent. Use a hogshair brush to remove dirt from any crevices. Remove the object from the bowl before you throw the dirty water away. Refill it and rinse the object well in clean warm water. Remove the object from the

bowl and gently mop up the surplus water with paper towels or a soft cloth, and allow it to dry in a warm place. Porcelain and stoneware may also be washed using the method described for objects that cannot be immersed in water. This further reduces the risk of damage.

● **CLEANING EARTHENWARE AND OTHER OBJECTS THAT CANNOT BE IMMERSED IN WATER**
Glazed earthenware and tin-glazed earthenware, gilded objects, objects with metal or ormolu mounts or objects that have been repaired can be cleaned using **cotton wool buds** with the water and detergent solution described in the Introduction (*see* p.21). Avoid cleaning any areas of on-glaze decoration that are poorly attached.

Cover a table or flat surface with a thick towel or similar padding. Do not use a very thick covering or the object will be unstable and could easily fall over. Support the

object with one hand and brush off the dust. Use a damp cotton bud as described in the Introduction (*see* p.21). An artist's hogshair paintbrush may also be useful for cleaning ornate decoration. If the surface of the object is rough, use a hogshair brush instead of cotton wool to avoid any fibres becoming caught. Rinse with a bud or brush dipped in clean water.

Pat the object dry with paper towels or an old, soft tea-towel, then leave it in a warm area to dry completely. Very ornate pieces can be dried with a hairdryer set on *Cool*.

Do not get metal or ormolu mounts wet. Dust the mounts with a soft brush (*see* ORMOLU), but clean the ceramic as described above.

● **CLEANING CERAMICS THAT SHOULD NEVER GET WET**
Unbaked clay or very soft objects, unglazed earthenware, ceramics with a flaking glaze or **iridescence** and painted earthenware

can be cleaned using a hogshair brush or a softer artist's brush to remove the dirt and dust, and a **swab stick** to pick off any soil or debris (*see* p.20). Take care not to remove the glaze or iridescence.

If the surface is flaking or paint comes off, it may be possible for a ceramics conservator to consolidate the surface. Remove what dust you can with a soft brush, but stop if you are dislodging the paint or flakes. Protect these ceramics from dust so that they do not need frequent cleaning.

● **REMOVING SOLUBLE SALTS**
Do not attempt to remove salts from ancient, rare, valuable or fragile objects or objects with a very delicate surface. These should be treated by a ceramics conservator. First, brush off the salts carefully. If they reappear after a few days or weeks, you may have to soak them out of the ceramic as they can be damaging, but where possible seek conservation advice rather than do it yourself. However, should you have an object, like a plant container, that has developed problems such as flaking glaze due to soluble salts, you can try washing them out.

To wash out the salts, leave the object to soak in clean tap water for two days:
● Place the object in a clean, dry plastic bowl.
● Using a jug, slowly fill the bowl with clean tap water until the object is submerged. Most ceramics are slightly porous, and the water displaces air trapped in the body. If the water is added too quickly, bubbles form which push off delicate surfaces when escaping. Similarly, placing the ceramic directly into a bowl of water can cause damage to the object.
● Change the water three times a day: remove the object, dispose of the water,

Washing salts out of a plant container.

replace the object in the bowl and add clean water as described above.
● If you live in an area where the water is chlorinated or very hard, use de-ionised or purified water for the last two rinses.
● Remove the object and allow it to dry. If, when it has dried out, a white bloom remains on the surface, repeat the washing procedure.

If you want to continue using a vase that you have washed free of salt crystals, place a container inside it or have a liner made to hold flowers in water.

● **REMOVING INSOLUBLE SALTS**
When ceramics are used as containers for pot plants, they very often develop a crusty deposit from the water similar to the scale found in kettles. Provided that a porcelain or stoneware object is in good condition, this can be removed using a small amount of kettle descaler applied to the surface with a dropper. You may also be able to remove some of it by picking it off with a **bamboo stick** (*see* p.20). Soak the object well in clean water when the scale has been removed.

Washing matt-surfaced ware with a stencil brush.

● **CLEANING BISCUIT AND PARIAN WARES**
The matt surface makes biscuit and Parian ware difficult to clean. Dust the object with a soft brush before washing it in a solution of detergent and warm water. It may help to remove the dirt by brushing the surface with a stencil brush. If washing does not clean the object, you may be able to remove the dirt by using a white spirit:water mixture or other water/**solvent mixtures** (*see* glossary, p.248) and rinse with clean water. If this is unsuccessful, consult a ceramics conservator.

Repair

If you break an object, which you might want to have professionally repaired, do not try to stick it together yourself. Collect all the pieces and wrap them up individually in **acid-free** tissue so that the edges do not knock against each other and become damaged further. Keep them all together in a labelled box until you can get them to a conservator. Repair is not as easy as some people believe and if you have any old, rare, fragile or precious ceramics, it is worth getting them repaired by a ceramics conservator.

Small repairs can be made using an easily reversible **adhesive**. Chips of missing glaze on the edges are characteristic of old tin-glazed earthenware, so if you have a piece restored it is not necessary to have every chip made good. Glaze sometimes comes away from the body; if this happens, consult a ceramics conservator.

Occasionally iridescence can be consolidated so that it is less obvious and the true colour of the glaze shows through, but this treatment should be carried out by a ceramics conservator. It is inadvisable to remove the iridescence, as it will make the surface uneven and marked; it may result in a very patchy appearance and can even remove all the glaze from some areas.

● **REMOVING STAINS**
It is seldom possible to remove stains completely from glazed earthenwares. If you try to do it yourself, it could make the appearance worse. Stain removal should be carried out only by a ceramics conservator. Stains are often an interesting indication of the former use of an object.

You could try to remove a discoloured crack in an item made from soft- or hard-paste porcelain, bone china or stoneware, provided it is in good condition. Do not try to do this if there is any gilding on the surface or on ware with a lustre finish or decoration, as the chemicals may remove or change the colour. Make sure that your object is not glazed earthenware, as this procedure can produce a bleached margin along the break that is even less attractive than the dirty crack. Never use domestic bleach or chlorine-containing bleaches, as they can change the colour of the object and cause long-term damage.

You can try to remove the stains with **hydrogen peroxide** at a strength of twenty volumes. Soak the object in clean water for about an hour before beginning. Always wear rubber gloves, eye protection and protective clothing as the peroxide can burn clothing and human tissue. Place the object on a plastic tray or ceramic tiled surface. Pour the hydrogen peroxide into a lidded glass or ceramic container and add a drop of ammonia. Pull some strips of cotton wool off a roll, about 1cm (½in) wide, and using tweezers dampen them with the hydrogen peroxide. Place the damp strips over the crack or stain using tweezers and leave them in place for about one hour. If the stain is still there, replace the old strips with new dampened ones. Continue to do this until the stain has disappeared. This may take several days and is not always successful. You should not let the cotton wool dry out on the object. If you leave the strips on overnight, put the object in a polythene bag. Once the object is as clean as you can get it, soak it in clean water for several hours and leave it to dry.

If this method does not remove the stain or your object is not suitable for this type of stain removal, take it to a ceramics conservator.

● **REMOVING OVERPAINT**

When an item is repaired, it may be retouched and painted over the original surface, and in time this overpainting is likely to become discoloured. It can usually be removed quite easily, but only where you are certain that there is ceramic underneath or if you are prepared to be faced with areas of filler. Do not try to remove overpaint from unfired or soft earthenware; seek conservation advice.

If the painting is on a sound glazed surface, it is sometimes possible to scrape it off by carefully using a bone or plastic scraper. Using a magnifying glass, check that you are not scratching the surface. Do not scrape paint off on-glaze or gilded decoration, as it is easy to remove these as well.

Removing overpaint from unglazed, gilded and enamelled pieces is more safely done with a solvent applied with a cotton wool bud. The **organic solvents** discussed in the Introduction (*see* p.21) are most commonly used. Test the solvent first. Do not use too much, as there is a danger that the paint will be pushed into cracks or the porous body. Dip a cotton wool bud in the solvent and roll it over the surface to soften the paint. Change the bud when it becomes dirty. Always use the solvent in a well-ventilated room, according to the health and safety suggestions supplied with the solvent (*see* p.23) and use personal protective equipment where necessary.

Removing paint from flaking glaze is difficult and should be undertaken by a ceramics conservator.

Outdoor Terracotta

Do not keep a terracotta statue of any significance outside if the temperature is likely to drop below freezing.

Terracotta statues, plant pots and containers can withstand exposure to mild weather quite well, but freezing conditions can cause spalling, cracking and even breaking. Spalling occurs when the water that has been absorbed by the terracotta freezes and expands, and lumps of terracotta, often circular, come off the surface of the object. Breaks can occur when the pot contains damp earth or water, as the pressure from the expanding ice causes the container to split.

If possible, move terracotta objects to a shed, garage or greenhouse before the onset of winter. Do not stand terracotta objects directly on a stone, brick or concrete

One of the basketweave terracotta pots, based on a Victorian model, that stand on the terraces of the garden at Powis Castle, Powys. Salt efflorescence from the soil inside the pot can be detected, together with slight frost damage around the lower edge.

Spalling and frost cracks on terracotta pots.

floor. Protect them from rising damp by placing them on wooden slats or cork and, if necessary, cover them with a **dustsheet** during storage.

If it is impossible to move the object for the winter, you can protect it from frost by wrapping the terracotta in bubble wrap or **polyethylene foam** during cold spells. Do not leave this wrapping on for longer than necessary as poor air circulation within the plastic can cause mould and algae to grow, and the terracotta may discolour.

If a terracotta pot cracks, it may be possible to continue using it, provided it is not moved; once you pick it up, it will fall apart.

Repairs to terracotta objects that are kept outside are seldom very successful, unless they are carried out by an experienced conservator who uses materials that are appropriate for the exterior environment. Damaged terracotta statues should be treated by a conservator experienced in this field.

Ceramic Wall and Floor Tiles

Tiles are usually matt or glazed, and are used as decoration for floors and walls both inside and outside buildings. During the art nouveau and art deco periods, they were used widely to decorate fireplaces and front porches. Many people now collect individual tiles.

Wall Tiles

Damp walls can cause tiles to deteriorate to the extent that the glaze flakes off and white salt crystals form in the tile itself or the

Tile by Edward Bawden, dating from the 1920s, in one of the bathrooms at Coleton Fishacre in Devon. Very fine craquelure is visible through the glaze.

grouting. Check that the damp course (if there is one) has not been broken or bridged and that gutters and drainpipes are not leaking. The salts and flaking surface may not become apparent for a long time, but the effect can be dramatic once the damage starts. If the damp problem is not rectified, the deterioration will continue. Do not attempt to stick the flaking pieces of glaze on to a tile without solving the underlying problem or before the tile dries out completely, as this can make the situation worse. If the source of the damp cannot be stopped, the tiles may have to be removed and mounted elsewhere or remounted *in situ* with damp-proofing behind them. This should be carried out by a conservator.

When the cause of the damp has been eradicated, allow the tiles plenty of time to dry out. It is difficult to quantify the time needed, as it depends on the temperature, thickness of wall, degree of damp, etc., but it will certainly take weeks and possibly months. A rough guide for drying time is 1 month per 2·5cm (1in) of wall thickness. Occasionally brush any crystals off the surface with a soft brush, taking care not to dislodge any glaze. If the damage is quite severe, or if the tiles are antique, rare or precious, or are part of an historic decorative scheme, a conservator should be called to check, clean and consolidate them.

Any soluble salts in the tiles may continue to be a problem if the **relative humidity** in the room is not kept stable. If the problems continue once the cause of damp has been repaired and the tiles have dried, you will need conservation advice.

Feathers

Bird feathers have been used as an adornment for costume in many cultures around the world. In the eighteenth and nineteenth centuries, decorative panels, referred to as featherwork, were produced, mainly by amateurs, and the later ones were often fashioned into realistic representations of birds.

Feathers are primarily made up of a protein, keratin, as are horn and tortoiseshell, and they are constructed of a central stem (rachis) from which branch fine strands (barbs) on both sides. They are naturally coloured by the inclusion of pigments in their structure and by the optical properties of the keratin, but they may also be dyed or painted. They vary in appearance from loose and downy to a more rigid flight form.

Problems

The colour of feathers fades readily in light, they are very vulnerable to insect attack, especially from clothes moths and carpet beetles, and mould can develop in damp conditions. Feathers, particularly the more flamboyant ones, are very hard to clean, so feathered objects should be protected from dirt as dust embrittles them and will permanently stain pale-coloured feathers.

Handling

Feather objects are usually very fragile, so handle them with extreme care. Always have clean hands and wear clean cotton **gloves**, provided they do not impair your dexterity.

Display

Display feathered objects in the same conditions as textiles. Costumes and head-dresses should be supported for display

LEFT: *A decorative featherwork panel, featuring a parrot, in the Shell Gallery at A la Ronde in Devon. The remarkable sixteen-sided cottage was built for two Georgian ladies, the Miss Parminters, in 1798, and they spent years decorating the interior with feathers, shells, marbled paint, cut paper, sand, seaweed and straw. The featherwork shows all the characteristic problems – fading, insect attack, water damage, and detachment following the disintegration of the glue.*

and storage, using **acid-free** tissue to pad them out. *See* TEXTILES.

Small feather objects should be displayed in glass or cases made of **acrylic sheet** or deep frames to protect them from dust.

Storage

Store feathers in a cool, dry, clean, dark, well-ventilated area. Wrap the object loosely in **acid-free** tissue or a clean **dust-sheet**. Make sure the feathers are not squashed or bent. Protect them from and check for insect attack (*see* pp.14-15). *See* TEXTILES for more information.

Housekeeping and Maintenance

Protect feathers as much as possible from dust and daylight. Check regularly for insect attack (*see* p.15). If insects are found, isolate the object until treatment can be implemented.

Feather costumes, ethnographic feather objects and rare and precious objects should only be cleaned by an experienced conservator, as feathers are delicate and are easily damaged beyond repair.

If you have a fairly modern object, such as a fan, which is in good condition, you can gently remove dust from the feathers with an artist's soft paintbrush. A gentle puff of **compressed air** may help to remove the dust, but practice away from the object first to ensure that the pressure of the air is not too strong.

Gently tease the feathers back into position with a **brush** or **bamboo stick**.

Cleaning

Further cleaning is difficult, but you could try **powdered eraser** gently rubbed with your finger tips. Work in the direction of the barbs, away from the central stem. Rub in one direction only, rather than back and forth. Clean both sides and then brush off the powdered eraser with a soft brush.

Repair

Feathers are extremely difficult to repair. Old, rare and precious objects should be repaired by a conservator.

When re-sewing feathers on to a backing, use cotton thread as other threads may cut through the stem or barbs. Take care not to pierce the stem or the barbs with the needle.

Feathers stuck on to featherwork can be re-adhered with a neutral pH emulsion **adhesive**.

Glass

It is thought that the first glass was made in the Eastern Mediterranean before 3000BC. It was a highly regarded material and was used primarily as a substitute for precious and semi-precious stones. Hollow glass vessels date from about 2000BC and were made by forming the glass around a core or by casting. Before the process of making glass was invented, glass was used in its natural forms, one of which is obsidian, formed during volcanic eruptions. Glass became a less precious commodity with the invention of glass-blowing in the first century AD, probably in Syria. It was mainly used to produce bottles, jars, bowls and other vessels. Apart from making vessels, glass is used for windows and mirrors, jewellery, lamps, lenses, paperweights, mosaic tesserae and many other decorative and utilitarian items.

Glass is made by fusing silica, in the form of sand, flint or quartz, with an alkali (potash or soda), and a small amount of calcium oxide (lime) at a high temperature. Together they form a clear liquid that, on cooling, forms a transparent solid.

Glass is frequently coloured by adding metal oxides such as cobalt, which turns it blue, and copper or iron, to provide a greenish tinge and other colours. Some metal salts, particularly lead and tin, turn the glass white and opaque.

Lead oxide has been an ingredient in glass since early times, but its effect on the properties of glass were better understood in the seventeenth century when it was used in the manufacturing process of what is known as flint glass or crystal. This is easier to cut and is ideal for producing highly decorated cut-glass items. Lead glass is bright, sparkles when cut and gives a clear ring.

Glass can be decorated by engraving and cutting with wheels, etching with acid or sand, moulding, firing on enamel colours or applying paint, silver or gold. It can be formed into cased or cameo glass, which is made by fusing a coloured layer of glass on to a clear base glass; a design is then cut or etched into the outer layer to reveal the layer below. Mosaic glass is made from

slices cut from coloured rods and fused together. It is most commonly seen in paperweights and dishes.

Problems

The most common cause of damage to glass is physical – breaking, cracking and chipping. Glass can be quite soft, so the surface may become abraded and the surface decoration can wear off. Enamelled, painted and gilded decoration may be poorly adhered to the glass.

The chemical durability of glass depends on the composition of the glass and the surrounding environment. Most glass, if kept dry, can remain in good condition for centuries, but high humidities (over 70% RH) or exposure to damp for a period of time can cause the surface to corrode. This shows first as interference colours (like the rainbow effect of oil on water) that gradually develop to creamy white iridescent corrosion layers peeling off like onion skins. Glass stored in a very damp environment or exposed to condensation can corrode quite quickly. The water or water vapour leaches out some of the chemicals from the glass, leaving behind a slightly pitted surface. The deterioration of buried glass is also predominantly due to water and can often be seen on bottles recently found in the ground. Look for **iridescence**, creamy white corrosion or a pitted surface.

The composition of glass is important for its durability and a slight change in the proportions of the ingredients can greatly affect this. Some glasses may deteriorate very quickly in either damp or dry conditions. Venetian glass is particularly vulnerable.

Unstable glass may either 'weep' or 'crizzle'. Weeping occurs in glass made with an excess of alkali and too little lime. The glass absorbs water from the air; it may develop a soapy feel and small tears of liquid can form on the surface. Gradually very fine surface crazing forms on the glass, the transparency is reduced and the glass can be described as 'crizzled'. Early Venetian glass often weeps. Crizzling can also occur on unstable glass that does not show signs of weeping when it is brought into a dry environment. It will dry out and the surface can become covered in small cracks to the extent that some small pieces of glass may fall off. Look for small hairline cracks in the glass. If crizzling has become severe, the glass will lose its transparency and eventually disintegrate.

Dust and dirt expose glass to risks of physical damage during cleaning; gaseous pollution does not have a direct effect on glass. Some nineteenth-century glass is affected by light, which may change a colourless glass to a purple or brown colour. This is seen mostly in the window glass of old houses rather than in objects.

Vibrations of certain wavelengths or intensity, such as from high speed aircraft, can cause glass to shatter, but general vibrations may also make windows crack or objects fall. Mould does not usually develop on clean glass but can be found on objects kept in high humidities or on damp and wet surfaces. A white cloudiness can form inside a decanter that has been left damp with the stopper in it; if alcohol is left in a decanter, a white deposit or even a dark stain can appear.

Check glass objects for previous restoration. Old adhesives may have discoloured to yellow or brown, but new repairs are harder to see. Look also for cracks, flaking enamel or paint and loose gilding and crazing in the glass. Check for a slippery feel. High temperatures can soften adhesives used in repairs, so handle glass objects with particular care.

Handling

Glass is very vulnerable, therefore before picking up any object, check for parts that are easily knocked off or for repairs which may come apart, as adhesives do not always hold. Never lean over an object to pick up another one, but move the front one out of the way, and make sure long necklaces, lockets and objects hung around the neck such as spectacles and pens do not knock anything. It is advisable to remove jewellery, especially rings with mounted stones. Unpack glass objects over a table that has been padded with a thick cloth or **polyethylene foam**.

Do not pick glass objects up by their rims, handles, knobs or projecting parts. Do not pick drinking glasses up with the finger and thumb on the rim. Use both hands to carry an object: cradle the body with one hand and place the other under the body. Some glass objects are very elaborate and have a lot of projecting decoration. This snaps off very easily. When you handle such objects, hold them under the base and do not grasp the decoration. Cased or cameo glass cracks and chips very easily, so handle it with great care.

Glass with iridescent layers and glass with gold or silver decoration or flaking enamel should be handled as little as possible (*see* Paintings on Glass). If either the layers or the metal decoration come off easily on your fingers, pick up the object using a piece of tissue paper or wear a thin rubber or vinyl **glove**. Make sure that you support the object securely at the base so

LEFT: *Glassware in the cupboard of the Servery at Blickling Hall, Norfolk. Acid-free tissue has been placed on the shelves, and the same type of glasses stored together so that they can be taken from the front of the shelves, avoiding accidents. The decanter and glasses on the butler's tray are set on a linen cloth.*

ABOVE: *Early twentieth-century glass bowl, 29·5cm (11¾in) in diameter, by the French master René Lalique in the Drawing Room at Killerton in Devon. This is in fine condition, but care must always be taken when handling glass items, with support underneath, and a good grip to prevent slipping.*

that the glass does not slip out from between the paper or your gloved fingers.

Where possible, remove lids and loose pieces before turning an object upside down. If you cannot take the lid off, always support it with one hand. A loose lid should be wrapped and packed separately.

Do not move objects quickly from a damp place to a dry one, as the glass could crizzle. This is particularly the case with some types of seventeenth-century glass.

Carry only one object at a time. If you need to carry several glass objects, pack them carefully in a box or tray with a lot of padding between them. Make sure that

they do not damage each other. It is better to make several journeys than to risk damaging the objects.

Set glass down very carefully so that it does not jar and break. Take particular care with glasses on stems, such a wine glasses, as it is easy to misjudge where the foot is.

Display

Glass objects are not usually harmed by light, but do not put them in direct sunlight or shine a spotlight directly on them, because the heat could dry them and cause them to craze or crizzle. Glass should be

washed and handled as little as possible to reduce the risk of damage. Therefore, avoid places such as mantelpieces and shelves over radiators and other heat sources where dust collects. Heat can aggravate

BELOW: *Nineteenth-century Nailsea glass pipes in the Justice Room at Clevedon Court, Somerset. Nailsea glass was made locally to Clevedon, and consisted of fragile objects such as walking sticks, rolling pins and smoking pipes in pastel colours shot through with spirals and twists. The fragility of the glass makes it difficult to display, and the iron grips shown here are rather too robust.*

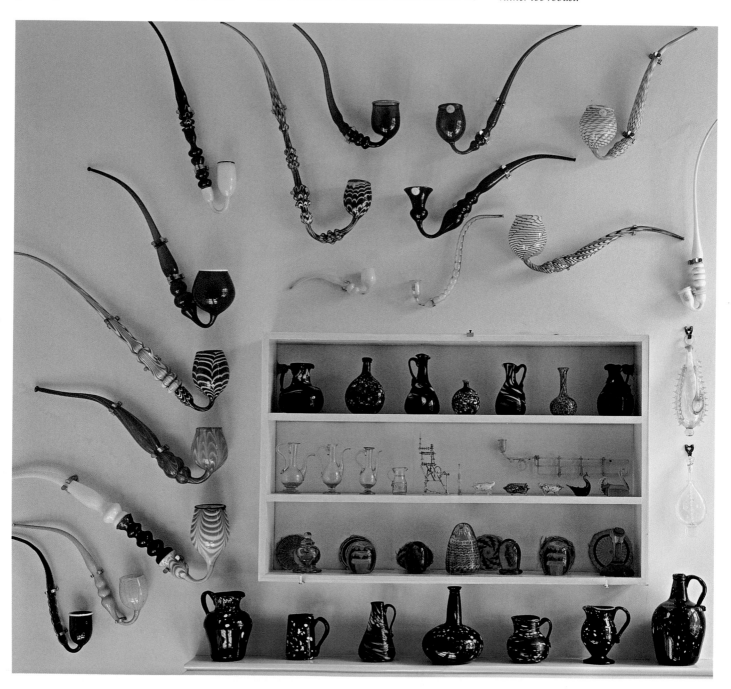

unstable glass. Unstable, weeping glass must be kept in conditions of controlled **relative humidity**, about 50% RH. This can be achieved by creating a suitable microclimate using a sealed display case. Seek conservation advice.

Glass-fronted cabinets are good places to display glass. Engraving shows up well when the glass is placed in front of a dark colour or backlit. Diffused lighting from above or below shows off cut glass. However, lights that do not cause the temperature to rise should be used when displaying glass, as the heat given off by tungsten bulbs and most fluorescent tube lighting can make some glass crizzle when used in a confined area. Take care that spotlights, which can generate a lot of heat, do not warm up an object (*see* p.18). Repaired glass should be kept out of direct sunlight and protected from ultraviolet light to lengthen the life of the repair, as adhesives and fillers often fail and discolour in sunlight.

Make sure that glass is placed towards the centre of the table, where it can not be knocked by passing people. Some floors are quite springy and when walked on make the furniture move up and down slightly. This can cause objects on tables or in display cabinets to move around and 'walk' to the edge of a shelf or table and fall off or rub against each other. Keep objects far enough away from flapping curtains or heavy doors that could slam.

Early hand-blown glass may have a sharp edge on the base where it was broken off the iron rod, or pontil, during manufacture. This 'pontil mark' can scratch furniture, so it is a good idea to place a glass, felt or cork mat under the glass.

See CERAMICS for more information on displaying glass and ceramic objects.

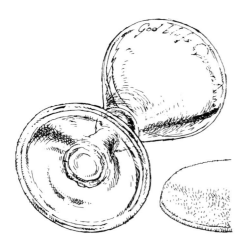

The pontil mark on the base of a glass.

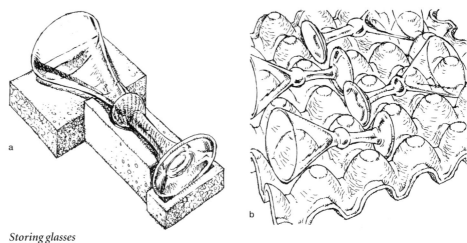

Storing glasses
(a) *Supported on polyethylene foam* (b) *Supported on an egg tray.*

Storage

Keep glass objects in a clean, dry area. Weeping and crizzling glass should always be stored in as constant a **relative humidity** as possible (40–60% RH). **Sealed plastic boxes** with some preconditioned **silica gel** will provide a good microclimate for these vulnerable objects. Decanters or bottles with stoppers should be stored without the stopper in. Cover the decanter with a handkerchief, piece of muslin or **acid-free** tissue held on with string or cotton tape to keep out the dust. Make sure that you keep the stopper with the decanter or bottle. Dry objects well before putting them away. Also remove any metal hangers or other attachments before storing glass objects.

Keep the dust off objects. Cover them loosely in **clear polyester film** or tissue paper cones. Do not wrap glass objects in cling film or sealed polythene bags. If you are packing them in a box, wrap them loosely in **acid-free** tissue. Tissue paper can absorb moisture, so do not wrap the objects too tightly. Label any wrapped pieces so that you do not have to unwrap them whenever you are looking for something. Do not pack glass objects in cotton wool or other fibrous material, as they hold moisture and the fibres can become attached to the glass surface.

Place glass objects on shelves as discussed in CERAMICS.

Store objects in the most stable position. This might mean storing a glass with the bowl down if the foot is small or wobbly, although there is a danger of the rim chipping if handled carelessly. Occasionally it may be necessary to store an object on its side, in which case the weight must be evenly distributed. Do not allow too much

weight to rest on the rim. Also make sure it will not roll over. A glass object can be supported on **polyethylene foam** or an egg tray. If you use foam, you will need to cut out a hollow to accommodate the shape of the glass. Small wooden or polyethylene foam wedges will also prevent cylindrical objects from rolling over. Archaeological glass or thin sherds should be stored on a tray or in a shallow box and should be padded with acid-free tissue for support.

Housekeeping and Maintenance

If the object is in good condition, dust it with a brush as described in the Introduction (*see* pp.19–20). Hold the object steady with one hand.

Cleaning

Most glass objects in perfect condition can be washed in water. Do not immerse objects that are 'weeping' or crizzled, glass with enamel or gilded decoration, painted glass, **archaeological** glass, glass with **iridescence**, conserved glass or glass with metal or ormolu mounts. Adhesives in repairs can come apart and metal and ormolu mounts will corrode if they get wet.

Never put antique glass in the dishwasher. It is also not advisable to put modern lead crystal in a dishwasher, as it tends to chip and may develop a bloom on the surface that is hard to remove.

Dust the glass first. Only wash one object at a time. It is safer not to wash objects directly in the sink but to use a plastic bowl large enough to hold the whole object. If you are unable to find a bowl of the correct size and have to use the sink, wrap the taps with cloth or foam plastic to prevent the object from being chipped.

Place a folded towel or some foam rubber at the bottom of the bowl or sink. Fill the bowl with warm, not hot, water and a few drops of a **conservation-grade detergent** or a mild household detergent. Gently immerse one object at a time and use a hogshair brush to remove dirt from any incised decorations or crevices. Remove the object from the bowl before you throw the dirty water away. Refill it with clean warm water and rinse the object well (*see* p.34).

Do not put undue pressure on any one part of the object, particularly the rim. If you wear rubber gloves, take care that the glass does not slip out of your hands. Avoid leaving glass in a bowl unattended, as someone else may not see it and put something else into the bowl and break the object.

Having rinsed it well, place the object to drain on a tea towel or paper towel to stop the glass from sliding around on a wet surface and to absorb the excess water. Dry the object with a linen cloth or paper towel. Do not use cotton or a fluffy material, as fibres will be left on the glass surface. Polish the glass gently. Rims of bowls and stems break easily, so do not apply pressure to them. Wine glasses often break when they are held by the base of the stem while the bowl is dried using a twisting movement, so hold the bowl, not the stem, and dry by wiping up and down the glass rather than round it.

Prevent your working area from becoming overcrowded, otherwise the glasses may knock against each other and chip or break. Do not leave glasses damp as they may become stained.

Repaired glass, glass with applied decoration which is in sound condition and glass with metal or ormolu mounts can be cleaned successfully using cotton wool swabs or buds. Cover a table or flat surface with a thick towel or thin **polyethylene foam** (0·5cm/¼in thick). Do not use a very thick covering, as the object will be unstable and may fall over easily. Support the object with one hand and carefully remove the dust with a soft brush. Wipe the object with cotton wool swabs dampened with warm water containing a few drops of conservation-grade detergent or a mild household detergent. Work from the bottom of the object up. Renew the swabs when they get dirty, and change the water frequently to keep it clean. Rinse with clean swabs moistened with clean water. To clean intricate areas, use a cotton wool bud or twist a few fibres of cotton wool round a **bamboo stick**. A hogshair brush is also useful for cleaning ornate decoration. Pat the object dry with paper towels or an old, soft tea-towel. Then leave it in a warm area to dry completely.

Never allow weeping glass, glass with layers of iridescence or glass with unsound applied decoration to get wet. These should be cleaned by a conservator or following their advice. Layers of iridescence or a thin opaque layer of deterioration should not be removed. If you scrape it off, you are removing actual layers of glass and you will be left with a rough surface. Mud or dirt can be carefully picked off glass that has an iridescent surface using a wooden cocktail stick, but it must be done very delicately.

Repair

Repairing glass is very difficult and pieces of any value should be conserved by a glass or ceramic conservator. If you break an object that you might want to have professionally repaired, do not try to stick it together yourself. Collect all the pieces and wrap them up individually in **acid-free** tissue so that the edges do not knock against each other and cause further damage. Keep them together in a labelled box until they can be delivered to a conservator.

Decorative glass can be repaired with an easily reversible **adhesive**. The join will be very weak as glass does not bond well, so handle the object as little as possible. It is unwise to use repaired glass vessels. *See* CERAMICS.

- Make sure the edges of the break are clean and dry before applying the adhesive.
- Secure the pieces in position using thin strips of self-adhesive tape.
- Mix up some easily reversible adhesive as described on p.52.
- Apply a drop of adhesive to the break line and allow it to run into the break (*see* p.52).
- Remove excess adhesive with a clean paper towel.

Occasionally iridescence can be consolidated so that it appears less obvious and the true colour of the glass shows through, but this treatment should be carried out by a ceramics or glass conservator. It is inadvisable to remove the iridescence as it will leave the surface uneven and marked.

Bottles

Chinese snuff bottles are frequently painted on the inside. Do not wash them out. If they are very dirty, clean the inside with a dry cotton wool bud, but stop if the paint begins to come off. Clean the exterior with a cotton wool bud dampened with a washing solution of water and **conservation-grade detergent**. Rinse with a clean bud dampened with water and allow to dry in a warm place.

Bottles from archaeological excavations should not be cleaned until all scientific examinations have been carried out on the objects and contents. Sometimes the contents of bottles are interesting and should not be removed. Occasionally the contents of a bottle may be toxic, so always wear latex **gloves** and handle them with care. Bottles that have been found in the garden and appear to be in good condition can be cleaned by soaking them for no longer than two or three hours in warm water containing a small amount of **water softener** and a little **biological washing powder**. This solution should help loosen the dirt. You may need to use a bottle-brush to get at some of the dirt on the inside of the bottle. Wear rubber gloves, but take care that the bottles do not slip through your fingers. Rinse the bottles very well in clean water and dry.

If this cleaning solution does not clean the bottle, try using a solution of **borax**. Borax can be harmful, so make sure that you wear rubber gloves and do not breathe in the dust – follow the health and safety instructions on the packet. Put 25g of borax in 600ml of water (1oz in 1pt). Leave the bottles to soak for two hours in the solution and then rinse them very well in changes of clean water.

Decanters

A decanter should be washed, rinsed and allowed to drain upside down. Placing it in a high-sided bowl or saucepan will help to ensure that it does not topple over. If necessary, dry the decanter with a hairdryer set on *Cool*, never *Hot*. Do not leave a clean decanter with the stopper in, *see* Storage.

Any cloudiness on the glass could be either deposits from the contents or deterioration of the glass. If it is a deposit, it may be removable. If the glass surface has been etched from the decanter being left damp, however, it is usually irreparable. You can try to remove the deposit by using either vinegar or **water softener**. Try vinegar first, and if that does not work, try the water softener.

Pour some undiluted clear (water white) vinegar into the decanter and leave it

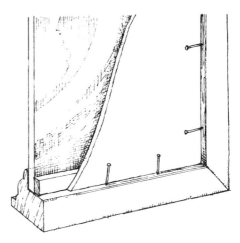

Fillet of acid-free card in a frame.

Nineteenth-century glass decanters in a box in the China Closet at Tatton Park in Cheshire. The gilding is showing wear, principally around the necks of the decanters where they have been handled. One of the stoppers has been chipped.

overnight. Pour away the vinegar, rinse the decanter very well and leave it to dry. If the vinegar does not remove the stain, put one teaspoonful of the water softener into a jug and pour on about 600ml (1pt) of warm water. Stir the solution until the water softener has dissolved completely. Fill up the decanter with the solution and leave it to stand for 2–3 hours. Empty out the solution. Rinse the decanter thoroughly and leave it to dry.

If either of the methods appear to be having some success, you may need to repeat the treatment, but if neither of the solutions removes the staining, you could try a mechanical method. Use the copper beads that are available commercially or swirl some crushed eggshells in water around the decanter. Dry the decanter at frequent intervals to make sure that the stain is going. You will not be able to see any progress while the decanter is wet.

STUCK STOPPERS

If a stopper is stuck in a decanter or stoppered bottle and some liquid remains inside, it is likely that the liquid has dried around the stopper and is holding it in place. Try turning the decanter over and leaving it in a pan, so that it does not topple over, for a few hours. The liquid may penetrate between the neck and the stopper and dissolve the residue. Gently *turn* the stopper to try to loosen it. Always turn the stopper; never pull it. If the decanter is dry or this is unsuccessful, put some penetrating oil or **spray oil** round the edge of the stopper. The oil should penetrate the neck and allow you to twist and remove the stopper. It is very easy to break the neck of a decanter, so be particularly careful. Wash and dry the decanter to remove the oil (*see* GLASS, Cleaning).

Paintings on Glass

Paintings on glass date from Roman times, and often come from countries in the Far and Middle East, such as China, Iran and India, although some types of European furniture and American clocks have painted glass panels. Glass painting was a popular leisure activity in nineteenth-century Europe. The picture is painted on the reverse side of the glass so that you look through the glass to the painting. The paint is frequently either an oil, resin or wax based paint but more recent examples may be acrylic paints. The back of the painting may be protected by varnish, paint, metal foil or another sheet of glass. The paint often crazes and flakes off and it will scratch very easily. It is very difficult to conserve paint or to repair a broken glass.

Do not place painted glass pictures where they are likely to get hot or where there are severe changes in temperature and **relative humidity**, such as near a fireplace or radiator in use or in the kitchen or bathroom.

Paintings on glass are usually framed. Make sure that nothing is pressing against the painted surface. There should be a fillet around the edge of the glass to prevent the backboard from touching the painted surface directly. A fillet can be cut from **acid-free** card. The frame must hold the glass securely so that the picture does not move around in the frame, thus preventing the paint from being abraded. The fixings of the frame need to be secure and checked regularly. A specialist framer with experience in this type of work will be able to help.

When handling or packing an unframed painting on glass, do not touch the back and make sure that the paint is not rubbed by any packing material. Place the glass face down on to polyester foam or a padded surface.

Clean the front of the glass by brushing off any dust and wiping it with a dry **microfibre cloth**. If the glass is very dirty, use a cotton wool swab barely dampened with a 2:1 mixture of water to **alcohol** rather than a commercial glass cleaner, which contains chemicals that may harm the paint or frame. Hold a piece of thin card against the inside edge of the moulding to protect the edge of the frame. Polish the glass lightly with a dry swab or soft cloth. Liquid should not penetrate behind the glass. Do not attempt to clean the back or painted side of the glass, as you may damage the paint.

If the paint is flaking or has mould spots or the glass is broken, it must be treated by a conservator specialising in this type of work. Do not attempt it yourself, as it is easy to make the problem worse.

Stained Glass and Window Glass

Stained glass was first used in churches, and by the eleventh century the designs and technology were already quite sophisticated. Some of the most magnificent stained glass was made between the twelfth and seventeenth centuries. After the mid-seventeenth century, the art began to decline, but in the mid-nineteenth century it was revived and stained glass became popular as a feature in houses and other secular buildings as well as in churches. It is still commonly seen in the front doors of many town houses. Around the end of the nineteenth century, stained glass was also used to make lampshades and other decorative panels.

Basically there are two ways in which glass is coloured. The colouring can be mixed into the molten glass to give an evenly coloured sheet of glass. Alternatively, a layer of coloured glass is fused or flashed on top of a colourless sheet of glass. The top colour can then be etched out with acid, creating a two-coloured design on one sheet of glass. Coloured glass can be painted, enamelled, stained, etched or engraved. The enamel colours and paint are both fired on to the surface of the glass.

Sometimes the side of stained glass that has had the decoration 'painted' on it will have a slightly matt surface. This surface can sometimes be very easily scratched. The other side will be smooth. On doors or window panels made in the late nineteenth and early twentieth centuries, the painted design is frequently confined to a central motif, while the borders are made from coloured molten glass which is coloured throughout its thickness.

Problems

Window glass, whether coloured or clear, suffers from the same problems as other glass, but to a greater extent, as it is exposed to the elements. Extremes of temperature, humidity and light cause it to deteriorate faster. Some very ancient glass can become discoloured, brittle, corroded

Detail of a glass ceiling light, c.1900, in the Upstairs Lobby at Sunnycroft in Shropshire. The black paint has been chipped, a common occurrence. But the glass panel is held securely by the lead, which can often become fragile and distorted with time.

and pitted. Layers of general grime, soot and weathering products can also build up on the glass.

Stained glass and leaded windows are made up of three different components: glass, lead and putty. The putty usually deteriorates fastest. The lead normally remains in good condition, as the window frame keeps it in shape. Sometimes the lead corrodes, which will weaken the window (*see* LEAD). As the lead deteriorates, the window will begin to bow out of its vertical shape. When leaded glass is stored unframed the lead often deteriorates, as the window is unsupported and the lead bends and buckles. In each case there is very little that you can do about this, as the window may need to be re-leaded. A stained-glass conservator should be able to advise you.

Church windows and good stained glass should never be touched by an amateur and should always be dealt with by a stained-glass conservator.

Display

Panels of unframed stained glass will need additional support before being displayed. A metal frame is recommended, as wood, particularly oak, can cause lead to corrode (*see* LEAD). Avoid placing the framed panels in direct sunlight or near any form of heat source, as the heat can increase problems in glass that has deteriorated.

Ultraviolet-absorbent varnish or film, often used on windows to protect objects within the room, should not be applied directly to stained-glass windows. It may be applied to leaded windows if cut to the shape of each pane. Ultraviolet protection can be provided using ultraviolet-absorbing **acrylic sheets** fixed on the inside of the window. The method of fixing will depend on the structure of the window, but care must be taken to allow for good ventilation between the acrylic sheet and the window glass in order to prevent condensation.

Storage

Sound stained-glass panels in a frame can be stored vertically. Fragments will need to be supported in a frame or stored flat. Keep them in a cool, dry place and away from organic acid vapours (*see* LEAD). Rest the objects on **polyethylene foam** or other **acid-free** materials.

Bowed and distorted panels should be stored horizontally with polyethylene foam padding underneath.

Housekeeping and Maintenance

The cleaning and care of medieval church glass should be done only by a qualified conservator.

Regularly brush other windows lightly to remove dust and debris as described in the Introduction (*see* p.19), and wash the undecorated side of the glass regularly (*see* Cleaning). The decorated side will need cleaning occasionally when there is a build-up of dirt.

Cleaning

If the glass or lead is badly corroded, it is unsafe to clean it. This should be dealt with by a conservator.

Glass that is coloured on the surface by paints and enamels should be cleaned with care, as the colour can sometimes come off easily. Heraldic designs and other ornate decoration, particularly of the seventeenth and eighteenth centuries, are especially vulnerable. Always test each colour on the glass before cleaning it.

Never use commercial window cleaners for cleaning stained-glass or leaded windows, as the chemicals they contain can affect the glass, the lead and the putty. Some leaded windows have very little strength, so do not rub them very hard.

Clear leaded glass or glass that is coloured throughout and has no paint enamel decoration can be cleaned by first brushing off any dust with a hogshair brush or clean household paintbrush. Most marks and dirt can then be removed by gently rubbing with a dry or damp **microfibre cloth**. A window that is extremely dirty can be cleaned with cotton swabs or a well wrung-out cloth dampened with 2:1 water to **alcohol** mixture to remove grime, then gently polished with a lint-free or microfibre cloth. Work from the bottom of the window upwards, making

Early seventeenth-century painted glass now set in a window in the Great Hall at the Treasurer's House in York. Originally the painting was probably all one piece, but has been repaired at some stage with lead. The cement from the lead has spread onto the glass. If leading has a problem, always consult a stained-glass conservator.

sure the cleaning solution does not get behind the lead.

When cleaning glass that has paint or decoration on one side, clean the non-decorated side first, as above, making sure that the cleaning solution does not get on to the decorated side of the window. To clean the decorated side, first check the surface carefully for flaking enamel or colour. Avoid cleaning any flaking areas, as you may pull off more decoration. You will need conservation advice for consolidation. Test the cleaning procedures carefully before continuing. Assuming the decoration is sound, brush off any dust that may be on the

surface. Sometimes the water/alcohol mixture used above will clean these surfaces successfully. Carefully test each colour on the painted surface in an inconspicuous spot with a **cotton wool bud**. If there is any sign that the colour or paint is coming off, do not continue, but if it is sound continue as above. In cases where the washing solution disrupts the colour, you may be able to remove some dirt with a dry microfibre cloth or **chemical sponge**. Test first, to make sure that it does not pull off any of the colour. If the test is unsuccessful and the colour comes off, clean only the other side.

Lampshades made of stained glass can be

cleaned with a dry microfibre cloth. If necessary, remove the shade from the lamp and wash it in the way described above.

Repair

Rare, old, fragile or precious stained or window glass should be conserved and restored by a stained-glass conservator.

If your stained glass is not very old or valuable, it is possible to consolidate a broken or cracked piece. Choose a dry, cool day; if it is very hot, the adhesive will harden too quickly. Clean the glass (as described above) and fix the pieces into their correct position using a few thin strips, about 0·5cm (¼in) wide, of self-adhesive tape across the join. Make sure that the adhesive tape is on the glass side and not the side with the surface paint or decoration. Turn the strips over at one end so that you have an unstuck bit to hold on to when you come to pull them off.

To consolidate the cracks in the glass squeeze a little easily reversible **adhesive** into a clean, small container. Do not use adhesives such as epoxy resins, as they eventually discolour and are hard to remove. Mix the adhesive with **acetone**, using a clean **bamboo stick** or something similar, until the mixture has the consistency of single cream. Take a fine artist's paintbrush (no. 0 or 1) and, on the glass side, not the decorated side of the panel, run a small amount of the diluted adhesive along the cracks. Capillary action will pull the dilute adhesive into the cracks. It should not come through to the other side. Allow the adhesive to dry for at least 24 hours. Carefully cut away any excess adhesive on the glass side with a razor or scalpel blade. Take care not to scratch the glass and do not push on the glass. Should any adhesive have gone through to the decorated side of the glass, it may be possible to remove it with acetone, but first, in an inconspicuous area, test that the acetone does not remove the colour. Then gently wipe a cotton wool bud moistened with acetone over the excess adhesive. Turn the bud as you go and discard it when it becomes sticky. If any colour comes off at all, stop at once – a little extra adhesive will not look as unsightly as a bare piece of glass. Leave the glass to dry for twelve hours before removing the adhesive tape. Do this by pulling it at right angles to the direction of the tape. Any repair will be weaker than the original unbroken glass, so take extra care when handling or displaying repaired pieces.

Horn

Horn is a tough, versatile and long-lasting material that is the outgrowth of skin that comes from **bovids** and antelopes. It is built up in layers over a bony core and has a characteristic fibrous structure. Horn, like hair, tortoiseshell and feathers, is made up of the protein keratin. Cattle and buffalo horn were most commonly used to make horn objects, but rhinoceros horn, which differs from other horn in that it is made up of compressed hair, is occasionally found on items such as dagger hilts.

By heating it in water, horn can be split into thin translucent sheets; these can be joined together using heat and pressed into a die or mould to form shaped objects. Oils rubbed into the thin sheets make the horn more translucent and were used for lanterns (as in lanthorn) and windows. The flexibility of horn was exploited in the manufacture of archers' bows. Horn is also used to make drinking vessels, jewellery, buttons, buckles, knife and fork handles, spoons, powder horns, spectacle frames and dagger hilts, and as a veneer on boxes. In North America in the nineteenth century buffalo horn was used to make chairs and small tables.

Horn is sometimes painted or inlaid. It has also been used as an inlay in furniture. Horn is sometimes dyed and coloured to imitate tortoiseshell but the two can be distinguished because horn is more fibrous, less translucent and usually greyer than tortoiseshell.

Early nineteenth-century horn-windowed lantern with a rushlight holder in the Firehouse at Townend in Cumbria. Horn is vulnerable to scratches and liable to crack, so dust with care to avoid fibres catching. The iron part of the rushlight holder is showing signs of corrosion.

Problems

In damp or very dry environments, horn can exfoliate or split and sheet horn may warp. Horn is seldom prone to insect attack, although occasionally it can be a food source for carpet beetle and clothes moth larvae (*see* p.15). Mould will grow on horn in a humid environment. In the long term, light will deteriorate the surface causing a white/grey bloom to develop. Paint does not adhere well to horn because of the oils in its structure.

Handling

See IVORY AND BONE and CERAMICS. Although horn is rather tougher than ivory or bone, it should still be handled with care, particularly if it is splitting or delaminating. Where horn is decorated with paint, avoid touching the surface as much as possible to protect the paint.

Display

Do not place horn objects in direct sunlight, or over a radiator or a fireplace in use. They should not be kept in very damp or dry conditions; the humidity should be as steady as possible.

Storage

Store horn objects in a cool, dry, dark area. Wrap smaller objects in **acid-free** tissue. Protect from and check for insect attack (*see* pp.14-15).

Housekeeping and Maintenance

Remove the dust from a horn object with a hogshair brush and vacuum cleaner (*see* pp.19-20). If the surface of the horn has become a little dull, a small amount of **microcrystalline wax** paste or **beeswax polish** applied to the surface and polished off with a soft cloth should help restore the sheen. If horn is painted, it should be dusted carefully. Do not wipe or polish the surface, as paint may become detached.

Cleaning

Never immerse old horn objects in water as it can delaminate, deform or split. To clean horn in good condition, wipe the surface with a cotton wool swab or bud dampened with warm water containing a few drops of **conservation-grade detergent**. Do not use household detergent. Rinse lightly with clean cotton wool swabs or buds and clean water. Do not allow the object to become very wet. Dry the horn with a soft cloth.

If the surface of the horn was originally polished but is now a little scratched, you may be able to revive the sheen by gently polishing it using a **fine abrasive paste** on a soft cloth or cotton wool. However, this does remove a small amount of the horn, so a very fragile, old or valuable object should not be polished at all and other horn objects should be polished only once. If the surface is very scratched, polishing will not help. Use a little **microcrystalline wax** if necessary to give a sheen.

Repair

See IVORY AND BONE and TORTOISESHELL.

BELOW: *Eighteenth-century cutlery handles carved as figures in bone, in the Store Room at Chirk Castle, Clwyd.*

Ivory and Bone

Ivory and bone are both made up of the protein collagen and an inorganic calcium salt (called hydroxyapatite), as is antler. True ivory is the tusk of an elephant or mammoth, but 'ivory' often refers to any similar hard, white or cream-coloured substance, such as the tusks of hippopotamuses, walruses and narwhals. Ivory is dense, close-grained and has a layered structure. It has very characteristic markings which show when the ivory is cut transversely. The markings are known as 'lines of Retzius', also sometimes referred to as 'engine turning', and are a regular pattern made up of finely contrasting material. When ivory is cut in section, the markings form crossing arcs. The difference between ivory and other teeth is that ivory has no outer layer of enamel unless the animal was very young. Remnants of old blood vessels and age cracks, collectively known as 'shakes', can sometimes be seen on surface ivory taken from the edge of the tusk. They show as brown or black flecks and

can be confused with the dark flecks found on bone.

Because of its structure, ivory has been a favoured material of carvers, but it can also be etched, stained, painted, gilded, inlaid with metals and with precious and semi-precious stones or used to inlay wood and metal and other materials. It can be highly polished and when cut into thin sheets it is translucent. Ivory has been used to construct or embellish a wide range of decorative and fine art objects from furniture to jewellery, including billiard balls, sculpture, miniatures, book covers, dagger and knife hafts and piano keys.

Long limb or rib bones are most usually used for making bone objects. They consist of a shaft of compact bone that surrounds the marrow cavity, with more porous bone at either end. Only the dense bone was used for objects. There are tiny holes in bone formed from blood vessels and these often show as dark flecks on the surface. Bone from the skull and vertebrae does not have a marrow cavity. Some bone has a layered structure, although it is not usually as pronounced as in ivory.

Most bone objects are quite small because of the limited size of the dense section bones, except those taken from whales and elephants. Occasionally pieces are joined together to make a larger object. Bone is used to make small carvings, decorative boxes, knife and corkscrew handles, mah-jong tiles and buttons. It is also used for inlay in furniture, particularly

ABOVE: *Indian ivory furniture collected by Lord Curzon during his time as Viceroy of India (1889–1905), and now on display at Kedleston Hall in Derbyshire. Large areas of ivory were made by cutting slices through ivory tusks and joining them together. Cracks can be seen in the pierced circular panels in the back of the settee.*

escutcheon plates round keyholes. In antiquity, bone was used for needles, combs and other domestic objects.

Artificial ivory – ivorine and Xylonite – was invented in the late nineteenth century. Good-quality imitations are difficult to detect, but they often have pseudo lines of Retzius which are more striking than those of real ivory.

Ivory bust of Lord Chancellor Somers, 20cm (8in) high, made in 1706 by David le Marchand, in the Library at Wimpole Hall, Cambridgeshire. The bust is showing splits along the grain, typical in ivory and not a cause for concern. Care has, however, to be taken in cleaning to avoid getting dirt into the cracks, and ivory should be kept away from sources of heat.

Handling

Always have clean hands, or preferably wear **gloves**, when handling ivory and bone, as bone in particular can be quite porous and will absorb dirt. Do not move ivory or bone objects directly from a cold, damp area to a hot, dry one, as ivory in particular may split. Handle ivory and bone objects as you would CERAMICS.

Bone or ivory inlay can shrink and fall out of position, so check the packing carefully after transporting or storing such an object.

Display

Although ivory is more sensitive than bone to light and changes of humidity and temperature, both materials need to be displayed under similar conditions. Do not place them where sunlight can fall on them and display them in a room where the temperature and humidity are as steady as possible. Avoid positioning them by fireplaces in use, radiators or other heat sources (*see* p.18). Do not display objects in bright light, and protect them from light as much as possible (*see* pp.16-17).

Thin pieces of ivory, such as ivory miniatures, are particularly sensitive to their environment and should be stored in optimum conditions (*see* MINIATURES).

Elaborately carved ivory or bone objects are difficult to clean and therefore are best displayed under glass to protect them from dust and dirt.

Storage

Store ivory and bone in a cool, dry and dark area. It is important that it is neither too damp nor too dry and that the temperature and humidity are as steady as possible. Wrap small objects in **acid-free** tissue and store them in an **archival quality** box. Do not wrap ivory and bone objects in cotton wool or cloth, as these can absorb moisture and fibres can become lodged in carving. Never wrap ivory or bone in coloured materials as they may stain the object.

Protect large objects from dust by covering them with a clean, white **dustsheet** or washed calico or by draping acid-free tissue over them. Raise them off the floor at least 5cm (2in) by using wooden slats, cork or similar materials.

The objects should be examined periodically for insects and mould (*see* pp.14-16).

On ageing, and with handling, ivory and bone acquire a yellow or brown **patina**. The surface of ivory can be artificially stained to simulate this patination. This is often found on Japanese netsuke.

Whale teeth, whale bone and walrus tusks which are engraved or lightly carved are known as scrimshaw. The design was enhanced by darkening it with **Indian ink**. Scrimshaw was mostly produced in the mid-nineteenth century, but examples are known from the late seventeenth century. Scrimshaw was particularly popular in North America, but was also carved in Britain, Australia and New Zealand. It is associated with whalers and other fishermen, but it was also carved on dry land.

Problems

Ivory and bone are very susceptible to moisture and heat, although bone is slightly less sensitive than ivory. Changes in temperature and humidity may result in warping, cracking and the breaking up of the surface. Ivory will tend to crack along the grain, giving rise to onion ring-like splits. When ivory and bone become very dry, they shrink, crack and distort. Light can cause ivory to discolour to a yellow colour and may bleach bone.

Paint or gilding on ivory and bone do not adhere well and often remain only in the depths of carving. If any decoration does remain, it is likely to be delicate and poorly adhered.

lacquer is applied as a varnish over a painted decoration.

Indian and Sri Lankan lacquerwork is made from shellac, as is some Persian (Iranian) lacquer. The lacquer is often applied by holding the coloured solid resin against the turning wood surface. The heat from friction causes the lacquer to melt and coat the surface, usually producing annular designs.

Problems

Lacquered and japanned objects are sensitive to changes in **relative humidity**, because the carcass expands and contracts according to the amount of water vapour in the air (*see* pp.17–18). Over time this movement causes the lacquer or japanning to crack and flake, and it may eventually peel off.

Water on the surface of japanning, in particular, may cause a permanent stain or white bloom, so water spilled on the top of a table should be wiped up immediately.

Light can change the colour of *urushi* and japanning and may cause the surface to deteriorate so that it becomes dull and uneven. It may crack and break up and become powdery, or it may develop a white bloom.

Dust and pollution can dull the surface permanently and frequent cleaning may also damage the surface. *Urushi* and japanning can be indelibly marked by fingerprints. Inlay may fall out.

Very often japanned and lacquered objects have been restored and layers of varnish or paint applied over the original surface or in patches. This may discolour or peel off.

Handling

Handle japanned and lacquered objects carefully and do not knock them as they chip very easily. Always wear cotton **gloves** when handling these objects, but avoid touching any of the raised decorative surfaces. Take care that they do not slip from your grasp.

LEFT: *Early eighteenth-century japanned bureau bookcase by the London furniture maker, John Belchier, in the State Bedroom at Erddig, Wrexham. Although faded on the outside, the inside reveals a brilliant scarlet. The exterior also shows scratches and chipping.*

Display

Japanned and lacquered objects should be displayed only where the **relative humidity** remains quite steady. Do not place them in direct sunlight, in windows or in any bright light nor near any direct heat source such as fires or radiators. Display a collection under controlled lighting (*see* pp.16–17).

Take care that chairs and other objects are not pushed back hard against lacquer screens. Avoid displaying flowers and plants on japanned or lacquered furniture. If iced drinks are placed on a japanned surface, put a large coaster under them to prevent drips from condensation running on to the surface. Do not put hot objects directly on japanning or lacquer.

Storage

Japanned and lacquered objects should be stored in a clean, dry, dark, well-ventilated area where the **relative humidity** remains steady. *See* WOOD.

Housekeeping and Maintenance

Japanned and lacquered objects in sound condition can be dusted using a dry **microfibre cloth** or lint-free duster, but make sure that the cloth does not catch on raised

The conservator pulling out a drawer from a lacquered secretaire at Osterley Park, Middlesex, is wearing vinyl gloves. These, rather than cotton gloves, are recommended because they do not mark the surface. Always avoid handling the lacquer itself by holding the top and bottom edges.

decoration or edges and pull the surface off. If the surface is cracked and lifting, it is safer to remove the dust with a soft brush and vacuum cleaner (*see* pp.19–20). Also use this method to brush the dust off carved decoration.

Cleaning

Rare, old or precious japanned or lacquered objects or those that have a cracked or flaking surface should be cleaned only by a conservator. Do not clean highly polished *urushi* as the surface is easily damaged and the shine lost.

If, after dusting, the surface is very dirty but otherwise in good condition, it may be possible to clean it further using a dry **chemical sponge** carefully rubbed on the surface. There is, however, always a risk that the surface may bloom or be scratched by the cleaning process. Test the surface very carefully before cleaning. Use a cotton bud dampened with a mixture of water, **white spirit** and **conservation-grade detergent** (*see* solvent mixtures). Do not use household detergents, as the chemicals they contain can cause long-term damage. First, test the surface in an inconspicuous spot to check that none of the japanning is being removed and that the surface is not being stained by the water. Carefully roll the cotton bud barely dampened with the mixture over the surface. Take particular care in the painted and decorated areas that they are not rubbed off or removed by the cleaning fluid. Small spots of dirt can be removed with a cotton wool bud dampened with saliva.

After cleaning the object, gently roll a clean cotton wool swab barely dampened with clean water over the surface, and dry it as soon as possible by blotting the surface with a clean cotton wool swab or soft white cloth. It is important not to get the surface very wet and to dry it quickly and thoroughly, otherwise a bloom may form. Make sure you do not leave fibres on the object and that you do not catch rough edges with the cotton wool.

Cleaning off overpainting and old repairs is difficult and it is easy to damage the *urushi* or japanning. Consult a conservator.

Repair

If the surface of a japanned or lacquered object is flaking or crumbling, do not attempt to repair it yourself. Ask a conservator specialising in lacquerwork for advice. When a small piece of inlay, lacquer or japanning becomes loose, it can be fixed again into position using a neutral pH emulsion **adhesive**.

Some japanning can become very dull and a light application of **beeswax polish** or **microcrystalline wax** may help to revive the sheen. Check first that the solvent in the polish will not remove any decoration. *Urushi* should not be polished with wax as it may cause damage to the surface.

Vernis Martin

Vernis Martin is the name for the brilliant translucent lacquerwork perfected in France in the eighteenth century by four brothers of the Martin family who had begun life as coach painters. It was used on extremely elaborate and valuable pieces of furniture, carriages, sedan chairs and numerous small decorative objects such as fans and snuffboxes. It has a beautiful surface and can range in colour from pearl grey, pale green or lilac to a Prussian blue. Sometimes gold dust was applied beneath the surface to give a sparkling effect.

Genuine *vernis Martin* objects are rare and therefore, if they are in good condition, they are likely to be valuable. Apart from careful dusting, they should be cleaned and conserved by a conservator.

Leather

Leather and skin products have been used widely throughout history for domestic and military objects, as well as for decorative items, clothing, bags, harnesses, belts, footwear, gloves, boxes, jugs, mugs, wall hangings, screens, seat covers, book covers, table covers and hinges, and in machinery and scientific instruments. Before synthetic compounds were developed to produce non-breakable materials, leather was used to make such things as water bottles, buckets and washers.

Leather is the hide or skin of an animal that has been treated to convert it into a product that resists putrefaction and retains, in whole or part, some of the open fibre structure of *in vivo* skin. The skin fibres undergo chemical modification in a process known as tanning. Without treatment the skin would be stiff and would putrefy. The part of the skin used for making leather is the middle layer, or corium, between the epidermis or thin outer layer and the subcutaneous fatty tissue beneath. Technically, leather only refers to skin products that have been fully tanned, but it is not always easy to tell whether the skin is untanned, semi-tanned or fully tanned.

Almost any animal skin can be tanned, but those most commonly used are goat, cattle and sheep, while skins such as ostrich, snake and reptile are used to make more exotic leathers. The skin taken from the carcass of larger animals is usually referred to as hide, while that of smaller animals remains 'skin'. Generally sheepskins are used for clothing and gloves, calfskin and goatskin are tougher and used for footwear and book binding, while bull hides were traditionally used for making belt drives and textile machinery components. Once removed from the carcass, the skin or hide is treated by removing the subcutaneous fatty layer and the epidermis and hair.

There are a number of methods of preserving the hide. Smoking was one of the simpler methods, in which the hides were suspended over a wood fire. The common preserving processes are:

• Chamoising or oil-tannage: a method of preservation where certain oils or oil-containing materials, such as tallow, egg yolk and animal brains, are rubbed into the hide. This produces a soft pale leather used for clothing and car leathers. The source of the leather is usually sheep or deerskin, and no longer necessarily the chamois antelope.

• Alum tawing: immersing or rubbing in a mixture of alum and salt produces a pure white leather. This type of leather may be used for gloves, footwear and some book-binding.

• Vegetable tanning: the pre-treated skin is soaked in a bath containing tannins obtained from trees or shrubs, including oak, acacia, chestnut, sumac, mangrove or larch. In Britain, oak bark was used traditionally for heavy leather products, while the sumac leaf was for lighter skins.

• Mineral tanning: the skin is treated with aluminium or chromium salts, a process developed in the mid-nineteenth century. Chrome leather is very durable, but not as easy to mould as vegetable-tanned leather and so is used less for bookbindings. Most leather is now mineral-tanned.

Tanned leather can be stiff and liable to crack and so was often finished by giving it an oil dressing to make it more flexible. Dubbin is an oil dressing made from tallow and marine oil and is still used for waterproofing boots and shoes.

Chamoising, alum tawing and vegetable tanning have been used for millennia. The exact processes and results depend on the type of leather available as well as local vegetables and minerals. Parchment and vellum (*see* p.66) are made from splitting sheepskin and calf skin, and treating them with a variation of tanning.

Leather is often decorated and can be coloured by dye or lacquer, grained or embossed to create a surface pattern, or 'glazed' to obtain a shiny smooth surface. It can be stretched over shapes to make scabbards or pieces can be joined by sewing or riveting them together to make water bottles, jugs and pails. It can be moulded, punched, incised, carved, scorched or bruised over a relief of carved wood. Motifs can be applied to the surface with a stamp, gold leaf can be impressed into the tooled decoration, paint can be applied to the surface and metal inlaid into the leather. Not all leathers can be treated or decorated in the same way; much depends on how they have been tanned and dressed.

Fur pelts are usually tawed or oil-dressed and worked mechanically to make them softer. Suede is made either by splitting the hide longitudinally to remove the grain and then rubbing to a nap, or by working the flesh side of a hide to produce a fine nap.

Leather has a characteristic grain caused by the arrangement of the hair follicles and the structure of each skin. This can be used to identify the animal origin of the leather. The type of leather and its tanning process can usually be identified by a leather conservator or a supplier of leather.

Problems

When kept in the right conditions, leather can be very durable, but it is prone to damage from wear, tear and handling, from exposure to moisture and high humidity, insects or other pests, and heat or low humidity (*see* Introduction). Signs of deterioration include an abraded or flaking surface, brittleness, cracks in the surface and reduction of flexibility. Mould may develop on leather kept in humid conditions.

Alum tawing is an effective preservative for as long as the alum remains in the hide, but it is easily washed out with water. If this happens, the leather will become hard and brittle.

Some leathers have 'red rot', which is a form of deterioration associated with atmospheric pollution. The fibres in the leather crumble into a red powder. Red rot usually occurs on vegetable-tanned leather made in the last half of the nineteenth century, although it can also occur in modern leather. It is frequently seen on nineteenth-century bookbindings. The rot first develops a pinkish colour but, as it gets worse, the colour darkens to dark red. No satisfactory solution has yet been found to treat or reverse red rot, although research continues. If you find red rot on a rare or valuable object or on one with applied decoration, such as gold leaf, paint or lacquer, ask a conservator for advice.

Leather is frequently used in conjunction with other materials including wood, metal, textiles and paper. It also often has surface finishes such as gold leaf, varnish, silver leaf and paint. These materials must be taken into account when caring for leather and any treatment applied to the leather should not harm the other materials. Similarly, the leather must not be harmed or stained by, say, metal polish or woodworm treatment.

Leather and skin products are vulnerable to attack from insects, including the biscuit beetle, *Stegobium paniceum*, the spider beetle, *Ptinus sp.*, carpet beetles *Anthrenus sp.* and cockroaches. Insect attack is usually associated with high humidity (*see* p.14).

ABOVE: *The Luggage Room at Lanhydrock in Cornwall offers an array of late nineteenth- and early twentieth-century leather pieces. The 'Gladstone' bag would benefit from being padded inside to prevent development of permanent folds, and thus cracks. Vigilance should be maintained concerning pests in this environment – avoid pushing objects into the corners where insects flourish.*

Leather can also be damaged by wood-boring insects when it is used to cover a wood carcass in items such as trunks, furniture and scabbards. As the adult insects emerge from the wood, they bore through the leather.

Handling

Old leather often looks more robust than it is, so always handle it with care. It may tear and split very easily. Do not try to unroll or flatten leather that is hard or brittle, as it may break. Old and rare objects should not be used for their original purpose and should be handled as little as possible. Ask for advice from a conservator.

Frequent handling and use can cause leather to deteriorate. Always wash your hands before touching leather and do not use hand cream, as the oils will mark. Grease and oil stain leather very easily, particularly if the leather has a dry appearance, usually caused by red rot, so take care not to get them on the surface. If the leather has red rot, handle it with **gloves**.

Do not stick adhesive labels or tape on to leather, as they may pull the top surface of the leather away when you remove them.

Display

Leather objects should be displayed in a stable environment that is neither dry nor damp (50–65% RH). It should be protected from sunlight and bright lights and not placed over fireplaces, radiators or other heat sources (*see* p.18). Make sure wall hangings and screens are not placed where sunlight can fall on them. Shaped leather objects, such as costume and shoes, need some support while on display or in store. This can be provided by rolled up **acid-free** tissue or by custom-made supports fabricated from an inert material such as **polyethylene foam**.

Storage

Store leather objects in a cool, dark, well-ventilated area which is neither damp nor dry. Do not lock them away in a cupboard or chest without ventilation. Check the collection frequently and clean any storage areas regularly to prevent insect attack. Leather should be protected from dust and dirt, so wherever possible box it in **archive quality** containers or cover it with clean **dustsheets**.

Leather is a flexible material which may stretch and distort. If it is folded, it will develop creases. Leather clothing and soft leather objects should be stored in a similar manner to TEXTILES. They should be supported by padding them out with **acid-free** tissue paper, laid flat with minimum folding or hung with padded hangers. Place wads of acid-free tissue along any folds so

that creases do not develop. Bags, hats and shoes should be padded with acid-free tissue to support their shape.

Housekeeping and Maintenance

Do not attempt to clean a fragile or deteriorating object. Remove the dust from a leather object using a soft brush. If the piece is very dusty, hold the nozzle of the vacuum cleaner in your other hand to catch the dust (*see* pp.19–20). Take care not to damage the leather with the end of the nozzle. If the surface of the leather is cracked or broken, place **nylon net** over the vacuum cleaner nozzle to prevent fragments from being sucked up. A can of **compressed air** is useful for blowing away dust from cracks and crevices on small objects and from inside hollow objects.

● **DRY LEATHER**

In the past, attempts have been made to treat cracked or dry leather using a leather dressing, usually a mixture of oils, wax and water, but it is now understood that these dressings can be more damaging than helpful. Although some leathers can benefit from the addition of certain oils, in other cases considerable damage can be caused. Leather does not need 'feeding' in the way that many people believe. It is safer not to apply a dressing. If you have a particular problem with an object, seek advice from a conservator who specialises in leather conservation.

If you are especially keen to improve the appearance of an object, such as a seat cover or suitcase, a little clear **beeswax polish** can be applied to the surface using a soft cloth or your fingers. First test in an inconspicuous spot to ensure that the wax does not remove the colour. Use only beeswax polish and only a very small amount. Beeswax furniture polish is preferable to leather creams, as it does not penetrate into the leather. Do not oil or wax painted or gilded leather, as the decoration may come off.

● **INSECTS**

Check leather objects regularly for insect attack (*see* p.15). If you see signs of insect attack in your leather, the object should be treated by freezing or eliminating oxygen (*see* pp.14–15). Liquid insecticide used on the leather may cause permanent staining. Isolate the object until you can get some conservation advice (*see* p.23).

Cleaning

How leather should be cleaned and treated depends very much on how it was tanned and dressed. Old, rare or precious objects should only be cleaned and treated by a conservator. Frequent or vigorous cleaning can damage leather. Museum scientists have recently discovered that many of the cleaning and preservation techniques used in the past are harmful. Research is being undertaken on the best methods of cleaning and preserving leather, but in the meantime only the simplest methods are advocated.

With age, leather develops a **patina** as a result of use, wear and care. The surface may be darker or lighter in some areas and slightly damaged. It is not usually desirable to try to change this nor to clean an old piece.

When cleaning and treating leather objects, care must be taken that the treatment does not affect any support material, adhesives or metal attachments and linings. Do not rub gold tooling vigorously. Paper linings in leather-covered boxes or trunks may be cleaned using **powdered eraser**, *see* PAPER. Consult a conservator if the lining is a textile and requires cleaning or repairing.

Some leather can be damaged by water, therefore conservators prefer to use dry or mechanical methods where further cleaning is necessary after brush-vacuuming (*see* Housekeeping and Maintenance). Powdered eraser or a dry **chemical sponge** can remove surface deposits when gently rubbed over the dirty areas. A soft plastic **pencil eraser** can sometimes be used for stubborn dirt, but the rubbing action is an aggressive treatment and may lift the grain. A cotton wool bud moistened with saliva may remove small spots of dirt.

If the leather remains dirty after dry cleaning and is in good condition, it may be possible to remove the remaining dirt using de-ionised or distilled water and a few drops of a **conservation-grade detergent**. Try it on a small test area first to make sure that the colour is not affected. Apply the cleaning mixture with a barely damp cotton wool bud or a small sponge. Do not get the leather very wet and avoid rubbing it. Just roll the swab over the surface or gently stroke it with the sponge. Rinse by wiping it with clean water on a clean sponge or swab. Allow it to dry naturally.

Modern leather that becomes soiled from use can be cleaned with commercially available products but do not use these on old leather as they can be very damaging. Test the leather for colourfastness before cleaning and follow the manufacturer's instructions.

If the surface of the leather has a nap or velvet finish, such as doeskin or suede, remove any surface dirt with powdered eraser. Modern suede can be cleaned with proprietary suede cleaners; follow the manufacturer's instructions. Do not use these on old suede, as they usually contain silicones, which can be damaging.

Stains such as ring marks or oil spillage are difficult to remove from leather. It is often better to leave the stain than to risk creating a paler area where you have tried to remove it. Do not use bleaches, as they can damage the structure of the leather.

Mould will grow readily on leather in damp conditions. If an object has mould on it, take it outside and brush off the mould with a hogshair brush. Wash the brush after cleaning off the mould so that it does not spread mould spores on to other objects. The mould should not reappear unless the conditions remain damp. As mould can cause discoloration of surfaces and general deterioration of objects, it should be removed and conditions improved as soon as possible.

Reptile leather with a varnished surface that is not very dirty can be cleaned after dusting by rubbing the surface gently with a little **beeswax polish** on a soft, lint-free cloth. Check first that the varnish does not come off. Cases and boxes covered in reptile skin are often lined with skiver, which is very thin leather stuck on to the framework and usually varnished for protection. Clean and polish skiver with beeswax.

Repair

Rare, old, precious or very fragile leather objects should only be repaired and treated by a conservator. Do not try to restore the colour to leather, as it is nearly impossible to achieve a good colour match and easy to make the appearance worse. However, there are some repairs that you can do yourself to less important pieces.

● RE-SEWING

Leather is usually stitched together and often the stitching wears out before the leather does. The leather can be re-sewn using the existing needle holes. If the leather is split along the sewing holes, it should be patched before sewing. To sew

thick leather you should use a strong thread, such as button thread, bookbinding thread or waxed linen thread specifically made for sewing leather. Very thick leather may need to be sewn with a harness needle. Thinner leather will require finer thread.

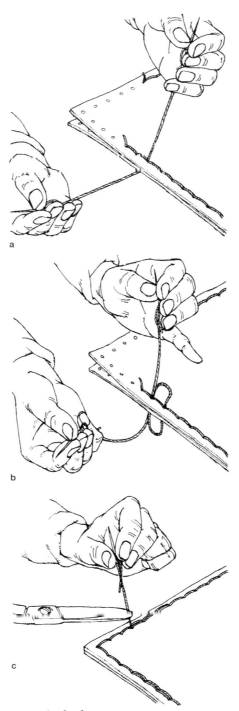

Re-sewing leather
(a) *Use a double stitch, preferably saddle, with needles on each end of the thread*
(b) *Using the existing holes, start before the area requiring re-stitching to prevent unravelling*
(c) *At the end, sew back over the last few stitches and cut the thread.*

The colour should match the colour of any remaining thread. A thread that is not waxed should be pulled across a block of beeswax to make it easier to work. Do not use thread much longer than 60cm (2ft).

A double-stitch technique should be used, preferably the saddle stitch using a double needle thread. Thread a needle of an appropriate size on each end of the thread. To ensure that no more of the old thread unravels, start sewing a few stitches before the area that needs re-stitching. Work towards your body. Using the holes that are already in the leather, push one needle through a hole and pull the thread half of its length until the hole is in the centre of the thread. Push both needles through the next hole, they will go through the hole from opposite sides of the leather. Keep the right-hand needle on top of the left as they pass through the hole. If both needles cannot go through the hole at once, push them through one at a time. Take care not to tear the holes and not to sew through the thread. Pull the stitch tight. Continue in this way to the end of the seam. When you reach the end, sew back over a few stitches. Cut the thread. Start a new thread in the same way. Do not make new holes or the edge of the leather will be weakened.

● PATCHING LEATHER

Torn or split leather is patched not sewn. Leather should be patched from behind. This means that leather upholstery or leather attached to a frame, such as a screen, may have to be disassembled. The latter work should be done only by an experienced conservator.

Gummed linen tape can be used to make the patch. Cut out a patch slightly larger than the tear. If necessary, colour it a similar colour to the leather using acrylic paints or watercolours so that it will not show as bright white.

Prepare a space where the object will be able to lie flat with a weight on the tear. Place some heavy-duty **blotting paper** on the table or bench top and **silicone paper** on top of that. Place the object on the table so that the tear is over the silicone paper. Adjust the tear so that edges are aligned. If one of the edges is frayed, gently use a needle to place the frayed edge under the hard edge. Lightly dampen the tape with purified water using a sponge and apply the patch to the reverse of the leather behind the tear. Lay silicone paper over the patch, followed by some heavy-duty blotting

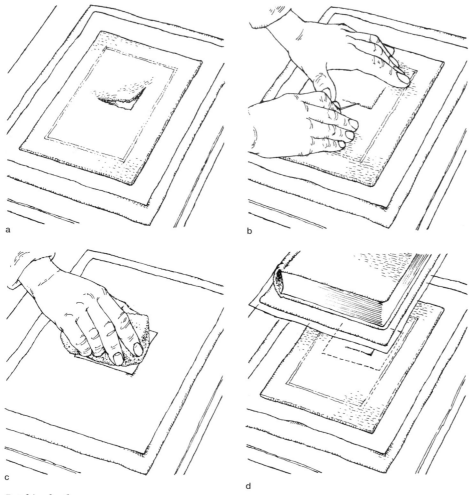

Patching leather
(a) *Place leather on a base of silicone paper over blotting paper* (b) *Adjust the tear, using a needle if necessary to position the frayed edge* (c) *Lightly dampen a piece of gummed linen tape and apply the patch to the leather* (d) *Lay silicone paper, blotting paper and a weight over the patched leather, and leave overnight.*

paper. Press the patch with a **weight** to ensure that the tape sticks well to the leather. Leave it overnight. This technique is difficult to carry out successfully and, if possible, ask a leather conservator to carry out the work or to advise you.

● **RE-STICKING DETACHED LEATHER**
The leather on leather-topped desks and leather-covered boxes can become detached from the wood carcass and, provided the object is in generally good condition, it should be re-adhered before the problem gets worse. If the leather or the whole object is in poor condition, seek conservation advice. Also seek conservation advice if the wood is weakened by insect attack or structural damage, as it is very difficult to repair the carcass without damaging the leather. Only re-adhere leather that was originally stuck down. If it was held in place with tacks or pins and the leather is now torn

Removing old adhesive from under leather before re-sticking.

or the pins are missing, you should seek conservation advice, as the leather will probably need some reinforcement.

The leather can be stuck on to the wood using a neutral pH emulsion **adhesive**. Remove old adhesive from the wood and leather (*see* below, left). Paint a little of the emulsion adhesive on to the wood, taking care not to get it on the surrounding wood surface. Press the leather down from the centre out towards the edges. Cover the area with a sheet of silicone paper, then **blotting paper**, and **weight** it down until the adhesive has set completely – at least twelve hours. Heavy-duty blotting paper between the silicone paper and the weight prevents the surface from being marked by the weight.

Sometimes leather is stretched over metal. Provided there is no corrosion on the metal, the leather can be stuck down in the same way. Stick the leather to the metal only if this was the original method of manufacture; if it was not, seek conservation advice. It is difficult to treat corroded metal without damaging the leather, so this work should be done by a conservator.

Archaeological Leather

Archaeological leather, whether wet or dry, should always be examined, cleaned, and treated by a conservator.

Bookbindings

See BOOKS.

Jugs, Tankards, Bottles, Flasks, Buckets, Helmets and Shields

These types of objects are usually made from vegetable-tanned cattle hide about 2–4mm (under ⅛in) thick. They generally survive in good condition but may be brittle, so handle them with care. Very little can be done to objects such as these. Clean them with a soft brush and vacuum cleaner (*see* pp.19–20), using **powdered eraser** if necessary. If they have a sealed and polished surface, buff it gently with a dry chamois leather. Protect the objects from dust.

Leather Screens

Leather screens were very fashionable at the end of the nineteenth century. Unfortunately, a great deal of the leather used is prone to red rot and becomes very brittle. If pressed against the screen, the corners

of furniture and backs of chairs will indent or tear the leather. Once the leather starts to tear, particularly along frame edges, it is sensible to get it repaired as soon as possible. The leather is likely to be weak, and on this occasion a stitch in time really does save nine. Once screens begin to split and tear, very little can be done by the amateur. Dust screens carefully as for WALL-HANG-INGS (*see* below). Do not apply any leather dressing.

Leather Wall-hangings

Protect leather wall-hangings from direct sunlight, heat and damp walls. If the wall-hanging is in good condition and the decoration is well adhered to the leather, you can keep it clean by using a soft brush and vacuum cleaner (*see* pp.19–20). Do not knock the leather with the nozzle. Do not attempt any further cleaning or any other treatment yourself. Consult a conservator.

ABOVE: *Detail of the early eighteenth-century, English Cordoba leather hangings in the Dining Room at Bateman's, the Sussex home of the writer Rudyard Kipling. Kipling purchased the leather in 1902, and wrote to his cousin, 'It is lovelier than our wildest dreams and will need immense care.' His daughter, however, remembered the hangings being brought back in a car, sticking out of the back like rolls of lino. The hangings now show the problems of painted leather, with flaking and cracking; it is important that leather is kept well away from heat.*

Shagreen

Shagreen is made from the skin of smaller sharks and ray fish. It was popular in France (known as *galuchat*) and England from the late seventeenth century, when it was used to veneer small cases, particularly those for surgical and draughtsman's instruments. The natural surface is grey and rough; this roughness also made it suitable for sword grips. By the eighteenth century it was often rubbed smooth to give a granular appearance of small circles or cross-hatching and dyed black or, more usually, green. Shagreen continued to be used through the eighteenth, nineteenth and early part of the twentieth centuries, particularly for covering boxes, including tea caddies and spectacle cases, as well as for picture frames, umbrella handles and other decorative objects.

The dye can be soluble in organic solvents or water, so test the skin in a small area before cleaning or waxing. Shagreen should be dusted and cleaned, if necessary, using a cotton wool swab damped with water containing a few drops of **conservation-grade detergent**. Rinse the shagreen with clean swabs dampened with clean water and dry it with a soft clean cloth. Polish with colourless **beeswax polish** applied with a soft cloth. Re-polish occasionally. Small repairs can be made using an easily reversible **adhesive**.

If shagreen becomes too dry, it may warp and split and small scales may start to detach. If it does, it can be treated by an experienced conservator.

Display, store and handle shagreen as for CORAL and IVORY AND BONE.

Untanned Skin

Untanned skin includes parchment and vellum (*see* below). Untanned skin is found on musical instruments and ethnographic objects as well as some luggage. As it is not tanned, it is not true leather. Although it has been through a preserving process, it can still be adversely affected by water or damp and is more liable to deterioration than leather if it is kept in inappropriate conditions. Untanned skin should not be treated in the same way as leather.

Skin should be cleaned and repaired by a conservator. Make sure it is kept in a controlled environment, as damp conditions will make it distort and deteriorate and dry conditions will cause it to crack and shrink. Skin is particularly vulnerable to insect and rodent attack.

Upholstery

Leather upholstery should be dusted regularly (*see* p.19). If the leather is very dirty, clean it as you would leather. Do not use saddle soap or cream dressing (*see* Housekeeping and Maintenance). Modern LEATHER, upholstery should be cleaned and treated according to the manufacturer's instructions.

Vintage Car Upholstery

Vintage car upholstery is often restored to pristine condition; this is very invasive and involves stripping off old finishes with alkaline chemicals and refinishing it. Specialist firms dye or lacquer leather to match the original. They also supply lacquer for touching up worn leather and will re-sew car seats. This degree of restoration is not advisable for vehicles in original condition.

Parchment and Vellum

Parchment is made from untanned animal skins that have been soaked in lime-water, de-haired, scraped and dried under tension to produce a relatively thin, firm sheet. The word vellum (from the same Latin source as the word *veal*) is properly used to describe parchment made from calfskin only, though historically the two terms have been used somewhat indiscriminately. Other than calf, the skins of goat and sheep are the most commonly used, but all are found, with a great variety of finish, thickness and stiffness, in the manufacture of books, both as page and covering material. Sheep parchment, often made from the inner or flesh side of a sheepskin split into two layers, was typically used until the middle of the twentieth century for important legal documents. Fine white parchment (usually from young calves or sometimes kids) has also been used for paintings, drawings and prints, and parchment is also used on other objects, such as boxes and even furniture.

Problems

Parchment and vellum are vulnerable to attack by rodents, insects and mould. They can also be badly damaged by inappropriate temperatures and **relative humidity**, and will distort or become very hard, brittle or even crack if kept too dry. Since parchment is dried under tension during manufacture, it is very susceptible to excessively damp conditions (higher than 65% RH). Moisture releases the tension, allowing parchment to expand and cockle, soften, and, if kept very damp over long periods, gelatinise, or dissolve into glue. Paint and gilding on the surface will lift and flake if the parchment or vellum cockles or distorts due to changes in relative humidity. When framed parchment distorts, pushing the paint layer against the glass, the paint may become stuck to the glass. Pastels on parchment are easily attacked by mould, so they should be inspected frequently.

Ink used on manuscripts and documents was often made from mixing galls from oak trees with ferrous sulphate and gum arabic, referred to as iron gall ink. It is sometimes very acid and the ink can destroy the skin, making holes in it and even causing the letters to drop out. These documents should be treated by a paper or document conservator who may be able to prevent further decay (*see* PAPER).

Handling

Parchment and vellum should be handled as little as possible, *see* LEATHER and PAPER.

Personal documents and deeds should be carried on a tray or in their box to wherever they are going to be read. With clean hands, carefully unfold the document, taking note of how it is folded. When putting it away, fold it up again in the reverse order.

Display

Parchment and vellum are very sensitive to their environment, so it is important that they are displayed in the correct conditions. They should be displayed where the temperature and **relative humidity** will remain as constant as possible and neither high nor low (ideally 50–55% RH). Keep them away from outside walls, entrance doors, heating pipes, radiators and fireplaces. Protect them from direct sunlight or bright lights. *See* PAPER.

Documents should not be put on display unless they are framed or in glass-fronted cabinets to protect them from dirt and pollution. *See* PAPER for methods of mounting and framing.

Parchment documents or other two-dimensional works are difficult to mount for framing as the parchment needs to be

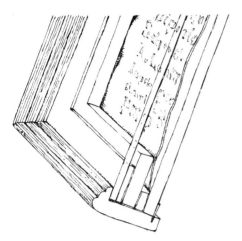

Mounting parchment or vellum in a frame, using acid-free mounting card thick enough to prevent it touching the glass.

ABOVE: *The licence to crenellate Oxburgh Hall in Norfolk, issued by Edward IV to the Bedingfeld family in 1482, and now on display in the King's Hall. The dimensions of the document are 19cm × 36.2cm (7½ × 14¼ in), the seal is 11.2cm (4½ in) in diameter. If a vellum document is not shown flat, the weight of the seal, suspended on its narrow tab, should be supported.*

kept under control within the frame. It must be done by a conservator specialising in this kind of work. Poor framing can cause damage to the paint surface or even allow mould to grow. **Acid-free** mounting card should be used to protect the skin from touching the glass. The card surrounding the skin must be thick enough to accommodate the wrinkles and distortions of the parchment, normally between 3–5mm (⅛–¼ in). The more buckled the skin, the thicker the card should be.

Parchment documents with seals attached present additional difficulties and should be mounted by a specialist framer or conservator. The seal will need to be supported so that it does not put strain on the document.

See LEATHER for the display of three-dimensional objects made with parchment.

Storage

Store parchment and vellum in a cool, dry, well-ventilated, dark area. The storage area should be kept clean to discourage insects and rodents. Unframed pages or documents should be interleaved with **acid-free** tissue and stored horizontally. Acid-free boxes provide the best protection, but a cupboard or trunk can also be used, provided it is not damp. Folded documents are best preserved if stored flat and unfolded but where this is not practicable, they should be stored wrapped in acid-free tissue. Parchment- or vellum-covered objects should also be wrapped in acid-free tissue. It is very important that the conditions should be carefully controlled. Monitor the storage area regularly for rodents and insects. Parchment-leaved books are best kept under light pressure in specially designed drop-spine boxes made to fit the books exactly.

Legal documents, such as house deeds, and others, such as family genealogies, are often written on parchment and stored in a safe place in the house. Metal shelves and boxes are not ideal, because they do not buffer the environment and there is a danger that when the **relative humidity** is high, rust may stain the parchment and mould will develop. However, if a metal safe or deed box is the safest site, line the shelves with acid-free card. If the local environment is damp, include some dry **silica gel** in the box (*see* p.18) and check it regularly to make sure it is keeping the safe dry.

Housekeeping and Maintenance

Old, rare, precious and fragile objects made from parchment or vellum should be cleaned and cared for by a conservator.

Dust can be removed from the surface with an artist's soft paintbrush. Always check that the paint or gilding is sound before touching the surface. Never allow water to come in contact with the skin. Do not apply any kind of leather dressing.

Cleaning

Do not attempt further cleaning of painted or fragile, old, rare or precious documents. If necessary, this should be done by a conservator. If the surface is in good condition, further cleaning of three-dimensional objects such as bookbindings or luggage can be carried out using **powdered eraser** or a dry **chemical sponge** (*see* LEATHER).

Repair

Do not attempt to repair parchment or vellum.

Metals

Most metals are found in nature as ore, and are extracted by smelting and are then further refined. However, some metals, such as gold, silver, copper, platinum and meteoric iron, also occur naturally, and it is likely that this is why these were the first metals to be used by man. Few metals are used in their pure form. They are usually mixed with other metals to make an alloy to improve their appearance, working properties and strength, and for economic reasons. For example, copper is very soft and is alloyed with other metals, such as lead, tin and zinc, to make harder bronze and brass. There are numerous alloys, each with slightly different characteristics, but steel (iron and carbon), pewter (tin and lead) and sterling silver (silver and copper) are common examples.

The malleability of metals often allows them to be shaped by hammering, stamping and bending, but they can also be cast by pouring the molten metal into a mould. Metal can also be turned and cut on a lathe. Very often a combination of methods is used to fashion objects.

Metal is joined mechanically by riveting or folding; by welding, whereby heat and/or hammering joins two pieces together; and by soldering, where an alloy with a melting point lower than the metal being joined is melted along the join. The melting point of hard solders is only just below that of the metal being joined and subsequently

BELOW: *Detail of the late nineteenth-century fireplace in the Housekeeper's Room at Upark in Sussex, once presided over by the mother of the novelist H.G. Wells. The stove is of cast iron with stove blacking. The kettle on the left is of steel, tinned on the outside; the kettle on the right and the saucepan are of copper.*

they form strong bonds. Soft solders are usually alloys of lead and tin and have much lower melting points and provide a weaker join. Historically adhesives were used to join a second material to metal, such as gems or bone knife handles. Adhesives are now used widely in the conservation of metal objects because soldering and welding expose the object to the risk of further damage, and the heat involved in either process may alter the structure of the metal. However, soldering and welding usually create a stronger join than adhesives so they will be used in repair work when necessary – for example, on the handle of a jug in regular use.

Metal is decorated in a number of ways. The surface can be painted, lacquered, gilded or waxed both for protection and decoration. Other forms of artificial patination (see below) are also found. A more decorative or stable metal – gold, silver or tin, for example – can be used to coat the surface. A design can be cut or engraved into the surface or a low relief design can be pushed out from sheet metal using punches. This process, known as repoussé or embossing, is often carried out from the reverse and then the detail is added to the design by 'chasing' with finer punches. Contrasting coloured metal or other materials such as ivory or tortoiseshell can be inlaid into channels or on to roughened areas cut in the base of the metal. Enamel, gems and some other materials can be applied to the metal surface (see ENAMEL).

Most metals are unstable and react with oxygen, water and other agents in a process commonly known as corrosion. Some metals corrode more readily than others; for instance, under normal circumstances, iron corrodes more readily than lead. In some cases, the corrosion protects the surface of the metal and slows down the rate of corrosion of the rest of the metal. Aluminium very quickly forms a protective layer on the surface which prevents further corrosion, and once copper roofs develop their characteristic green colour the rate of corrosion decreases. Pure gold does not corrode at all.

The term tarnish is generally used to describe the thin, smooth, coloured surface corrosion found on silver and copper and its alloys. Corrosion is more disfiguring and destructive than tarnish. Layers of corrosion can build up and completely obliterate the original shape of the object, the detail may be lost and the surface pitted. The form of corrosion varies from metal to metal. Rust, the corrosion on ferrous metal, can build up thick layers on the surface and has a much larger volume than the metal it replaces, while copper corrosion is more dense, retaining more of the shape of the object. Some metals, such as zinc, form small dots. The term **patina** is used to describe corrosion that has either formed naturally or been deliberately induced as a metal to enhance its appearance. The patina found on copper alloys can be black, brown, blue or green and is often highly valued.

Problems

The major problem associated with metals is corrosion, which requires oxygen, water vapour and, depending on the metal, other agents, such as sulphide gases or an acidic environment. Wherever possible metals should be kept in dry conditions and not exposed to pollutant vapours (see p.19). **Archaeological** metalwork is particularly vulnerable to corrosion and may have to be kept under carefully controlled conditions.

When two metals are joined together, one may protect the other from corrosion but will itself corrode more rapidly than if the object were made only out of that material, and not attached to the other metal. For example, a steel bolt used in a brass object will rust more rapidly than the same steel bolt in a steel object.

Another form of corrosion, known as electrochemical corrosion, can be set up when the metal is exposed to certain chemicals. This is a particular problem for metal objects kept outside.

Metals are also vulnerable to physical damage. Although most metals are not as brittle as ceramics and glass, they can easily be scratched, dented or crushed; they can also tear and break.

Fluctuating temperatures may be a problem for some metal objects, because metals expand and contract with each change, but

A toilet set, probably French c.1684, in the State Bedroom at Powis Castle, Powys. The gilded brass boxes and brush handles are decorated with champlevé *enamel in imitation of oriental work. The large box is showing wear to the gilding.*

the coefficient of expansion (*see* **thermal expansion**) is different for each metal. This rarely affects objects made of more than one metal, but if metals are used with other materials, frequent cycles of expansion and contraction can cause a cleavage between them. The rate of corrosion or tarnish increases with the temperature; therefore, wherever possible, prevent the temperature from becoming too high.

It is thought that the rate of silver tarnish may be increased by light, but generally speaking light is not damaging to metals, provided they are not painted or used in combination with **organic materials**. Similarly, pests are not a problem for metals, although bat, fly and spider droppings can encourage corrosion.

Ancient jewellery might look very strong, but this may be deceptive. It could be badly corroded and weak and can break very easily. It is inadvisable to wear ancient jewellery, but if you really want to, ask a metal conservator to check that the piece is strong enough to wear. Do not open and close clasps more than is essential. Ancient gold jewellery may be made from almost 24-**carat** gold. This is softer than modern gold and marks, scratches and bends very easily.

Handling

Always wear **gloves** when handling metal objects to protect the metal from the oils and moisture deposited by your hands, which can etch the surface and cause corrosion. Where possible, wear thin rubber or vinyl gloves rather than cotton gloves, as the moisture can soak through the cotton on to the metal. However, if you do not like wearing vinyl or latex gloves next to your skin, wear cotton gloves underneath them.

Do not stick adhesive tape or labels on to a metal surface, as they may cause corrosion or tarnish, for example on silver, and can remove the patina when they are removed from bronze, lead and other surfaces.

Metal objects, particularly antiquities, may appear to be a lot stronger than they are. Internal corrosion is not always visible, but it can make an object very brittle. There are certain copper alloys used in antiquity that shatter if dropped or placed abruptly on a table. Joins may become weak in time and solders may corrode away.

Metal objects should be handled like other objects (*see* p.12), taking care to support them securely and not to grasp the objects by handles, spouts, arms or other protruding parts. Also take care that pieces which stick out do not knock into doorways when an object is being carried – bows, spears and horse's tails are particularly vulnerable. Remove your belt, watch and jewellery before handling metal objects to prevent them scratching the surface.

Carry candlesticks so that the weight is supported from underneath. Many candlesticks are not made of solid metal: they have a core of a natural resin or plaster of Paris and they are therefore not very strong. Handle them very carefully. Do not set them down hard on the table, as the core can crack and the metal may break at the waist. When putting candles into branched candlesticks, support the socket by placing your hand under it.

Check that mounted sculptures are secure on their mounts. If the base is not firmly fixed to the object, it may well fall off when you pick up the sculpture.

When moving a metal object that is too heavy to lift, use a trolley or sack barrow or suitable carrying equipment. Always make sure the barrow is well padded with clean blankets or **polyethylene foam**, as grit and dirt can damage the surface or patination. Set the object down on wooden blocks or battens, as this makes it easier to lift and means you can set it down squarely without getting your fingers trapped.

Moving large metal objects is a specialist skill and should be undertaken by experienced art handlers and shippers, otherwise it is easy to damage yourself, the objects and the surroundings. When large objects are being moved, the floors and doorways may need protection. This is often done by laying down sheets of hardboard on the floor and **polypropylene twinwall board** to protect walls and woodwork.

Display

Most historic metal objects, as opposed to antiquities, are relatively stable and can be displayed almost anywhere, but some metals do not survive well outside or may need regular maintenance or protection (*see* individual metal entries). Metal objects should not be displayed in a damp environment – conditions should be under 65% RH, but antiquities and archaeological metalwork are better preserved under 45% RH.

Do not display metal objects where they are in direct contact with another metal, as the metals interact and set up corrosion problems. Where metal is used in conjunction with **organic materials** the object must be displayed in conditions that are also suitable for those materials.

Avoid placing metal objects on mantelpieces or above radiators, where they will become dusty and may tarnish quite quickly. Place small objects far enough back on tables and sideboards so that they cannot be knocked off on to a hard floor.

Do not put metal objects directly on to stone or brick floors that have no dampproofing, as the damp in the floor can be damaging. Stand them on cork mats or wooden slats. Large objects, in particular, should be on a plinth to raise them off the floor, to protect them from vacuum cleaners or from being kicked, and to enable them to be moved when necessary.

If you are using metal bowls or urns for houseplants, use a plastic liner or place a plastic container or a saucer in the bottom of the bowl so that the water from the plant does not come into direct contact with the metal. Larger metal containers used for exterior planting should be raised off the ground. In the case of lead cisterns, a bed of flat stones, such as paving stones from a garden centre can be placed under the cistern so that the gaps between the stones are small enough (maximum 2cm/¾in) to prevent the lead from sagging into them. Stronger metals can be raised on wood or stone blocks, but these must extend for the full width of the container. Replace the wood if it rots to ensure that the support remains stable. There should be one or more drainage holes in the bottom, which must be checked to ensure that they are not blocked and that the water can run out freely. The container should also be lined with a plastic liner about 5cm (2in) smaller than the internal measurements of the container and with a drainage hole, otherwise the metal will corrode rapidly. If the weight of the soil is too great, particularly for lead urns, the container may twist, buckle or split.

Storage

Keep metal objects in a dry area. Wrap small objects in **acid-free** tissue to prevent them from being knocked and to help protect them from tarnishing. If they are to be boxed, use an acid-free cardboard box. Do not wrap objects in bubble wrap, cling film or sealed polythene bags, because condensation may form inside and cause corrosion. Silver can react with cling film,

ABOVE: *Dancing figures in the Library at Anglesey Abbey in Cambridgeshire. The piece has the very shiny patina fashionable in twentieth-century bronzes – this can easily be damaged by aggressive abrasives.*

and if stored in it for any period of time the film will bond with the metal. Metal used in conjunction with organic materials should be stored under conditions to suit both the materials; this usually means in a stable environment that is neither too dry nor damp (40–65% RH). Metal objects should not be in contact with other metals.

Special **corrosion-inhibiting bags** (*see* p.246), pouches and rolls are now available for storing all types of metal. Some are plastic and change colour when the corrosion protection is no longer effective.

Do not stand objects directly on a stone, concrete or brick floor, as the damp from the floor can cause corrosion. Place objects on wooden slats, cork or Polythene sheeting. Cover large objects with a **clean dustsheet**, **calico** or **Tyvek** to protect them from dust.

Small metal objects that are very prone to corrosion can be kept dry by storing them with **silica gel** in **sealed plastic boxes** Inspect them regularly and replace the silica gel when necessary (*see* p.18).

Housekeeping and Maintenance

Remove dust using a soft brush and vacuum cleaner (*see* pp.19–20) or a dry **microfibre cloth** for flat objects. **Compressed air** is useful for blowing dust off intricate areas. Check metal objects at least once a year for signs of active corrosion and tarnish. Some metals are protected with a wax coating that can be reapplied every 12 or 18 months (*see* individual metal entries).

Cleaning

How much a metal is cleaned may vary from metal to metal and according to taste. For example, in some parts of the World, silver is left to go black, because cleaning it removes a small amount of the silver, and if it is cleaned regularly the decoration and detail can be worn away. Ancient bronzes are never polished but are admired for the brown or green **patina**, while brass is often kept bright; however, some modern sculptors intended their bronze pieces to have a shiny surface. Many people prefer metals not to be too sparkling so that they do not look too new, and allow them to develop a patina. Cloths are available for cleaning polished metal such as silver, copper, brass and gold which are very useful for maintaining a shine. They have been developed for use with the specific metals identified on the packet and should not be interchanged.

Some door furniture can have finely chased or etched decoration. This may have been worn away by constant polishing. Keep the fittings clean with a microfibre cloth and brass polishing cloth and polish less frequently.

Brass can be used as an inlay on furniture, grandfather clocks, decorative boxes and many other objects. This inlay should never be cleaned with brass polish, as it will stain the wood. If the inlay is very dirty, try cleaning it by rubbing with a dry cotton wool bud. Stubborn spots may be removed using a **bamboo stick**. Sometimes rubbing the surface with a soft **pencil eraser** will remove tarnish and help polish the brass.

Once it is cleaned, the inlay can be buffed using a soft duster or brass metal polishing cloth when you clean the object, but take care that the cloth does not catch on and lift loose or damaged inlay. Brass inlay on armour should be attended to by a conservator. However, if the armour is in very good condition, the brass can be waxed with microcrystalline wax for protection.

Pinchbeck

Pinchbeck is a type of brass but with a lower percentage of zinc (20 per cent rather than 30–40 per cent). It was invented by a watchmaker, Christopher Pinchbeck, in the early eighteenth century and was used for making snuffboxes, watch-cases and small items. Some pinchbeck objects were gilded, but it is difficult to see where the gilding has worn off on the edges and high spots, as its colour is very similar to gold unless it has tarnished. If you can tell whether the pinchbeck is gilded, handling, cleaning, display and storage are similar to ORMOLU. If the object is not gilded, handling, cleaning, display and storage are similar to BRASS. Take care when cleaning, as the surface is often finely detailed and this can be lost with polishing. It is also difficult to get all the polish out of the detail, which may leave the piece looking unpleasant.

LEFT: *Brass locks and hinges in the Balcony Room at Dyrham Park in Gloucestershire. These lovely fittings, decorated with flowers, were bought by William Blathwayt in 1694, and were probably made by John Wilkes of Birmingham. The wood surrounding the locks is slightly marked with the residue of polish. Traces of green corrosion caused by old polish can be seen around the flowers.*

Scientific Instruments

Many instruments have brass fittings (*see* SCIENTIFIC INSTRUMENTS). The original lacquer should not be removed and the brass is not usually polished. You could buff it slightly with a soft cloth.

Bronze

Bronze is an alloy of copper and tin, often with other metals, particularly zinc and lead. It has excellent casting properties and is ideally suited to making statues.

Bronze has been used from the earliest times, since the Bronze Age (1000–500BC in Britain). When bronze is cast, it can vary in colour, depending on the composition of the alloy, from a copper to a golden or silver tone. If it is left to tarnish naturally, it will eventually darken to a dark brown. Atmospheric pollution can turn the surface a pale green or even a blue, but corrosion like this is more commonly seen when a bronze has been buried. Many bronze sculptures have the surface coloured artificially by the application of chemicals and/or heat. More modern sculptures may be painted. The patina on indoor bronzes ranges from a golden brown to a brownish-black colour, although a few may be green. Ancient bronzes are more likely to be green. The **patina** on bronzes is highly prized and should not be removed.

As well as sculpture, bronze has been used for domestic and decorative objects, such as firedogs, early cooking pots, tables, decorative fittings on furniture, clock mounts, weapons, cannon and coins. Bronze can be used in combination with ivory, silver, marble and other materials.

Problems

A patina will protect bronze from tarnishing, but the metal can corrode in high humidity or when there are chloride compounds (found in salt or chlorinated water) or acid vapours present. Under these circumstances, spots or patches of green will appear; in time, the whole surface can be covered. There is a particularly destructive corrosion known as 'bronze disease'; small areas can corrode quite quickly, producing pitting in the surface. Bronze disease appears as bright green powdery spots on the surface of the bronze. The green is brighter than the other corrosion products and is usually only found on ancient or buried bronzes. Salt can cause

rapid bronze corrosion even on modern pieces; it can come from your hands, the sea, chlorinated water and other sources. For this reason, bronzes kept outside by the sea or near a chlorinated swimming pool will need frequent maintenance and wax protection.

Handling

See METALS and p.12.

Display

See METALS. Bronzes can be displayed almost anywhere in the house, but it is best to avoid bathrooms and conservatories or anywhere with a very damp atmosphere. Do not place bronzes close to windows that are frequently opened, as cool, damp air will form condensation on the bronze. Do not place vases of flowers or houseplants that need to be sprayed with a fine mist of water close to bronzes. The spray may drift on to the bronze.

Storage

See METALS.

Housekeeping and Maintenance

The only cleaning that bronzes should require is a light dusting. If the bronze is very dusty, the dust should be removed with a soft brush and vacuum cleaner (*see* pp.19–20). Flat surfaces can be dusted with a dry **microfibre cloth** or lint-free duster. Remove any dust from crevices and decoration with a hogshair brush or **compressed air**.

BRONZE DISEASE
Bronze disease, although rare, may be found on ancient bronzes, but very occasionally it occurs on more modern bronzes, whether they are displayed outside or inside. It is difficult to distinguish bronze disease from other harmless corrosion products, so, where possible, ask advice from a conservator. If you find a small area of bronze disease, keep the object in a dry environment and monitor the corrosion to see if it gets worse. One way to do this is to darken the light spots so that if another bright area appears you know that the corrosion is continuing. To tone down the spots of corrosion, using a very fine brush (00), paint a little raw umber watercolour or acrylic paint on to the light areas only. If the

bronze disease gets worse, if more spots appear or the existing spots get bigger, ask a conservator for advice. If the bronze disease is severe, keep the object as dry as possible and ask a conservator for advice.

Cleaning

Old, rare or very valuable bronze sculptures should be cleaned only by a metal conservator.

Never use abrasive cleaning materials, such as metal polish, on a bronze. Never use water or **alcohol** or any **solvent** on an indoor bronze, as these may remove surface colouring such as wax and lacquers.

Avoid rubbing a bronze too vigorously, as raised surfaces can become highlighted and dirt can still be left in the depths. To remove caked dirt from crevices and hard-to-reach areas, take a few fibres of cotton wool and wrap them round the end of a **bamboo stick**. Dampen them with saliva. Gently push the bud along the crevices, turning it as you go so that the dirt is not ground into the surface. Replace the cotton wool as soon as it is dirty. Ready-made buds are not very satisfactory for this work as they are too soft and unravel.

● WAXING INDOOR SCULPTURE

If a bronze statue has a dull surface from having been in an unsuitably damp place, it may be revived by taking a soft bristle brush and lightly waxing the surface. Touch the surface of the bristles with **microcrystalline wax**; there should be hardly any wax on the brush and, if necessary, wipe off any excess on a clean piece of paper towel. Then, very lightly, brush the wax over the surface of the bronze and lightly polish it with a soft, clean cloth. Do not use a brush that has been used for waxing bronze on any object made of a different metal.

If a bronze has a green patina that has been either chemically induced or painted on, check a small area to see that the wax will not take the colouring off. Make sure you use only a very small amount of wax.

Repair

Bronze can be repaired by brazing or soldering, but a great deal of damage can be done to bronzes by the layman trying to repair them. Always take a damaged bronze to a metal conservator. Small repairs can be made by using an epoxy resin **adhesive** or an easily reversible adhesive.

Lead solder and adhesive are potentially weak, so do not use these methods to repair structural parts, such as handles or candelabra arms. If lead solder was used in the original fabrication or in old repairs, these may fall apart if you use much heat (*see* BRASS).

Outdoor Sculpture

Bronze is frequently used for outdoor sculpture. Compared with many other metals and alloys, bronze is reasonably resistant to corrosion, but it is not immune to the heavily polluted atmospheres of industrial cities, which contain corrosion-inducing chemicals. Some corrosion may be washed away by rain, thus exposing the surface of the bronze to further attack. The shape of the sculpture can also affect the way it corrodes. For instance, contaminated water can drain into and remain in crevices such as the folds of clothing. This water is

Bronze urn modelled in the late seventeenth century by Louis Ballon and originally in the garden of the Château of Bagatelle. It now adorns the Formal Garden at Lanhydrock in Cornwall. The surface has acquired a patina through corrosion.

likely to be strongly corrosive. The water can also seep into the bronze through pit holes in the surface, resulting in the inside of the object becoming very corroded. The underneath of a statue can also deteriorate badly. Examine all of these areas – small gullies, folds of material and the underneath – as well as the major part of the statue to make sure that the metal has not completely corroded away, leaving holes.

Some bronzes have internal iron armatures. These will rust and expand and can eventually split the bronze, particularly in narrow parts of the sculpture such as the legs and arms. Check for orange or brown iron staining on the surface and any sign of cracks in the bronze. Keep an eye on the iron staining. If it gets any worse or if the bronze is cracked, you should consult a metal conservator as soon as possible.

The combination of rain, dust, soot and tar can cause unsightly streaks, stains and pitting on the surface of a bronze. Streaks occur particularly on bronzes positioned underneath trees.

Display

Outdoor bronze sculpture is usually displayed on a plinth. A new plinth should have a damp-proof membrane, such as polythene, lead or slate, and should stand square to the statue to prevent the statue from leaning and developing unnatural stresses. A plinth in poor condition should be repaired and a damp-proof membrane added if this is not too disruptive to the sculpture.

Do not place lawn sprinklers near bronze sculpture and, where possible, prevent trees and bushes from growing too close to a bronze. Overhanging branches can scratch the surface. Also, if a sculpture is overhung with a canopy of greenery, the air around the sculpture stays quite damp and this can cause the sculpture to corrode unnecessarily quickly. Water dripping off the trees will cause disfiguring streaks in the patination.

Housekeeping and Maintenance

Regularly remove leaves and other debris which collect in crevices, as they hold water and speed up corrosion.

Once the bronze sculpture has been thoroughly cleaned and waxed (*see* below), it should be washed and waxed at regular intervals. Brush off any loose dirt or bird droppings with a dry brush as necessary.

Wash and wax the sculpture about once a year. This should keep the statue in good condition. If a statue has been badly neglected, you should ask a metal conservator for advice.

Cleaning

Outdoor bronze statues in good condition can be cleaned by washing. Choose a warm, dry day. Where there is a stone base, protect it from being stained by the dirty cleaning water by covering it with polyethylene sheeting securely taped into place.

Remove as much as possible of the grime and bird droppings before washing with a dry, medium stiff bristle scrubbing brush. Do not use a brush that is too stiff or you could scratch the surface of the bronze. Then scrub the bronze with a paintbrush or stencil brush using warm water containing a few drops of **conservation-grade detergent**. Scrub off any further deposits that did not come off when dry.

Rinse the sculpture really well with clean, warm water – a clean garden spray bottle is useful for this – and examine the entire surface of the bronze for any further loose material. Pay particular attention to sheltered parts, including the underside of the figure, and to ledges or crevices where water may have collected. If necessary, wash the sculpture again, then dry it as much as possible with clean, dry cloths or a chamois leather and allow it to dry completely in the sun.

If the sculpture has unsightly green streaks or patches, it may be possible to tone them down by mixing powdered artist's pigment with **microcrystalline wax**. Raw umber, burnt umber and black are probably the most useful colours. Mix the colours into the wax with a spatula or knife. First wax the entire sculpture with uncoloured wax. Then rub the coloured wax well into the pale streaks and they should go darker.

After cleaning outdoor bronzes, they should be waxed for protection. Waxing should be carried out thoroughly and often.

● **WAXING AN OUTDOOR BRONZE SCULPTURE**

Microcrystalline wax is recommended for bronzes as it protects the metal and dries hard, so dirt does not stick to it as much as to beeswax, which, although excellent for wood, is too soft and sticky to be used on metal. Silicone waxes should not be used on antiques or antiquities as they are very

difficult to remove and give an inappropriate gloss.

Make sure that the bronze is completely dry. Apply microcrystalline wax on a bristle stencil brush. Make sure the wax covers the entire surface, including underneath and all crevices, folds and ledges. Polish the wax as you go with a soft bristle brush or a soft, dry cloth. Do not apply all the wax and then polish, because once the wax has dried it becomes very hard and difficult to polish. If you are not certain that you have covered the entire surface, apply a second coat of wax in the same way an hour later.

Bronze Cannon

Bronze cannon are generally kept outside and, with time, a green patina can form on them. Sometimes more active corrosion is set off by atmospheric pollution. When bronze cannon were in use, they were allowed to tarnish to a dull bronze colour and were not kept polished. If you have a cannon in this condition, maintain the colour with regularly cleaning and waxing, *see* OUTDOOR SCULPTURE. Cannon should not be placed directly on the ground. If there is no cannon carriage, mount it on wooden blocks. The bore is normally inclined downwards, or blocked at the mouth with a closely-fitting plug to prevent rainwater from collecting inside it.

Cold-cast or Simulated Bronze

Modern resins make it possible to create what are known as cold-cast or simulated bronzes, which are cast in a mould. They are made of a synthetic resin filled with a bronze powder and then coloured to look like genuine bronze. They can be very like real bronze. However, because they are made of resin, they can be treated in the same way as plastic. One thing to bear in mind is that a cold-cast bronze is not nearly as strong as a genuine bronze, so parts like legs, arms and tails are very vulnerable and may snap off easily. An armature may have been used in the construction, which will provide a little extra strength.

Cold-cast bronzes should be cleaned by dusting them with a soft, clean cloth. If they need further cleaning, they can be washed in warm water containing a few drops of **conservation-grade detergent**. First, test a small inconspicuous area to see that the surface colour does not come off. Use a cotton wool swab dampened with the washing liquid. Carefully wipe the test area. If any colour comes off on the swab, do not continue to wash the object. If the colour does not come off, wipe the surface with swabs of cotton wool dampened with the washing solution. Rinse the object by using clean cotton wool swabs dampened with clean water. Dry it with a soft, clean cloth.

Cold-cast or simulated bronzes can be displayed and stored indoors under most conditions. Avoid direct heat sources or direct sunlight, which could affect any surface colouring.

Chromium

Chromium is a hard white metal that can be polished to a high shine. Chrome plating is applied to a variety of metal surfaces, usually brass or steel, to provide a decorative or protective finish. Plastic may also be chrome plated. It is mainly found on twentieth-century objects, such as art deco figurines, clocks, lamps, car mascots and bumpers, furniture and bathroom fittings, as well as on more modern plastic objects, including toys. Silver and chrome, when highly polished, can look very similar. Chromium is also an ingredient in various other alloys, such as stainless steel.

Problems

Chromium itself does not corrode. However, if the chrome plating is broken the metal underneath will corrode. Where the original layer of plating is thinly applied, tiny air bubbles left in the chrome layer can cause breaks in the chrome surface. The base metal may corrode in these breaks, forming small pimples that appear on the surface of the chrome as black or grey discoloration. In severe cases, the chrome can peel off.

Handling

See METALS. The chromium plate layer may be very thin, so do not scratch it or treat it roughly.

Display and Storage

See METALS.

Housekeeping and Maintenance

Art nouveau and art deco objects were often protected with a lacquer, so take care not to remove this during cleaning. Loose dust or grit should be brushed off with a soft brush.

Cleaning

Do not clean an object where the chrome is flaking off the base metal, as the cleaning process may remove the chrome and exacerbate the corrosion. Consult a metal conservator.

Provided the object is in good condition, grimy, greasy dirt can be removed by washing the chrome with a soft bristle brush dipped in warm water containing a few drops of **conservation-grade detergent**. Never use wire wool or any other abrasive cleaner on chrome, as it will scratch the surface. Rinse thoroughly with clean warm water and dry with a soft, clean cloth. If this is not effective, use the white spirit and water mixture (*see* **solvent mixtures**). To make sure all the water is removed, dry with a warm – not hot – hairdryer.

On art deco objects particularly, chromium was used in conjunction with other materials, such as ivory and plastic. Wipe the chromium of such objects with a cotton wool bud dampened with the warm washing solution, rinse with a clean bud dampened with clean water and dry the object thoroughly with a soft, clean cloth. Do not allow the cleaning solution to spread on to the ivory or other materials. Do not dry the object with a hairdryer.

To remove areas of discoloration, clean the chromium surface with a **fine abrasive paste**. Apply the cleaner on small wads of cotton wool or a **cotton bud** on a swab stick and polish with a circular movement. Buff with a soft, clean cloth.

Do not try to remove or flatten any pimples, as this will break the chromium layer

BELOW: *Two model seaplanes in chromium, in the Book Room at Clouds Hill, T.E. Lawrence's remote cottage in Dorset. The smaller model is a Schneider Trophy plane (Lawrence was involved in the race of 1929), the larger model is a Handley-Page flying boat. Chromium must not be cleaned too aggressively, lest the metal underneath is revealed. There are signs of this on the engine of the left-hand side of the biplane.*

even more. Once the chrome is polished, they will not look as disfiguring.

It is possible to have objects re-chromed, but this is not recommended for antiques and historical objects, because the colour and appearance of the chrome will alter as the method of plating has changed.

Repair

Chromium-plated objects have to be repaired in a way that suits the base metal (*see* relevant section). Small breaks can be repaired using an epoxy resin **adhesive**. Do not try to solder chromed objects, as any heat will discolour and blister the surface. If the chrome layer is peeling off, you will need to get professional advice.

Copper

Copper is thought to be the first metal to be widely used by man, because native copper is occasionally found in pieces which can be worked immediately without smelting. Small objects made from native copper have been found in early archaeological sites (9000 and 7000 BC). Copper is more commonly smelted from ores.

Copper is a pinkish red colour; it is a very soft, ductile metal and a good conductor of heat and electricity. It does not cast well unless it is alloyed, but sheets can be cold hammered to form cooking pots, jewellery and other objects. Because copper corrodes, the inside of food vessels are frequently coated with another metal, usually tin. The base metal of Sheffield plate is copper. Copper has also been used extensively as the base for enamel painting.

Copper is alloyed with other metals, particularly tin to make bronze and zinc to make brass. It is also alloyed with silver and gold. It is most often made into domestic objects, kettles, coal scuttles, bed warmers and warming pans, saucepans and engraved printing plates.

Copper will tarnish to a brown colour or corrode to green or occasionally blue. This green, which can be seen on copper roofs, is often carefully preserved for its appearance. Copper objects are often thought to be more attractive when they have been allowed to tarnish slightly.

Problems

Copper corrodes as described in BRASS and BRONZE.

Old cooking pots and bowls are often used for holding plants. Check that the seams have not corroded through or split, otherwise the water from the plant will leak out. Use a liner to protect the copper.

Handling

See METALS. Copper is a very soft metal and is easily scratched and dented by careless handling. Do not set round-bottomed copper bowls down hard as they can dent and crack.

Display and Storage

See METALS.

Housekeeping and Maintenance

See BRASS. A copper **metal polishing cloth** can be used on lightly tarnished objects.

Cleaning

Old, rare or precious copper objects should be cleaned by a metal conservator, but other copper objects can be cleaned as described in BRASS.

Do not polish your copper too often, as it is very soft and will wear away. Do not press too hard when you polish thin copper, as you could make a dent in the object.

Copper is also inlaid into silver and brass. This copper inlay can be polished at the same time as the object itself. *See* BRASS.

Copper can be protected from tarnishing with a coat of clear **lacquer**. *See* BRASS.

Repair

Do not attempt to repair old, rare or precious copper objects. This should be done by a metal conservator.

Other copper pieces can be repaired using lead solder and a soldering iron or gas torch as described in BRASS, but unless this is done well it can look unsightly and may change the structure or colour of the metal (*see* p.75). If lead was used in the original fabrication or there are old repairs, these may fail if you use much heat.

Electrotypes

Electrotyping is a method of reproducing an object by depositing metal electrolytically into a mould. Electrotyping was

developed in the mid-nineteenth century and is a similar process to electroplating. The difference between the two is that in electroplating a surface of gold or silver is plated on to a finished base metal object; in electrotyping the whole object is made by depositing metal into a mould coated on the inside with graphite. The deposited metal becomes the body of the object, and is usually copper, although gold or silver can be used. The metal is very thin, so it is often backed with plaster of Paris or another metal, usually lead, to give it strength.

Most electrotypes are made in several pieces, backed with lead and then joined together to make a complete object. With a coin, the obverse and reverse would be made separately and then soldered together. The copper base is often plated with another metal, such as gold or silver, or may be chemically patinated. Occasionally electrotyped objects are left copper-coloured. Very fine detail can be obtained by this process and nowadays many reproduction reliefs, medals and small ornaments are electrotypes. Large objects such as furniture and life-sized sculptures have also been made by electrotyping.

If the surface of the finished object is copper, treat it in the way you would copper. If it is gold- or silver-plated, *see* GOLD or SILVER. Always bear in mind that the body of the object is very thin, so handle electrotypes with great care. In addition, any metal plating will be extremely thin and will wear through quickly, exposing the copper.

Printing plates

Printing plates are usually made from copper, but whatever they are made from, they should never be polished, as the action of polishing will soften the lines of the engraving and the polish will fill them up. Wash them in warm water containing a few drops of **conservation-grade detergent**. Rinse them well in warm water and pat them dry with a soft cloth. For protection, apply **microcrystalline wax** with a soft cloth or brush and polish off with a soft cloth.

Tinned copper vessels

Polish tinned copper vessels occasionally with a copper **metal polishing cloth**. Frequent polishing of any kind will wear away the tin. Do not polish the tinned areas.

Gold

Gold is regarded as the most precious of the historical metals. Very occasionally pure gold objects were made, but normally it is too soft and too expensive in its pure state to be used, so it is alloyed with other metals. The amount of gold in the alloy is expressed in **carats**. Pure gold is 24 carats. The other standards used are 9, 14, 18 and 20 carats. The number represents the proportion of gold out of 24 parts.

The colour of gold varies according to the type and quantity of metal in the alloy. Gold is usually alloyed with silver, which gives it a pale greenish colour, or copper, which gives a reddish tinge. When both copper and silver are used, the metal is more yellow than the pure metal. Platinum makes it silvery and a 25 per cent platinum 75 per cent gold alloy produces 18-carat white gold.

Gold, like silver, can be decorated by engraving, embossing or enamelling. It has been used for jewellery, decorative objects, coins and medals, and statues. Gold can also be coated on to other metals and made into gold leaf for decorating frames and furniture, ceramics and glass, and for illuminating manuscripts. It is used as an inlay to decorate other materials and can itself be inlaid with a variety of materials.

Problems

Pure gold does not tarnish, but when it is alloyed with a high percentage of another metal, the surface may be tarnished by the corrosion of the secondary metal.

Handling

See METALS. Gold is a very soft metal and, even when alloyed with other materials, will dent and scratch easily. Gold objects should therefore be handled very carefully.

Display

See METALS. Ancient gold objects with a lot of copper in the alloy must be kept dry.

Storage

See METALS. Gold can withstand almost any environmental conditions, but the other metals in the alloy will corrode or tarnish if the conditions are not suitable. Therefore, keep gold dry and away from atmospheres harmful to SILVER.

Where there are a number of objects stored in one box, make sure that the weight of those on top does not crush those at the bottom.

Housekeeping and Maintenance

Dust with a soft brush, a soft, clean cloth, a **microfibre cloth** or a gold **metal polishing cloth**.

Cleaning

Old, rare or precious gold objects should only be cleaned by a metal conservator. *See also* COINS AND MEDALS.

Before cleaning gold objects, check that the object is solid gold and not silver gilt, ormolu or gold-plated. These types of object can be severely damaged if cleaned incorrectly. For cleaning gold-plated objects, *see* ORMOLU.

Grimy, greasy dirt can be removed by washing the object in warm water containing a few drops of a **conservation-grade detergent**. Rinse the object well in clean warm water and pat it dry with a very soft, clean cloth. Where gold is used in conjunction with another material, such as ivory, use cotton wool swabs or **cotton buds** with the washing solution, and take care not to wet the other materials.

Tarnish can develop on the surface from the silver in the alloy. Very gently remove this with a gold **metal polishing cloth**. Do not use a cloth made for other metals. As gold is so soft, it can be worn away by rubbing.

Gold is often decorated with enamel and gemstones or other applied decoration. These should not get wet and should not be cleaned by immersing them in water or **solvents**, as the liquid trapped under the enamel or stones can cause the enamel to separate from the metal and staining to appear under the stones.

Do not try to clean **archaeological** gold. Some ancient gold is covered in green copper corrosion products from the copper in the alloy. Do not attempt to remove this. It should be cleaned by a metal conservator. A red patina is also sometimes found on gold and generally is considered to enhance the object.

Repair

Repairs should be carried out by a metal conservator or a goldsmith.

Iron and Steel

Iron is one of the most common and utilitarian metals. It can be cast, forged or rolled, or made into steel. Steel is used to make tinplate by coating it with tin, but it can also be coated with other metals. Iron and steel are frequently referred to as ferrous metals. They were first used for weapons and domestic utensils and later for decorative objects. They have been used for cannon balls, ornate shoe buckles, jewellery, cooking pots, door hinges and armour, fire grates, ornamental railings, garden furniture, wall lights, machinery, vehicles, ships and more. Ferrous metals may be inlaid with gold and silver and used to make decorative objects.

Ferrous metals are silver-grey, ductile and malleable. They are also magnetic, which differentiates them from other metals, although some stainless steels are non-magnetic or only weakly magnetic. Even with heavily corroded objects, if you place a small magnet near the object, you will feel the slight pull that indicates that it is made of iron. However, if the metal has completely corroded away, the magnet will have no effect.

IRON

Iron is either cast or wrought. Cast iron has a high carbon content, making it too brittle to forge. Objects are made by pouring the molten metal into a mould. They consist usually of one piece or of several pieces bolted together, as cast iron cannot easily be welded. As it is brittle, it will not bend, and it breaks easily. When cast iron is broken, the inside may range in colour from black to silvery white and is rather coarse. Iron that has been badly cast will have air bubbles trapped in it, which give it a spongy appearance. Examples of cast-iron objects are ranges, firebacks, fire-irons and fire surrounds, though cast iron can also be made into small decorative objects and is sometimes inlayed with gold and silver.

Wrought iron has a low carbon content and is malleable. When red-hot, it can be hammered into simple patterns, twisted or curled or flattened. These pieces are then

RIGHT: *The nineteenth-century dairy at Ham House, Surrey. The marble overshelf is supported on cows' legs of cast iron: these rest on stone blocks to avoid rusting. The decorative ceramic tiles show some signs of wear on the decoration, but are otherwise in good condition.*

Problems

Lead is very durable, unless it is exposed to organic acid vapour, which is produced by many types of wood – oak and sweet chestnut in particular – or other materials such as household paints and cardboard boxes. The organic acids cause the lead to corrode; the surface of the metal becomes milky white and, if the corrosion continues, it expands, pushing the lead out of shape so that the object becomes distorted. The corrosion product is toxic.

Lead is so soft that it often cannot sustain its own weight. Most lead sculptures are supported by an internal iron armature that will corrode in high humidities. This is sometimes evident in garden sculpture in which the iron becomes so weak that the statue begins to collapse under its own weight. The lead may split or the sculpture may lean from the knees or ankles. A metal

conservator accustomed to dealing with lead can rectify this problem. The conservator may have to replace the original iron armature with one made of stainless steel.

Toys and models, if they have survived their original owners, are quite stable as long as they are not stored in an acid environment. They often suffer from physical damage and missing or flaking paint.

Handling

See METALS. After handling lead objects, make sure that you wash your hands well, even when you have worn gloves.

Display

See METALS. See BRONZE, Outdoor Sculpture for lead sculpture that is displayed outdoors.

ABOVE: *Detail of an early eighteenth-century lead statue of a young shepherd boy attributed to Jan van Nost in the Green Court at Canons Ashby in Northamptonshire. He has been painted over on at least one occasion to protect the lead. Lead statuary requires careful maintenance.*

Lead objects should not be displayed in the proximity of materials producing organic acids, such as oak, cardboard, emulsion paint, chipboard, **MDF**, sweet chestnut and vinegar. Although oak is not recommended for use with lead, lead can be displayed on, not inside, antique oak furniture if there is a good circulation of air around it. However, new oak furniture is potentially more damaging and should not be used. Do not put lead objects back into a room that has been newly decorated until the fumes have disappeared. A display case

ABOVE: *Late nineteenth-century collection of lead toy soldiers in the School Room at Calke Abbey in Derbyshire. Despite some flaking of the paint, and distortion where the metal has been bent in vulnerable places such as the carriage, they are in very good condition. The fact that they retain their original box and wood wool packing has helped, even though wood is not ideal for lead.*

or shelves should ideally be made of metal, glass or **acrylic sheet**; avoid painted wood, oak, plywood, MDF or chipboard.

Storage

See METALS. Never place lead objects in oak drawers or cupboards, boxes made of cardboard or wood products that give off corrosive vapour. Use **archival quality** boxes or **sealed plastic boxes**. Do not pack too many objects in a box nor pack the box too tightly, as some of the objects will be squashed. Use plenty of packing material.

If outside lead objects are to be stored, say over the winter, place them in a dry area, free from frost. Lead statues should be kept upright, because if they are laid down, protrusions may be squashed. Raise the object off the floor using wooden slats, cork, etc.

Housekeeping and Maintenance

Dust with a soft brush and vacuum cleaner (*see* pp.19–20). Flat surfaces can be dusted with a **microfibre cloth** or soft, lint-free cloth.

Outdoor sculpture should be washed at least once a year to remove general grime and bird droppings (*see* BRONZE, Outdoor Sculpture). Use a soft bristle brush. Never use a nylon brush, because it may score the surface. Lead can easily be damaged by over-vigorous polishing or scrubbing with a hard brush, so treat it gently. A protective coating such as wax is not recommended.

If the object has spots of severe corrosion, or shows signs of splitting or distortion, seek advice from a metal conservator. It is important to check that the storage or display conditions are not causing the corrosion. Move the object to a better environment if you suspect they are.

Cleaning

Rare, old and precious objects should be cleaned only by a metal conservator.

If indoor lead objects need further cleaning, wash them by wiping the surface with cotton wool swabs dampened with warm water containing a few drops of a **conservation-grade detergent**. Rinse well with clean swabs dampened with clean water and dry with a soft, clean cloth. If this is not successful, try the water:**acetone** mixture (*see* p.21 and **solvent mixtures**). Take care not to remove the surface **patina**. If it is flaking off, seek conservation advice.

See PAINTED METAL for cleaning painted lead objects.

Always wear clean gloves and wash your hands well after cleaning lead. Never eat or drink while you are working on a lead object.

Repair

Do not attempt to repair lead. Inappropriate adhesives can cause harmful corrosion; soldering and lead burning should be carried out only by a metal conservator.

Although toys and models may look scruffy, they are not usually repainted. It is also not advisable to straighten any bent pieces, such as arms and guns, as they may snap off. Ask a metal conservator for advice if you feel it is imperative that some parts should be straightened.

Ormolu

Ormolu is mostly used to make mounts on furniture, ceramics, glass and clocks. True ormolu is cast brass or bronze that is chased and **mercury gilded**. There are numerous imitations of ormolu, including lacquered brass and electro-gilded zinc (or spelter).

Where the gilding on true ormolu is worn through, the base metal will be the golden-brown colour of tarnished bronze or brass, or the colour of polished bronze or brass. If the ormolu is made of spelter, the base metal will be grey. On spelter-based mounts, there may be tiny pimples breaking through the gilding, causing white or black discoloration. This never happens on true ormolu mounts. It is very difficult to differentiate between good quality imitations and true ormolu.

RIGHT: *An Empire gilt bronze and ormolu tazza with circular bowl, one of a pair signed by 'Thomire à Paris', in the Dining Room at Hinton Ampner in Hampshire. The tazze are 18·5cm (7¼in) high, 23·5cm (9¼in) in diameter. Hinton Ampner has a fine collection of ormolu pieces built up by Ralph Dutton, and this piece is in very good condition.*

Problems

The fixing pins and screws may work loose. If ormolu is incorrectly cleaned, the gold will be lost. The base metal may corrode (*see* the appropriate metal entry).

Handling

Handle ormolu as you would BRASS and BRONZE, but remember that the gilding is very thin and that the more you handle it, the faster the gold will wear away.

Display and Storage

See METALS. The display and storage conditions must suit any other materials used in the object.

Housekeeping and Maintenance

The surface of ormolu is very vulnerable, as the gold is very thin. The coloured lacquer on bronze mounts is also thin and scratches easily. Ormolu should never get wet nor be rubbed or polished. To remove the dust from ormolu, brush it with a soft brush. **Compressed air** may help to remove dust from crevices. Do not use a duster, as the rubbing may remove the gold and the cloth may snag on edges or fixings.

Cleaning

To remove a build-up of old polish and dirt in ormolu, *see* METALS, Removing Wax.

Avoid letting candle wax run down

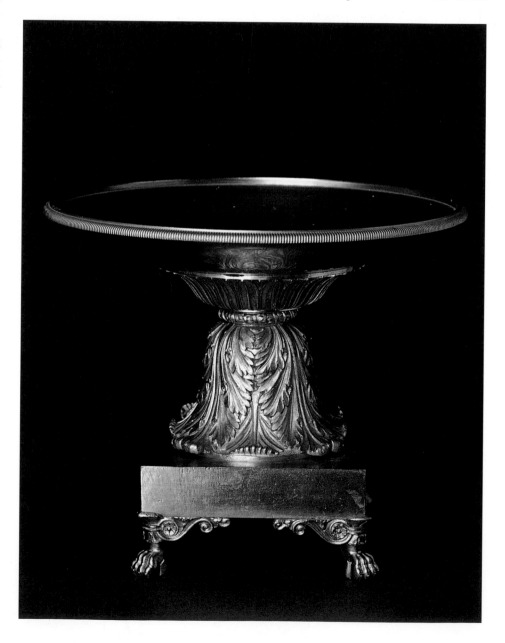

ormolu candlesticks. Protect them by placing plastic or glass wax-catchers on the candleholder.

The gilding on ormolu will often have worn through on the raised areas of the mounts. It is not recommended that these areas be retouched or regilded as the appearance will be changed. In order to regild the ormolu, the original gilding has to be removed, and modern gilding is a different colour from the original mercury gilding. *See also* SILVER GILT.

Repair

All repairs to ormolu should be carried out by a metal conservator or silversmith experienced in this kind of work. Never let anyone use lead solder on ormolu. Once on, it is virtually impossible to remove.

Pewter and Britannia Metal

Pewter is an alloy of tin with copper and lead. Pewter was known in Roman times and has been used extensively since the Middle Ages for domestic objects such as plates, tankards, bowls, spoons and candlesticks. The colour varies according to the percentage of lead in the pewter. Cheap, low quality pewter contained a high proportion of lead, was blackish-grey in colour and was dangerous to eat from because of the toxicity of lead. Better quality pewter contained copper but no lead and was nearly as bright as silver when polished. Pewter became popular for making art nouveau objects and was often used with other materials, such as wood and ivory. Old pewter mugs and plates should not be used for drinking or eating from because of the lead content.

Modern christening mugs and similar items are sometimes called pewter or hard pewter but should more correctly be referred to as Britannia metal, which does not contain lead. It is a tarnish-resistant alloy consisting mainly of tin and antimony, and is used to make christening cups, napkin rings, tankards and other objects.

Problems

Although pewter is harder than lead, it is very soft and is easily dented or scratched. Pewter that contains lead will corrode in

Miss Chichester was a great amasser of collections, still to be enjoyed at Arlington Court in Devon. Her collection of pewter concentrates on British ware with a few Continental examples. The first picture (ABOVE) shows three Bavarian flagons from the sixteenth century in an advanced state of corrosion. In such a condition, they need careful handling, both for the object and for the handler as pewter is an alloy of lead. Always wear latex or vinyl gloves.

The second picture (BELOW) is of an English charger from the seventeenth or eighteenth centuries, together with some pewter spoons, one brass-plated with a white metal. Pewter is very soft and can scratch easily – it would be melted down and reused on a regular basis for kitchen and dining ware.

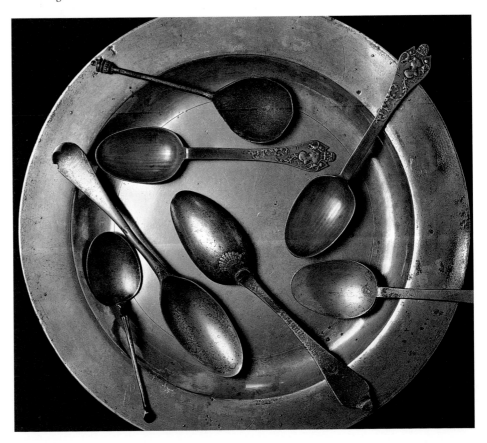

patches if it is exposed to organic acid vapours (*see* LEAD).

Pewter can develop a surface **patina** that may come off if an object is badly handled. Self-adhesive tape or labels stuck to the metal may take off the patina when they are removed.

Handling, Display and Storage

See METALS and LEAD.

Housekeeping and Maintenance

Dust pewter with a soft brush and vacuum cleaner (*see* pp.19–20).

Cleaning

Do not clean any rare, old or precious pewter objects yourself. These should be cleaned by a metal conservator. Where further cleaning of other pewter objects is necessary, *see* LEAD. Where pewter is used in conjunction with other materials, take care not to get the washing solution on them or in the joints.

If the surface is stained or looks dull, you can improve the appearance of the pewter by rubbing it with a soft cloth. If this is unsuccessful, you can use a **fine abrasive paste** on cotton wool or a soft cloth. Gently polish the surface of the pewter in a circular motion, and wipe it off with a clean, soft cloth. Brush off the polish and remove any remaining polish with cotton wool swabs moistened with **white spirit**. Do not use the abrasive frequently, as the metal surface will wear away, and do not press hard on the surface, as the metal may dent. Old pewter should not be given a high polish; it should have a dull gleam.

Some old pewter may have wart-like growths on the surface. If these spots have a hard skin and do not have any white powdery corrosion round them, it is safer to leave them alone. Do not be tempted to grind them off. If a white powder should appear in small spots or the surface shows any sign of flaking, consult a metal conservator.

Repair

Do not attempt to repair pewter. Adhesives can cause a lot of harmful corrosion and soldering should be carried out only by a metal conservator.

Silver

Silver is a soft, white, precious metal which has been used since about 3000BC. It is too soft to use alone and so is alloyed with at least one other metal, usually copper. English sterling silver contains about 92.5 per cent silver mixed with copper. Britannia silver contains 95.8 per cent silver with copper and electrum is made up of 25–40 per cent silver to 75–60 per cent gold.

Silver has been widely used over the centuries to make household and religious objects that can vary in size from thimbles and plates to large candelabra and even altar-frontals and furniture. Silver may be decorated by engraving and embossing, precious stones can be set into it and enamels can be applied to the surface. Silver can also be used as a thin coat on a base metal and on glass and ceramics. It can be beaten into silver leaf to decorate picture frames, statues, leather and similar materials, and is frequently used as an inlay to embellish wood or other metals or can itself be inlaid.

Niello is a black compound of silver, copper, lead and sulphur, fused with heat into incised decoration on the silver. It is frequently used to decorate silver objects, such as jewellery and other decorative objects, particularly those made in India and the Far East.

Problems

Silver objects may be heavily used and so are vulnerable to physical damage, resulting in dents, scratches and worn decoration from vigorous polishing. Pins securing the handles of teapots and jugs work loose and joints can come apart. Keep broken off or loose parts in a safe place, and label them, so that they will not be lost before the object can be conserved.

Silver tarnishes very easily. The tarnish is silver sulphide, which appears first as a yellow film but soon becomes brown, eventually purple and then black when it is quite thick. It is caused by sulphur-containing compounds, such as hydrogen sulphide, which are produced by some industrial processes and by our bodies. Sulphur-containing compounds can also be found in paints and rubber compounds and some textiles; wool, silk and some dyes will cause tarnish, but cotton and linen do not. Some foods such as eggs, sprouts, vinegar and salt also tarnish and corrode silver, so they should be washed off cutlery, mustard pots and salt cellars as soon as possible.

Silver may develop a waxy purplish corrosion, most often found on buried silver. Silver containing a large proportion of copper, either as an alloy or as a base metal for silver plate, may form green copper corrosion products, particularly if it is stored in damp conditions.

Silver is usually alloyed with copper, which will corrode when exposed to organic acid vapours (*see* COPPER).

A silver object decorated with other materials, such as gems, paint, enamel or inlay, must be examined to make sure the gems are secure and the paint or inlay are not coming away from the metal.

Handling

See METALS. In the past, butlers and other staff handling the silver would wear cotton gloves when they were polishing and carrying the silver to prevent leaving fingerprints on the surface. This still applies and **gloves** should always be worn when handling silver objects, although this is not practical when you are using silver for its original purpose.

Do not leave tea, coffee or mustard pots or any other objects with hinged lids upside-down on a draining board with the lid open after you have rinsed them out. This puts all the weight on the hinge and may eventually tear it out. Wash salt, mustard or sauces out of silver containers after use as, even if they are glass-lined, the food can corrode the silver.

Hollow objects such as candlesticks are sometimes filled with natural resin, as are some cutlery handles. The resin will soften in hot water, so do not wash these objects in the dishwasher or hot water.

Display

See METALS. Some materials used in the construction of display cases can cause silver to tarnish quickly. They can continue to emit silver-tarnishing products for several years. If possible, try out the cabinet before displaying a lot of silver in it. You can do this by cleaning two similar silver objects, such as two pieces of cutlery, in the same way. Then place one inside the cabinet and leave one in the room. If the one in the cabinet tarnishes faster, you know that the cabinet is not suitable for displaying silver.

If you are making a new cabinet, you can do a similar test to check the fabric with which you want to line it. In this case, wrap the objects in the different fabrics and see

which tarnishes first. Leave one unwrapped piece in the room for comparison. Allow some weeks for this. Many museums and historic houses test materials for use with silver; your local museum may be able to identify suitable materials for you.

A well-sealed case made from pollution-free materials is the best way to display valuable silver. It is possible to buy products that inhibit silver tarnishing by giving off a vapour. These are usually in capsule form or strips of impregnated paper and are placed inside the display case or storage

area. However, they can cloud or craze the surface of Perspex and may adversely affect copper objects. If you use these products, always follow the manufacturer's instructions carefully.

Storage

See METALS. In the past chamois leather, baize or felt were used to wrap silver, but these materials can give off sulphur compounds that tarnish it. Bags, wraps and roll-ups made from good quality cotton or

ABOVE: *Fish from the collection made in the late nineteenth and early twentieth centuries by Geraldine Hervey, wife of the 3rd Marquess of Bristol, now on display in the Museum Room at Ickworth in Suffolk. These tiny jointed fish, mostly silver, but with examples in silver-gilt and* cloisonné *enamel, were used as scent bottles and vinaigrettes. These are in very good condition, with only a few signs of worn gilding. Take care when cleaning and polishing objects like these, to avoid catching edges.*

silver protection cloth are more suitable, as they protect silver both from tarnishing and against physical damage. They are most effective when they totally surround the silver. The impregnated cloth becomes less effective as the chemicals are used up, but their life appears to be at least ten years. This material should not come in direct contact with lead and pewter objects. Small plastic bags made with a tarnish inhibitor are available for smaller objects such as coins and medals.

Housekeeping and Maintenance

Remove dust with a soft brush and vacuum cleaner (*see* pp.19-20). Silver can be lightly polished using a silver **metal polishing cloth**, soft linen cloth or **microfibre cloth**. Dust lacquered objects with a soft brush.

Cleaning

Rare, old, archaeological or precious silver objects should be cleaned only by a metal conservator.

Whenever a layer of tarnish is polished off silver, a small amount of silver is removed. Eventually, the silver will wear away and engraved designs can be polished away altogether. In the case of plated silver, the silver can be worn off, leaving the base metal exposed. The surface of highly decorated silver is often finely textured, but this can easily be lost by polishing. Therefore, try to keep silver in conditions which reduce the tarnishing and thereby cut down on the need for cleaning. The cleaning materials used should also be as non-abrasive as possible. Some silver cleaning materials leave a protective layer on the surface that helps slow the rate at which silver tarnishes. You should clean silver only when it actually needs it, not as a matter of course.

● PRECAUTIONS
Before cleaning, the piece should be examined for delicate surface texture, niello or other deliberate colouring, as these are easily removed by cleaning. Hold the object in the light and move it around slowly; you should be able to see any patterns against the reflection of the light. Niello is difficult to detect on heavily tarnished silver, as it is the same colour as the tarnish, but it does have a different surface texture. It is usually less reflective than tarnished silver and a denser colour.

Twentieth-century silver is sometimes deliberately coloured by the manufacturer, particularly on modern jewellery; this could be an overall colour or colours, or a blackening in the depths to emphasise relief decoration. Modern coloured surfaces are not easy to detect, but they are usually harder to remove than tarnish. When you are cleaning a piece that you suspect is deliberately coloured, look for areas that clean with more difficulty than other areas, as they may be the deliberate colouring.

Before cleaning, also check the object for tears, breaks and broken pieces. If these are caught by the polishing cloth, further damage can be done.

Objects with hollow areas, such as feet, handles or rims, where water or cleaning solutions can gather must not get very wet, so cleaning and washing solutions have to be applied with cotton wool swabs and removed with clean swabs. This is particularly important if Silver Dip is used as the chemicals in it can cause corrosion if left in hollows. Similarly, other materials combined with silver, for instance wood, ivory and basketry, should not get wet. You must be careful that the cleaning substances for the silver do not get on to these materials as they will be stained and damaged.

Take care when you are cleaning and polishing a thin silver object that you do not put undue pressure on any area, as the silver will gradually cave in. Support each area with one hand while you clean with the other.

● PREPARATION
Before cleaning silver, always cover the table, including the edges, with a soft towel or blanket so that the object is not dented or scratched by the table. Wear rubber or vinyl **gloves**.

● CLEANING
First, with a soft brush, remove any dust and grime, as they can scratch the silver. If the object is made entirely of silver and is very dirty with greasy grime, wash it in warm water containing a few drops of **conservation-grade detergent**. Rinse the object well in warm water and dry thoroughly with paper towels, a soft, lint-free cloth or an old tea towel. Where the silver is combined with another material, such as plaster, wood or bone, as in candlesticks or cigarette boxes, wipe the surface with cotton buds or swabs dampened with the washing solution. Rinse with clean swabs dampened with clean water. Dry with a soft, clean cloth.

Very lightly tarnished silver should be polished with a silver **metal polishing cloth**. This will be sufficient to keep it looking good.

Silver Foam is a cleaning agent with a fine abrasive and is supplied with a sponge. It is useful for removing tarnish and may be used on silver that can be washed. Follow the manufacturer's directions carefully. Apply the foam to small objects using cotton buds or a soft natural bristle brush rather than the sponge. Rinse it off well in warm water or use damp cotton wool swabs for objects that cannot be washed. Dry and polish the silver with a soft cloth. Take care not to wet or stain other materials. The advantage of Silver Foam is that there is no residue once the object has been thoroughly rinsed.

Silver Dip has the advantage over polish in that it is not abrasive, but it too must be washed off thoroughly, otherwise the silver will re-tarnish rapidly. Pour a small amount of Silver Dip into a glass or plastic container. Apply the dip with cotton wool buds or swabs, or use a soft hogshair brush for tooled decoration and difficult-to-reach areas. Clean a small area at a time and rinse it with water, using swabs. Reapply the Silver Dip if necessary. Continue cleaning the whole object, rinsing off the cleaning solution as you go. It is very important to make sure that all the dip is washed off, otherwise severe tarnish will form again soon after cleaning. When the cleaning has been completed, rinse the object in clean water if it is suitable to do so. Otherwise, rinse well with swabs of clean water. Dry the object with a soft, clean cloth and polish it with a silver metal polishing cloth.

The manufacturers of Silver Dip recommend that you dip objects directly into the solution, but if it is re-used too often it may deposit silver back on to the surface of the object. The deposited silver has a different texture and colour, looks unpleasant and is *very* difficult to remove. If you are using it to dip small objects, decant some of the dip into a second container and throw the dip away after use. Silver Dip can stain stainless steel.

If the silver is to be stored after cleaning, it is a good idea to leave the object in a warm place for at least two hours to make sure it is completely dry before wrapping it up to store.

Proprietary silver polish is not recommended for general or regular cleaning, because it is abrasive and very difficult to

remove from all the crevices and decoration; if it is not removed, it can cause metal corrosion. An exceptionally tarnished and dirty piece of silver could be cleaned with polish.

Use a good quality silver polish. Apply the polish with a soft cloth. When it is dry, polish it off with a soft, clean cloth or brush. Make sure all the polish is removed, particularly from the crevices. A soft silver polishing bristle brush (a plate brush) is very useful for a final polishing and for removing any polish from the crevices.

Do not use nylon brushes, particularly toothbrushes, as they are likely to scratch the silver.

● DECORATED OBJECTS AND SILVER ENAMEL

Silver is frequently decorated with enamel, gemstones or other applied decoration. These objects should not get wet and should not be cleaned by immersing them in water or other solutions. A silver metal polishing cloth and/or a soft **pencil eraser** should remove most of the tarnish and will

ABOVE: *Cleaning a silver pot using a silver polishing cloth to remove the light tarnish. The padded surface is important to protect the object.*

not abrade the surface. If this is unsuccessful, use a cotton bud with a small amount of **fine abrasive paste** and polish it off with cotton wool. It is essential that polish, cleaning fluid or water does not run under the enamel, gems or decoration, as corrosion and irreparable damage may follow.

A soft pencil eraser may be all that is needed to clean the highlights of heavily embossed and chased objects. Take care not to soften a textured surface. Silver Dip (*see* p.94) should be used if more cleaning is necessary.

Clean an object decorated with niello using a soft pencil eraser and/or a silver cloth. Do not use Silver Dip, as it may remove the niello.

Cleaning the textured surface of silver with a soft pencil eraser.

• **ACCUMULATED POLISH AND DIRT**
Often highly decorated pieces have accumulated dirt and polish in the decoration. You may want to leave it, as it can be part of the attraction of the piece, but if it obscures the decoration, it can be removed. Carefully remove the accumulation with a **swab stick**; never use a metal point. A swab stick with a few fibres of cotton wool wrapped around it and dampened with Silver Dip or a small amount of Silver Foam (*see* p.94) can then be used in the crevices as described above. Rinse off the Silver Dip or Foam well.

Very stubborn deposits of polish can be removed by using a mixture of **alcohol** and a few drops of **ammonia** (two or three drops of ammonia to an eggcup of alcohol). Apply the solution with a swab stick with a few fibres of cotton wool wrapped around it or a cotton bud. Rinse the object well and dry it. Do not use ammonia solution on silver-plated objects as the ammonia can damage the copper.

• **ELECTROCHEMICAL CLEANING**
Cleaning silver electrochemically is not recommended. The process of using aluminium sheet or milk bottle tops can remove more silver than is necessary and

can be detrimental to the object. With modern cleaning materials this method is now obsolete.

Protection

Silver can be protected from tarnishing by applying a coat of clear **lacquer**. This protection is only suitable for objects on display that are not used. The lacquer is applied with a brush, but do not attempt to lacquer an object if you are not practised at brushwork. If the lacquer is not applied evenly over the entire surface, the object may begin to tarnish in patches and the lustre of the surface may be lost. Where possible you should ask a conservator to lacquer objects for you. Should you have your objects lacquered professionally, check that the lacquer used will not be cured by heat or a catalyst but will be air-dried and remain soluble in **organic solvents** so that it can easily be removed. There are lacquers available for use on silver that air dry and are designed to provide protection against sulphur-containing compounds. Do not use polyurethane lacquers, as they discolour and are hard to remove.

The protection afforded by lacquer does not last indefinitely but, provided the surface is well prepared, the lacquer is well applied and remains intact, the silver should remain untarnished for several years. Objects on display are suitable for lacquering, but those in use are not, as the lacquer coating is more likely to get scratched or damaged.

Lacquer is particularly useful for protecting Sheffield plate, silver plate and silver plaques with light engraving which can be worn away by frequent polishing. However, lacquer does slightly reduce shine and brilliance and is very difficult to apply well.

If the lacquer coating is poorly applied, scratched or damaged, the exposed areas of silver will tarnish rapidly and the silver surface can become pitted. The lacquer has to be removed before the silver can be cleaned. Both lacquers and their solvents can be harmful to health if they are not used correctly.

Do not use long-term silver-cleaning products before lacquering an object. They leave a tarnish-inhibiting deposit on the surface of the metal, which may stop the lacquer from working effectively. Polish the silver with Silver Dip or a **fine abrasive paste** for heavily tarnished objects before lacquering it.

After cleaning the object well (*see* above),

remove all traces of polish using warm water with a few drops of **conservation-grade detergent**, then rinse it with clean water and dry it. Use swabs on objects such as candlesticks that cannot be immersed in water. Leave the object in a warm area to dry thoroughly.

Degrease the surface by wiping it with cotton wool moistened with **acetone** or **alcohol**. Make sure that all the fibres from the cotton wool have been removed. Take care that your bare hands do not touch the silver surface.

If you have an icing or pottery turntable, it will make lacquering much easier, as you can rotate the object. Make sure that the working surface is clean. Place the object on **silicone paper** to prevent the lacquer from sticking to the table-top.

Apply the lacquer with a brush. For a lacquer to be effective, it must be applied very carefully. It is best to try to complete the lacquering with one coat, as it is very difficult to apply a second coat without disturbing the first.

APPLYING LACQUER
• Use a new, soft, fairly thick, clean brush, preferably made of split bristles, camel or badger hair. **Brushes** are available for use with lacquer. Ideally, the lacquer should be about the consistency of light machine oil. If necessary, thin the lacquer with a reducer supplied by the manufacturer of the lacquer. Do not make the lacquer too thin or the protection will not be effective.
• Work quickly in a warm, dust-free, well-ventilated room. For a good coating, the room should be 15–20°C (59–68°F) and the **relative humidity** not higher than 70–75%. Try not to paint the same area twice. Stipple the lacquer into the depths, but do not let too much settle in them. Allow the lacquer to dry completely, ideally about 24 hours.
• For health and safety reasons, the room must be well ventilated and appropriate health and safety procedures must be followed. *See* p.23.

REMOVING LACQUER
When a lacquer is poorly applied, old, or damaged, patches of tarnish may develop. The lacquer will have to be removed and fresh lacquer applied. Before you can remove a lacquer, you need to establish what solvent to use. Acetone is generally successful for most air-dried lacquers, but other organic solvents may be more suitable. If you have a record of the lacquer that was

used, the supplier or a conservator may be able to advise you on the solvent.

Many commercially applied lacquers are chemically cured on the metal, are not soluble in the usual range of organic solvents and are difficult to remove. This type of lacquer is frequently found on bedsteads and door handles (*see* below).

When you have established what solvent is needed, pour it into a suitably sized glass or metal container. Do not put your fingers into the solvent; wear solvent-resistant **gloves**. Many organic solvents are flammable and toxic, so use them according to the health and safety information provided by the supplier. Do the work in a well-ventilated room and away from naked flames. Small objects can be dipped into the solvent and agitated slightly. Touch the surface with a paintbrush and you can usually feel if the lacquer is still there and sticky, or if most of it has dissolved off. Once the lacquer has dissolved off, remove the object from the container. Rinse it in clean solvent applied with a brush and leave it to dry.

Place objects that cannot be dipped, such as larger objects or those made of several materials, on a metal tray or in a large metal or glass container. Wipe the surface with the solvent on swabs of cotton wool or apply the solvent with a brush and agitate it to soften the lacquer. Replace the swabs when they become sticky and continue until all the lacquer has been removed. You can also use a **pipette** to wash the solvent over the surface.

Discard the swabs into a lidded container (*see* p.21). This prevents the solvent from continuing to evaporate into the room. When you have finished, put the container outside, remove the lid, and allow all the solvent to evaporate before putting it in the dustbin.

A lacquer that is not easily soluble is much harder to remove. A metal conservator is the best person to remove such lacquers from precious or valuable objects. The product most likely to remove this lacquer is a water washable **dichloromethane-based paint remover**. It can be applied to objects of little value, such as door furniture. The paint remover will damage paint, plastics and finishes on wood, so great care must be taken not to get it on to any other surface. Wear solvent-resistant gloves and work in a well-ventilated room.

Test a small area first to make sure the process will not damage the object. Apply the paint remover with a brush. Leave it for a few moments until the lacquer has bubbled up. Wash it off with cool water or wipe it off with a swab of **white spirit**. Apply the paint remover to any remaining lacquer. Wash the object thoroughly in warm water with a drop of mild conservation-grade detergent and rinse in clean water. Dry thoroughly.

Repair

Silver objects should be repaired by a qualified silversmith or a metal conservator. To repair silver well is a difficult and skilled job so, unless you are very experienced at this sort of work, do not attempt to solder pieces together yourself. Never use lead solder on a piece of silver; use silver solder. Lead solder runs over the surface very easily and is virtually impossible to remove. It also makes future restoration particularly difficult.

Should you ever need to stick a loose piece back on to an object, use an easily reversible **adhesive**. These are often strong enough; they will not harm the silver and are easy to remove if the object needs to be repaired in the future. If you need extra strength, use a quick-setting epoxy resin adhesive.

Archaeological Silver

Silver that has been buried in the ground is frequently covered in a thick layer of a black, grey or purple waxy corrosion and possibly green copper corrosion products. Archaeological silver can be very fragile and brittle and should be handled with the utmost care. It must be cleaned by a conservator, as the object can easily be ruined by an untrained person.

Store archaeological silver in a **sealed plastic box** with a bed of **acid-free** tissue paper to protect it from physical damage.

Silver Inlay

Silver is frequently used as an inlay to decorate wood, iron, brass, ivory, lacquer and other materials. Cleaning silver inlay is not easy, as the surrounding material can be damaged or stained by silver cleaning agents. If possible, polish the silver with a silver **metal polishing cloth** and/or a soft **pencil eraser**. Take care not to catch and lift any pieces of inlay which may be loose and proud of the surface. Where possible, stick them down before cleaning. If polishing the inlay with a cloth does not clean it enough, use a **fine abrasive paste**, not a liquid metal polish, applied with a few fibres of cotton wool wound round a **swab stick** (*see* p.21). Do not get the paste on the wood or stuck in the depths of the inlay. It is better for the inlay to remain slightly tarnished than to leave unsightly remnants of polish. Alternatively, wrap a few strands of **impregnated wadding** for silver around a **bamboo stick**.

A thin coating of wax will help to protect the silver from tarnishing, but must be applied carefully, so that it does not spread on to the other materials.

To repair silver inlay in furniture, wood or other **organic materials** see WOOD. Extensive damage to silver inlay on a metal object must be repaired by an experienced conservator. Small raised pieces of inlay should be stuck into place as soon as possible. Clean out any debris in the channel with a bamboo stick and degrease the area with a small swab of **acetone** or **alcohol**. Apply a small amount of an easily reversible **adhesive** and hold the inlay in place until the adhesive has set hard. *See* WOOD for more information.

Sheffield Plate

Sheffield plate was produced from about 1740 until 1840. It was made by fusing silver on to a copper base and then rolling it into a thin sheet. Initially, the copper base was silvered on both sides. Nowadays, the silver is deposited on to the copper using electro-plating, which produces a different colour. Sheffield plate was used mainly for making candlesticks, coffeepots, biscuit barrels and other domestic items. Ribbons of solid silver wire were applied to the places most likely to wear through, such as the rims and edges.

The coating of silver is very thin and will eventually wear away, exposing the copper underneath. Sheffield plate should therefore be polished as little as possible or, even better, not at all. Clean it in warm water containing a few drops of a **conservation-grade detergent**, taking care that the soapy water does not soak into the inside of candlesticks and other hollow areas. Do not immerse these objects; use cotton wool swabs dampened with the cleaning solution. Rinse thoroughly and dry with a soft, clean cloth. The objects can then be buffed with a silver **metal polishing cloth**. If the Sheffield plate is very tarnished, clean it with **Silver Dip** on a cotton wool swab as described for SILVER and wash it well. Then buff it with the silver metal polishing cloth.

The solid silver wire applied to the rims and edges sometimes lifts and it is easy to catch it with a cloth. This can tear off the wire, which is very difficult to re-lay. Therefore, take very great care when drying and polishing the edges.

Sheffield plate benefits from being lacquered, as it very much reduces the amount of polishing necessary. *See* SILVER, Protection. Do not use long-term products if you intend to lacquer the object. Worn Sheffield plate should not be replated as this will change the appearance and reduce the value.

Silver Gilt

Silver gilt objects have a thin layer of gold covering the silver; parcel gilt is only partially covered with gold. The gold is used to cover the inside of bowls, tumblers and salt cellars and to make wine labels, jewellery and other decorative items. It is also used to highlight decoration.

The gold itself does not tarnish and it will help to protect the silver from doing so, but occasionally the silver will tarnish through the gold. This tarnish is usually a range of colours, a little like a rainbow or the effect of petrol on water, rather than the black tarnish found on silver.

Ideally, silver gilt should never be cleaned with any sort of metal polish or **Silver Dip**, because these wear away the gold. Clean silver gilt objects with warm water containing a few drops of **conservation-grade detergent**. Use a cotton wool swab if necessary. Rinse thoroughly and dry with a soft, clean cloth.

If you have a silver gilt object with silver tarnish on it which does not come off with washing and you are unable to take it to a conservator, clean it very carefully with a gold **metal polishing cloth**.

Sometimes, the gilding will have worn off parts of the silver. It is not advisable to re-gild the object as the methods used now for depositing gold on to the surface are different from the original **mercury gilding**, and the gold is therefore a different colour and texture. Mercury gilding is dangerous and seldom carried out because of health and safety restrictions.

Silver Plate and Electroplate

Silver plate or electroplate is made by depositing a thin layer of silver electrolytically on to a base metal, such as brass, bronze, nickel silver or Britannia metal. As the base metal is often silver-coloured, it is not always easy to tell when the silver has worn away. Electroplated silver has been produced since the 1840s. It is often stamped EPNS (Electroplated Nickel Silver) or EPBM (Electroplated Britannia Metal). Items marked A1 have a particularly thick layer of plating, which was used for objects subjected to significant wear. Plated silver tarnishes more easily than sterling silver and should be carefully stored and protected.

The coating of silver is even thinner than that on Sheffield plate and therefore easily wears away. To clean it, *see* SHEFFIELD PLATE. Like Sheffield plate, electroplate is a good candidate for lacquering.

Modern silver plate, particularly cutlery, can be replated when it has worn through. Replating early EPNS or other plated silver may affect its value, however.

Silver on Porcelain and Glass

White metals, usually platinum or white gold but sometimes silver, were occasionally used to decorate porcelain and glass in a similar way to gold, by firing a very thin layer into the glaze. If the metal tarnishes, it is not usually possible to bring back the silver appearance. Where the layer has worn thin or completely away, it is virtually impossible to restore it successfully. Silver or aluminium leaf can be applied, but it never has the same sheen as the original silver and usually looks tatty. The object is better left untouched.

Tin

Tin is a soft, white metal, which is normally quite stable, although it will slowly react with the atmosphere so that the surface will become a dull grey. This layer reduces the rate of corrosion. Tin has been used since early times both on its own and as a constituent of alloys such as bronze, pewter and Britannia metal. Plates, mugs, jugs, coins and buttons can be made from tin. It has also been used extensively for coating thin sheet iron to preserve it from rust; this is known as tinplate (*see* TINPLATE). Tin was also used as a coating inside copper and bronze cooking and eating vessels to prevent the food from reacting with the copper and producing poisonous compounds. In antiquity, bronze was coated with tin to make jewellery.

Problems

Tin is less dense than lead but not as soft, and it will not mark a piece of paper as lead will. Small pimples of corrosion can form on tin; very little can be done about this.

Handling

Handle objects made from tin carefully so that the protective corrosion layer is not broken. Take care not to dent or squash them. *See* PEWTER.

Display and Storage

See PEWTER.

Housekeeping and Maintenance

If tin jugs, plates or buttons have gone a dull grey colour, it is best to leave them alone, as their grey layer of corrosion protects the tin from further deterioration. Tin objects should be dusted when necessary with a soft, clean brush or cloth. If the object looks very grimy, it can be washed in warm water containing a few drops of a **conservation-grade detergent**. Rinse thoroughly in clean water and dry with a soft, clean cloth. Ensure the object is thoroughly dry; if necessary, leave it in a warm place overnight. Never use an abrasive to polish tin, as the metal will wear away.

The layer of tin on copper vessels can be polished with a soft cloth, although frequent polishing of any kind will wear away the tin. Do not use the cloth for polishing other metals.

Cleaning

Rare, old and precious tin objects should be cleaned only by a metal conservator.

Tinplate

Tin has been used extensively for coating thin sheet iron to preserve it from rust; this is known as tinplate or tinned sheet. Tinplate is used to make toys, such as early cars and trains, moneyboxes and manufacturers' containers for biscuits, cakes, polishes and so on. It can be painted or have a coloured surface decoration. *Moiré metallique* is a very decorative form of crystalline tinplate, usually protected with a tinted varnish, which is used to make small boxes and needle-cases.

ABOVE: *A nineteenth-century slipper bath in the Silk Dressing Room at Tatton Park in Cheshire. The main body of the bath is of tinned zinc. The inside of the bath is enamelled to look like marble. The water was kept hot by a compartment filled with red-hot charcoal in the toe, from which a flue led to the chimney. Also in this photograph is the coal box, of painted metal with gilded decoration making it look like toleware, a cast-iron fireplace, wrought-iron tongs and poker, and a brass water can.*

Problems

The layer of tin on the surface of tinned sheet is very thin. If this is broken by scratches or dents, the iron base will rust quickly. As the iron sheet is also thin, it will bend and dent easily. The paint or ink on the surface may chip or peel off or be worn away.

Handling

See METALS. Handle toys and tin containers carefully. Do not knock them against each other, as this dents the metal and then breaks the seal of the tin or scratches the paint. Once the rust starts, it will push through any painted decoration there may be on the surface. Handle tinplate objects as little as possible to prevent the decoration from being worn away. Take care not to cut yourself on any sharp edges.

Display and Storage

See METALS.

Housekeeping and Maintenance

To clean painted tinplate, remove dust and grit with a soft brush.

Cleaning

Tins and painted tinplate are often very dirty. As it is preferable to keep them dry to prevent iron corrosion and accidental removal of paint, try cleaning them with a dry **chemical sponge**. Check first that the surface is sound and the sponge will not pull off the decoration.

If this is unsuccessful, you can try wiping the surface with cotton wool swabs dampened with water containing a few drops of **conservation-grade detergent**. First check

Six-sided 'Damascus' table, inlaid with ivory and mother-of-pearl, in the Hall at Standen in Sussex. The most common problem with mother-of-pearl is that the inlay falls out or becomes detached.

Display

As mother-of-pearl will flake in a dry atmosphere, do not place objects in direct sunlight or over radiators and fires.

Although the bathroom is a good environment for displaying individual shells, it is not recommended for objects covered in mother-of-pearl because the backing glue may soften in the damp atmosphere or may grow mould. *See* SHELL.

If you display mother-of-pearl in a wood display cabinet, test the cabinet first for acid fumes (*see* LEAD).

Storage

Store mother-of-pearl in a cool, dry, dark area. Wrap individual objects in **acid-free** tissue paper and preferably store them in acid-free boxes, not ordinary cardboard. If you use polythene boxes for storing smaller objects, pierce holes in the lid or sides or leave the lid slightly open to prevent condensation.

Keep the dust off larger objects by draping them with acid-free tissue.

Housekeeping and Maintenance

Remove dust with a soft brush (*see* p.19). **Compressed air** may be useful for removing dust from crevices.

Cleaning

Old, rare, fragile or precious objects made from mother-of-pearl should be cleaned by a conservator.

Mother-of-pearl should not be cleaned with **solvents**, such as **acetone**, **alcohol** or **ammonia**, or acids. Do not soak mother-of-pearl in water. All of these things can cause the mother-of-pearl to flake.

Often the most effective way of cleaning mother-of-pearl is to rub it with your finger or a wooden stick; this should remove the dirt and give the surface a shine. If this cannot be done or is ineffective, try cleaning the surface with a cotton wool bud moistened with saliva.

Old wax sometimes accumulates on mother-of-pearl inlay in furniture. This can be removed with a cotton wool bud dampened with **white spirit**. Take care not to let the white spirit run on to the surrounding surface.

If you have a modern piece of mother-of-pearl, extremely stubborn dirt can be removed by gently rubbing the mother-of-pearl with a **fine abrasive paste** on a cotton wool bud. Remove the cleaner with a soft, clean cloth or a cotton bud. This is not recommended for antique pieces, as the abrasive can wear away the top surface.

Cutlery with mother-of-pearl handles should not be immersed in hot water nor placed in the dishwasher, as the heat and chemicals can cause the mother-of-pearl to disintegrate.

See also TORTOISESHELL, Piqué work.

Repair

Small repairs can be made using an easily reversible **adhesive** or a neutral pH emulsion adhesive.

To replace small pieces of mother-of-pearl inlay, *see* WOOD, Furniture Repair and SILVER INLAY. For refixing a knife handle on to cutlery, *see* IVORY AND BONE.

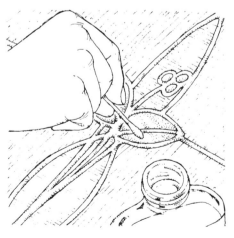

Removing old wax from mother-of-pearl inlay with a cotton bud.

ABOVE: *Some of the books in the Library at Felbrigg Hall in Norfolk. Belonging to William Windham II and dating from the mid-eighteenth century, they reflect his interest in architecture, natural history, military drill, wood-turning and fireworks. Fold-outs should be folded out only very occasionally, and need support.*

Screen de
Derbyshi
the probl
some of t

The sec
together
like a b
clean ha
packing
clean ta
space to
coffee,
risks aw

If the
one edg
card o
work a
vided t
sheet o
When
hold it
paper o

Paper, Prints, Drawings and Manuscripts

Paper was being made in China by the beginning of the second century AD. Paper-making had spread to the Arab world by the eighth century, and then through Europe via Spain to England in 1494, although it was certainly used in England for writing purposes by the second half of the fourteenth century. The spread of printing in the late fifteenth century led to a steep increase in output through Europe. Paper can be made from a wide range of materials, from rags, hemp, wood bark and maize, as well as from wood pulp. European papers were made from rag until the nineteenth century, when wood pulp was also used. Paper has to be treated, or sized with materials such as gelatine, so that it can be written or drawn on.

Paper is used as a support for many things, including manuscripts and documents, watercolours, gouache, drawings, prints and maps. It is used to make greeting cards, fans, models, posters, screens, lampshades and even clothes.

Some types of paper are very durable while others, such as wood pulp paper, contain materials that may decompose to form acids, and may only last a short time. For instance, you can very quickly see the change in colour of a newspaper if you leave it lying around for a few days. The paper turns yellow and eventually dark brown; it also becomes very brittle. Generally, paper made before 1870 is more stable than later paper. Damage from acids can also come from the ink or from the surrounding atmosphere, and sometimes from display or packing materials.

Papier Mâché

Papier mâché is a light but tough material that is prepared from pulped, layered or chopped paper, glue and fillers. It is shaped in a mould, baked and then either varnished or **japanned** for protection and decoration. Papier mâché may also be painted and gilded, or inlaid with mother-of-pearl or semi-precious stones and decorated with metal foil.

Papier mâché was introduced into England from France in the seventeenth century and used extensively during the nineteenth century to make almost every sort of object, from painted panels for coaches and bedheads to bookcases, screens, tables, trays, chairs, mirror and clock frames, miniature chests of drawers, work-boxes, and small domestic objects such as pen boxes.

In the middle of the nineteenth century papier mâché was made for internal architectural decoration. The method of manufacture was patented under the name of *carton-pierre* and was used extensively for the moulded decoration of ceilings and walls and for dolls' heads and other toys.

A chair made from papier mâché in the Organ Lobby at The Argory, County Armagh. Given the fragility of the material, it is in remarkably good condition, supported on wooden legs, around which the papier mâché has been built up, and on castors. This is a grand and large piece, but the painted decoration is similar to that applied to boxes and trays.

Problems

Papier mâché is sensitive to humidity and, like lacquered and japanned objects, the protective surface will begin to crack and flake if the object is exposed to changing **relative humidity**. Papier mâché is easily damaged by water and may become soft and distort if it is allowed to get wet or is kept in a damp environment. Low humidities will also cause the papier mâché to shrink and weaken.

The paint or japanning may crack or lift, particularly on trays and table-tops where hot liquid or dishes have been put directly on to the surface, or there may be white marks from water rings or hot objects. The material is not very strong, so the rims of trays or the edges of objects are often damaged and the decorative paint on trays is frequently worn off from use.

Papier mâché can be attacked by wood-boring insects or silverfish (*see* p.15). If evidence of insects is found, isolate the object until it can be treated (*see* pp.14–15). Do not use proprietary woodworm killers, as the spirit base can affect the finish on the papier mâché.

Handling

Papier mâché will chip or bruise easily if it is knocked or dropped. If you use a papier mâché tray for carrying things, bear the weight from underneath as the edges are not very strong. *See* JAPANNED AND LACQUERED OBJECTS.

Display, Storage, Housekeeping and Maintenance

See JAPANNED AND LACQUERED OBJECTS. After cleaning you can protect the surface by applying a very light coating of **microcrystalline wax** or **beeswax polish**, but test a small inconspicuous area first to ensure that the solvent in the wax does not remove the paint.

Cleaning

See JAPANNED AND LACQUERED OBJECTS.

Repair

Small repairs can be made using a neutral pH emulsion **adhesive** or an easily reversible adhesive.

Plaster of Paris

Plaster of Paris or gypsum plaster is produced by heating gypsum, alabaster or selenite (a hydrated calcium sulphate) to form calcium sulphate hemihydrate which, when mixed with water, sets hard. It is cheap, easy to pour into moulds, takes detail well and holds paint. It is therefore ideal for mass-producing statues and ornaments. Until the advent of modern materials, plaster was used for making moulds and casting. The Victorians used plaster moulds to cast copies of monumental friezes and statues, such as those from the Parthenon. Plaster is brittle and breaks easily, therefore objects are often strengthened with metal armatures, wood battens or hessian.

Painted plaster figures were very common until the advent of synthetic plastics. A decorative layer was often added to the plaster to simulate marble, bronze or terracotta. This coating can be very realistic and distinguished from the real thing only by careful examination, and sometimes by weight and coolness to the touch, as plaster is warmer and lighter than stone and metal.

ABOVE: *A gilt plaster model in the Outer Hall at Ightham Mote in Kent. This was the model for a life-sized bronze statue of the Black Prince by the nineteenth-century sculptor, Edward Lantéri. The plaster of Paris has been decorated with bronze paint, with metal additions for the spear and sword. It is very fragile, needing support – in places the wire armature is showing through the plasterwork – so it needs to be dusted with the greatest care.*

Detail of an early eighteenth-century scagliola table-top decorated with trompe l'oeil *playing cards, in the Velvet Drawing Room at Saltram House in Devon. The decoration is produced by scooping out the plaster and filling with another colour. The surface is vulnerable to scratches and staining. Here the spades in one of the playing cards have been damaged.*

pilasters and other interior architectural features. Scagliola can be very soft and it scratches, chips and bruises very easily, although some scagliola can be as hard as stone.

It is not easy to differentiate between scagliola and marble, but the former may be softer and warmer to the touch. If in doubt, make a tiny scratch in an unobtrusive area; scagliola will scratch very easily and the exposed surface will be powdery.

Clean scagliola in the same way as unpainted plaster. Saliva on a cotton bud may remove areas of stubborn dirt. *Never* use paint remover to clean scagliola, because it will destroy it. Water may also stain or damage the surface and so is not recommended. If the surface looks dull, polishing it lightly with **microcrystalline wax** will improve and protect the finish. Handle as for MARBLE, but bear in mind that scagliola is more delicate. Protect it from water as for WOOD.

Plastics and Rubber

The term plastics now refers to synthetic materials which can be extruded or moulded. Modern plastics have developed from rubber and mouldable materials made of an organic binder, such as shellac, blood or casein, mixed with a filler for strength and bulk. Previously horn and hoof were moulded, manipulated and coloured to make flat sheets or three-dimensional objects. Bitumen has now been superseded by plastic, but was also used from antiquity to the twentieth century. When modern plastics were developed, they were used for making moulded objects, such as buttons, picture frames, jewellery, toilet sets, walking stick handles and imitation jet.

Natural rubber is exuded from the tree *Havea braziliensis*. The earliest recorded rubber objects are rubber balls from the sixth century found in Central America. There are reports from the early seventeenth century of the Aztecs also using rubber for shoes and clothing.

Rubber was introduced into Europe in the mid-eighteenth century and was mostly used for rubberised cloth. Unfortunately, rubber was sticky when warm and rigid when cold. Around the mid-nineteenth century, it was discovered that sulphur can modify rubber to improve its properties.

Around this time, a hard, rigid, thermoplastic material, called vulcanite, ebonite or hard rubber, was produced. It was used very widely for electrical insulation, decorative matchboxes, brooches, musical instruments, pipe stems and a variety of objects. It is usually black.

Gutta-percha is also extracted from tropical trees and was first imported into Europe from the Far East in the 1830s. It was used not only as the insulation for undersea telegraph cables, but also for moulding materials such as picture frames and hose-pipes.

In the mid-nineteenth century, a moulding compound, called *bois durci*, using egg white or blood and fillers, was developed in France to produce desk accessories and plaques. These objects were said to be difficult to distinguish from carved rosewood or ebony. In the second half of the nineteenth century, there were a lot of mouldable materials being developed, including papier mâché and *carton-pierre*, along with gutta-percha, rubber and shellac. Shellac is an insect resin from India used as an adhesive, a surface coating and to make moulded objects, particularly daguerreotype and ambrotype cases, for which the resin was reinforced with wood flour.

The first man-made plastic to be developed was cellulose nitrate (Celluloid, Parksine, Xylonite) which was developed in the mid-nineteenth century. For a long time it was the only synthetic plastic and its use continued until very recently for table tennis balls and spectacle frames. When celluloid was first developed, it was used to imitate bone, ivory and tortoiseshell, which were becoming increasingly rare or expensive, as well as to make billiard balls, collars, cuffs, photographic negatives and film. Celluloid was also used for dolls' heads, cutlery handles, dental plates, buttons, toothbrushes, dice, fountain pens, bicycle pumps, piano keys and floating toys. It can range in colour from translucent, almost

Old telephones are now collectible items that need careful attention. This example can be seen at the home of the modernist architect, Ernö Goldfinger, 2 Willow Road in Hampstead, London. The plastic of the telephone can be scratched through abrasive cleaners. The rubber covering of the flex should be protected from heat, dust and light. This picture also shows an anglepoise lamp in aluminium. No corrosion problems here, but the possibility of scratches.

the twentieth century. Bakelite was used for electrical insulation, so plugs and light fittings were made from it, as were wireless cabinets, eggcups, tobacco jars, electric clock cases and many other items.

Similar, totally synthetic materials made from urea-formaldehyde were developed which were white and could be moulded. This meant that objects such as cups and picnic-ware could be manufactured in pale and marbled colours.

By the mid-1930s melamine (melamine formaldehyde) had been developed. It was and is still used for making moulded tableware and picnic-ware, as well as Formica and other laminates.

It is difficult to differentiate Bakelite from early melamine, although Bakelite is usually brown or mottled. Objects made from urea are usually a pale colour and mottled.

The plastics industry really developed after the 1930s. Polyvinyl chloride (PVC), polystyrene, polyethylene, epoxies, polyester, nylon and acrylics were all made in large quantities. Many are thermoplastic, which means that they can be heated until they soften, they can then be worked and will return to their original characteristics when cool. The advantage of this is that they can be made into fibres, rods or sheets, or moulded and used to make a vast range of objects. New plastics are being developed all the time for specific purposes.

Problems

A great deal of modern jewellery is made from polyester, acrylic and epoxy resins. These resins are fairly stable, but like other plastics may discolour with exposure to light and time, and can be affected by **organic solvents** or vapour. Some plastics are much less stable than others. Usually they begin to flake, craze or crack because the organic binder breaks down; sometimes the plasticiser comes to the surface, making it sticky.

Ebonite and most early plastics are affected by moisture in the air as well as by light, both of which can cause the material to break down. Ebonite, for example, fades to a dull, grey-greenish brown colour. As the earlier plastics become older, they also become more fragile and brittle and are harder to conserve. Celluloid can decompose in sunlight and at room temperature, giving off acidic fumes which, in a confined space, will harm other objects. It is also a fire hazard, as it is flammable

water-like white to pastel shades or darker, or it can be mottled or have a pearl-like appearance. Celluloid can be identified by its characteristic smell of camphor. If the smell is not immediately obvious, you will be able to smell it if you carefully scrape an unobtrusive area very slightly.

At the turn of the century, cellulose acetate was patented. One of its main advantages over cellulose nitrate was that it was much less flammable. It was used until recently as a base for films, and for cutlery handles and fountain pens.

Casein was introduced a few years later. It was used mainly for buttons and knitting needles. Casein has a characteristic taste, which you would recognise if you had ever sucked casein buttons as a child, but this would not be considered good conserva tion or analytical procedure!

An imitation ivory known as 'French ivory' was made of a mixture of cellulose nitrate, casein and pigments. It looks very like genuine ivory and even has the characteristic fine lines of ivory. These lines are produced during the manufacturing process and are likely to be more evenly spaced than those on genuine ivory.

These first plastics were based on natural materials. The first completely synthetic resin was Bakelite (phenol formaldehyde), which was produced at the beginning of and cellulose nitrate film can self-ignite. If cellulose nitrate (celluloid) starts to deteriorate, metal fittings on the object or nearby metal objects will corrode noticeably. This is particularly apparent on 'tortoiseshell' toilet sets or strings of 'amber' or 'ivory' and metal beads.

Handling

Handle plastics with care, as the early plastics can be very brittle. Do not put them down sharply on a hard surface. The surfaces can scratch easily. Wear **gloves**, as fingerprints can mark the surface. Do not knock plastic objects against other objects. *See* CERAMICS.

Display

Most plastics, particularly celluloid, discolour if placed in direct sunlight or exposed to warm temperatures. Display plastic objects out of direct sunlight and do not place them near a radiator or fire. Keep objects in a steady **relative humidity**. Do not use spotlights close to the object and keep the light levels as low as possible (*see* pp.16–18).

Most plastics will fade; if you place objects on or against them, they will fade unevenly. Celluloid should never touch any other object. If a celluloid object is displayed on polished furniture, stand it on a cork mat to prevent it from harming the surface.

Storage

Celluloid and early plastics must be stored where the ventilation is good so that the harmful gases given off are slowly removed. Never store these objects in plastic bags or sealed containers. Wrap them in **acid-free** tissue to keep them free from dust.

Store celluloid away from other objects, particularly metal, which may be corroded by any gases given off. Keep plastic objects, particularly celluloid, in a cool, dark, dry place with a steady temperature.

High temperatures perceptively increase the rate of deterioration of plastics. Celluloid in particular should be stored at a low temperature, *see* PHOTOGRAPHS.

Housekeeping and Maintenance

Brush off any dust with a hogshair brush.

Cleaning

Do not immerse early plastic objects in water. Wipe the surface with a cotton wool swab or cotton bud dipped in warm water containing a few drops of a **conservation-grade detergent**. Rinse the object with a clean cotton wool swab or a cotton bud moistened with clean water and dry it with a soft cloth. Do not use heat to dry the object. Do not clean deteriorating cellulose nitrate or cellulose acetate, but seek conservation advice.

Solvents, such as **acetone**, **white spirit** or **alcohol**, affect many plastics, so do not use them to clean objects. However, the sticky deposit from a label may not come off with water, so you may have to try white spirit, lighter fuel or alcohol on a cotton swab. Use a minimum amount of solvent and test the surface carefully first.

If the surface is very scratched, it may be possible to improve it by rubbing lightly with a little **fine abrasive paste** on a cotton wool swab or bud. However, extensive polishing can remove the original surface, leaving it more vulnerable to deterioration. Wipe the polish off with a moist swab of cotton wool and pat the object dry; if you try to polish the abrasive off, the surface of the plastic may become charged with static electricity and pick up dust and fluff. Do not use abrasive polishes, such as those for metals or car paint, as the solvents can harm the plastic.

If you have objects made from **acrylic sheet**, flick or brush the dust off rather than wiping it off. If you rub the plastic, it will become charged with static electricity and pick up more dust and it may scratch. Non-static cleaners are available for modern acrylic sheet.

Repair

The deterioration of plastics is not well understood, so the best method to treat a plastic object that is cracking or flaking is not yet very clear. If you have an object that is degrading, seal it in a glass jar and keep it away from other objects. Loosen the lid of the jar periodically to allow the fumes to escape. Consult a conservator who has had experience of working with plastics.

A broken plastic object is difficult to repair. Most modern adhesives will not hold pieces together for long. Whether or not an adhesive will work on a plastic object very much depends on what the adhesive and the object are made from.

Easily reversible **adhesives** (p.244) contain solvents which can soften some plastics. Epoxy resin adhesives do not stick most plastics. Cyanoacrylate instant adhesives do stick some plastics. If you have a valuable piece, it would be sensible to leave it alone until more is understood about the deterioration of plastics.

It is sometimes recommended that you should try to weld plastics together. Do not attempt to do this. They are flammable and would soon be ruined by welding.

Quillwork

Quills can either come from the hollow stem of large wing or tail feathers or from the needle-like spines of spiny animals such as the porcupine. Porcupine quills are cream and black-brown in colour. Like feathers, quills are predominantly made up of the protein keratin.

Quills have been used to decorate small boxes, such as jewellery and writing boxes, and they are also found on ethnographic objects. On quillwork boxes, the quills are cut into short lengths and held in position by a band of wood. The wood may be inlaid with ivory or bone.

In North America, quills were used to decorate clothing and furniture and were also used to make jewellery. Quills can be dyed or used with their natural colour intact.

The term quillwork is sometimes applied to the technique of paper filigree or quilling. For advice on this, *see* PAPER.

Problems

Although quills are basically quite tough, they become very brittle with time. A very dry environment may cause them to become loose or detached from the carcass. Mould may develop in a damp environment. Deterioration will be accelerated by strong light.

The wood banding on quillwork boxes holding the quills in place may be missing or loose, so that the quills may fall out.

Handling

Follow the general guidelines for handling (*see* p.12). Clothing decorated with quillwork must be handled as recommended for embroidered and sequinned costume (*see* TEXTILES).

Shoulder decoration from a Canadian Indian coat in the costume collection of Charles Paget Wade, now at Berrington Hall, Herefordshire. The red border is made up of flattened, dyed porcupine quills. The embroidery is made from moose hair sewn onto wool. The fringe is red dyed fibre held in bundles by tinned iron cones.

Display

Do not display quillwork in direct sunlight or near spotlights, particularly if it is dyed. It should be displayed in an area with a steady humidity and temperature (*see* pp.17–18). This is most important for quillwork used for clothing or backed on to another material. Do not display over a fireplace, radiator or other heat source.

Storage

Quillwork should be stored in a cool, dry, dark, dust-free area. Although not common, quillwork can be attacked by the larvae of clothes moths and carpet beetles, so check objects regularly for insect attack (*see* pp.14–15). Protect the objects from dust by wrapping them in **acid-free** tissue.

Housekeeping and Maintenance

Remove any dust with a soft brush. Brush the quills from the base towards the sharp tip. **Compressed air** may help to remove the dust from crevices.

Cleaning

If the quills are still dirty, wipe them from the base to the tip with a piece of dry **chemical sponge**. If this does not remove the dirt, try a small swab or cotton bud moistened with saliva. Wipe again with a clean swab barely dampened with water to rinse and leave the object to dry. Do not get the quills very wet. If the quills are dyed, do not wash them, only dust them with a soft brush, as the colour will come off very easily.

Repair

Quills on boxes are usually held in place by the wood and should not need fixing. If you do need to use **adhesive**, try an easily reversible adhesive or a neutral pH emulsion adhesive or Scotch glue.

Shell

Shells have been used to decorate ethnographic costumes, weapons, figurines and musical instruments. Since the late eighteenth century, seashells have been used to make elaborate pictures and three-dimensional works of art, as well as to cover clock cases, boxes and other ornaments.

Like mother-of-pearl, shells are made up of the protein conchiolin and a crystalline inorganic calcium salt known as aragonite.

Problems

The delicate colour of shells will fade in light.

In humid conditions, marine shells can develop a crystalline coating comprising a mixture of salts, known as Byne's disease, which will weaken and spoil the shell. Acids will harm shell, so do not display or store them in cupboards and boxes that may give off organic acid vapour, such as oak and cardboard boxes.

If shells are kept in very dry conditions, they eventually become brittle and flake, but otherwise they are generally quite robust.

Heat and damp may soften the adhesive used in shell pictures or decorations. If the environment is too dry, the adhesive may become brittle, causing shells to detach.

Handling

See p.12.

Display

Protect objects from dust by using frames and glass domes. Also protect them from strong light and display them away from direct sunlight, radiators or open fires (*see* p.18).

Storage

Store objects made from shell in a cool, dark, dry place and protect them from dust. Use **acid-free** storage materials. Use tissue paper or **polyethylene foam** padding rather than cotton wool.

Housekeeping and Maintenance

Clean shell objects by brushing off the dust with a soft brush and vacuum cleaner (*see* pp.19–20).

Cleaning

Compressed air may help to remove dust from crevices. Wipe any remaining dirt off

Removing dust from shellwork using a photographer's puffer.

ABOVE: *Amongst Miss Chichester's many collections at Arlington Court in Devon is her collection of shells. This shellwork box, on display in the Morning Room, is in good condition, but there are places where the shells are becoming detached because the glue has failed.*

the shells using a cotton wool swab or bud barely dampened with warm water containing a few drops of **conservation-grade detergent** or a mild household detergent. Rinse the shells with a clean swab or bud dampened with clean water and allow them to dry. Do not get the shells very wet or the water may soften any adhesive fixing the shells into position.

Where there are salt crystals on the surface of the shells (Byne's disease), move affected shells to a drier environment and seek conservation advice. Do not wash them if the shell is in poor condition, but brush off the crystals with a soft **brush**, and improve the environmental conditions to eliminate any source of acid vapour. If the problem is only very slight, remove the crystalline growth by rinsing in de-ionised water.

Repair

If many shells become loose or fall off or the object is badly damaged, you should take it to a conservator to be repaired, but if you want to replace one or two shells, use an easily reversible **adhesive** or neutral pH emulsion adhesive or Scotch glue. *See also* NATURAL HISTORY, Shells.

Straw Marquetry or Straw-work

Straw-work is the decoration on small boxes, mirror frames and small pieces of furniture which was formed by cutting lengths of bleached and coloured straw and forming geometric patterns or landscapes. It was practised in Europe from the seventeenth century onwards and in France particularly in the late eighteenth century. It is still being made today.

Problems

The colours will fade in light. High humidity may soften the adhesive and cause mould to develop. Low humidity can cause the straw and adhesive to become brittle and detach from the carcass.

Handling, Display and Storage

See WOOD, Tunbridgeware.

Housekeeping and Maintenance

Clean the straw by removing the dust with a soft paintbrush. Never use a duster, which will catch the ends of the lengths of straw and pull them off.

Cleaning

Avoid wetting the straw, as the colour is fugitive and will come off and the straw will soften. **Compressed air** may help to remove dust from the crevices and any remaining dirt may come off with a dry **chemical sponge** rubbed gently along the straw-work.

Repair

Replace loose pieces of straw with a neutral pH emulsion **adhesive** or Scotch glue.

Stone

Many different types of stone have been used to create works of art and decorative features, as well as to construct buildings and make tools. It is broadly classified by the process of formation and by its composition and texture. Stone is made up of one or more minerals and varies widely in hardness, porosity, colour, translucency, texture and durability. Some stones are very hard and can take a high polish, while others, such as alabaster and soapstone, are soft enough to be cut with a knife. Limestone, used widely for buildings and sculpture, is more porous and granular compared with granite, which is hard but coarse-grained, while jade is glass-like in appearance although very tough. Generally, stone can support a lot of weight, but is brittle and can easily be broken or chipped.

The surface of stone sculpture and interior ornament was often decorated with paint or gilding. For example, evidence indicates that classical sculpture and medieval European cathedrals were heavily painted. The remains of decoration is sometimes found in the folds of drapery or other crevices. If you find any remnants of paint on an object, you must get advice from a conservator before carrying out any cleaning.

Problems

Stone objects kept inside a building usually survive very well; the greatest risk is from physical damage, such as breaking, cracking and chipping, or from staining. All stone is porous to some degree, even marble

ABOVE: *Old Father Time showing distinct signs of age, in the gardens at Anglesey Abbey in Cambridgeshire. A number of repairs have been made to his weak points, his arms and wrists. Lichen and moss have both grown on the surface, along with a black crust caused by pollution. A skin has developed over the limestone, as can be seen in the drapery under his left wrist.*

which, though it may not look porous, can be stained by dirt and handling. Limestone and marble are damaged by acidic liquids, such as fruit juice or wine, which can etch into or stain the stone surface. Acidic vapour can also destroy these stones.

ABOVE: *Statuary in the North Gallery at Petworth House in Sussex. Most of the pieces shown here are antique, collected by the 2nd Earl of Egremont in the 1760s, though some 'modern' early nineteenth-century works were added by his son, the 3rd Earl. This is a display on a grand scale, but the pieces show characteristic problems, with old repairs using iron clamps that cause staining on the marble, as seen on the left knee of the standing figure on the right.*

Stone objects can have a surface **patina**, which may be deliberately applied or has developed over time from handling, use and cleaning. As with furniture and bronzes, it is generally considered desirable to retain the patina and essential if it is known to have been deliberately applied by the creator of the piece.

Stone objects inside buildings can deteriorate if they are exposed to a damp environment or to damp entering the stone. This is seen mostly in churches where a monument may be placed on a stone floor or against a wall where there is no damp-proof course; similar damage can also occur to any stone piece placed directly on a stone or brick floor without damp-proofing.

The stone will deteriorate even faster if it contains soluble salts (*see* CERAMICS). These are chemicals within the stone which form whitish crystals when the stone is dry and the humidity low, but when the humidity is high the crystals dissolve. Gradually the repeated cycle of crystallisation causes the surface of the stone to break up and become powdery, to the extent that the whole object can disintegrate. The salts can be absorbed into the stone from a number of sources, such as atmospheric pollution, previous treatment or cleaning materials, fresh cement or concrete, or sea air. Sometimes the original use of the building or object can be the source of the salts; stables suffer from problems of salts, as do containers used for preserving pork or eggs. Salts are often found in archaeological stone, for example, from Egypt.

Stone objects that are displayed outside are exposed to rain, wind, pollution and frost, which cause gradual deterioration; even heat causes the stone to break down slowly, although this phenomenon is most evident in hot climates. The stone can be worn away by rain-water, corroded by pollution in the air and abraded by wind and dust. The surface of most stone may become powdery, while marble can become crystalline, like sugar. This often occurs on the underside of carving, where the surface will feel rough and granular to the touch.

Although stone generally does not appear to be very porous, some types, such as limestone and sandstone, can absorb quite a lot of water. If this wet stone is exposed to freezing temperatures, it can spall (pieces, often circular, break off the surface) or break up. This type of damage can also occur to wet stone containers exposed to freezing temperatures.

Limestone sometimes forms a skin as a result of weathering. If this skin is removed or broken, the stone underneath is powdery and the surface detail will be lost.

Mould, algae and lichen can grow on the surface of stone that is damp for any length of time. The roots of algae and lichen can break stone down, so, although it can enhance the appearance of objects, it may eventually be destructive and is usually, but not always, removed from sculpture and ornament.

An object, such as a stone sculpture, may be made of several pieces of stone secured together by metal dowels, often made of iron. In a damp atmosphere, the dowels may corrode and rust-coloured stains can develop; eventually the dowels will expand, causing the stone to split. Copper or brass dowels or fittings will leave blue or green stains.

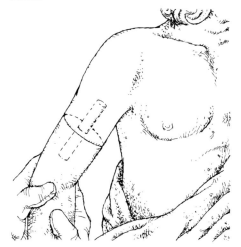

Metal dowels, usually of iron, secure pieces such as arms and legs onto the body of a stone sculpture.

Marble pedestals are often made by boxing together thin slabs of marble around a brick core to give the appearance of being made of a solid piece of marble. In time, the adhesive used to stick the marble to the core can give way and the marble veneer can come off. Check that the veneers are sound by looking along the joins to see that they are tight and there are no gaps. Gently tapping the surface can sometimes help, as a hollow sound can indicate that the adhesive is failing.

Alabaster and plaster can dissolve in water, and so may be damaged by cleaning them with water. However, they are not always easy to distinguish from marble. It is important, therefore, to make absolutely sure that what appears to be marble is neither alabaster nor painted plaster before you start to wash it. First look carefully at the surface; if there are any small chips that look a powdery opaque white, it may be plaster. Very carefully scrape a tiny area in a discrete spot with a sharp knife or scalpel. If the object is small enough, lay it on its side and scrape the underside. If the sculpture is made of plaster, it will be soft, opaque white and powdery. If it is alabaster, you will be able to scratch it easily, but it is more translucent and slightly harder than plaster, though not as hard as marble. It is difficult to be certain without comparative materials.

Stone objects should be protected as much as possible from becoming dirty and from physical damage. Objects outside may need some protection from extreme weather conditions. If the stone is deteriorating, the humidity should be kept as steady as possible. Light is not a major problem for stone unless it is painted, but artificial lighting should not increase the temperature of the object. The signs of damage to look out for on stone are: blistering, flaking or a crumbly surface, old repairs, cracks and chips. If it is painted, check whether the paint or gilding is sound or flaking, lifting or powdery.

Handling

Wear clean gloves or have clean hands when handling stone, as dirt and grease from your fingers will be absorbed by stone and can be difficult to remove. Move stone carefully, as it breaks and chips easily. Before picking up a stone object, check it for repairs or pieces that could be knocked off and check its weight to ensure that there are enough people available to carry it safely.

Smaller pieces can be carried and handled using the same care and methods as for CERAMICS; *see also* p.12.

Moving large stone objects is a specialist skill and should be undertaken by experienced art handlers and shippers, otherwise it is easy to damage yourself, the object and the surroundings. When large objects are being moved, the floors and doorways may need protection. This is often done by laying down sheets of hardboard on the floor and **polypropylene twinwall board** to protect walls and woodwork.

Do not push or drag an object made from stone; always lift it. To move anything other than a very small stone object, carry it on a truck or barrow well padded with clean, soft blankets. Tie the piece to the barrow with clean webbing or rope. Put padding, such as **polyethylene foam**, between the statue and the webbing or rope to prevent it from marking the object. Arms, legs, necks, hands, fingers and any other projections may extend beyond the side of the truck, so make sure that they do not bang into doors or pieces of furniture along the way. You also need to check that the weight of the object is evenly distributed and not resting on an arm or fold of garment.

It is usually safer to keep a stone piece upright when you are moving it. If this is impossible, for instance if the doorways are too low, ease the piece into a horizontal position to move it. The danger of this is that any weak area on the piece, such as ankles or a repair may break or bend under the strain. If you have to lay the object down, make sure that it does not rest on any projections and that the padding is arranged so that the weight is evenly supported. Stone table-tops should be carried vertically, otherwise they can snap under their own weight. If you are in doubt, and if the statue is of importance, consult an art handler.

Statues or busts on bases or pedestals are not always fixed to the base. They could be standing on the base, bolted or stuck to it or held in place with a dowel that is not fixed, so it can be turned and lifted off the base. Small statues and busts are often fixed in the latter manner. Always check whether the base is loose. Even if it appears to be fixed, take precautions to prevent it from dropping off during moving, as the movement may cause it to separate from the

Statue on a dowel.

object. If the sections can be separated, do so before moving them.

Move one object at a time. Do not carry stone objects on the same trolley as more delicate pieces, because if the trolley lurches, the stone may damage the other objects.

Should an object become damaged, make sure that even the smallest pieces are collected and put in a safe place until it can be repaired. When the object is conserved, it is much easier for the conservator to use the original material, no matter how small the bits, than to have to make up missing areas.

Display

● INDOOR DISPLAY

Avoid placing stone where dust may be deposited, such as above fireplaces in use, radiators and other heat sources.

Stone reliefs or other flat pieces can be displayed on a strong wall, but they must be prepared, with suitable fixings, by someone experienced in displaying heavy objects, such as a mount-maker or stone conservator. Make sure that the wall is not damp and that it is strong enough to carry the weight of the stone. The object may need to be supported from underneath and secured at the top. Use stainless steel brackets covered with plastic tubing or a layer of **polyethylene foam** to prevent the metal from marking the stone.

Objects need to be placed where they will not be knocked or hit and where they do not get too much handling. They should be raised off the floor just enough so that the base will not be damaged from cleaning the floor or from being kicked; they will also be easier to move in the future. Usually wood or stone plinths or battens are advised for this.

Avoid placing marble or alabster in a damp part of the house, such as a bathroom, near frequently opened windows, by indoor swimming pools or in conservatories as the surface can be corroded and iron stains may develop.

If you have houseplants near marble objects or on marble table-tops, make sure that wet leaves do not rest on the marble surface as they can mark it. Do not spray houseplants with water if they are standing on or near marble, as the fine mist may eventually cause the marble to stain; take them away from the marble to water them. Place a glass or ceramic mat under a vase, plant or other object displayed on a stone surface to protect it against scratching and staining.

● OUTSIDE DISPLAY

Stone objects that are displayed outside will deteriorate more quickly than those that are inside; but if the object is placed in a suitable spot and properly maintained, deterioration should be slow. Marble can stain when outside and may deteriorate quite rapidly, so it is recommended that marble sculpture should be displayed under cover or inside wherever possible. Never put alabaster outside (*see* ALABASTER).

When setting a piece outside for the first time, prevent damp from rising through a plinth or the object by laying a damp-proof membrane made of polythene, lead or slate at the base. If possible, dig a small trench round the plinth and keep it filled with small pebbles to improve the drainage. Do not let plants grow over the pebbles. Carved stone benches should also have a waterproof membrane under their feet.

Outside statue with a damp-proof course.

Ideally, plinths should be level horizontally to prevent the object from leaning and producing stresses in the stone. Sometimes the earth settles under a plinth and the plinth shifts; this will need to be rectified.

Make sure that statues that are displayed on the top of walls are securely fixed with mortar and/or stainless steel fixings to the wall so that they cannot be knocked or blown off.

Avoid placing stone sculpture too close to trees and bushes. Overhanging branches can scratch the surface of a sculpture. Keep an eye on the length of the branches and trim them back if necessary. If a stone sculpture is displayed under trees, the water dripping off the leaves and branches will cause uneven staining on the piece; algae may grow on the surface of sculpture placed under overhanging ivy or trailing plants

due to the poor air circulation caused by the tent-like effect of the foliage. Do not let ivy grow up stone objects, because its roots will destroy the surface of the stone.

Storage

Store stone objects in a dry place where the humidity and temperature are not extreme. Protect them from dust or dirt by covering them with tents of **acid-free** tissue paper. Large objects can be covered with a clean, white **dustsheet**, **calico** or Tyvek. To pack small objects away, wrap them in acid-free tissue and pack them in acid-free boxes or plastic crates. Do not put too many in a box or crate, as it may not be able to take the weight and the lower pieces may be crushed. When placing stone objects on shelves, make sure that the shelves are strong enough to take the weight. **MDF** shelves bend over time and metal shelves, if they are not strong enough for the weight, can also bend, causing the objects to roll into one another. Use metal shelves of a suitable gauge that will take the weight. Avoid covering stone objects in polyethylene sheet or bags, as polyethylene can attract dust. Also, do not store objects in sealed polythene or bubble wrap, as the lack of air circulation can cause microorganisms to develop and some stone to deteriorate.

Keep small outdoor stone sculptures and objects under cover when they are not on display. Outbuildings, sheds and garages are suitable if they are dry and clean. Put the sculptures far enough back in the storage area, and not too close together, so that you do not have to keep moving them to get at other things and to prevent them from being damaged by everyday comings and goings, or by being knocked by moving the lawn-mower or other equipment. Cover the sculptures with a clean dustsheet, calico or Tyvek to keep off the grime and bird droppings. Raise them off the ground by placing them on battens or pallets, both to make moving easier and to protect them from damp or flooding.

Outdoor stone objects that are too difficult to move into storage should ideally be covered for protection during the winter. You could make, or have made, canvas or wooden covers to go over them, but ensure that the covers have ventilation holes in the sides to prevent condensation. Alternatively, wrap them tightly in Tyvek, which is porous and should not cause condensation. Put the covers on before the winter is really in its stride, and while the object is completely dry.

Before winter sets in, empty stone urns and troughs of earth to reduce the likelihood of them being split by frost and ice. Where possible, use fibreglass liners for plant troughs.

Housekeeping and Maintenance

Before cleaning an object, check the condition and whether there is any patination. If the condition is poor, for example if the surface is powdering, or there is a **patina**, do not proceed without getting conservation advice.

- **INDOOR STONE**
First remove dust and loose dirt, using a dry, clean, hogshair brush and vacuum cleaner (*see* pp.19–20). Make sure that the nozzle of the vacuum cleaner does not catch the surface of the stone.

Regular dusting is necessary to prevent the stone from becoming very dirty; always use a brush rather than cloths or dusters, as they tend to rub the dust into the surface and may smear greasy dirt. Do not use feather dusters, because the feathers break and the broken ends of the spines can scratch the surface.

- **FIREPLACES**
Maintain the condition of the fireplace by dusting regularly. Occasionally wipe the surface with a damp cloth. Once or twice a year re-wax the fireplace, but use very little wax (*see* Cleaning Indoor Stone).

- **OUTSIDE STATUARY**
It is not always easy to tell how sound the surface of limestone and sandstone is because the 'skin' formed by weathering will actually appear sound. If you tap it gently, it will sound hollow. Never clean limestone or sandstone in this condition and take care not to knock the surface or it will break off. If the stone surface is powdery or flaking you may damage it more by cleaning. In both cases, get advice from a conservator.

On stone in good condition, regularly brush off loose dust, dirt, bird droppings and leaves as necessary using a hogshair **brush** or a natural bristle brush. This may be once a week or once a month, depending on the site. Examine the statue at least once a year in spring to assess whether further cleaning is necessary.

If further cleaning is necessary, first dampen the surface with a fine mist of water using a garden spray, then wash with a few drops of a **conservation-grade detergent** in water. Gently scrub the surface with a soft, clean brush and work on a small area at a time; start from the bottom and work upwards. Sometimes the dirt takes a while to soften, so keep the area wet for a few minutes. Avoid letting water run down the surface, as this can result in a streaky appearance; do not use too much water; and hold a paper towel or clean cloth below the area being cleaned to mop up any drips. Rinse the detergent off with clean water. If you find that particles of stone are becoming detached by the cleaning process, it is best to stop and seek help from a conservator. Do not wash a stone object in the winter when there is a danger of frost.

Cleaning

- **INDOOR STONE**
Never clean rare, ancient, precious stone objects or stone that has a deteriorating surface, nor objects with a patina; this should be done by a conservator. Any traces of paint on ancient or antique stone can be completely lost by cleaning. Always ask for advice from a conservator before cleaning such an object.

Acids and alkalis, no matter how dilute, attack marble, limestone and sandstone and should *never* be used on stone. Also, do not use proprietary stone- or marble-cleaning agents, as many of them contain acids or alkalis and may damage the stone.

First move the piece right away from any furniture or objects that might be damaged. Always remove loose dust and dirt, as described above, before any further cleaning. The following cleaning methods should be carried out only on stone in good condition.

A **chemical sponge** can be very effective at removing layers of grime. Rub it gently over the surface after dusting.

If the object is still grubby, it can be washed using warm water containing a few drops of a **conservation-grade detergent**; do not use household detergent but you must remove all dust and loose dirt first. Before washing marble, make absolutely sure that it is neither alabaster nor painted plaster (*see* Problems). Dampen the whole surface of the object with clean water – a fine garden mister is useful for this – and then wash as described for Outside Statuary (above). Pat dry any excess with paper towels and allow the object to dry. If you

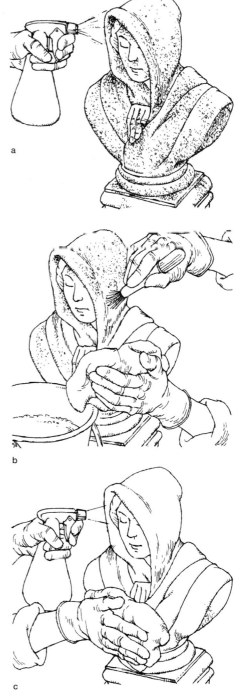

Cleaning outside statuary
(a) *Dampen the surface with a fine mist and detergent* (b) *Starting at the bottom, gently scrub with a soft brush, using a towel or cloth to catch the drips* (c) *Rinse off the detergent with spray mist.*

are cleaning a large object *in situ*, you may need to protect the floor with polythene or **dustsheets**.

Sometimes greasy dirt can be removed from stone by wiping the surface with swabs of cotton wool dampened with a

1:1 mixture of purified water and acetone or the **white spirit**:water:detergent mixture (*see* **solvent mixtures**). Rinse as you go by wiping the surface with clean swabs of cotton wool dampened with purified water. Clean a small area at a time. There may well be areas of a statue or fireplace that will not clean as well as the rest. To prevent over-cleaning some areas and the stone looking patchy, lightly clean the statue all over once and then, if necessary, go over it again. The result will be much more satisfactory than cleaning 'thoroughly' the first time and perhaps being left with a blotchy object.

Do not use very wet swabs and do not let the cleaning liquid run on the surface. Discard the swabs as soon as they become dirty. Wipe in one direction only and do not rub the surface. Use **cotton buds** for small objects or intricate surfaces.

If the stone remains dirty and you feel further cleaning is appropriate, consult a stone conservator who may be able to do it for you.

Removing stains from any material can be difficult, as there is a danger that the appearance will be worsened rather than ameliorated. Iron and copper stains found on stone are very difficult to remove. Therefore, seek the advice of a conservator if the stone is stained.

A marble object in good condition that has old wax, household paint or varnish on it can be cleaned by using a water washable **dichloromethane-based paint remover.**

First examine the object carefully and make sure it is stone and not composition or plaster. Stone was often painted to imitate marble, and it is not advisable to remove historic paint schemes. If the paint is chipped, you may be able to see original decorative paint, but otherwise it is difficult to detect and you should seek conservation advice. The paint remover may take off all the layers of paint, so check carefully before you start. Remove any spots of paint, wax or other dirt on the surface of the marble, scraping off as much as possible with a plastic spatula or wooden **bamboo stick**, and taking care not to scratch the marble surface.

Wear rubber **gloves** and protect your eyes. Take care not to get any remover on your skin. If you do, wash it off immediately in cold water. If possible, work outside to protect yourself from the fumes of the paint remover. If you are working on a fixed object such as a fireplace that cannot be removed, open all the windows in the room and make sure that there is good ventilation. Read and follow the health and safety instructions on the can.

Apply the paint remover to a small area (approximately 12 × 12cm or 5 × 5in) of the marble with a clean, long-handled paintbrush. Brush it on lightly so that the dirt is not pushed into the pores of the marble, leave it on the surface for only a few minutes, and wipe it off with clean cotton wool swabs dampened with water or white spirit. Then wipe the area again with clean, dry swabs. Apply more paint remover as needed. Do not allow the paint remover to dry on the surface of the marble. Apply the paint remover to the next area and repeat the procedure. Place the dirty swabs in a lidded container and allow them to evaporate outside before putting them in the dustbin (*see* p.23). When the entire surface has been cleaned, brush it with warm water containing a few drops of conservation-grade detergent, rinse with clean water and dry. Do not use a blowlamp or hot-air stripper for removing paint, because it is easy to scorch the marble and the stone can deform at quite a low temperature.

Do not use paint remover on porous or open-grained stone, such as limestone or sandstone, or on stone with a rough surface, as the paint will be pushed further into the pores and it is difficult to remove the paint remover from the stone. Seek expert advice.

Some fireplaces have an original decorative paint surface. If the paint is in sound condition, these should be cleaned as for PAINTED STONE. If the painting is fragile, it is better to leave it alone or ask a conservator for advice.

Some marble table-tops and fireplaces do not always clean using the above methods. A fine abrasive may clean the surface, although even these abrasives can abrade polished marble, so work with care and use a magnifying glass to check that the surface is not being scratched. Use a **fine abrasive paste** and work on a small area at a time. Rub it evenly over the surface of the marble with a circular movement, using a clean stencil brush, cotton swab or cotton bud. Wipe off the cleaner with swabs of cotton wool dampened with white spirit before the abrasive dries, and polish the surface with a soft, clean white cloth. Never use any other abrasive, particularly not household and bathroom cleaning powders and creams, because the chemicals they contain can harm and discolour the marble and the abrasive will scratch the surface. Do not clean porous stone, such as limestone and sandstone, using an abrasive.

When you have finished the treatment and the object has dried, apply a light coat of **microcrystalline wax** with a clean bristle brush and polish with a soft, clean white cloth to help protect the marble. Stone takes a long time to dry, so leave it for a week before waxing.

● STONE FLOORS
Patented floor cleaners can contain acids or silicones which may eventually damage the stone, so they should be avoided on historic floors, as should household cleaning agents, particularly creams or scouring powders. Matting placed at entrances will help collect dirt and cut down on the need to clean the floor. Regularly vacuum up the dust and grit in and under the matting and on the floor.

Floors should be washed often enough to prevent a build up of dirt; precisely how frequently this is will depend on the amount of use it gets, the weather, and its position within the house. Wash the surface using water either on its own or containing a few drops of a conservation-grade detergent or a mild household detergent. Do not make the floor too wet or get water on skirting boards or furniture legs. Remove chairs and light furniture, or raise them off floor level, and wipe the floor around and under the furniture that cannot be moved by hand with a floor cloth. Use two buckets, one with the soap solution and one of clean water. Wash and ring the mop out regularly in the soapy water to remove the dirt. Change the water in the bucket before it becomes very dirty. Rinse the floor well as you go with clean water after washing it with detergent.

Stone floors can stain very easily and it is worth having a new stone floor sealed with a commercial stone sealer. Do not seal an historic stone floor without consulting a building conservator first, as the sealer could ruin a floor that is damp and might alter its appearance permanently.

● PAINTED STONE
Do not clean antiquities and historic sculpture that have traces of paint, as the paint will be lost. Seek advice from a conservator with experience of working with painted stone objects.

A more modern painted piece can be cleaned, but first check that the paint is sound and not powdery, flaking or lifting. Remove the dust and loose dirt with a ponyhair brush. You can then follow this by wiping with a dry chemical sponge. For further cleaning, try a solution of conservation-grade detergent on a cotton bud and/or the white spirit : water mixture (*see* **solvent mixtures**) on a bud, but first test each paint colour with a small swab to check that the paint will not be removed. The other cleaning agent that is sometimes very successful is saliva. Always rinse the surface with clean water on a swab.

● OUTSIDE STATUARY

Brushing and washing regularly as described above should keep outdoor sculpture in good condition. If a stone object is covered with lichen or algae, it can sometimes be controlled just by washing as described above. If the growths are not controlled, their roots can penetrate the stone and cause considerable damage. In cases where the rhizomes of the lichens have penetrated deeply, the object should not be cleaned, as flakes of stone may become detached.

Biocides produced to restrict the growth of lichen and algae may be used only by people with the appropriate training; therefore, you will need help from a suitably qualified stone conservator if you choose to use these chemicals.

Repair

Do not try to repair a statue of any value or an object in poor condition.

Small pieces, such as fingers, broken off a stone object displayed inside can be stuck back into place using an easily reversible **adhesive**. If the piece is too heavy to be held by the adhesive or the angle of the join is awkward, it would be safer to have it repaired by a conservator. Do not use too much adhesive or it will squelch out; hold the piece in position until it has set. Remove any excess adhesive from round the join with a sharp knife or scalpel. Take care not to scratch the stone. Larger repairs are difficult to carry out so that they look good and are strong and safe. They should be carried out by a stone conservator.

Repairing outdoor objects is a specialist skill, as particular adhesives and mortars are required so as not to initiate or exacerbate any deterioration. Water vapour moves through exterior stone and it is important that it should not be prevented from doing so; therefore, do not try to repair outdoor sculpture with epoxy or other synthetic resins. Seek advice from an experienced stone conservator.

Areas of a stone floor may begin to break up and should be repaired as soon as possible to prevent the floor from getting worse. Do not use cement or synthetic adhesives, as they can make the damage worse. A suitable lime mortar mixture can be used, but the work should be carried out by a stone conservator or a builder familiar with the use of hydraulic lime, as it is a difficult material to use without experience.

Soluble salts often cause powdery and flaking surfaces. Sometimes the salt crystals are visible. A stone conservator may be able to treat such pieces; do not attempt to do this yourself as it is easy to exacerbate the problem.

Agate and Onyx

Agate is a form of silica. It usually has a layered structure, each layer differing in colour and translucency. Agates occur in a range of colours, including red, brown, yellow, green and white. Agates can also be dyed.

Onyx is a form of agate with distinct parallel banding of white with dark brown or black. Onyx marble is a form of calcium carbonate sometimes known as calcite alabaster. It is translucent and banded, and ranges in colour from white to red, brown and black. It can also be dyed. Onyx marble is used for ashtrays, desk sets, art deco figurines, table-tops and other small carved ornaments.

Check onyx carefully for cracks and chips. The dye (in dyed pieces) can be removed by inappropriate cleaning and may change colour when exposed to light. Handle, Clean, Display and Store it as for BLUE JOHN and JADE.

Alabaster

Alabaster is a translucent stone. Softer and less granular then marble, it is made up of calcium sulphate (gypsum), except for Egyptian alabaster, which is calcium carbonate (calcite). There is seldom any distinction between the two types of alabaster, but calcite alabaster is usually more durable than gypsum alabaster.

Alabaster is usually white or creamy in

Various forms of decorative stone, the result of a shopping tour of Italy in the 1840s, now in the bay window of the Great Hall at Charlecote Park in Warwickshire. The superb, translucent alabaster vase and marble and porphyry plinth came from Florence, the red and white marble floor from Venice.

colour, but it can be yellowish, orange or even red, often with darker veins running through it. When alabaster is cut into sheets, it is translucent. Alabaster is very soft and can be carved with a knife; it can also be polished.

In houses in Yemen and in Byzantine churches in Ravenna, alabaster is still found instead of glass in the windows. Alabaster is used to produce a wide range of objects, including religious carvings, sculpture, clock cases, lamps and vases, pedestals, tourist souvenirs and architectural ornaments such as altarpieces and columns. Religious carvings were often painted and gilded.

Alabaster is soft and can be scratched with a fingernail; it is also slightly water soluble. If it is heated, it can become opaque and white and very fragile. This is often noticeable on alabaster lamps.

Handle alabaster very carefully. Do not set it down hard or it will crack or crumble. See STONE for further information on handling. Before cleaning alabaster, check for fragments of paint or gilding, particularly on historic or ancient pieces. Such decoration is very easy to remove, so do not clean gilded or painted alabaster but seek conservation advice.

Remove dust as described in STONE. Do not clean alabaster with water or water-containing mixtures. Dirt can usually be removed from the surface using white spirit, but try **alcohol** if this is not successful. Dry it with a paper towel or a soft, clean white cloth. If further cleaning is necessary, consult a conservator. If the surface of the alabaster looks dull, apply a little **microcrystalline wax** and buff gently with a clean, soft white cloth.

Alabaster urns are sometimes used as lamps by placing a light bulb inside them. If too much heat is generated by the light bulb, the alabaster will deteriorate, so always use a low-wattage bulb and check that the alabaster does not crack or start to become crumbly.

Display alabaster as described for STONE. An alabaster object should not be displayed in a damp room and never display alabaster objects outside.

See STONE for Storage and Repair.

RIGHT: *Early nineteenth-century Blue John urn on a black marble base in the North Drawing Room at Hinton Ampner in Hampshire. The urn is made up of five pieces of Blue John stone, and stands 41cm (16in) high.*

Blue John

Blue John is a highly decorative, translucent stone made from the mineral fluorspar with bands of colour ranging from blue/violet to light brown and yellow. It is found in Derbyshire and is also known as Derbyshire spar. Blue John was particularly popular in France, which imported large quantities of it, calling it '*bleu-jaune*' (blue-yellow), hence the English name Blue John. Although Blue John had been used earlier, it was employed extensively in the late eighteenth century, when urns, boxes, jewellery and other objects were made from it, often with intricate metal mounts made of ormolu or bronze. Blue John is not usually found in large pieces, so often a number of segments were joined together with shellac or animal glue to make a large object.

The surface of the stone can be quite soft and scratches easily. A Blue John object should not be cleaned by immersing it in water, as it may be made of several pieces that can come apart. Clean it by removing the dust with a brush and then wiping the surface with cotton wool swabs or buds moistened with warm water containing a few drops of **conservation-grade detergent**. Rinse with swabs or buds dampened with clean water and dry with a soft, clean cloth. Saliva may also be used on cotton buds to clean the surface and must be rinsed off with clean water on a cotton bud (*see* p.21). If the stone is in ormolu mounts, take care not to rub or wet the ormolu. *See* ORMOLU.

If the surface is dull, apply a light coating of **microcrystalline wax** with cotton wool and polish with a soft clean cloth.

Small pieces of broken Blue John can be repaired with an easily reversible **adhesive** but more serious damage should be dealt with by a conservator.

Breccia

Breccia is a type of rock comprised of angular fragments of one or more rock types cemented into a matrix. Breccias often contain different coloured materials and some can be polished, so they have been used to make decorative objects, particularly panelling, plinths, table-tops and inlays, as well as vessels and knife handles. Breccia should be cleaned as for STONE.

Chalk

Chalk is a type of limestone and is composed of almost pure calcium carbonate. It is fine-grained, white or grey and usually soft. Chalk can be carved and has been used for architectural decoration.

It is extremely fragile and friable, damages very easily and readily absorbs water and dirt. Treat it as you would PLASTER OF PARIS.

Composition or Artificial Stone and Coade Stone

Artificial stone can be made either from stone dust and fragments mixed together with cement or lime mortars or from a fired clay mixture. Eleanor Coade developed the fired material called Coade stone in the eighteenth century to make sculpture and architectural elements. Nowadays stone dust is mixed with modern resins

Coade stone urn dating from 1805 in the garden at Killerton in Devon. This urn is in very good condition, a tribute to the durability of the formula created by Eleanor Coade.

and cement to produce a very convincing artificial stone.

It can be quite difficult to distinguish between limestone, sandstone and composition stone, but if there are any signs of air bubbles in the surface of the piece, it is definitely composition stone. Pieces cast in composition stone often have lines, known as flash lines, on the surface from where the sections of the mould join. Artificial stone is often reinforced with an iron armature which may show at breaks.

Composition stone can be cared for in the same way as LIMESTONE AND SANDSTONE.

Gemstones

Gemstones are minerals prized for their rarity and beauty. They may consist of a large crystal of a particular mineral or a combination of minerals. Gemstones are hard and durable. There are many different ways that stones are cut. The different cuts are intended to show the stone at its best. However, not all stones will take an elaborate cut, as they shatter.

Stones are 'set' or fixed into a piece of jewellery using different techniques. There are open and closed settings. An open setting, such as a claw setting, allows light to shine and reflect through the stone. A closed setting encloses the base of the stone. In many cases, metal foil was placed under the stone to help reflect light. Adhesives of various types were often used to hold a stone in a closed setting. If this type of setting is immersed in water or other liquid, the adhesive could be dissolved or loosened; similarly, liquid could get trapped under the stone and cause the metal to corrode. Do not try to reset stones; this should be done by a jeweller or a metal conservator.

Granite

Granite is composed predominantly of the minerals quartz, feldspar and mica. It is one of the hardest and toughest rocks and is very dense and durable. Its texture is quite coarse-grained and it occurs in a range of colours from pale grey and pink to blue-grey, red, dark grey or almost black. It can be carved and polished to a hard shine.

Granite is generally used as a building material, but it can also be used to make tombstones, monuments, basins and garden urns, as well as table-tops and fire surrounds. The Victorians used granite extensively.

Clean granite in the same way as MARBLE. Because it is much tougher, it can be scrubbed with a bristle brush, but do not use a wire brush.

Jade

Jade is a term loosely used to refer to jadeite and nephrite, which are different minerals but very similar in appearance. Jade is a very hard, smooth and translucent stone; it ranges in colour from dark spinach green through brown to buff and white, which is known as 'mutton fat' jade because of its lardy appearance. Jade can be carved and may be highly polished.

Jade has been used extensively by many cultures, including the Chinese, Mughals of India and the Aztecs of Mexico. Although jade is very tough and was used to manufacture axes, it can be brittle at times and so should be handled carefully.

For Cleaning, *see* BLUE JOHN. Unless the jade has stones set in it, or metal inlay or mounts, the object may be immersed in the washing solution.

For Display and Storage, *see* GLASS.

Rare, precious or old jade should be repaired only by a conservator, but small repairs can be carried out using an easily reversible **adhesive**.

Jet

Jet is composed of fossilised wood; it is black and can be carved and given a high polish. The deposits of jet in Yorkshire, England, have been worked from the neolithic period. Jet has been prized since then and was very popular in the nineteenth century, particularly for mourning jewellery. It is very hard, but fractures easily and may split in very low **relative humidity**.

Throughout antiquity there have been many imitations of jet made from lignite, coal, glass, vulcanised rubber and plastic (*see* PLASTICS AND RUBBER).

To clean jet, brush the dust off and clean the object with a cotton wool bud dampened with saliva or water containing a few drops of **conservation-grade detergent**. *See* BEADS for cleaning jet beads. Very stubborn dirt can be removed using a **fine abrasive paste** on a cotton bud.

Small repairs to jet can be made using an easily reversible **adhesive**.

Limestone and Sandstone

Limestone is a composed mostly of calcium carbonate. It exists in a wide range of densities, textures, porosities and colour, from cream to grey or brown. It is a fairly soft stone and is used extensively for buildings and architectural carvings, as well as sculpture. Limestone was often painted and remnants of early paint may remain in undercuts and detail.

Sandstone is made up of grains of quartz sand cemented together by calcium carbonate, quartz or iron oxide. In appearance it is similar to limestone, but it comes in a wider range of colours and the texture is generally coarser. Sandstone is also used for buildings and sculpture, particularly in the eighteenth and nineteenth centuries, when garden ornaments became available to the general market. Objects made from sandstone include urns, sculptures, sundials, fountains, garden seats, tombstones, tiles and flooring. Sandstone is often harder to carve than limestone, as it blunts chisels more readily, so limestone, where available, was usually the preferred stone.

Both limestone and sandstone are affected by atmospheric pollution, which weakens the surface so badly that it will eventually flake off, exposing a soft, crumbly layer underneath. When this happens, the surface detail is lost. There is as yet no completely satisfactory way of dealing with the problem, but a conservator working with

stone should be able to make some improvements for you. Do not clean sandstone or limestone that is not in sound condition. Both types of stone can be quite porous and pick up grease and dirty easily. Handle, Clean, Display and Store as for STONE.

Malachite

Malachite is an opaque green mineral composed of copper carbonate and is usually very patterned with black or pale veining. It is used to make a wide range of decorative objects, particularly in Russia, where it is found with azurite in some quantity. Large pieces are uncommon, but the stone could be sliced and used in a manner similar to a veneer to make table-tops, columns and vessels, as well as smaller items. Malachite is often found in *pietre dure* pieces and was used extensively by Fabergé.

It can be damaged or destroyed by acid-containing liquids or gases. Handle, Clean, Display and Store as for BLUE JOHN.

Marble

Marble is a hard, crystalline stone made up mainly of calcium carbonate and is often highly polished. Some decorative stones, referred to as marbles, may actually be polished limestone or granite or another polished stone. True marble is usually white or grey, but there are many varieties of ornamental marble, ranging in colour from black through green, yellow and red. Marble occurs throughout the world and has been used for buildings, ornament and sculpture. It is also used for fire surrounds, for floor and wall tiles, for tops of tables and washstands, decorative friezes, pedestals, vases and urns, sarcophagi and monuments. Marble can be carved and polished, painted, inlaid with other marbles or precious and semi-precious stones or with gold and silver. Marble is very susceptible to being damaged by acids, such as polluting gases, and liquids, such as fruit juice or wine.

Pietre Dure

The term *pietre dure* applies to objects such as ewers, busts and vases that are made from hard or semi-precious stones, such as lapis lazuli and agate. These objects can either be made from one stone or several different types of stone and often have elaborate ormolu or other metal mounts.

Comesso di pietre dure or, as it is known

ABOVE: *Detail of a parrot from a pietre dure cabinet in the Drawing Room at Charlecote Park in Warwickshire. George Hammond Lucy collected a whole series of* pietre dure *pieces, including seventeenth-century Florentine cabinets from the great sale of William Beckford's collection at Fonthill in 1823. This detail from one of the Beckford cabinets shows the skill of the craftsmen in matching brightly coloured stones against the black background*

in English, Florentine mosaic, are decorative panels made by setting hard or semi-precious stones on to a stone base to produce a design. These designs are often highly elaborate, depicting flowers, birds, fruit and insects in a way similar to marquetry. The most impressive panels come from Florence and show scenes, landscapes and portraits. The panels are used to make table-tops, boxes and pictures, or to decorate the front of cabinets.

Objects made from *pietre dure*, or Florentine mosaic, can be cleaned in the same way as Blue John. To protect the surface from stains, wax it lightly with **microcrystalline wax** applied on a soft, lint-free cloth.

If any of the stones are loose, they can be relaid using an easily reversible **adhesive**.

Rock Crystal

Rock crystal is a naturally occurring, very hard, transparent crystalline form of quartz. It resembles glass in appearance, but can be distinguished from glass by its hardness (it is harder), and by the flaws and inclusions in it. It is used to make objects such as dagger handles, chandeliers, small bowls, small carved ornaments, beads and jewels. Occasionally, large pieces of rock crystal have been found and have been carved into vases and larger objects. Clean and treat rock crystal objects in the same way as BLUE JOHN and JADE. Handle as for GLASS,

but always test the weight before carrying an object, as it is often heavier than you might expect.

Slate

Slate is a dense rock that easily splits into sheets. Slate can vary in colour from grey to red and green. It is used for roofing, floors, writing tablets, fire surrounds, table-tops and headstones, and as a base for carving inscriptions. Slate is sometimes painted. It is easily chipped and broken and is particularly susceptible to frost; it also easily picks up oil, dirt and grease from handling.

Clean slate as for STONE. If a slate surface looks dull after cleaning, rub on a thin layer of colourless **beeswax polish** or **microcrystalline wax**. Use only a small amount and rub it in well.

Painted slate should be cleaned in the same way as Painted Stone. Take particular care when watering plants on a painted slate surface and mop up any spills immediately. Do not put anything hot directly on to a painted slate surface or the paint may lift off.

Slate pictures should be dealt with by a painting conservator and should be framed and unframed by a framer.

Soapstone or Steatite

Soapstone is a very soft stone, even softer than alabaster. It comes in a variety of colours, ranging from white and yellow to a bluish-grey or green, and it feels rather soapy, hence its name. Soapstone is used to make small carvings and is found particularly in Inuit art. Sometimes soapstone is hardened after carving by heating it. It is then less easy to identify.

Clean as for ALABASTER.

Textiles

Textiles are made by interlacing yarns or threads. This group of materials includes fabrics made by weaving, crocheting, knitting, lace-making, braiding, knotting (carpets) and embroidery, as well as non-woven materials such as felt. The fibres used to make textiles fall into three main groups: plant fibres, such as cotton and linen; animal-derived fibres, such as wool and silk; and synthetic fibres. Textiles can be used to make a vast range of things, from clothing, carpets, wall hangings and bags to the linings of suitcases and boxes.

Weaving is usually done on a frame or loom using spun or twisted yarns or threads. The warp yarns are stretched

RIGHT: *Hardwick Hall in Derbyshire is the home of a remarkable collection of textiles, some dating back to the sixteenth century and belonging to Elizabeth Hardwick, Countess of Shrewsbury. This group of furnishings dates from more recent times. Bottom row: eighteenth-century chairback and table-top worked in wool and silk on canvas. Middle row: valance in red silk damask woven in Marlborough designed by Owen Jones, 1872, and a late nineteenth-century silk tassel from curtain ties. Top row: case covers dating from the 1860s–80s of glazed roller-printed cotton.*

Apart from some fading on the upper right, these textiles are in very good condition. The area along the bottom of the canvaswork is brighter and cleaner, probably as a result of being folded under.

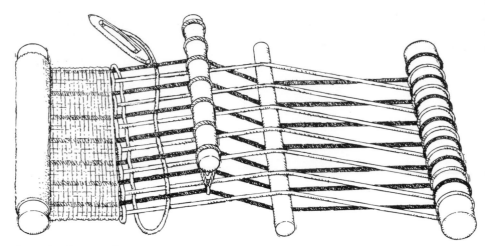

Loom showing warp threads stretched lengthways, and weft woven through by a shuttle.

lengthways on a loom, forming the threads through which the weft yarns are woven. The most simple weave is a criss-cross of the weft threads under one warp thread and over the next, but a pattern can be woven into the textile by altering how the weft threads interlace with the warp.

Coloured designs can be woven into the fabric by dyeing some of the yarns. Designs can also be printed or embroidered on to the fabric after it has been woven. Metal threads are sometimes used for decoration and can either be woven into the fabric or added later.

Problems

Textiles are delicate and easily damaged by light and insects, as well as by dirt, mould and poor repairs, handling and packing. Ideally, textiles should be kept dry, clean and in darkness, but in everyday life this is unrealistic, as they are often in use or on display. The main aim of textile care is to minimise exposure to light, dirt and damp, and to prevent attack from insects, mice or other pests.

Light, both visible and ultraviolet, fades colours and weakens the fibres. As with most chemical reactions, the higher the temperature, the faster the reaction; therefore, the rate of disintegration increases with temperature. Fading is the first sign of light damage, but it is also a sign that the fibres themselves are weakening. Some white textiles can become more yellow when exposed to light. The effect of light is gradual but irrevocable and is rarely noticed until the damage has been done. You can often see if a textile has been damaged

ABOVE: *Walnut chair, part of a suite upholstered by the London craftsman Thomas Phill, 1714–16, in the Tapestry Room at Canons Ashby in Northamptonshire. The original embroidered cover has survived in remarkably good condition, with some evidence of repairs only at the corners of the seat. The vivid colours of this piece, and of the rest of the suite, have survived because they have always been kept under case-covers. The tapestry behind, on the other hand, is showing signs of fading, especially the yellows.*

by light by comparing the areas exposed with hidden areas, such as the back and front of rugs and embroideries and the underside of upholstery and costumes. Only those rare pieces that have been stored in darkness for most of their existence show their original colours. Any fading indicates that the textile will be weakened and will need particularly careful handling.

Decay may also be due to the materials used in the textile's construction. Some dyes destroy the thread; this is very noticeable on some carpets, patchwork quilts and printed fabrics. Browns, in particular, are a problem as they are dyed with an iron fixative or mordant, which accelerates the weakening of the fibres. Unfortunately, it is not normally possible to stop this sort of deterioration, except by avoiding overexposure to light or moisture.

The chemicals used in finishing fabrics and residues of soap and detergent can be potentially harmful and may also cause white fabrics to yellow. Pollution, particularly acid from wood or cardboard, may weaken threads (*see* p.19).

The grit in dust can physically harm textiles by causing minute cuts in the fibres and will greatly increase the rate at which textiles in use will wear. For example, walking on carpets that have dust and grit in them will wear them out faster than walking on clean carpets. Dust and dirt are also potentially acidic and can accelerate decay in the textile; for this reason, it is important to ensure that no dust is penetrating through gaps in the front or back of framed textiles and that stored objects are protected from dust. Cleaning textiles exposes them to extra physical wear and tear. Textiles should, therefore, be prevented from getting dirty as much as possible so that cleaning can be kept to a minimum.

Textiles can be damaged by the way in which they are folded or displayed. They will weaken along fold lines or at a point that is taking a lot of weight. Thus displaying and storing textiles correctly is very important.

Corroding pins and fastenings can cause staining and weakening of the textile, so any extraneous pins must be removed. Not all metal fittings can be removed, as they may be an integral part of the object.

● INSECT DAMAGE
The insects most likely to damage textiles are some types of moth larvae, carpet beetles, silverfish and cockroaches. The damage is caused by the eating habits of the larvae of moths and beetles rather than the adult beetle, and by the nymph and adult cockroach and silverfish. Some damage or staining can result from the insects' excrement, especially that of cockroaches and flies.

The materials most at risk are wool, fur and feathers. Fur and feathers should always be stored separately from other fabrics, because they are particularly prone to insect attack.

Moth damage appears as small, irregular-shaped holes and is caused by the larvae that hatch from eggs laid by the adult moth. Where there are traces of moths, such as white cocoon wisps, larvae cases, frass the same colour as the textile and dead moths or damaged fabric, there are probably moth eggs or active larvae. The larvae of the carpet beetle feeds over a much larger area than the moth, so the holes are likely to be further apart. The holes are small and neat, there is no frass and the cases of the pupae, known as woolly bears, can often be found near a damaged spot. Grazing on the surface of the fabric will accompany holes. Silverfish usually graze on the fabric and seldom form holes.

Insects rarely attack clean, dry fabrics, but old food, stains, dirt and dust attract moths and beetles. The most important aspect of insect control is good housekeeping and ensuring that storage and display areas are clean and free of dust. Insects will breed in areas where dust collects, such as under furniture, so these areas must be vacuumed at least once a year.

● MOULD
Mould often appears as fuzzy-edged spots – black, grey or white – which can stain and weaken fabric. Mould, of which mildew is only one form, is encouraged by poor ventilation and damp conditions. Burst pipes, leaking roofs and damp basements can all start mould growth in previously clean, dry fabrics, as mould spores are always present in the air. Storage in polyethylene bags can lead to mould growth as a result of condensation inside the bag. Inappropriately framed embroideries, samplers and lace may also suffer, especially if they are hung on outside walls or in humid kitchens and bathrooms where there is condensation. Mould can start growing where framed fabrics are in contact with the glass. Stone, brick or terracotta-tiled floors may be damp, so check regularly under rugs and carpets that are on floors laid directly on earth, or wherever damp is suspected.

It is essential to remove the cause of the damp if the problem is not to recur, so improve the conditions by repositioning frames, curing sources of damp and improving the ventilation of the storage area (*see* p.14).

● SIGNS OF DETERIORATION
Look for faded colours, yellowing of cotton or linen fibres, dry and brittle or fraying threads, staining, insect attack, mould, dirt, tears and localised wear. Carpets and rugs often become worn along edges or creases. Look for insects in areas of costume that may have had food or body fluids on them, such as under arms, collars, fronts of shirts, crotches of trousers and in dark folds or underneath other objects.

Framed textiles need to be checked for mould and dust and for discoloration or weakening caused by a build-up of acid vapour within the frame from the wood and framing materials.

Handling

All textiles should be handled as little as possible. Unnecessary handling puts a strain on the fabric and dirt from hands will inevitably transfer on to the textile. Always have clean hands and make sure that any surface you lay the textile on is clean and dry and covered with a clean **dustsheet**.

If curtains are closed regularly by hand they will soon develop patches of wear. Use pulley strings or a drawing rod for curtains on rings and poles. Lift floor-length curtains well clear when polishing or vacuuming the floor; for instance, you could rest them over the back of a chair.

When moving large objects, such as carpets or curtains, do not drag them; roll carpets (*see* p.150) and carry curtains supported on a dustsheet so that there is no strain on the fabric.

Keep sharp objects such as watches, jewellery and belt buckles away from textiles. Also avoid smoking, eating, drinking or using ink, felt-tip or ball-point pens near textiles; use pencils if you need to write near a textile. When laying large objects on the floor, always cover the floor with clean sheets.

Display

Because light is so damaging to all textiles, museums and historic houses try to eliminate most of the ultraviolet light and

Group of nineteenth-century needlework tools from the Rachel Kay-Shuttleworth collection at Gawsthorpe Hall, Lancashire. It is tempting to display such attractive pieces, but beware of tarnishing of metals, fading of threads and light on the painted packets. Needles have been traditionally sold in black paper which is naturally acid-free.

employ low levels of visible light for permanent and temporary exhibitions. They also rotate the objects on display by changing them for other examples, so individual items do not become badly damaged. Rotation should take place every six to twelve months.

Use of blinds and ultraviolet-absorbing film will help to protect textiles within a room (*see* pp.16–17). Position objects where they will receive a minimum of light, but make sure that, if they are against an outside wall, air can circulate between the object and the wall (*see* p.18).

Traditional methods of protecting upholstery are still effective, such as using **dustsheets** or loose covers. Move rugs and carpets around to prevent one area from receiving more light than another and to spread the wear.

Textiles must be protected from heat, moisture, dirt and dust, as well as from light. They should be displayed away from draughts carrying dust and never above radiators and fireplaces in use.

Never use pins, drawing pins, tacks, wire staples or any other metal fixings to secure textiles. These are very damaging, as they can cut the fibres, and may corrode, staining the textile.

Antique embroideries or other textiles are best protected if they are framed for display mounted on a cloth-covered board. The disadvantage of displaying them on a stretcher frame is that too much strain is put on the fabric and the centre is not supported; dirt can also penetrate from both sides. If your textile is already framed in this way, consult a conservator who can advise on methods of improving support and protection without changing the appearance.

Ideally, flat textiles should not be hung, as the weight of the textile can cause the threads to weaken and break. They should be displayed horizontally or slightly inclined, though realistically this is not always feasible. Very fragile textiles should never be hung or displayed vertically as they are not robust enough to withstand the strain on the threads. When flat textiles are hung, it must be done in such a way as to provide adequate support to reduce the risk of damage to a minimum (*see* CARPETS AND RUGS and TAPESTRY).

The original mounts and framing materials of an historic needlework often provide evidence about the maker and provenance, so consideration should be given to the importance of an old mount before replacing it. If you decide to replace an old mount, draw or photograph it to keep a record of the construction. You might also store the old mount as a record.

● TO MOUNT AND FRAME A TEXTILE

Flat textiles, other than large carpets and tapestries, should be mounted on cloth-covered boards and framed and glazed so that they are well supported and protected from dust. A large mounted textile will be heavy and cumbersome; it is best to seek professional assistance in mounting and framing pieces that are over 1m (3ft) long. It is difficult to mount a textile successfully so that it is not secured too tightly, and it does not sag. Conservators are skilled and experienced at doing this so, wherever possible, ask a conservator to carry out the work for you. If the object is very old or fragile, the mounting definitely should be done by a conservator, but you may be able to mount more robust pieces yourself if you can sew finely and neatly.

The support can be made of thick card known as **museum board** (conservation grade). If you need to use something slightly stronger, you can use a type of **medium density fibreboard** (MDF) with zero formaldehyde content; this is preferable to wood or standard MDF, which may emit acids that can harm the textile. The board should be big enough to provide at least a 2cm (¾in) margin around the textile, but you will also need to consider the size and depth of the frame rebate, as well as the aesthetic requirements for a border. As a precaution against acid from the MDF damaging the textile, the board should be wrapped in aluminium foil and secured at the back with self-adhesive archival tape.

It is usually recommended that some padding be placed between the board and the backing fabric; flannelette sheeting makes excellent padding. Avoid using polyester wadding, which can make the mount look too much like a cushion.

A linen or heavy-duty cotton fabric can be used as the background fabric. Before covering the board with your fabric, check that it is colour fast. Do this by laying a

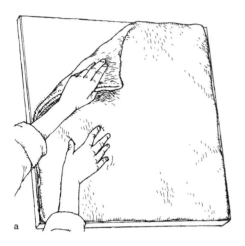

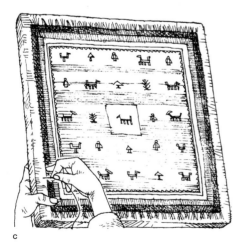

Mounting and framing a textile
(a) *Place padding on backing board* (b) *Wrap the backing fabric over the board and secure* (c) *Secure the textile on the board with pins and sew into place.*

piece of the textile on to white **blotting paper**. Prepare a solution of water with a few drops of **conservation-grade detergent**. Place a small swab of cotton wool soaked in this solution on the textile and leave for about 20 minutes. Examine the blotting paper and the cotton wool carefully. If there is any trace of colour, the textile should not be used as your backing fabric as the colour may bleed into your object.

You will also need to wash the dressing out of the backing fabric before using it. Dressing is a stiffening that is often added to textiles during manufacture and in some cases can be damaging in the long term to your object or to the backing fabric itself. Iron the fabric after washing.

The backing fabric will need to be larger than the board so that it can easily turn over the edges. Stretch it over the board and secure it at the back with double-sided archival tape or a neutral pH emulsion **adhesive**. It is important to keep the weave of the mounting fabric as straight as possible and parallel to the edges of the board, and to keep the fabric as tight as possible to prevent it from sagging.

Position the object temporarily using fine stainless steel pins. Do not pierce any threads of the object with the pins; make sure they go through the spaces between the threads. Start pinning the object from the centre of each side and work towards the corners to help keep it straight. The object should be aligned with the edges of the board and the threads should run parallel to those of the mounting fabric. Positioning the object is tricky, so proceed slowly. Always remove the pins before altering the position of the textile; do not try to force it into place. Do not stretch the textile, but make sure that it is sufficiently taut so it will not sag when it is hung up.

Use a fine curved needle and fine thread to sew the textile in place. Do not use monofilament nylon thread, as it will cut the textile. If possible, use a thread made of the same fibre as the textile. Sew around the edges of the object, again starting from the centre of each edge rather than the corners. Use small support or herringbone stitches quite close together. Do not pull them too tightly; they should be just tight enough so that the textile will not drop.

Ideally, the textile should be framed. The materials used within the frame should be **acid-free** or **archival quality** and the backboard and glazing well sealed to prevent dust from entering. The frame can be glazed with either glass or acrylic sheet. Seal the glass into the frame with gummed **brown paper tape**. Some objects, such as stump-work or heavy embroidery, are almost three-dimensional. They will need a box frame, which should be specially made by a frame-maker. Box frames made from **acrylic sheet** can be effective, although acrylic sheet should not be used with very fragile textiles as static electricity can pull off small, weak fragments of thread. The textile must not touch the glass, so the rebate must be deep enough to allow for a space between them. It may be necessary to use a fillet or a sub-frame of museum board or **polyethylene foam** between the mounted textile and the glass (*see* PAPER, Mounting and Framing).

Cover the back of the mounting board with a backboard made from museum board and hold it in place with small picture framing tacks. Seal the edges with **gummed linen tape** to prevent dust from entering the frame from the back.

For hanging larger textiles, *see* CARPETS AND RUGS and TAPESTRY. For displaying clothing, *see* COSTUMES AND CLOTHING.

Storage

The ideal place to store textiles is in a cool, dry, dark and clean area, free of pests and with a steady humidity. Store textiles away from light and sources of heat and moisture. Do not store textiles in or near wood that has been recently treated for woodworm with a residual insecticide, as it may penetrate the textiles and stain them or cause them to deteriorate.

When textiles are in store, they should be checked regularly for signs of insects and they should be protected by placing them in **acid-free** boxes or covering or wrapping them in calico or **Tyvek**.

Avoid storing important or historic textiles in an airing cupboard, which is usually warm and fluctuates from moist to dry. Basements are too damp and attics are unsuitable, because the temperature and humidity fluctuate too much unless they are well insulated. Cupboards in the main part of the house, such as a spare bedroom, are often a suitable storage space.

Items should be cleaned before storing them to deter insects. Insects rarely attack clean fabrics, but it is important to check the objects regularly and to put in place preventive precautions as necessary (*see* pp.14–15).

Remove any steel pins, brooches, staples

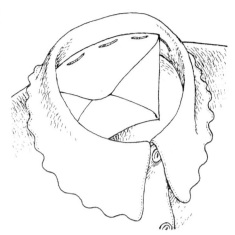

Sew an acid-free envelope containing labels and trimmings onto the garment or container

or metal fastenings and trimmings, as they can damage other textiles and corrode, stain and rot the fabric. If you are storing a number of textiles, you should keep those with metal fastenings away from the others. Slip some acid-free tissue or thin card between the textile and metal fastenings.

Keep any labels, bills or notes with the fabrics, as they often add to their historical value, but do not attach them with pins. Put any pins, trimmings, buttons, notes, etc. in a white, acid-free envelope and sew it loosely on to the garment or attach it to the storage container. This is safer than pinning things directly on to the fabric.

Use acid-free tissue for padding and wrapping. Never use coloured tissue or old paper packing material that is yellowing or becoming brittle.

Avoid folding flat textiles; it is preferable to roll them, if possible, as damage often occurs along fold lines. Squashed folds

become permanent creases that will in time crack and tear. Large textiles, including rugs and tapestries which cannot be stored flat, should be rolled rather than folded. Painted textiles must be stored flat.

If items must be folded, place wads of acid-free tissue along the fold lines to lessen creasing. Pad bags, shoes, hats, etc. with acid-free tissue so that they retain their shape.

Where several small textiles are stored together, label the box clearly with the contents and order of packing. Use lidded storage boxes, preferably made from acid-free card. Always line boxes with acid-free tissue.

Do not store coloured and white fabrics together in case they become damp accidentally and the colours run.

● **ROLLING A TEXTILE**

Flat textiles are often stored by rolling them around a tube, which can then be suspended from brackets. Ideally, the tube should be acid-free, but this is only possible with smaller objects for which small acid-free card tubes are available. The cardboard tubes for commercial carpets, which can be acquired from carpet shops, are useful for large objects. PVC tubes or drain pipes can be used for large objects, provided the diameter is large enough and they are supported on a metal pole to prevent the tube from sagging under the weight. Non-acid-free tubes, such as PVC or cardboard, should be covered in **clear polyester film** or aluminium foil to help protect the textile from acid vapours. Wrap the tube in several layers of acid-free tissue. It may be easier to use fabric on the larger tubes instead of tissue. The tube can be covered with calico

rolled around it tightly and sewn in place. The fabric or tissue, whichever is used, must be smooth and firm around the tube.

The larger, thicker and stiffer the textile, the greater the diameter of the tube must be. Most textiles can be rolled on a tube with a diameter of between 10–12cm (4–5in). A very fine fabric may be rolled on a smaller tube unless it is extremely fragile, but never on one less than 5cm (2in) in diameter. The tubes should always be longer than the length or width of the object being rolled so that there is always at least 5cm (2in) of the tube protruding beyond the edge of the textile to prevent the edges of the object from being damaged. Carpets and large objects need a wider margin, as they are seldom perfectly square and straight; the diameter of the tube should be about 20–30cm (8–12in).

Roll all items with the right side outwards. If the textile has any pile, it must be rolled in the direction of the pile. Similarly, kilims, carpets and tapestries should be rolled in the direction of the warp. Cover the reverse side with acid-free tissue as the rolling proceeds and smooth out creases and folds as you go. As at least two or more people, and sometimes as many as six, are needed to roll most carpets and large objects, you must make sure that everyone rolls at the same speed. You may have to stop occasionally and level the tube so that it remains at right angles to the warp.

Cover the roll with acid-free tissue, washed calico, Tyvek or an old, clean sheet and secure it with 5cm (2in) wide strips of white cotton tape or **hook and loop fastener**.

The rolls must be kept horizontal and suspended so that there is no weight

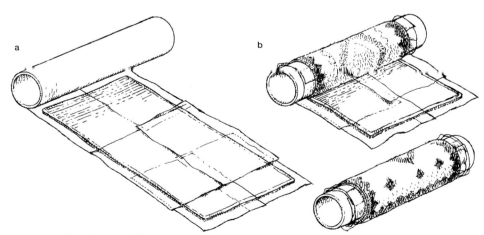

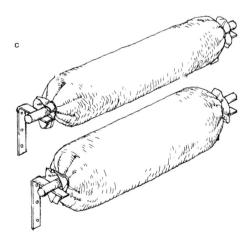

Rolling and storing a textile
(a) *Select an appropriate tube, cover reverse side of textile with acid-free paper* (b) *Roll, ensuring textile remains straight* (c) *Suspend heavier rolls on a pole on brackets.*

crushing the underside of the textile. This applies particularly to heavier textiles, such as carpets, but ideally every rolled textile should be stored in this way. To suspend a rolled textile, fix a couple of brackets securely to the wall. Push a pole through the tube and rest the ends of the pole on the brackets, or support the ends of the pole on wooden blocks.

Housekeeping and Maintenance

Very fragile or precious textiles should be cleaned only by a textile conservator.

Dirt and dust not only make the object less attractive and dull the colours, but they also encourage decay and insect infestation. Regular vacuuming is important for

Bedspread being cleaned by low-suction vacuuming, using nylon microfilament to protect loose threads.

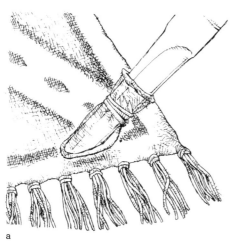

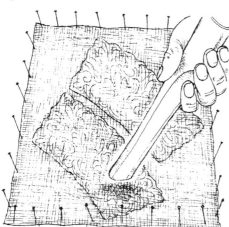

Cleaning textiles
(a) *When cleaning textiles with loose ends and tassels, such as rugs, cover the end of the vacuum cleaner with fine nylon net*
(b) *Protect small pieces of textile, such as lace, from the vacuum cleaner by covering them with net that has been pinned down.*

looking after textiles, but cleaning should not be carried out unnecessarily frequently, as over-frequent cleaning can do more damage than the dirt and dust.

Surface dust may be removed by gentle vacuuming, which is safe for strong textiles, but very fragile fabrics should not be vacuumed. If the fabric is strong enough, lightly brush it or pat it before vacuuming to loosen some dust and make the vacuuming more effective. Never beat carpets or upholstery. *See* CARPETS AND RUGS.

Use a vacuum cleaner on which the strength of the suction can be controlled. There are special 'museum' vacuum cleaners that are useful if you have a big collection, but a good quality cleaner, with some control over the power setting, should be sufficient. One of the dangers of vacuuming is that tassels, fringes and loose threads, or even the textile itself, can be sucked into the vacuum cleaner. By covering the crevice tool with fine **nylon net**, this danger can be reduced; hold the net in place with an elastic band over the crevice tool. Gently move the crevice tool just above the surface of the textile (about 0·5cm/¼in) and take care not to rub the nozzle against the fabric. Make sure you go over the entire surface. By holding the nozzle at a 45° angle, the area of textile being vacuumed can be seen at all times so that you can check that there are no problems.

Smaller pieces of textile, such as samplers or lace, can be protected from the vacuum cleaner by lying them flat on a soft, clean, **acid-free** board and covering them with

net that is pinned down around the textile, not to it, and vacuuming as before. Alternatively, you can make a square of stiff net, such as fly netting, about 30cm (1ft) square; tape the edges so they do not catch, place this over the object and vacuum through it. You must use stiff netting for this, otherwise the net will be sucked into the nozzle.

To remove mould, dry and air the affected fabric and then vacuum off the powdery spores as described above. Take care not to spread the spores or they will infect other materials, and wash the vacuum tools when you have finished (*see* p.16). It may be possible to remove any resulting staining by washing the textile if it is suitable (*see* Cleaning), otherwise you will need advice from a textile conservator.

● **PREVENTION AND TREATMENT FOR INSECTS**
Good housekeeping is the best way to prevent insects from taking hold of your textile collection. Regular cleaning of dark and hidden areas, such as heating ducts, cupboards, cellars and attics, boxed-in radiators, the edges of fitted carpets and under furniture, as well as the more accessible places, is essential. If you suspect that you have insects in an object or group of objects, remove the affected items from the rest of the collection and seal them in a polyethylene bag until you can deal with them; do not leave them for more than about two months in the bag as mould may develop. Always check newly acquired

objects for insect damage and keep them away from your collection until you are certain they are insect-free.

Where evidence of insects is found, it is almost certain that there will also be minute eggs, virtually invisible to the human eye. If these eggs drop on to other objects, the infestation will spread. First clean off all the debris and larvae with a vacuum cleaner. Where possible, clean the object outside. To avoid scattering eggs as you go through the house, carry the textile in a polyethylene bag. Thoroughly clean the display or storage area where the object is kept to remove dust, dirt and any eggs. Throw the vacuum cleaner bag and the net into the dustbin as soon as you have finished cleaning the textiles and the cupboards and thoroughly wash the vacuum cleaner nozzle.

The professionals looking after collections of textiles now prefer not to use chemicals to kill insects, but instead employ methods such as freezing or oxygen-free atmospheres. This is both to protect the textiles and to prevent people from being exposed to potentially toxic chemicals (*see* pp.14–15). These treatments should be carried out by a conservator or specialist to avoid damage to the objects.

There are some insecticides based on **permethrin** that have been developed for historic collections and are used by spraying the solution on to shelves, floors and storage materials. They help to protect a collection by acting on insects that are in contact with the treated surfaces. These insecticides should not be used directly on antique textiles.

Insect inhibitors, such as mothballs (napthalene) and paradichlorobenzene, do repel adult clothes moths and carpet beetles, but only when used in very high concentrations and they do not function as insecticides. The health and safety aspects of these chemicals are under review and their use with textile collections is no longer recommended.

Dichlorvos strips can be used as an insecticide and insect repellent, but only in an enclosed space and at the concentration recommended on the pack. For example, one brand recommends 1 small space strip for 6m³ (200ft³). If it is used in higher dosages and/or at a very high **relative humidity**, it can cause colour changes in dyes and metal corrosion. Make sure that the strip is not in contact with any of the objects. Do not use dichlorvos strips in bedroom cupboards or a kitchen or any

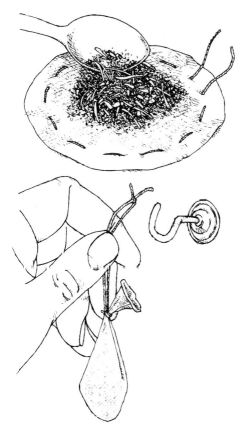

Place herbs in a circle of muslin to make a bag that will protect textiles from insects.

room that is heavily occupied, because this poses a potential health hazard.

There is some evidence that lavender oil and cedarwood oil in high doses act as insect repellents and there are now some commercially available **sachets** for this purpose. It is not safe to assume these will protect your textiles, but they may act as a deterrent. An old-fashioned pot-pourri of aromatic herbs may also discourage insects, but there is no scientific evidence for this yet. The herbs traditionally used to protect textiles from insects include: mint, sage, rosemary, bay, mugwort, lavender, thyme, santolina, southernwood, woodruff and sweet marjoram. You can make a bag from just one herb or from a mixture and place it with the stored textiles, but not in direct contact with them.

To make a single-herb insect repellent bag, put a heaped tablespoon of dried lavender, mint, rosemary, mugwort, southernwood or woodruff on to a circle of thin muslin about 7·5cm (3in) in diameter. Add a few pieces of chopped orris-root or a teaspoon of crushed cinnamon stick; gather the muslin and tie the bag with cotton tape. To make bags with a mixture of herbs, you can use either a tablespoon of sweet

marjoram and woodruff and 2 tablespoons of lavender flowers or equal quantities of rosemary, southernwood and sage and a few pieces of chopped orris-root.

Large objects, such as tapestries or carpets, can be treated for insects, but this should be done by a conservator. Annual vacuuming of the reverse as well as the right side will help discourage infestation.

Cleaning

Textiles may need deeper cleaning than vacuuming, particularly when newly acquired, or before putting them into store. A textile can hold harmful compounds that are formed during the deterioration of the fibres and other damaging products that are absorbed from the atmosphere. These compounds, along with dirt and stains that remain after vacuuming may be removed by washing but care must be taken as washing can cause unexpected damage. Therefore, wherever possible, get advice from a textile conservator before embarking on cleaning. Textiles should not be cleaned frequently, as too much cleaning can weaken the threads and change the dyes.

There are two types of washing: with water – wet cleaning; or in a cleaning solvent – known commercially as dry cleaning. Strong fibres can be wet cleaned if the dyes are colour-fast and the construction of the textile is suitable, while most types of fabrics can be solvent cleaned. Textiles containing metal threads should not be washed (*see* p.161).

The two methods of cleaning remove different types of stains. Solvent cleaning removes grease and oil-based stains, but has little effect on water-carried stains, such as perspiration. Wet cleaning has little effect on oil-based stains. Commercial dry cleaning fluids often contain some water so that most dirt can be removed.

The advantage of solvent cleaning is that special finishes, such as glazed chintzes, are not affected and fewer dyes will run. Dry cleaning solvents are less harmful to pile fabrics, such as velvets, and do not remove pleats or tucks set in with heat and steam. Dry cleaning firms will always clean 'at the owners' risk', so only send strong textiles for cleaning and then use only specialist firms and explain that the piece is old. Do not send valuable or antique textiles to a commercial dry cleaner. Try to find a dry cleaner where the drum does not rotate fully but moves gently back and forth using an action similar to the 'hand wash' programme of many washing machines. The solvents used for cleaning are changing, so it is difficult to recommend any particular solvent at this stage, but make sure that your dry cleaner will use *clean* solvent and has some interest in and experience of cleaning old textiles. There are some dry cleaning firms that specialise in conservation dry cleaning. Your local museum or **Area Museum Council** may be able to advise you of suitable local dry cleaners. If you are in doubt about whether a textile can be dry cleaned, consult a textile conservator.

Contact a textile conservator about fragile, ancient or rare textiles that need a more specialist cleaning. Not all textile conservators have the facilities to carry out solvent cleaning, but they should be able to recommend someone who can take on the work.

● WET CLEANING

Although wet cleaning can help the preservation of textiles, it is very difficult to tell whether threads and dyes will be enhanced or damaged by wet cleaning. It is also hard to assess whether the structure of a costume will hold up to being washed. Textile conservators always carry out extensive tests on objects before cleaning them and it is not possible here to discuss all the dangers of wet cleaning, therefore the advice is to clean white cotton or linen only. Simple cotton christening gowns or night-dresses, cotton covers, household linens and lace are the sorts of items that can usually be washed safely, although even with these there can sometimes be problems.

Never wash silk or satin, banners, flags, tapestries, silk or satin embroideries, or textiles which show any sign that the base fabric has weak areas. Do not wash textiles that are light-damaged, have metal threads, metal fastenings or decoration, or have been repaired. These should be cleaned by a textile conservator. Only wash a textile yourself if you are absolutely sure that it is suitable and strong enough. If you have any doubts about whether a textile can be washed, it is better to be cautious, as a mistake can cause irreparable damage. Consult a qualified conservator for advice about washing textiles.

For plain cotton and linen items these are some basic rules for hand washing:

● Remove as much dust and loose dirt as possible by vacuuming prior to wetting.
● Never machine wash.
● Use soft water or purified, distilled or de-ionised water. Hard water can be softened slightly by boiling it in a kettle, allowing it to cool and then adding a small amount of **water softener** before use. Dehumidifiers provide a source of purified water that you can store in the dark until you need it. If you do not store it in the dark, algae will begin to grow in the container.
● Water should be no warmer than lukewarm.
● Use a liquid **conservation-grade detergent** designed for low temperatures with no added enzymes, perfumes or whiteners. Such detergents are available for use with delicate fabrics or for people with very sensitive skin. Never use commercial detergents, including biological washing powder, which, although suitable for everyday clothes, contaminates fabrics with additives that can promote yellowing and decay.
● Never use bleach, because it weakens the fabric.

● Whenever possible, separate the lining and wash it separately.

Use a large, shallow container. Plastic ones from garden centres and photographic shops are excellent. Alternatively, use a bath for larger objects. Do not use a metal container. Fill the container with soft or purified water (distilled or de-ionised) which is cold or no more than lukewarm. Use enough water to allow the object to be covered easily so that dirt can float out rather than be squeezed out. Add a few drops of the detergent. Do not use too much, otherwise you will need to rinse the fabric a great deal.

Textiles are at their weakest when wet. Anything other than the most robust textile must be laid on a piece of **nylon net** or plastic netting, such as gardening net, to act as a support when it is lifted in and out of the water. Cut a piece of net rather larger than the size of the textile, lay the textile on

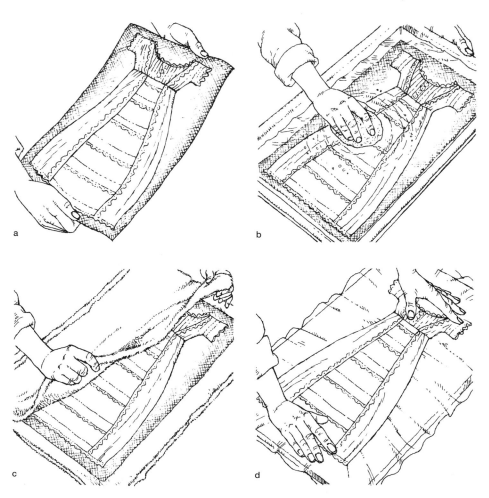

Washing a textile on a net
(a) *Place on a piece of nylon net or plastic netting* (b) *Lower into water, dab with sponge and rinse* (c) *Lift out of the water and lay on one towel with a second on top* (d) *Dry on a board covered with polythene or clear polyester film.*

it and lower it carefully into the water. Gently submerge the textile and, when it is completely wet, gently dab it with a sponge. This will encourage the dirt to come out. Press and release the sponge along the whole length of the textile. Do not squeeze or rub it with your hands.

When the whole textile has been washed, lift it out of the dirty water. Use two hands and hold each end of the net so that there is no strain on the textile. If it is a large textile, two people will be needed, one at each end of the net. Always lift the textile out of the water before tipping the water away.

If the textile is very dirty, wash it once more. Rinse it very thoroughly with two or three changes of clean, lukewarm, soft water, then give it a final rinse with distilled or de-ionised water. Some rust spots that are found on textiles are thought to be caused by iron impurities in ordinary tap-water, so it is important to use distilled or de-ionised water for the final rinse.

Lay the net and the textile on a clean white bath towel, lay another towel on top and press down gently to absorb the excess water.

Dry the textile by laying it flat on a smooth surface, such as a sheet of Formica or glass or on a board covered with poly-thene or **clear polyester film**. The textile should be dried with the right side facing upwards and smoothed into shape while damp. Dry it naturally, away from sunlight and artificial heat. Good ventilation speeds drying, so an electric fan that is not heated may help. Avoid or minimise ironing by smoothing out the fabric before it dries.

Lace and similar fabrics, such as fine crochet, need to be held flat to keep them in shape while drying. After washing, place the lace on a piece of soft board or **poly-ethylene foam** larger than the object, covered with polyethylene, clear polyester film or white **blotting paper**. Gently smooth the object into shape starting from the centre. Cover the lace with a piece of **nylon net** that is several centimetres (eg. 7·5cm or 3in margin all round) larger than the object. Stretch the net taut over the lace and secure the net with weights or pins. If you pin it, the pins should be at a slight angle with the heads pointing away from the centre of the object. Use pins that will not rust, such as brass lace pins or stainless steel pins. To get the best result, the pins should be quite close together. The net holds the lace to the flat surface and dries it flat. If you are going to use weights to hold the net, place them close to the edge of the

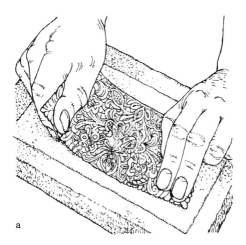

a

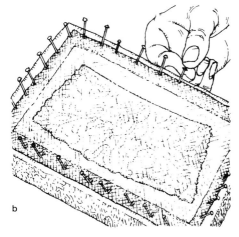

b

Drying lace
(a) *Place lace on soft board or polyethylene foam covered by polyester film or blotting paper* (b) *Cover lace with nylon net and secure with pins.*

lace but not on it. Glass weights or plastic-covered weights are best, as they will not rust or stain the textile, but weights from old-fashioned kitchen scales are also suitable, provided you make sure that they are not in contact with the object. This method of stretching net over the lace to hold it in place while drying is better than pinning the lace directly, as some lace is likely to shrink a little as it dries. This may put a strain on the threads as they pull against the pins. Allow the lace to dry naturally.

● **STAINS**
Any stains and spots that remain after cleaning are best left alone. In general, more harm is done by trying to remove them than by leaving them alone.

● **CANDLE WAX**
Candle wax gets spilt on tablecloths or carpets. To remove it from a cloth in good

condition, carefully scrape as much of it off as you can with a fingernail or blunt knife. Chilling the wax with ice in a polyethylene bag will make it more brittle and easier to remove. If the wax has gone right into the material, some will remain after the scraping and can be removed with blotting paper and an iron.

Place a sheet of blotting paper or paper towel on top of the wax and another sheet under the textile. Go over the surface with a warm – not hot – iron and the wax will melt and be absorbed by the paper. Change both sheets of paper continually until no more wax appears on either sheet. There is always a danger of this method driving the wax further into the textile, so it is import-ant to scrape off as much of the wax as possible first. Any wax remaining after this can be removed with **white spirit**. Care-fully dab the wax with a cotton wool swab dampened with white spirit. Finally, dry the patch by gently pressing it with a paper towel. This way, the wax should not be spread further into the material. Do not use this method on fragile textiles; seek conser-vation advice.

Removing wax from a carpet is more difficult, as the wax may penetrate the pile. Chill the wax with ice and pick off as much as possible. If you use a hot iron, there is a danger that the wax will penetrate into the pile, therefore it is safest to leave the re-maining wax.

● **ADHESIVES**
Modern adhesives leave a residue when dropped on to textiles that can be very difficult to remove. It may be possible to soften the remaining adhesive using **sol-vents** such as white spirit or lighter fuel. Before attempting this, test the solvent on each colour in an inconspicuous spot to ensure it does not cause the colour to run. Dampen a cotton bud with a small amount of solvent and gently roll it over the affected area. The adhesive may swell and become stretchy so that you may be able to ease some off. Make sure you do not pull up any threads. **Acetone** may also remove some adhesives. You will probably not be able to remove all the adhesive. Do not use these cleaning solvents on synthetic fibres, which can be dissolved or damaged by solvents. Do not try to remove adhesive from fragile textiles; seek conservation advice.

● **CHEWING GUM**
Chewing gum can sometimes be removed from modern textiles by chilling it. Put an

ice cube in a polyethylene bag and hold it against the chewing gum until it becomes brittle. When it does, it can be removed with a blunt knife, palate knife or fingernail. Do not do this to fragile textiles.

● MECHANICAL CLEANING
Fluff sometimes sticks to textiles, particularly velvet and velour, and it is difficult to remove from the fabric without damaging the pile. Self-adhesive tape will take it off, if it is pressed gently against the textile, but use this only on textiles in excellent condition.

● IRONING
Never iron very old or fragile textiles. As heat and moisture accelerate decay, it is advisable to iron only cotton and linen in good condition and to keep the number of occasions you iron one item to a minimum. Never iron a textile that has not been cleaned, because heat fixes many stains and seals in dust and dirt. Some pieces will need ironing after washing. Try to arrange the wet textiles so that they dry flat and do not need ironing.

Always use a lightweight iron at its lowest heat setting. At this temperature the iron will not hiss when you put a drop of water on it. Use a pressing rather than a rubbing action. A clean white linen teacloth placed between the textile and the iron will give further protection.

Often the creases in wool, silk or velvet will drop out if you hang the object in a steamy bathroom. Pile fabrics such as velvet should be ironed as little as possible. If you have to iron velvet, iron it on the wrong side with the pile lying against another piece of velvet.

● STARCH
Avoid using **starch**, which is a food for insects. It also causes damage, as stiffened fabrics are brittle and can crack easily. Old-fashioned starch, which is rice starch, can be used for christening dresses or wedding veils, but always wash the starch out before storing them again. Never use spray-on stiffeners or plastic starch, because they cannot be washed out easily.

Repair

Repairing textiles well is a difficult and skilled job. Rare and precious items should always be repaired by a textile conservator.

Never use adhesives on textiles; they can be damaging and are difficult to remove.

Any repairs must be done by sewing, but do not darn or sew up tears as the stitches may cause further damage to the textile. Textile conservators will strengthen torn and weak fabrics by carefully sewing them on to a suitable backing material; sometimes very weak fabrics are also protected by net sewn on the front. This process, when done correctly, supports the textile without putting strain on any of the threads. However, it is very skilled work and can be damaging unless done by an experienced conservator who will choose the right type of needle and yarn to suit the object. Often such yarns are not readily available to the non-professional.

Beadwork

Beadwork is the term used to describe the decoration of textiles with beads. Beads can be made from a wide range of materials including glass, metal, plastic and bone. They can be strung on a single thread in a definite order and can then be knitted, plaited, woven or even crocheted into the fabric as it is made. Alternatively, they can be woven into the fabric or they can be stitched individually on to a backing material.

Beaded clothing dates from very early times. In the sixteenth and seventeenth

Mid-nineteenth-century floral beaded bag from the Snowshill costume collection of Charles Paget Wade. This example is in good condition, but needs careful support to retain its shape – the effects of lack of padding can be seen in the upper right corner.

centuries, beads became very popular in Europe to decorate dresses, looking-glass frames and small caskets. The Victorians used beadwork extensively for pictures, cushion covers, footstools, chair covers, tea cosies, purses and jewellery. Dresses were beaded in the 1920s, and beaded dresses, bags and accessories still make their appearance on the catwalk today.

Problems

The problems most often encountered with beaded objects are broken threads; cracked, broken or corroded beads; or the weight of the beads weakening the support material.

Handling

All beadwork should be handled with care, because the threads holding the beads are fragile and may break easily. When handling beaded dresses, carry them horizontally so that the weight is evenly supported. Do not carry them by one small area, such as the shoulders. Beaded dresses of the 1920s often had a chiffon support which may disintegrate.

When carrying beaded chairs or stools, take care not to press your fingers or thumbs into the beadwork as you lift them, as the pressure may break the threads holding the beads. If possible, lift a stool by holding the legs and lift a chair by placing your hands under the seat rail on each side, unless there is fringing, in which case carry it by the legs.

Display

It is particularly important to make sure that beaded dresses or other garments are well supported so that the weight of the beads does not cause a strain on the fabric (*see* COSTUMES AND CLOTHING).

Housekeeping and Maintenance

If beadwork is very dusty, use a soft brush and direct dust towards a vacuum cleaner with net over the nozzle (*see* p.144). Never vacuum beadwork directly, as you are likely to suck the beads off.

Cleaning

Never wash beadwork. If it needs further cleaning, take it to a textile conservator.

Repair

Beadwork is very difficult to repair and this should be done by a conservator. If you have a beaded dress that you want to wear, make sure that the beads are secure and the backing fabric is strong enough to support them. If it is not, the whole dress should be supported by sewing it on to a lining of silk crepoline or very fine nylon net. Ask an accomplished seamstress to do this.

If the beadwork is unravelling, make sure that you secure the end of any loose threads, either by stitching through several beads or by tying the thread ends to catch the beads that are loose.

Carpets and Rugs

There is no real difference between carpets and rugs except that the term 'rug' tends to be used for ethnographic pieces. However, most people when referring to rugs think of them as being smaller than carpets.

Most carpets and rugs are made either with a knotted pile or a flat weave such as that found in kilims and Indian dhurrys. Hooked rugs are made by poking the tufts of wool into a pre-existing loosely woven fabric, whereas in carpet weaving the knots are inserted as the weaving proceeds. Carpets are usually made from animal fibres, such as wool, silk, goats' hair, and vegetable fibres, such as cotton, jute, linen. Frequently, carpets have a warp and weft made in a different fibre from the pile; usually the pile is made from animal fibres and the warp and weft from vegetable fibres. Carpets can also be made from, or include, synthetic fibres. Whatever materials are used to make them, the basic care of carpets and rugs is the same.

A knotted-pile carpet is made by wrapping tufts of wool around one or more warps so that the tufts project at right angles to the plane of the weaving. The tufts are knotted or tied, a row at a time, and held in place by wefts. The method of knotting causes the tufts to lie in one direction towards the bottom of the carpet; this is the direction of the pile. You can establish the pile direction by moving your hand on the surface of the carpet towards both ends. The direction in which the pile seems smoother is the direction of the pile.

Problems

Carpets will wear at heavy traffic points, for example in doorways, by telephones or cupboards; they can also be marked by furniture legs. Ridged or rucked carpets will wear along the top of the ridge. The ridges can be caused by the carpet being too large for the space, by uneven underlay, small bits of underlay not butting closely together or deteriorating rubber underlay sticking to the carpet. Ridges also occur in tribal rugs where the tension of the warp is lost as the loom is moved. Such ridges are woven in and cannot be removed, so avoid placing these rugs where they will be exposed to heavy wear which will result in splitting. Repair usually involves making a dart in the rug. The side cords on the edges of carpets often become weakened and worn, and the end fringes can break off, causing the knots to loosen and the pile to come away.

A carpet may fade unevenly if furniture protects it from light in some areas, or where sunlight falls on one spot.

Insects may establish themselves under a carpet or under furniture in an area which is seldom cleaned. If carpets are laid on stone or tiled floors, check for damp, which encourages mould growth and insects.

Axminster stair carpet in Mr Straw's House in Worksop, Nottinghamshire. This carpet was bought in 1923, the year after the discovery of Tutankhamun's tomb which resulted in the rage for all things Egyptian. Despite the vulnerability of stair carpets, this example had survived well until the National Trust took over the house in 1990 and feet of visitors very soon affected the condition. Compression of the top tread, for example, can be seen in this photograph, while the risers are largely undamaged. (The carpet has now been taken up to protect it.) To prevent this happening, adjust the position of the carpet up and down.

Handling

When moving large heavy carpets, they should be rolled and lifted rather than dragged, otherwise weakened threads may give way.

Do not fold carpets, as creases are likely to form, which will cause the carpet to wear unevenly when relaid, and it may cause splits and cracks along the fold line.

Before being rolled small carpets can be turned over, but very large carpets should be pulled back on themselves. This operation will require at least two – more likely four – people.

● **TO ROLL AND TURN A LARGE CARPET**
The carpet is rolled in the direction of the pile. Prepare the roll as you would for Storage (see p.152). Start at the end facing the direction of the pile. Have everyone stand side by side on, or facing the end and pick up the edge of the carpet and walk backwards, pulling it with you for several steps. Put the carpet down, place the tube on the wrong side of the carpet at the end you were holding and start to roll it away from you. Cover the underside of the carpet with

acid-free tissue as you roll. Then walk back another few steps, carrying the tube with the carpet rolled round it, put it down and then roll up the next bit of carpet. Carry on in this way until you reach the end of the carpet. This will give you a carpet rolled in the correct way without having to turn the whole carpet over before you start. Several people may be needed to carry the roll of a very large carpet, as it becomes increasingly heavy. The carpet can then be moved to its new position and carefully unrolled by the same number of people. Place the edge in position, lift the roll and gradually unfurl it as you walk backwards.

Display

Valuable or rare carpets and silk carpets should be used only in rooms with light traffic, not halls, passageways, on stairs or in sitting rooms. Dining areas are also unsatisfactory for carpets, as there is the risk of staining from food and drink, the table and chairs concentrate wear on small areas of the carpet and the pushing back of chairs at the end of a meal causes great strain.

Shoes with narrow diameter heels can cause considerable damage to carpets, so try to discourage people from treading on fragile, rare or valuable carpets with heels smaller than 2cm (¾in) in diameter. Avoid placing carpets where they will be exposed to direct sunlight.

Most floor surfaces that are smooth, dry and clean are suitable for carpets. Always make sure that a carpet sits flat, otherwise the top of any wrinkles will soon begin to be worn bare.

All carpets need some form of underlay. Underlay reduces the wear of carpets by cushioning them from the unevenness of the floor. The best underlay to use is a felt made from natural fibres and not one made of synthetic rubber, which tends to disintegrate and become tacky, and then sticks to the carpet and the floor. The underlay should always come to the edge, or preferably beyond the edge, of the carpet and should ideally be in one piece. If it is necessary to use two or more bits of underlay, make sure that they butt closely together but do not overlap, then fix them in position by sewing them together using

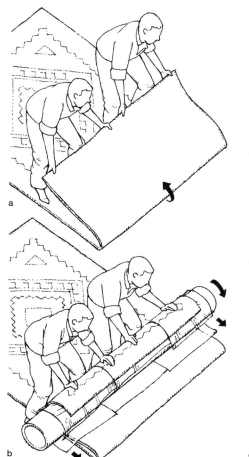

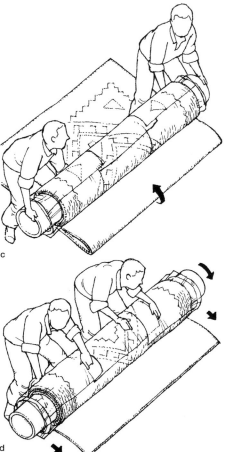

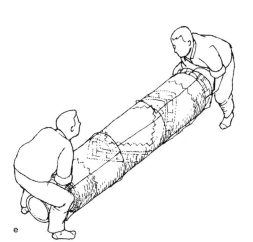

Rolling and turning a carpet
(a) *Fold back the end of the carpet* (b) *Place tube on reverse side at right angles to the warp and roll forwards, covering reverse with acid-free tissue. Keep the roll straight and an even tension on the carpet* (c) *Walk back a few steps with the tube* (d) *Repeat the process until the end* (e) *The roll can then be turned.*

The carpet in the Saloon at Kingston Lacy, drawn back to show the underfelt. This provides good support and prevents slippage and uneven wear. On top of the carpet is a drugget; the National Trust uses these to protect carpets that are part of the visitor route in houses. Strips of wood are also installed in some houses to prevent movement of the carpet.

Small, lightweight carpets in good condition make good wall hangings and can be hung either by being mounted on to a board covered in a suitable material, or by being hung from the top using a sleeve for a hanging pole, or they can be fixed using **Velcro**. Fragile or damaged carpets should not be displayed vertically.

● **MOUNTING A CARPET**

A small carpet can be mounted on a board as described above (*see* p.141). Make a basic wood frame, seal the wood with sanding sealant (available from a hardware or DIY store), then fix **museum board** on to the face of the frame using staples or pins. Larger objects will need a frame made with cross bars so that the museum board can be cut into suitably sized pieces and stapled to the frame. If you use zero formaldehyde **MDF** instead of museum board it must be prepared by covering with aluminium foil (*see* p.141). Pad the board with old or flannelette sheets as described above, before covering the board with the background material. When sewing on the carpet, take

heavy duty thread and a herringbone stitch. Trim the underlay with scissors to fit irregular rug shapes. Underlay will spread with time, so trim it again when necessary. It is sensible to fit a non-adhesive **anti-creep tape** on the underside of the underfelt for carpets on slippery floors or use non-slip underlay under the ordinary underlay.

On stone or wooden floors, a heavy-duty damp-proof paper, available from carpet shops, should be put down between the floor and the underlay. This helps to protect the carpet from rising damp and from the dust that rises between floorboards.

If a carpet is too long for a room, never fold it in under itself. Roll the excess, right side out, on to a tube covered with **acid-free** tissue.

Carpets that are placed on top of a larger or fitted carpet have a tendency to 'walk' in the direction of the pile of the fitted carpet. The best solution is to sew a heavy canvas, slightly smaller than the top carpet, to the fitted carpet; if this is not practical, place polyester wadding underlay between the carpets and replace the wadding annually.

When furniture is placed on a carpet, particularly if it has metal castors, use furniture cups underneath the legs. This will help to spread the weight and so minimise the denting in the carpet. The cups can be made of wood, plastic or glass, or you can cut out small circles of plywood about 5cm (2in) in diameter, which can be painted to match the carpet. Move the furniture from time to time to allow the squashed pile to revive.

Sparks and falling embers will damage a fireside carpet, so always make sure that there is a good fireguard in position.

Carpets can also be used as table coverings, but the edges of the table must be padded with a blanket or felt underlay to prevent them from biting through the carpet. Polyester felt underlay provides very effective padding.

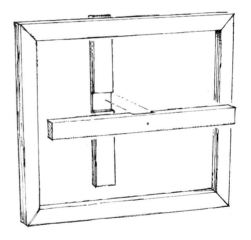

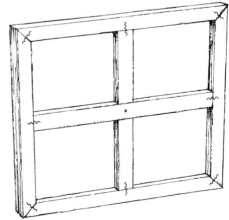

Making a frame with cross bars for mounting a carpet.

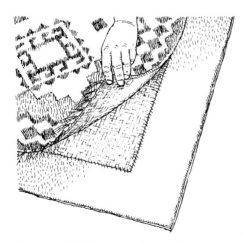

Canvas on fitted carpet under a carpet.

care that the needle goes between the threads and not through them.

A mounted carpet can be glazed to protect it from dust and reduce the need to clean it. This is important for very old, rare or fragile carpets.

● HANGING A CARPET

A carpet in good condition can be hung vertically by supporting it along the full length of the upper edge. This is often achieved by sewing a sleeve to the carpet through which a pole is slipped. The pole must be at least 10cm (4in) wider than the carpet. Use herringbone carpet tape or soft cotton webbing about 5cm (2in) wide; if a thick pole is to be used, wider webbing will be needed. Cut a strip the width of the carpet. Stitch the top edge of the webbing across the back of the carpet about 2cm (¾in) from the top. Use buttonhole thread, a straight needle and a stitch, such as a stab stitch, which will go right through to the front of the carpet. Stab stitch is a short running stitch made by sewing straight down through the textile, between the threads, and straight up a little further along. Take care not to split the yarns by stitching through them; the needle must pass between the warps and wefts. Each stitch should cross two warps. The pile will hide the stitches. To calculate where to sew the bottom edge of the webbing, place a suitable hanging pole on the carpet inside the webbing and see where the bottom edge of the webbing falls on the carpet. Make sure that there is enough slack for the pole to slip in and out easily. Stab-stitch the bottom edge of the webbing straight across the carpet. Insert the pole and, using the protruding ends, hang it up with chains.

Hook and loop tape can also be used for hanging carpets from a wooden batten fixed to the wall; fastener 5cm (2in) wide can support most carpets. Sew the soft half or loop side of the fastener on to a length of cotton webbing long enough to reach across the width of the carpet. Stab-stitch both edges of the webbing to the carpet about 1·5cm (½in) from the top. Use buttonhole thread and sew as described for the sleeve. Fix the hook side of the fastener to a wooden batten with tacks or staples. Secure the wooden batten to the wall and press the two halves of the tape together.

Storage

Ideally, carpets should be rolled and suspended from strong brackets or wood

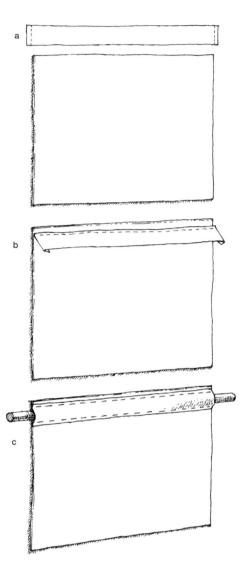

Hanging a carpet (1)
Making a sleeve: (a) *Cut a strip of carpet tape or webbing the width of the carpet* (b) *Using stab-stitching (see p.154), join the top edge of the tape/webbing to the back of the carpet* (c) *Stab-stitch the lower edge of the tape/webbing and insert the pole.*

blocks as in TEXTILES; the rolls should never be allowed to stand upright on their ends. The roll must be covered with calico, old sheeting, **Tyvek**, etc. and secured with wide tape or **hook and loop fastener**. Do not tie it with string, which will cut and distort the weave. If rolling is not possible, carpets should always be stored flat, lying horizontally so that they are evenly supported.

Do not store carpets directly on stone, brick or concrete floors. Always place some polythene sheeting under them to protect them from rising damp. See TEXTILES for Storage conditions.

Hanging a carpet (2)
Sew the loop side of the tape to the back of the carpet, and attach the hook side to a wooden batten.

Housekeeping and Maintenance

Antique carpets should be vacuumed regularly, but not as often as new carpets, to minimise the loss of pile fibre. How frequently they are cleaned depends on where they are placed and how much dirt and wear they receive. Vacuum only when necessary, and not as a matter of habit. In addition, about once a month vacuum the back of a small carpet and the floor under it, for this is where the dirt and grit collect. It is more realistic to clean the underside of a large carpet which has furniture on it once a year. Regular vacuuming should make the need to beat a carpet unnecessary. Beating may damage the carpet.

Make sure that the edges of the carpet are well secured before vacuuming so that they do not get sucked into the machine. Use a cylinder vacuum cleaner with a smooth nozzle on the lowest power setting. Do not use an upright vacuum cleaner or a head with rotating brushes. Vacuum the carpet in the direction of the pile, not against or across it. However, if a carpet is very dirty, occasionally vacuum against the pile, but this should not be a regular practice. Cleaning is more efficient if the dirt is loosened before vacuuming. This process is called tamping. Turn the carpet upside down and pat the reverse with the flat of the hand or a large, flexible rubber paddle. The dust that comes out can be vacuumed up.

Worn or frayed areas and very fragile carpets should be vacuumed through polyester or **nylon net** (*see* TEXTILES). Silk carpets should not be vacuumed too vigorously as they wear easily.

Make sure that there are sufficient and large doormats at strategic entry points in the house to take up the worst outside dirt. Vacuum these regularly so that the grit does not get taken into the house.

Turn carpets regularly to avoid uneven fading and wear.

Cleaning

Do not use commercial carpet cleaners, carpet shampoo or machines that generate steam to clean antique carpets, as they can cause harm. If your carpet really needs washing, ask a textile conservator, who will be able to advise you.

If you spill liquid on a carpet, mop it up as soon as possible using a dry cloth or paper towel. Avoid rubbing the carpet, as this may disturb the pile. Put the paper towel or cloth over the spillage and press it with your hands or, if it has spread over a wide area, tread on it gently with your feet. Replace the towel when the first one is damp. Repeat until no more liquid is absorbed on to the towel. This should remove all the liquid. If a liquid that might stain is spilt, such as tea, coffee or wine, first mop up as much as possible with towels as above, then dampen the area with a little soda water or water and continue the mopping.

Repair

Old, rare and precious carpets should be conserved by an experienced carpet conservator; seek advice from a textile conservator or a reputable carpet dealer. Inappropriate or poorly executed repairs can cause more damage.

Worn or fragile areas of a carpet are very difficult to strengthen because the support must cover the full size of the carpet. This is because patches can exacerbate the problems. The support is a linen or similar material stab-stitched to the underside of the carpet using buttonhole thread of an appropriate colour and taking care that the needle goes between the warps and wefts, not through them. The weak areas are then couched down on to the support. Couching is where the object is sewn on to the ground material using a fine thread and tiny evenly spaced stitches. This is very difficult to achieve successfully and is best carried out by an experienced conservator. Never use any adhesive, adhesive tape or iron-on binding on carpets.

● **SIDE CORDS**

The side cords of carpets usually wear through before the carpet does. They are the selvage on most hand-made carpets. When the carpet is being woven, the weft thread, at the end of each row, is taken round and back over several warp threads. When the carpet is finished, this edge is usually oversewn as well.

When the carpet is in use, the oversewing on the side cords will begin to wear. Once the oversewing has worn away, the core of warp threads will be exposed to wear. When you see this happening, you should replace the side cords as soon as possible. This will prevent the core warp threads from becoming worn.

● **STRENGTHENING WORN OVERSEWING**

Use a straight needle, such as a carpet or tapestry needle, and an appropriate coloured silk or wool thread according to the fibre of the carpet pile. You should start sewing 1cm (½in) or so from the worn area. To hold the thread in place, run the needle under the binding for about 2·5cm (1in), starting from the damaged area. Oversew the damaged area and about 1cm (½in) beyond on either side. Do not make the stitches too tight and always pass the needle between threads, not through them. Finish off by running the needle back through the oversewing for about 2·5cm (1in). Cut off the thread. If the carpet has a double side cord, use figure-of-eight stitches to oversew it.

● **REPAIRING THE CORE**

If the core of the side cord has broken and some threads are missing, you will have to strengthen it by sewing in some new threads. Do not cut off the broken threads. You will need to run some new threads parallel to the edge of the carpet in line with the existing core threads.

Use a cotton, linen or wool thread of an appropriate colour and thickness to match the surviving core threads. Run the needle under the undamaged oversewn cord in the direction away from the damaged area for about 2·5cm (1in). Leave a tail of thread about half the length of the damaged area. Bring the needle and thread out through the oversewing and then back under the cord to make a small straight stitch on the surface of the oversewing. The needle should then be in line with the next damaged warp thread and pointing towards the damaged area. Pull the needle across the damaged area and insert it into the cord on the other side in line with the same warp

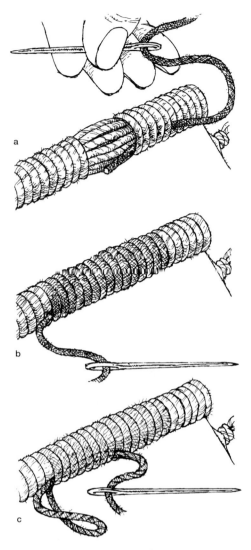

Strengthening worn oversewing
(a) *Start sewing 1cm (½in) from worn area. Hold thread in place by running needle under the binding, starting from the worn area* (b) *Oversew* (c) *Finish by running the needle back.*

Oversewing a double side cord, using figure-of-eight stitches.

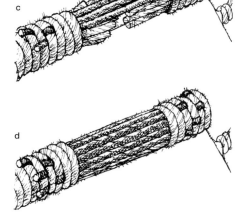

the needle back through the carpet so that it comes out with the next missing weft thread and parallel to the first thread, leaving a small straight stitch on the surface of the carpet. Loop the thread round the warp threads you have just replaced. Run the needle back into the carpet through the next weft thread and repeat the operation. The warp threads should be neatly bound by the replacement weft threads. Carefully push any loose tails of thread into the carpet using a blunt **bamboo stick** or similar instrument.

Finally, oversew the whole replaced cord as above.

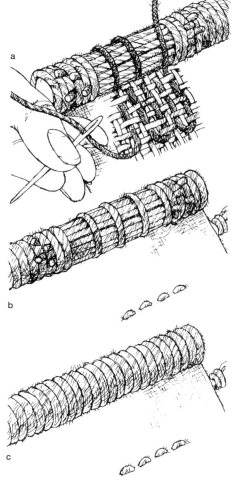

To replace worn fringe on a carpet, use the method for weft repair, but leave long loops to convert into fringe.

Repairing the core of side cords
(a) *Side cords, showing missing threads*
(b) *Add new threads by running the needle under the undamaged oversewing, leaving a tail* (c) *Bring the needle through the oversewing and back under the cord, leaving a small, straight stitch* (d) *Repeat this until the core is the correct thickness.*

thread. Run the needle into the undamaged oversewn cord and take your thread along for 2·5cm (1in). Bring it out through the oversewing and cut the thread, leaving a tail. Continue by repeating this procedure until the core is an appropriate thickness.

It is important that the tension of the threads is correct and does not distort the line of the side cord: too tight and the carpet will bunch, too loose and the cord will be misshapen.

The weft threads then have to be replaced. Run the needle into the carpet directly in line with the missing weft thread. Bring the needle out about 2·5cm (1in) into the edge of the carpet, leaving a tail of thread. Pass

Repairing the weft threads
(a) *Run the needle back and forwards into the carpet in line with the missing threads*
(b) *This will create small straight stiches on the surface of the carpet* (c) *Oversew the cord.*

● **WORN FRINGES**
The fringes of carpets are the ends of the warp threads. When they wear and break off, the weft threads and the pile will begin

to unravel. The fringes can be replaced. The technique used is similar to replacing the weft threads as described above. Instead of wrapping the thread round the core, a long loop is left, which is later cut to form the fringe. The loop should be longer than the

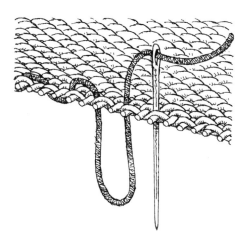

Stab-stitching a carpet or textile.

original fringe so that it can be trimmed to size. The replacement fringe should be knotted if necessary.

Kilims

Kilims are rugs without a pile. In many ways they are similar to a tapestry. Kilim is the Turkish name, the Indian equivalent is called a dhurry.

When the end of a kilim wears, the weft threads begin to break and unravel. Secure these threads to prevent the kilim from un-ravelling any further.

Use a buttonhole thread or wool thread of an appropriate colour and sew from be-hind so that the stitching shows as little as possible from the front. Sew along the entire edge of the kilim using blanket-stitches; each stitch should be about four warp threads wide. Vary the length of the stitches into the kilim to avoid disturbing the weft along one line. The needle must go through the spaces between the warp threads and not through the threads them-selves. Make sure that the stitches are even and not too tight.

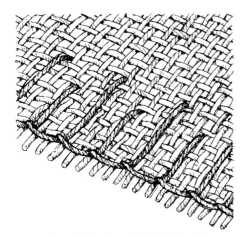

Strengthen the fraying end of a kilim with blanket stitches.

Rag Rugs or Mats

These were made by hooking pieces of available fabric, such as old bits of trousers, shirts and vests into a sacking type of ma-terial or, indeed, into an old sack. Because every sort of colour and type of material was used, it is impossible to say whether a rag rug is suitable for washing or not. They should therefore always be dry cleaned. These rugs should be routinely vacuumed as described in TEXTILES, Cleaning.

Costumes and Clothing

Costumes and clothing present particular problems for display and storage, so wher-ever possible consult a specialist textile or costume conservator for advice.

Handling

Old, rare or precious clothing should never be used for plays, films, etc. Make-up, per-spiration and handling quickly destroy fragile fabrics. People today are generally larger than those for whom the clothes were made, and we do not wear the same undergarments. We are therefore not the shape that the clothes were made for, so wearing them can put a strain on the seams and may cause splitting. Use old costumes and accessories as models to make replicas instead of wearing the originals. If gar-ments have to be worn, insist that they are professionally cleaned afterwards to remove perspiration (*see* Cleaning).

Display

See TEXTILES for general display recom-mendations. Ideally, costumes should be displayed in display cases to protect them from dust.

Never use metal pins for display and do not pin costumes directly on to the wall.

Whether on display or in storage, cos-tumes must be well supported or they can gradually loose their shape and split at the seams or along lines that support their weight. Tailors' dummies of the appropri-ate size can be used, but they will have to be carefully modified to fit the costume, as modern dummies are seldom the right shape: they are usually too large and the shoulders are too wide. A child-sized dummy can be padded to the correct size. Consult a conservator as constructing the correct form to support the costume is skilled work.

Storage

Costumes should ideally be stored flat and well padded in **archival quality** boxes. Most costumes should not be hung, as the weight of the textile may make it split or break up. Only menswear, female outdoor dress and some children's wear are safe to store by hanging for long periods. Beaded dresses should always be stored flat; if this is not possible, they must be supported from the waist by sewing cotton tape loops on to the waistband which can be placed over the padded hanger (*see* p.156).

Cardboard boxes used for storage must be **acid-free** or archival quality, have lids and be lined with plenty of acid-free tissue. The box must be big enough to prevent the objects from being squashed. Always put a final layer of acid-free tissue in the box before you put the lid on. Drawers should be similarly lined, since most woods give off acid vapours. Label boxes and drawers thoroughly to make it easy to locate items.

When packing items in a box, pad all the folds and creases with wads of acid-free tissue paper or stockinette (cotton knit fabric) tubes so that the folds will not be squashed flat. It is important to keep the folds as open and three-dimensional as possible so that creases do not develop (*see* TEXTILES).

Much damage can be caused by hanging costumes, so hanging should be considered only as a last resort, when packing or stor-ing them flat is not possible. Where they are hung, items must not be squashed together on the rail; there should be about 10cm (4in) between each item. Wrap acid-free tissue or some white cotton tape around the metal hook of a coat hanger so that it does not come in contact with the fabric. If the garment has a high collar, wrap extra layers of acid-free tissue round the hook in order to keep the collar in shape. Make sure the hanger hook is long enough so that the top of the collar is not pressed against the hanging rail. If necessary, you can use a piece of cotton tape tied to the rail to ex-tend it. The hangers should be padded.

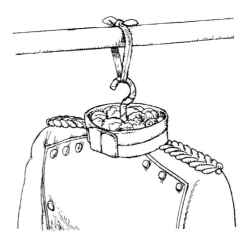

Protecting a high collar with padding.

Packing Textiles

PADS AND TUBES FOR PACKING

Acid-free tissue is used to pad out the folds and creases of garments when they are packed. The paper is scrunched up to form pads that can be inserted into the garment. Stronger tubes can be made with polyester wadding and washed stockinet or muslin. Cut the washed muslin or stockinet to the required length about 5cm (2in) wider than the circumference of the finished tube. The direction of stretch should be along the width. Cut a piece of polyester wadding about the same size. Roll the wadding into a tube and temporarily secure it with pins. Place the polyester wadding roll on the fabric and wrap the fabric around the wadding. Pin the fabric closed, but remove the pins from the wadding as you go. Sew the fabric closed, removing the final pins and making the seam as smooth as possible.

A padded hanger.

MAKING PADDED HANGERS

Use strong plastic, metal or wood hangers, as wire is not robust enough. Check the width of the hanger against the costume. If it is too wide, bearing in mind that the padding will add another 3cm (1¼in) or so, cut off the ends with a small hacksaw. Children's hangers are very useful. The hangers should be padded with polyester wadding covered in undyed washed cotton.

METHOD 1:
FOR COATS, JACKETS, ETC

Make sure that the hanger is smaller than the width required. Bind some polyester wadding tightly around the ends of the hanger and secure in position by sewing the ends. Cut out two pieces of polyester wadding in a roughly triangular shape, using the coat hanger as a pattern, to cover the hanger. Sew the wadding together along the sides leaving an opening for the hook. Turn it inside out so that the seam is on the inside and place it over the hook so that this triangle of wadding is covering the coat hanger and the padded ends. Make a calico, muslin or white cotton sheet cover for the polyester in a similar fashion and sew along the bottom edges of the triangle, turning the raw edges inside.

METHOD 2:
MOSTLY USED FOR CHILDREN'S CLOTHES

Wrap polyester wadding around the length of the hanger. Secure it in place by sewing the ends. Outline this shape on a piece of paper and use the pattern to cut out two pieces of washed calico, muslin or white cotton sheet in a triangular shape. Sew the pieces together with a 1cm (½in) seam along both shoulders, leaving an opening at the top for the hook. Turn the cover so the seam is on the inside and place it over the wadding, making sure that the seams lie flat. Sew along the bottom of the triangle, turning the raw edges inside.

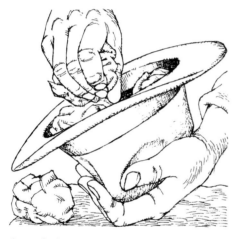

Scrunched acid-free tissue inserted as pads into a hat.

Supporting a garment from the waistband.

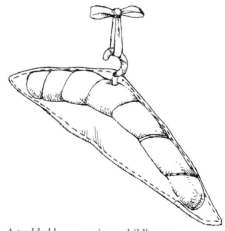

A padded hanger using a child's coat hanger.

Tubes of polyester wadding sewn into stockinet or muslin covers.

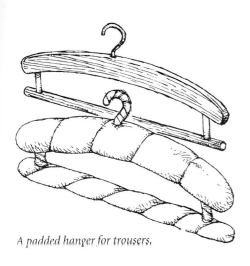

A padded hanger for trousers.

HANGERS FOR NON-TAILORED GARMENTS

Garments that are not tailored can be hung from a padded pole or tube. You will need a wooden pole or rigid plastic tube about 2·5cm (1in) in diameter and slightly longer than the width of the shoulders of the garment. Tie white cotton tape around the centre to form a loop for hanging. Wind strips of polyester wadding around the tube or pole to cover the length, securing both ends by sewing them to prevent the wadding from unravelling. Cover the pole with a tube made from washed calico, muslin or white cotton sheeting.

A padded hanger for untailored clothes.

DUST COVERS

Dust covers can be made from washed calico, cotton sheeting or **Tyvek**. Side opening bags allow easier access to the contents and are preferable to bottom opening bags.

MATERIALS:

Medium-weight, unbleached cotton calico, pre-washed and 137, 152, or 190cm (54, 60 or 75in) wide, depending on the required width of the finished bag. Most garments will fit in a bag made from 152cm (60in) of fabric.

2m (6½ft) of 1cm (½in) cotton tape per bag for closures

Sewing thread

With the garment hanging on its hanger, measure its length from the base of the hook of the hanger to the hem and add at least 15cm (6in) to get the length of fabric required. Measure the width of the garment, on its hanger, at its widest point, and add at least 15cm (6in) to get the width of bag.

Select the most suitable fabric width, which should be at least 15cm (6in) wider than twice the width of the bag.

Tear or cut off the length of fabric required.

Fold in one selvage to the width of the bag and pin it at the top and bottom.

Fold the excess fabric in the opposite direction and pin it.

Mark the centre of the width with a pin at the top and bottom.

Machine stitch across the top and bottom, including the excess fabric, leaving 2·5cm (1in) open in the middle for the hanger, about 0·5cm (¼in) from the edge. Reverse stitch at the ends to secure them.

Turn the bag inside-out so that a front flap is formed, and the extra fabric forms a fly inside, like on a pillowcase.

Press the seam open with your fingers and manipulate it to the edge of the fold. Pin, and stitch it about 1cm (½in) from the edge (like a French seam), running the stitching to the edges at the hook holes. Reverse stitch the ends to secure them.

Sew on the cotton tapes.

Also sew on an object identification label or mark the bag with a laundry marker. It is necessary at this stage to decide which side the opening should be on and therefore which hanger opening to use, as there is one in both ends.

Place the garment on the padded hanger, put the hook of the hanger through the hanger opening, hang up the garment and arrange the bag over it, tying it closed with the tape.

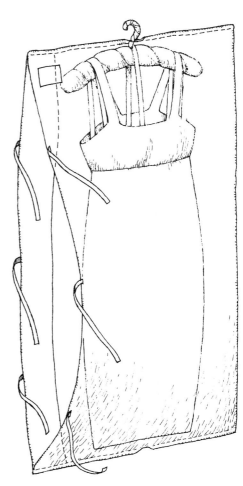

Dust cover for a garment.

Costumes in store should be protected from dust, abrasion and unnecessary handling by covering them with large bags made from washed calico, old sheets or Tyvek. These give the best protection from dust without reducing ventilation. Do *not* use polyethylene bags, as they attract dust. Condensation can form inside polyethylene bags that may cause mould growth, and some bags, such as black bin liners, give off gas and cause the cloth to disintegrate.

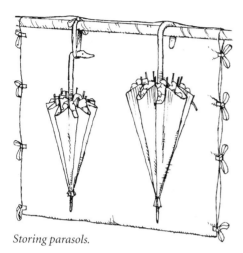

Storing parasols.

Pad hats, shoes, gloves and bags into the correct shape with acid-free tissue and store in acid-free boxes. Hang or stand parasols and umbrellas vertically with the handle uppermost and left slightly open. Pad the folds with acid-free tissue to prevent them from being creased. Make sure they do not touch each other. Drape acid-free tissue, washed calico or an old, clean cotton sheet over them to protect them from dust. Make sure there is no extra weight on the wire frame. Label boxes and covers clearly: photographs are useful, so that you can easily locate objects without having to look through the boxes needlessly.

Housekeeping and Maintenance

See TEXTILES.

Cleaning

Costumes and clothing should be cleaned before being stored or displayed unless there is a significant reason not to. Only very simple cotton or linen costumes should be washed. Other costumes should be professionally cleaned. *See* TEXTILES.

Display of lace from Chastleton House in Oxfordshire. This photograph was taken in November 1991, shortly after the National Trust acquired the house. It is not a good idea to display lace in front of a window, but if this is inevitable, then UV protection is vital. The caps should be given more support to avoid distortion of the brims.

Flags, Military Colours and Banners

Antique flags, military colours and banners should be cleaned, conserved and displayed only by a textile conservator as they are usually in poor condition and very fragile.

Handling

If you have an old flag that has been hanging in a hall or a church for some considerable time, do not take it down without first consulting a conservator, as a great deal of damage can be caused very quickly by inappropriate handling.

Display

Frequently, flags, military colours and banners are displayed so that both sides can be seen. They are usually displayed by being hung from a wood or metal pole slipped through the sleeve along one edge. Eventually, the textile weakens and shreds, partly because of the method of manufacture, but also from damage by light. If flags, military colours and banners are hung from an upright or diagonal pole, they will hang in diagonal lines and are likely to deteriorate faster along the folds than when hung from a horizontal pole.

The best method of display for flags, military colours and banners is in a glass case or frame and lying flat; however, this is not usually practicable.

Storage

Store as for TEXTILES.

Housekeeping and Maintenance

Modern or reproduction flags and banners should be cleaned and looked after as for TEXTILES.

Repair

It is possible for flags, military colours and banners to be lined almost invisibly with very fine net, but this should be done only by a textile conservator. Before embarking on the conservation of military colours, you should check that it is appropriate, as there is a tradition that colours should not be repaired.

BELOW: *Replica of Winston Churchill's standard as a Knight of the Garter, hanging in his study at Chartwell in Kent. The flag is hung from the top edge by curtain rings, and here creases are beginning to form.*

Painting on Textiles

Painting on textiles is another specialist area where treatment should be undertaken only by a textile conservator.

Painted textiles must always be stored flat. Sandwich them between layers of **acid-free** tissue paper. Never roll them, because the painted surface may be hard and inflexible and will crack and pull away from the textile when you attempt to roll it up.

Metal Threads

Metal threads can be found in embroidery, tapestries and carpets, or as decoration on uniforms and other clothing. These metal threads are usually made of thinly beaten metal wound round a core of silk or cotton thread. They can be made from alloys of gold and silver, but are more usually made from silver gilt or gilded or silvered brass or copper. Occasionally, the silver was coated with a yellow lacquer to make it look like gold. Care should be taken not to remove this lacquer. Strips of metal and metal wire wound round in a spiral, as well as metal sequins, can also be found in textiles. An object can be heavily encrusted with metal threads or have only a few strands running through it.

Storage

Where possible, textiles with metal threads should not be rolled, but if they have to be, use a cylinder of a greater diameter than you would normally use. Place a layer of polyester wadding between interleaved sheets of **acid-free** tissue. This will take up some of the differences between the raised metal decoration and the flat textile, allow the object to be rolled more evenly and prevent strain being put on a few small areas. The wadding must not come in contact with the metal, as the threads will catch and pull on the wadding. *See* Rolling a textile.

See COSTUMES AND CLOTHING and TEXTILES for Display and Storage.

BELOW: *Detail of an apron dating from the reign of Queen Anne (1702–14), from the Rachel Kay-Shuttleworth textile collection at Gawsthorpe Hall in Lancashire. The exquisite embroidery employs metal thread, which is particularly vulnerable to physical damage. The silver threads are tarnished, while some of the gold along the scalloped edges has been lost, leaving the core underneath.*

Housekeeping and Maintenance

Textiles containing metal threads should not be washed. Vacuuming, using nylon net for protection, will remove dust and dirt (*see* TEXTILES).

Cleaning

The metal is often dull from tarnish. *Never* use a proprietary metal cleaner to clean it. Do not clean metal threads with a glass bristle brush as sometimes recommended, even though it may make the metal nice and shiny. The bristles scratch the metal and damage the thread by scratching off gilding or silver. Do not try to clean damaged, broken or corroded threads.

You can gently wipe the metal threads with a dry **chemical sponge** to remove loose dust and dirt. A cotton bud moistened with saliva gently rubbed on the metal surface may remove dirt and tarnish. However, if this is not successful, consult a conservator, as cleaning metal threads is very difficult and damage can easily be done to the textile or the thread. Cleaning should be carried out only by a textile conservator, who is likely to suggest that you do not have it done at all, because in many cases cleaning the metal may cause damage.

Samplers and Other Embroideries

Before cleaning, check that the stitches are not broken or loose, as they may be sucked into the vacuum cleaner. Remove loose dust by vacuuming through a net covering the piece as described in TEXTILES. If further cleaning is necessary, consult a conservator, as washing samplers and embroidery is very risky. The dyes often run and some of the threads may shrink. It is therefore safer for a conservator to carry out tests before commencing work.

To frame embroideries, *see* TEXTILES.

RIGHT: *Montacute in Somerset is home to a fine collection of samplers, many from a very early period; this example is dated 1662. It is in remarkably good condition, with bright colours. Many samplers are faded, with the linen background becoming discoloured and brown with age.*

Tapestry

To many people, tapestry and canvas-work appear very similar, and the terms are often used incorrectly. Tapestry is a hand-woven fabric, usually made of wool, silk or linen, or a combination of these fibres and sometimes incorporating metal threads. The pattern or picture of a tapestry is created by the weft thread while the tapestry is being woven, and so becomes part of the structure of the tapestry. Tapestries are woven on a loom and are usually used as wall hangings.

Canvas-work, also known as needle-point, *gros* or *petit point*, is embroidery done with a needle and threads of wool or silk on a woven linen, cotton or canvas ground. Berlin work is a form of canvas-work in which the pattern is worked in coloured wools according to designs printed on the canvas or a chart. The basic structure of canvas-work is the woven ground with the pattern or picture added to it. Canvas-work is most often found on chair seats, backs and arms, cushions, stool tops and fire-screens (*see* UPHOLSTERY).

Problems

Tapestries attract dirt from the atmosphere because of their rough texture, and become dirty and dusty. They also may be brittle as a result of light and pollution damage. Areas woven in silk deteriorate more quickly than those woven in wool. However, brown wool, especially used in outlines, deteriorates quickly because of the dye used.

The sheer weight of a tapestry is one of its greatest problems. Historic tapestries are generally hung with the warp running horizontally so that the weft, which is the weaker thread, takes the weight; therefore, horizontal splits may occur between the warps. The top part of the tapestry is most vulnerable because all the weight hangs from it. The slits, which occur when two colours in the design meet, are another weak area. These slits were usually sewn up with cotton or linen thread, but when this weakens and the stitching gives way, the weight of the tapestry causes the slits to pull apart. These slits should be sewn up by a conservator as soon as possible to prevent the tapestry from becoming misshapen. However, some tapestries have small slits woven into the design to emphasise certain features. These were not sewn up originally and should be left unsewn.

Cotehele in Cornwall is furnished almost exclusively with tapestries, most dating from the later seventeenth century. This detail from a tapestry in the Caesar Augustus series was woven in Antwerp in the 1660s or 70s, and hangs over the fireplace in the South Room. It shows well the wear that comes with age, with tears, some of which have been badly repaired in the past, and with fading.

Tapestries are usually lined to protect the back from dust. Check that the tapestry is hanging square and flat. If it is not, it may be due to the lining having shrunk or because the tapestry is incorrectly hung. Consult a conservator and resolve the problem before further damage is caused.

Take care that furniture is not pushed back against a tapestry.

Handling

Tapestries become very brittle and split and tear easily under the strain of their own weight. They should never be folded but always rolled as described above (*see* TEXTILES and CARPETS AND RUGS) with the right side, i.e. the design side, outside.

Taking a tapestry down or hanging it can expose it to a lot of physical stress and strain. The process requires a scaffolding tower and a number of people so that the weight is supported. As it is difficult to handle the tapestry without causing damage, it is best to get help from a textile conservator before taking down a large tapestry. If the tapestry is in poor condition, it may not be possible to re-hang it without first undertaking conservation treatment at substantial expense. So, it is often advisable to leave a tapestry hanging undisturbed until this treatment can be carried out.

A small tapestry is easier to handle, but at least two people, at each end, will be needed to unfasten it. A further two people may be necessary to receive the tapestry and place it on clean white sheeting or **Tyvek** on the floor or a table.

Before rolling a tapestry for moving or storage, vacuum the back and the front while it is flat. Roll a tapestry in the direction of the warps, which run from side to side of the design, not top to bottom.

For further information on handling, *see* CARPETS AND RUGS.

Display

Tapestries, like other textiles, are very sensitive to light.

Try to place them where people will not rub against them.

Tapestries were frequently hung from rings, but hook and loop tape attached to two or three sides is now more commonly used, as it provides more support. Attaching the tape correctly is difficult and should be done by a textile conservator.

For further information on display, *see* TEXTILES and CARPETS AND RUGS.

Storage

See TEXTILES.

Housekeeping and Maintenance

Never attempt to clean an old, rare or precious tapestry or one in bad condition. This must be done by a textile conservator.

It is possible to remove surface dirt and dust from a hanging tapestry that is in good condition by vacuuming it through **nylon net** (*see* p.20 and TEXTILES).

Cleaning

If the tapestry needs further cleaning, consult a textile conservator.

Repair

Do not attempt to resew any unsewn slits on old, rare, precious or fragile tapestries. These must be dealt with by a textile conservator. However, on a more recent tapestry, you may want to sew up the slits yourself.

If the tapestry is in good condition, this work can be done while it is still hanging on the wall. Use buttonhole thread or appropriately coloured polyester thread with a count of 30. It is better to use a tapestry needle, because it has a blunt end, but you may need to use a curved needle if the slit is

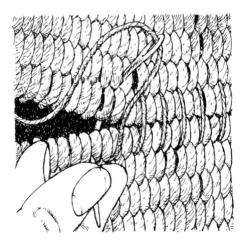

Mending a slit in a tapestry, sewing between the threads, but not through them.

very difficult to get at. Make sure that you sew between the threads not through them, particularly not through the warp threads. To secure the end of the thread, sew it twice round the warp thread at the end of the slit. Continue to sew along the slit so that the stitch will be straight on the front and diagonal on the back. Do not pull the thread too tight. Keep the tension even. Finish off by sewing twice round the warp thread at the other end of the slit.

Take conservation advice before carrying out any other repairs.

Upholstery

See also LEATHER.

Furniture has been upholstered since the late seventeenth century, but very little has survived from that date. The term upholstery includes everything from the simple covering of wood with fabric to a complex arrangement of webbing, springs, stuffing and wadding.

Problems

Upholstery is prone to the problems of light, dirt, insects, etc. discussed in TEXTILES, but there are additional factors affecting its condition.

Upholstery wears out quickly and is often altered to suit changing fashions, so original upholstery on antique chairs and beds is rarely found. Where it survives, the surface fabric and the total structure of the upholstery may have historical importance and should be preserved and carefully recorded.

The condition of the framework of the furniture is important, as a weak framework and loose joints put a strain on the covering fabric and the internal structure of the upholstery. Faults below the surface eventually affect the covering.

Upholstery usually develops worn or weak areas, fraying edges and piping, as well as loose fringes from use and handling. On more modern furniture which is in use, you may wish to have these repaired to prevent the damage worsening, but on historic pieces these should be left until they can be conserved by a textile conservator. Care must be taken when cleaning not to increase the damage.

If the frame has active woodworm, it will be necessary to treat it. This is most easily done where the upholstery can be removed, but when this is not possible you

will need the help of a textile or furniture conservator or upholsterer who specialises in treating historic objects. Insects can also attack the stuffing inside upholstered furniture, so if you have an infestation seek conservation advice.

Handling

See WOOD for additional information on handling and moving furniture.

Take care when moving upholstered furniture because the upholstery is easily damaged. Sharp edges of tables, door handles, keys in doors or even light switches may catch and rip fitted upholstery, particularly the backs of chairs and sofas.

Carry upholstered antique stools and chairs by the legs, particularly if they have tassels or braid round the edges. Larger pieces of furniture, such as chairs, should be carried by two people, lifting from under the seat, not by the arms.

Handle beadwork upholstery with particular care. *See* BEADWORK.

Display

Canvas-work panels, often used for seats and chair backs, are stitched with dyed wools or silks that are particularly susceptible to dust and light (*see* TEXTILES). Wherever possible, use loose covers to protect them and to protect important silk upholstery. The covers must be very loose to prevent pressure on fragile textiles and fringes.

Almost more than any other sort of upholstery, beadwork upholstery will deteriorate from wear and tear. Because of its age and structure, it is extremely fragile and should never be sat on. If the beads are coming loose, secure them as soon as possible.

Storage

Make sure the furniture is really well covered by **dustsheets** to prevent unnecessary dirt from falling on the upholstery.

Use lightweight dustsheets or loose covers, such as **Tyvek** or cotton lawn, over velvet upholstery or other fragile textiles to prevent the pile of the fabric or fringes from being crushed.

If upholstery becomes damp, make sure that it is thoroughly dried out before storing it, since the stuffing holds moisture and encourages mould growth.

If rooms are not in use for long periods, cover the furniture with clean cotton dustsheets. They are also essential when decorating or building work is in progress. If necessary, use polyethylene over the dustsheets, but not in direct contact with the upholstery since it attracts dust and condensation.

Housekeeping and Maintenance

Keep upholstery clean to protect it from damage caused by dirt and insects.

Vacuum upholstered furniture regularly using a vacuum with a clean, smooth nozzle attachment, not a brush. Protect antique and fragile upholstery and fringes from being damaged while vacuuming, either by placing **nylon net** over the upholstery or by covering the nozzle of the vacuum cleaner with net (*see* p.20 and TEXTILES). Keep the suction head away from fringes, which can easily unravel. Clean particularly in crevices and down the backs and sides of chairs and sofas and under furniture where insects can breed.

Remove the dust from around the buttons on button-backed chairs and sofas with a hogshair brush and vacuum cleaner.

Some upholstered furniture has exposed polished wood surfaces. During routine cleaning only dust the wood. When it is necessary to polish the wood, take great care not to get the polish on the upholstery, as it will stain the fabric and is nearly impossible to remove. Place a piece of card between the wood and the textile to stop the wax from spreading. Use a **beeswax polish**; do not use a spray polish. Apply the polish with a brush, and brush it off. Remove drop-in chair seats before polishing the frames.

Cleaning

Further cleaning to antique upholstery should not be done without conservation advice.

Do not be tempted to use special finishes that can be sprayed on to upholstery to make it 'dirt and stain resistant'. They may make future cleaning more difficult and may cause damage to antique fabrics.

Very fragile antique and valuable upholstery should be cleaned by a textile conservator.

Repair

Repair work to valuable upholstery should be done only by a textile conservator.

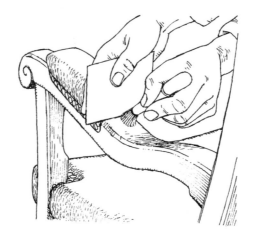

Polishing wood on upholstered furniture.

Minor damage, such as small tears and loosened braid or fringes, should be stitched up before they become frayed, unravelled or detached and can no longer be neatly repaired. Worn piping around the edges can be oversewn or re-covered. Always sew, never stick: adhesives are impossible to remove and make future conservation much more difficult.

Before re-covering drop-in seats, always remove the old covers unless they are original. If you do not, the seat will be slightly larger than it was before and when used it is likely to force the seat-rail joint apart.

Whitework

Whitework, as the name implies, is made only from white threads. The yarns used are usually linen or cotton. Whitework objects are often decorated, although the decoration is always in white threads. The most common whitework objects are lace, tablecloths, christening dresses, wedding veils and decorative pillowcases.

Whitework should be handled, displayed, stored, maintained, cleaned and repaired as described in TEXTILES. *See* COSTUMES AND CLOTHING for whitework clothing.

CHRISTENING DRESSES

Christening dresses, together with wedding veils, are among the few antique costumes that are required to be worn occasionally. However, always bear in mind that using them could expose them to damage.

After a christening dress has been worn, check to see that no snags or tears have occurred, particularly round the bottom edge. These can be repaired with a matching cotton thread.

After use, a christening dress must be washed, *see* TEXTILES. Dry flat or hang the christening dress to dry on a small hanger padded with polyester wadding or **nylon net**. Do not use heat to dry it. While it is drying, smooth out the creases with your fingers and ease it into shape. Make sure that the dress is completely dry before it is stored (*see* COSTUMES AND CLOTHING).

When the christening dress is next needed and brought out of storage, it should be allowed to hang from a small padded hanger for a few hours and any small creases will probably fall out. It may help the creases to drop out if you hang it in a steamy bathroom.

WEDDING VEILS AND LARGE LACE TABLECLOTHS

Wedding veils and tablecloths may be passed down through a family from generation to generation. They were usually made of cotton or lace, although modern veils are often made of man-made fibres.

After a veil or tablecloth has been used, it should always be repaired and washed before it is stored.

Handling

Carefully examine the veil or cloth for any weak or damaged areas before and after use. If it is very precious, or a great deal of repair is needed, a textile conservator should be consulted. If there are just a few snags and weak areas, you can do some minor repairs.

The size of a wedding veil or a very large cloth makes it difficult to handle and clean. Make sure when you are moving it about that the ends do not trail on the ground or become caught on sharp edges. It may help to carry it in a clean **dustsheet**.

In order to examine the cloth or veil satisfactorily, you will need a clear, flat area larger than the veil so that the veil can be laid out flat. You may need to move the furniture to make some floor space. Cover the area with a sheet of clean polyethylene or a clean sheet, preferably not white.

RIGHT: *White woollen bedspread from the late seventeenth or early eighteenth centuries, in the King Charles Bedroom at Cotehele, Cornwall. It is in good condition, with just a few small stains, probably iron. The stitching around the quilted sections is particularly vulnerable, and is beginning to become loose.*

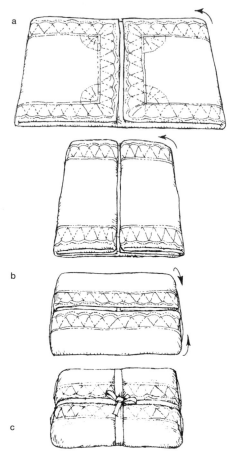

Folding a large whitework object
(a) *Fold left and right-hand edges to meet at centre* (b) *Fold top and bottom edges to meet at centre* (c) *Tie bundle loosely with cotton tape for storage or washing.*

● **FOLDING A LARGE WHITEWORK OBJECT**
After examining and repairing the object, spread it out again so that you can fold it up. Fold the left- and right-hand edges to meet at the centre. If the veil or cloth is rectangular, you may need to fold it again in the same way to make it squarish. Put rolls of **acid-free** tissue along all the folds so that they do not become sharp creases.

Fold the top and bottom edges to meet at the centre. Continue folding the left- and right-hand edges, then the top and bottom edges until the veil or cloth is the right-sized parcel to be stored or washed.

Storage

Veils or tablecloths should ideally be stored rolled rather than folded (*see* COSTUMES AND CLOTHING). See above for the best way to fold large textiles. Cover the object with **acid-free** tissue or washed calico or a clean sheet. Do not use polyethylene bags, as condensation may form inside.

Whitework objects should never be stored dirty, as the dirt will attract insects and mould. Any repairs that need doing should always be carried out before the object is washed.

Cleaning

Very large whitework objects can be easily damaged when they are wet. It is advisable to fold them before being washed so that they are not handled when wet. Wash the folded parcel in your bath or basin. Tie the bundle loosely with cotton tape. When the bundle is secure, it can be washed as described in TEXTILES.

When you have finished washing the object, place the parcel back in the centre of the sheet of polyethylene. Undo the tape and unfold the bundle in the reverse order to that in which it was folded up. This is made easier if you have one person at each side of the veil or cloth. Carefully smooth the veil or cloth into shape. Pat the object dry with a clean white towel and leave it to dry naturally and thoroughly.

If necessary, iron the veil or cloth with a lightweight steam iron set on *Cool*, but remove it from the polyethylene first. If it is easier to iron it on the floor, place the veil on a clean sheet.

Repair

Carefully go over the veil or cloth looking for damage. You can patch weak or torn areas with fine net that looks similar to the veil. Using a fine needle and polyester or cotton thread of a similar thickness to the threads of the object, sew the net on to the cloth. Take care to stitch with appropriate and consistent tension. If the stitches are too tight, they may cut into the old fabric, and if they are too loose, they will allow movement between the support and the cloth and be ineffective. Make sure you pass the needle through the holes in the lace, not the threads.

The edges of the veil are most likely to be damaged. If they are, you can strengthen them by sewing on an edging of fine net. If this is not possible, oversew the edge.

Tribal Art and Textiles

Most tribal art textiles or objects are coloured with vegetable dyes which fade or change colour very quickly. Be extremely careful when displaying tribal textiles that they are well away from any sources of direct light. The dyes on tribal textiles and the colours on objects are seldom fixed. They will run or streak very easily if they get wet or damp.

It is important to check tribal art for insect infestation, to which they are also prone. Imported insects can be very voracious, *see* WOOD.

Tortoiseshell

Tortoiseshell comes from the shell of sea turtles. The highest quality shell is said to come from the Far Eastern hawksbill turtle. The top layer of the upper surface is the part of the shell that is used to make decorative tortoiseshell.

The Romans used tortoiseshell as a veneer for furniture and it has been used extensively since then by furniture-makers. It was used by A. C. Boulle in conjunction with brass to make his furniture. Tortoiseshell can also be moulded into small boxes and cut into combs and Spanish mantilla combs, buckles, fans, pen nibs, shoehorns and buttons. It can be used as a veneer for dressing-table sets, caskets, mirrors and picture frames and can be inlaid into other materials, such as wood and silver. Gold and silver are sometimes inlaid into tortoiseshell; this is known as Piqué work.

Tortoiseshell is a hard, brittle, translucent material and can be polished to a high shine. It is usually mottled yellow and brown or black but sometimes has a red tint. When tortoiseshell is gently heated, it softens and can be shaped and moulded. While soft, sections can be joined together so that the joints are invisible when the tortoiseshell cools. The size of the sections of the turtleshell limit the natural size of the sheets of shell, but the joining technique enables large objects to be covered in what appears to be a single sheet of tortoiseshell.

It is now illegal to import turtles, tortoises or their shells into most countries. Genuine new tortoiseshell is therefore no longer available and moving antique objects from country to country requires a licence.

Many objects that appear to be tortoiseshell are, in fact, made from stained horn, celluloid and, more recently, other synthetic materials. It is not always easy to differentiate genuine tortoiseshell from imitation.

Tortoiseshell is thinner and more translucent and usually more flexible than horn. Celluloid may smell of camphor and other plastics sometimes have a resiny smell, which is not a characteristic of tortoiseshell.

Piqué work is the art of inlaying tortoiseshell, and sometimes mother-of-pearl and ivory, with gold and silver. The metal can be inlaid either vertically as small rods, which give a dotted effect, or horizontally as flat shapes and strips. Both techniques can be used singly or together to form patterns and decorative scenes. Piqué work was used for small decorative objects, such as candlesticks, clock cases, boxes, cigarette cases, spectacle cases, knife hafts, jewellery and dressing-table sets.

The tortoiseshell was heated and, while it was soft, gold and silver were inlaid into its surface. When the tortoiseshell cooled down and became hard again, it trapped the metal. It is occasionally possible to find plastic 'tortoiseshell' boxes with so-called piqué work on them, but this metalwork will usually be stuck on to the surface and not inlaid into it.

Problems

The surface of tortoiseshell can easily scratch. It can develop a grey, milky appearance if it is exposed to direct sunlight or other bright lights. Fluctuating or extremes of **relative humidity** and temperature will make tortoiseshell distort, crack and delaminate off any backing or out of any inlay.

ABOVE: *Detail of Boulle work combining tortoiseshell and brass, from a Louis XIV writing desk in the Drawing Room at the Treasurer's House, York. The brass has been heavily polished and scratched. The tortoiseshell, too, is damaged with cracks. This example, however, does not show a common problem with Boulle, when the material moves and distorts the inlay.*

In piqué work, the tortoiseshell may shrink over the years and, as metal does not, it may lift out of the surface. It is very difficult to re-lay this metal and repairs should be undertaken only by a silversmith or conservator experienced in this type of work.

Handling

See p.12.

Display

Do not display tortoiseshell in direct sunlight, in windows or over radiators or fires. Take particular care with objects on dressing-tables. Display objects where the **relative humidity** remains as steady as possible. This particularly applies to wood objects veneered with tortoiseshell, otherwise the tortoiseshell is likely to separate from the wood carcass.

Storage

Wrap tortoiseshell objects in **acid-free** tissue and store them in a cool, dry, well-ventilated place away from bright sun. Do not store tortoiseshell objects in sealed polythene bags or cling film. If they are placed in a **sealed plastic box**, make perforations in the lid to allow the air to circulate and to prevent condensation.

Housekeeping and Maintenance

Remove dust with a soft brush or wipe the surface with a dry **microfibre cloth**. When dusting larger objects covered with tortoiseshell veneer or inlay, use a **brush** rather than a cloth or duster, which may catch and pull up pieces.

Cleaning

Use swabs of cotton wool or cotton buds dampened with warm water containing a few drops of **conservation-grade detergent** for further cleaning. Do not use household detergent. Stubborn dirt may be more effectively removed with a little saliva on a cotton bud. Rinse with clean swabs or buds and clean water. Pat dry with a soft cloth or paper towel. If the object is inlaid, take care not to catch the inlay with the cloth. Do not soak tortoiseshell objects in water or get them very wet.

A little very **fine abrasive paste** gently rubbed over the surface of tortoiseshell with a soft cloth or cotton wool may revive the colour and shine if it is a little dull. This will remove a thin layer off the top surface and so should only ever be done once and not at all on a very old, fragile or valuable object. It is preferable to wax very lightly with **microcrystalline wax**. If tortoiseshell

has been exposed to sunlight for a long time and has become very grey and opaque, it is unlikely that you will be able to revive the colour and translucency.

Clean silver inlay using a soft **pencil eraser** or silver **metal polishing cloth**.

Repair

Loose tortoiseshell inlay or veneer can be re-laid as described in WOOD.

Wax

Wax has been used as a modelling material from the earliest times; wax figures exist from ancient Egypt, Greece and Rome. In Europe wax has had wide use in anatomical models for teaching medicine, dolls, medallion portraits and relief groups, sculptors' maquettes, displays of fruit and flowers and many other decorative and fine art examples, including Madame Tussaud's modelled heads of the victims of the French Revolution.

Waxes were coloured either by mixing a dye or pigment with the wax or by rubbing dry pigments into the surface of the wax; dolls were often coloured in this way. Sometimes the surface of the wax was painted.

Beeswax was predominantly used but was often combined with other waxes, such as carnauba, candelilla and spermaceti, to improve the properties of the mixture. The waxes were sometimes mixed with natural resins and an assortment of fillers, including lard and flour.

Most coloured seals found on documents of the eighteenth to twentieth centuries are, in fact, made from the natural resin shellac rather than wax. Earlier seals were either beeswax or a beeswax-rosin mixture. Wax seals should be treated as any other wax object. Seals are very brittle and are easily broken. If a seal breaks, it is important to make sure that all the fragments are collected and put in a safe place until it can be repaired. Documents with seals attached should be framed by a specialist framer, *see* PAPER.

Problems

Beeswax itself is a comparatively stable material but, as it was used in a variety of combinations with other materials, the durability of wax objects can be very

unpredictable. The surface of waxes can craze and vibrations can cause them to disintegrate. The wax can sweat and develop a brown film or a white bloom on the surface. Some waxes can become brittle.

Waxes can begin to soften at temperatures not too much higher than room temperature. Although the softening may not be noticeable, dust and dirt on the surface may be absorbed into the wax. Heat will soften wax so that it may distort and eventually melt; when cold, wax is very brittle.

The colour on waxes can fade in light.

Many wax models have internal iron armatures that may corrode. Some are on a backing such as glass that is vulnerable to breaking. If the wax is combined with **organic materials**, say on a wood backing, fluctuating **relative humidity** may cause the wax to separate from the other materials (*see* pp.17–18).

Handling

Wax objects are very vulnerable to physical damage and so must be handled with extreme care (*see* p.12). The warmth from hands can be sufficient to soften waxes, so carry wax objects in a tray or box. Remove watches, rings and other jewellery before handling a wax object.

Display

Wax objects must be kept away from sunlight and heat: a few minutes of sunlight falling through glass on to wax can be enough to melt it and the heat from a nearby radiator can cause the collapse of a hollow head. Spotlights and other heat sources must be avoided (*see* p.18).

As wax objects are difficult to clean, they must be protected from dust as much as possible by using glazed frames and bell-jars, glass domes or display cases.

Storage

Wax objects should be stored in a clean, dry, dark area where the temperature and relative humidity remain fairly steady. Waxes in frames should be carefully and individually wrapped in **acid-free** tissue and placed in individual containers so that they do not get knocked or jolted.

Never wrap a wax object in cotton wool. When the cotton wool is removed, it can pull delicate fragments off the wax. If it is left in contact with the surface for any

ABOVE: *Wax portrait of a lady in the Tapestry Room at the Treasurer's House in York. It is one of a pair; the other is of a gentleman, made in England c.1800. Wax is particularly vulnerable to damage because it is so soft, and this lady has suffered dents and scratches, with worn paint on the eye and mouth, and the silk damaged by light. There is also the possibility of insect attack to the textiles.*

length of time, the fibres can become attached and eventually embedded in the wax and it is virtually impossible to remove them. If unframed or unboxed waxes are going to be stored for a long period, any wrapping must not be left in contact with the wax surface. Place the wax in a plastic container or **archival quality** box without any packing. A useful cover can be made by cutting the top off a clean, dry plastic bottle and inverting it over the object.

Housekeeping and Maintenance

Provided it is in good condition, brush dust off the object using a soft brush and vacuum cleaner (*see* pp.19–20) or **compressed air**.

Cleaning

The cleaning of models, dolls, tableaux, portraits or any other sort of wax object is an extremely skilled job and should be carried out only by a conservator with experience in dealing with wax objects. Old wax is exceptionally brittle and even brushing with a soft brush can cause it to shatter.

Repair

The repair of wax objects is highly skilled and very complex. If you have a wax object which is broken, it must be dealt with by a conservator specialising in wax conservation. Sticking wax silhouettes back on to glass backgrounds should be left to an expert. Synthetic adhesives will not stick wax securely for any length of time.

Wood

Wood has been used by man for shelter, fuel and tools as well as to make fine and decorative articles. Wood is reasonably easy to work; it can be durable and is strong and flexible. Its uses range from architectural to carts, ships and trams as well as weapons, household utensils, furniture, musical instruments, carved ornament and sculpture. In fact, almost anything can be made out of wood. Pieces of wood are joined together in a number of ways, the simplest being binding with twine or leather, but screws, nails and dowels are also used. Two pieces of wood can be cut in such a way that they join by interlocking, as seen in mortise and tenon and dovetail joints. Wood can also be stuck together, traditionally using animal glue. Wood is shaped by being sawn, cut, planed, turned, whittled, or carved, and finished by being sanded and polished. It can be decorated by inlaying other woods, metals, tortoiseshell, ivory and precious stones, or it can be painted, varnished, waxed, gilded and lacquered.

Trees are divided into two main groups, the softwoods and hardwoods. Hardwoods come from broad-leafed trees, which can be either evergreen or deciduous and have enclosed seeds (angiosperms). Softwoods come from cone-bearing trees, usually with evergreen needle-like leaves and having 'naked' seeds (gymnosperms). The terms hardwood and softwood can be quite confusing, as balsa wood, for example, is a hardwood, despite being very soft and yew is as hard as some of the hardwoods, although botanically it is a softwood.

The hardwoods most commonly used for furniture and wooden objects were ash, lime, beech, birch, chestnut, mahogany, oak, rosewood, satinwood, teak and walnut. The most common softwoods were larch, various pines, spruce and yew.

Softwoods usually bruise and damage more easily; hardwoods are more durable and take better finishes. Softwood is often used for the carcass of a veneered piece of furniture or for the structure of gilded frames.

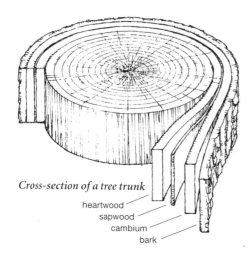

Cross-section of a tree trunk

heartwood
sapwood
cambium
bark

The trunk of a tree consists of a series of rings built up during each year of the tree's growth; these annular rings give rise to the grain in wood. A single layer of cells beneath the tree's bark, called the cambium, grows and divides to make new bark on the outside and sapwood on the inside. The sapwood is the living part of the tree. At the core of the trunk is the heartwood, which is no longer active and is preserved by chemicals produced by the tree. The heartwood is predominantly used for furniture and wooden objects because of its hardness and durability. By contrast, the sapwood is much softer and full of nutrients and for this reason is much more vulnerable to insect attack and rot. The variations in the cellular structure of woods give rise to their individual characteristics and colours. Food storage cells within the tree, radiating out from the centre of the trunk and known as medullary rays, produce an attractive figure on some woods such as oak.

When trees are cut down for use, the bulk of their water content will dry out, resulting in considerable shrinkage. This is often seen in the radiating cracks of firewood logs. To reduce the effects of shrinkage, timber is sawn into boards and seasoned for a number of years, which allows the sap to dry out with a minimum of cracking, leaving a residual moisture content of approximately 12 per cent. The boards are then ready for making into furniture.

Almost all woods have at some time been used for making objects, but the particular properties of certain woods lends them to be used for specific purposes. Beech was used widely for chairs, particularly turned rails; ash bends well and was used for chair backs; birch was used for upholstered chair frames, as it is tough and is not split by tacks. Lime, box, pine, olive and oak were often used for carving and sculpture, while decorative woods, such as holly, laburnum, fruitwoods, amboyna, sycamore, maple, kingwood and box were used for contrasting inlays, marquetry and Tunbridge ware. Oak was also used widely for furniture in Europe until the late seventeenth century. It is very durable and well known for its characteristic silvery rays and figuring; it is also hard and difficult to carve and does not hold paint, glue and gilding well.

From the mid-seventeenth century, walnut was used more widely for furniture, while oak was still used for the carcass and for drawer linings, although eventually it was replaced by pine. Walnut was also commonly used for furniture during the Italian Renaissance. Originally mahogany came from Cuba and the Honduras. It was used in Europe from the second quarter of the eighteenth century for furniture-making and soon replaced walnut as the most popular wood for furniture. Teak grows in India and Burma and furniture imported from the East was made from teak. By the mid-eighteenth century a lot of veneered furniture was being made; much was veneered with mahogany.

Furniture is often constructed by applying veneers to a carcass. The veneer is a thin section of timber that is sawn or sliced off the trunk and was first used in Europe in the mid-seventeenth century. Veneer is usually selected for its attractive grain patterns. Veneering makes it possible to match and reverse the grain patterns in the wood to form a decorative effect. Very often chests of drawers or tables were veneered from the same tree to give a matching or mirrored grain pattern.

Marquetry is made from different veneers cut to form floral or figurative scenes, sometimes with other materials such as bone or brass included, and applied to the furniture carcass or surface.

Sometimes an inlay of lines or banding of wood, bone, ivory, mother-of-pearl, tortoiseshell or metal is set into grooves cut into the wood. Parquetry is inlaid or veneered wood that has a geometric pattern made up of different coloured woods or the

Arts & Crafts-style sideboard, probably designed by Llewellyn Rathbone, in the Dining Room at Standen in Sussex. The main body is oak, decorated with marquetry panels that have been varnished, thus reducing the contrast in the pattern. The loop handles are of beaten copper on copper backplates. The silver-plated hot plate is by W. A. S. Benson.

same wood placed so that the grains lie in different directions. Wooden parquet floors are often made in this way.

Objects made from wood, furniture in particular, are usually finished with a protective or decorative coating. Furniture was often sealed and finished with wax, usually beeswax, or oil. Wax alone could be used, but often an oil polish or oil varnish made with linseed oil was applied. French polish (shellac varnish) became popular in the early nineteenth century. In the 1930s cellulose lacquers were introduced. A lot of furniture dating before 1820 has now been French polished, even though it would not originally have had a shellac finish.

Paint was sometimes used to decorate objects or to give an artificial appearance, say of polished stones or panelling, to wood architectural work. Gilding is often found on furniture, frames, sculpture and decorative carvings.

Problems

Wood is remarkably strong and when kept in the right conditions, durable.

After seasoning and use, wood remains sensitive to water vapour in the air no matter how old it is. It takes in or gives up water according to the humidity of the air and this causes changes in dimension, predominantly across the grain. Excessively dry conditions may cause wood to shrink and crack, joints to open and become loose, and veneer to lift. In damp conditions wood will swell, glue softens and again veneers may lift. Manufacturers learnt that furniture designs had to be able to incorporate these dimensional changes. For example, chests were made of frames and panels where the panels fitted loosely into the frame without nails or adhesives so that they could move without splitting.

Many of the problems found in furniture or wooden objects are the result of poor construction or the differential shrinkage of components. Wood sculptures are often constructed from a number of pieces of timber glued together, and these sections can sometimes separate with continuing fluctuations of humidity.

Painted or gilded finishes on wood do not change dimensions in the same way as the ground timber, so eventually the wood and paint layers may separate.

Most woods will change colour in light regardless of their surface finish. Some of the darker woods will bleach and the paler woods may become darker. Some

marquetry furniture was very colourful when first made, as the marquetry consisted of many different coloured or dyed woods, but now it appears in shades of brown because it has faded in sunlight. If you have a desk or cupboard on which the colour of the marquetry survives, expose it to as little light as possible to prevent the colours from disappearing.

Liquid spillage can leave white or dark stains on the surface depending on the type of wood.

Wood is prone to attack by wood-boring insects, particularly the furniture beetle. Surface mould (mildew) will stain the surface of wooden items and flourishes in damp and unventilated conditions. If wood gets very wet, it is prone to wet rot or dry

The eighteenth-century staircase, inlaid with exotic woods and ivory, at Claydon House in Oxfordshire is a tour de force *by the craftsman Luke Lightfoot. However, it shows all too clearly the effect of light on wood, with faded treads contrasting with the rich colour of the risers.*

rot, which over time can completely destroy its structure.

• INSECT ATTACK

Many woods are vulnerable to insect attack and the resulting damage, although some woods are more resistant to insect attack than others. Walnut and beech are particularly susceptible, but mahogany and teak are seldom attacked. Usually the heartwood is more resistant than the sapwood, because it contains chemicals, including tannins, produced by the tree that preserve it from insect attack and rot. Occasionally, you can see narrow bands of sapwood infested by woodworm, while the heartwood remains untouched.

The furniture beetle or woodworm *Anobium punctatum* is the insect most commonly found in temperate climates, but death-watch beetle and powderpost beetle are also found. Other wood-boring insects are common in other parts of the world and can occasionally be imported with wood.

It is not the adult insects that cause the damage to wood but their larvae. The female beetle lays her eggs in crevices, old joints and hidden corners and cracks. When the eggs hatch, the larvae burrow into the wood for food and protection. This tunnelling may continue for between one and five years, after which the larvae pupate and eventually emerge from the wood as mature beetles, leaving the characteristic round flight holes. This usually happens between May and August, although where there is central heating it can happen at most times of the year. However, wood-boring insects do not survive well if the moisture content of the wood is low. For this reason, furniture beetle is seen less frequently in centrally heated houses than in houses heated by open fires.

New flight holes are not always evident on the finished surface of an object. The beetle often infests unfinished wood or softwood, such as the backs and undersides of furniture and particularly the softwood backboards and divisions on cupboards and mirrors and the backs of drawers. Holes in the wood do not necessarily indicate that there is active woodworm in the wood, but it is wise to be cautious. New flight holes are clean and the edges of the holes are crisp. Old flight holes are likely to have darkened and their edges to have become less sharp. Sometimes you may find small piles of frass (powdery debris of insect droppings with wood dust) by a flight hole. This does not

necessarily mean that the hole is new, as the frass could be old but recently shaken out.

If you acquire a new piece of furniture or sculpture or even firewood, always inspect it for woodworm before bringing it into the house and, if necessary, keep it isolated from other objects until you are certain that it is insect-free or you have had it treated. Particularly check sculpture or carvings that have recently come from tropical or sub-tropical climates. The best time to treat wood for woodworm is in the spring or early summer when the pupae or beetles will be just beneath the wood surface and particularly vulnerable.

Some furniture and wooden objects are also vulnerable to other forms of insect attack, for example where they are upholstered or where paper, textiles or leather are an integral part of the structure.

These insects include silverfish, clothes moth larvae and carpet beetle (*see* p.15) which can cause considerable damage if not checked in time. For example, card tables, which usually have a lining of baize or leather and fold in half when they are not in use, are particularly vulnerable to textile-eating insects. Such tables should be opened and vacuumed at least once a year. Similarly, linings to boxes, desks and drawers should be checked and cleaned and treated as necessary.

• MILDEW AND MOULD GROWTH

Mould will grow on wood whenever the conditions are sufficiently damp, usually when the **relative humidity** is above 65%. The mould will appear as fuzzy grey/white and musty-smelling patches that almost always leave a stain when removed. Because

Moving a commode with the aid of cotton webbing slings. The four carriers wear gloves to protect their hands. Think about footwear when carrying heavy furniture; it should be sturdy with non-slip soles.

the mould feeds off the material on which it is growing, in severe cases it can weaken the object, particularly when it forms on associated textiles or paper. The best way to prevent mould growth is to make sure there is good air circulation around objects and to prevent the relative humidity being too high. Regularly check poorly ventilated areas, such as the insides or backs of cupboards, drawers, bookcases or pictures, particularly those next to outside walls.

Where possible, remove vulnerable objects from damp areas and open doors and drawers in spare rooms or those not in use to aid ventilation.

Handling

General observations for handling wood objects and furniture are discussed in the Introduction (*see* p.12). Only move one piece of furniture or object at a time and always lift it by the lowest solid part of the main frame or the body of the object. The most vulnerable parts of furniture are the arms and legs of chairs, the top edges and legs of tables and the feet and bases of chests and cabinets.

Recommendations for moving furniture are:

• Always lift furniture; never drag it across the floor, even if it has castors, as it puts a great strain on the joints.
• Do not stack one piece on top of another to carry them.
• Use two people to carry a piece where possible.
• Make sure that belt buckles cannot scratch the object as you carry it.
• Do not lift chairs by their backs or arms; place your hands under the seat on each side or on the legs, taking care not to apply pressure to the arms.
• Do not lift an object by its projecting parts.
• Lift a chest of drawers or table by the top support rail not the overhang.
• Lock or tie doors closed before moving cupboards. Use soft webbing rather than rope or string that can score or rub the wood.
• When moving a chest of drawers, empty the drawers, remove them and carry them separately.
• Do not turn a piece of furniture upside-down unless it is essential. It puts an unnecessary strain on the joints. If you have to turn it over for any reason, lift it right up off the floor, turn it over and then

Mahogany washstand in the North East Bedroom of Lindisfarne Castle, Northumberland. Made in England in the early nineteenth century, it is fitted with a blue-and-white slop bowl and soap dish. Water damage is evident on the upper surface where jugs have left rings in the varnish. The glass top was intended to protect the wood, but it can also cause damage by trapping water.

put it down squarely on a blanket on the floor. Do not tip it over on its legs.
• Remove marble tops, protective glass and other movable tops before moving a piece of furniture and carry them separately; always carry them vertically, as they can break under their own weight if they are carried flat.

The base (legs, feet, bottom rungs) of furniture is often damaged during floor cleaning by vacuum cleaners, mops, etc. Always move chairs and lightweight furniture and clean carefully by hand around the rest.

Do not fix anything, such as self-adhesive tape and labels, to the finished side of a piece of furniture, as they are difficult to remove without damaging the surface.

Display

Wood objects need to be displayed in as steady humidity as possible, one that is neither too low (below 45% RH) nor too high (above 65% RH) for any length of time (*see* pp.17–18). Wood should therefore not be displayed near radiators, in direct sunlight, over fireplaces, etc.

Try to keep wood away from bright light. If strong daylight falls on an object, it may fade and develop a patchy appearance from the resulting change in colour. Move the furniture around to prevent this but, better still, control the light using blinds and curtains (*see* pp.16–17).

Do not push furniture back hard against walls, curtains, and hangings. Always allow a small gap between them.

Very often sculpture, ceramics, photographs and other objects are displayed on furniture. Check that bases are not rough and do not scratch the finish. If they are, put a piece of brown felt or chamois leather under them.

Houseplants or vases of flowers on furniture should be placed on a waterproof mat that is larger than the base of the vase and big enough to catch pollen falling from flowers. Ideally, they ought to be removed from the furniture before watering. This is generally possible with houseplants, but with vases of flowers, particularly large arrangements, more water may be spilt when moving the vase than by carefully watering it where it is. Always use a long-nosed watering can and, if any water is spilt on the furniture, mop it up at once so that is does not mark. Make sure that the water does not run under the mat. Do not overfill vases. If you tuck the top of your finger over the edge of the vase you are about to fill, you will feel the water when it reaches your fingertip, before it reaches the top and spills over. Never spray plants with water if they are standing on wooden furniture. If you put houseplants on polished furniture, make sure that the leaves and flowers do not rest or drip on to the surface; be aware that pollen can damage polished surfaces. Never put houseplants or vases on gilded furniture, as the smallest drop of water can completely ruin the gilding.

Some finishes on wood, particularly French polish, are easily marked by alcohol or hot or cold objects. Use mats to protect the polish. Also, if you are using a table to write on, place some card or a blotter between the paper and the table, as the pressure of the pen can mark some finishes.

Storage

Wooden objects should be stored in a cool, dark area with adequate ventilation and as steady humidity as possible. Raise off the floor to protect from damp (*see* p.14). Keep the storeroom clean to help prevent attack by woodworm, mould or moths, and check stored objects at least once a year for woodworm and mould growth.

Wrap small wooden sculpture in **acid-free** tissue or, if it is a large piece, calico or **Tyvek**. Do not place wooden sculpture in metal or wooden cabinets unless they are well ventilated, because a lack of ventilation can cause mould growth (*see* pp.15–16). Do not stack objects on top of one another.

Housekeeping and Maintenance

Regularly monitor the condition of furniture and wooden objects, as problems should be solved as soon as possible to prevent them from getting worse. At least once a year, and preferably in the spring, check for woodworm infestation and mould.

Look inside drawers and cupboards and check crevices in softwood and all back-boards and other unfinished surfaces. Vacuum inside furniture and move furniture on carpets away from its usual position to facilitate cleaning underneath.

Look for splitting and warping, for lifting veneers and loose metalwork and inlay. Check for flaking, cracking and lifting surfaces, such as lacquer, gilding and paint. Make sure that joints, legs and stretchers are secure. Collect any detached pieces and put them in an envelope or small plastic bag, label the bag so you know where the piece has come from and place it either inside the piece of furniture or in a safe central place. If you are likely to forget where the pieces have been put, put a label inside or on the underside of the furniture telling you where they are.

● DUSTING

The surfaces of furniture and wooden objects are usually finished to give them an attractive polished shine or decorative finish. In normal circumstances, a flat surface only requires a light dusting to keep it free of dirt and dust. Use a clean, dry **microfibre cloth** or a duster with hemmed edges. Lint-free dusters with these edges are preferred over the household yellow duster, which can snag on rough areas and leave yellow fluff behind. The dust should be collected in the duster and not just swept off the object's surface. Dusters should be changed regularly and washed.

Dust is abrasive and can scratch more delicate surfaces, such as gilding, boulle, lacquer or marquetry. In these cases, it is better to use a ponyhair or hogshair brush with a vacuum cleaner (*see* pp.19–20) to dust the object. A **brush** is more effective for cleaning inlaid furniture or pieces with missing moulding or veneer, carved wood and sculpture. Take care not to pull off paint, gilding, inlay or veneer. In this way, you can efficiently remove the dust from the entire object, including difficult-to-reach areas such as crevices and deep carving.

Never use a feather duster, as it cannot be washed; the feathers tend to break and their spines can then scratch the surface. Long-handled fleece dusters often leave fluff on the furniture, so are not recommended.

● POLISHING AND WAXING

If a piece of furniture is old and has been waxed and polished over the years, the shine can often be revived by buffing-up

the surface with a soft, clean duster without applying any more wax. Old surfaces form the **patina** of a wooden object and this represents a considerable part of its attractive appearance and value. It is therefore vital that the surface is not worn away during cleaning and polishing. How highly polished a piece of furniture or wood should be is really a matter of choice, but a bright hard shine does not always show off the wood as well as a more mellow sheen.

Objects that have a natural 'raw' finish are not generally waxed. The surface can be cleaned after brushing away the dust by wiping it with a clean, damp cloth, wiping in the direction of the grain.

Similarly, an object with an oil finish, oil varnish, French polish or a modern finish only needs burnishing with a soft, dry cloth and a very occasional application of a little liquid wax.

Furniture is waxed to give a protective coating to the original finish and to provide a hard, shiny surface that the dirt and dust will not cling to, as well as to give the piece of furniture a well cared for and attractive appearance. A wax polish will also fill in any tiny scratches that may have been made on the surface of the piece of furniture and can be used to fill woodworm holes.

French polish, shellac, varnish, paint or lacquer finishes ideally should not be waxed but, when furniture is being used rather than displayed, a thin coating of wax will help to protect the surface from the hazards of everyday life. The wax will help to prevent spills of liquid and small scratches irreparably damaging the surface.

If too thick a layer of wax is allowed to build up, it will eventually dull the surface and collect dust. Only wax a piece of furniture if it really needs it rather than as a matter of routine. Waxing is necessary when the surface has become worn and dull and will not shine when buffed.

If a piece of furniture has lifting or cracking veneer or inlay, it is advisable not to wax it, as the polishing cloth is likely to catch on the edges of the lifting wood and pull it off. Also, if wax gets under the veneer, it will make it much more difficult to stick back the missing bits.

Use a **beeswax polish**. Apply a thin coat of wax with a soft duster or brush using a circular movement. Use a soft natural bristle brush on carved wood. Do not let the wax dry for too long or it may become difficult to polish and will remain streaky. Polish the wax with a soft, clean duster or use a soft brush on carved objects.

Try to match the colour of the wax to that of the wood. Pale yellow waxes used on a dark wood may show white in cracks and depths of carving when dry. It is better to use a darker wax in this case. Similarly, dark wax on a light piece of furniture wood will darken it and irreparably spoil the patination.

Aerosol polishes of any kind are to be avoided, as the solvent in the polish can cause white marks or a bloom on the surface of the wood, it can dissolve some applied finishes and the aerosol wax does not give much protection because it is such a thin coating. Most aerosol polishes contain silicone, which should not be used on anything other than modern synthetic finishes, as the shine is not appropriate to antique furniture and the silicone can build up in the crevices and is extremely difficult to remove. They may also cause a bloom.

Furniture creams can contain ingredients that are potentially harmful to a waxed or French polished surface, so check them carefully before using them. They can be useful for polishing and cleaning furniture that is not waxed, such as pieces with a cellulose lacquer or modern paint.

Cleaning

Dust and loose dirt should removed as described above.

Removing stains from wood is often very difficult without making the damage look worse. Stains on oiled, waxed or varnished wood can usually be removed only by taking off the finish. This then has to be replaced to match the original finish with a resulting loss of the **patina** and original surface. This work is best left to an experienced furniture conservator. Consideration must also be given to whether it is appropriate to remove an original finish and destroy a patina built up over years.

Before wetting the wood, you could try cleaning it with a dry **chemical sponge**, which may well remove enough surface dirt and prevent any risk of damage from using water. A very dirty object can usually be cleaned, once the dust and dirt has been brushed off, using water with a few drops of **conservation-grade detergent**. Wipe the finished surface with a barely damp swab to remove the dirt. Rinse with swabs dampened with clean water. Wipe the surface with a soft cloth or paper towel. Do not get the surface very wet. Allow it to dry naturally. An unfinished or raw wood surface

can be cleaned in the same way, but a soft brush may also be necessary. Mop up the water as you work so that the object does not get too wet, otherwise the grain will rise. Rinse with clean de-ionised water. Make sure that any metal associated with the object does not become wet.

The same method may be used for cleaning French-polished surfaces dulled with wax and dirt. Dip a soft cloth or cotton wool swab into the solution, squeeze it out and then gently rub at the dirt. Dry off the surface with a clean cloth and polish with a soft, clean cloth.

Wax often gathers in carvings and crevices. This can be removed by carefully using a **bamboo stick** or a plastic spatula to scrape it out. Do not scrape the wood or use a metal tool or sharp knife. **Solvents**, such as **white spirit**, should not be used as they will damage the surrounding wax polish before they soften the encrusted sections.

Candlewax can be removed from a polished surface by placing an ice cube in a corner of a polyethylene bag and holding it against the wax. After a few minutes, the wax should become hard and brittle enough to be removed with pressure from a fingernail. Re-polish the area with a cloth with very little polish on it and then buff it.

If the surface of a piece of furniture or wood object is in such a poor state that it needs to be re-polished, seek the help of a furniture conservator who will be able to judge whether the original surface can be revived and retained and will preserve or recreate the original intended appearance of the piece.

● REMOVING MOULD

An object with mould is likely to be damp, so it should be dried out slowly. Move the object to a drier part of the house or gradually improve the conditions within the room. Improved ventilation, including opening doors and drawers, may be all that is necessary. Do not dry an object too quickly, as this can set up stresses leading to cracking or lifting veneer.

Wherever possible, take wooden objects outside to remove the mould. This will stop the mould spores from spreading to other objects. Wear a face mask to protect yourself from breathing in the spores. Using a soft bristle brush, brush off the mould. If working inside, hold the nozzle of a vacuum cleaner in your other hand to catch any mould spores and dust. You can also wipe mould away with a soft, damp cloth, but carefully dry the surface afterwards.

Repair

Minor repairs can be done at home, but it is always advisable to consult an experienced conservator before tackling major repairs. Even for minor repairs, manual skills and an understanding of wood and the construction of the object are necessary, as a badly executed repair can be more damaging to the piece and reduce its value. Structural damage in furniture can be serious, especially if it is neglected.

For example, if a piece of furniture with loose legs, chair rails, slats, etc. is used, strain is put on the other joints and severe damage can be caused. These cannot be repaired successfully without working on the structure of the object. Temporary repairs are not recommended, as they may exacerbate the problem. The furniture should be taken to a furniture conservator. Try to get structural damage rectified as soon as possible and use the furniture as little as possible until that time. Good quality furniture and wooden objects should always be repaired or treated by a conservator.

There is often a tendency to want to fill the cracks of split wood in sculptures and panels, but when they are filled, the wood continues to swell and contract with changes in humidity, the crack opens up again or another split appears. Therefore it is preferable to leave a crack unfilled.

Choosing the right **adhesive** is very important when repairing wood. Many can cause more problems than they solve. Epoxy resins are too hard and strong and almost impossible to remove; commercial white PVA wood glue is very difficult to remove, may be too strong, may collect dirt and the bond may fail over time. The recommended glue is Scotch glue but fish glue and rabbit skin glue can be used for small repairs. Scotch glue has traditionally been used in the construction of furniture and wooden objects; it is very compatible with wood – strong but flexible and easy to remove when repairs are necessary. It takes a little time to prepare but is easy to use.

When pieces of wood are glued together, they must be held in place with clamps or weights while the glue dries. Before carrying out any small repairs, prepare some small flat blocks of wood or hardboard, which are used to prevent the clamp or weight from marking the surface, and some sheets of thin polyethylene or **silicone paper**, which are needed to prevent the blocks from sticking to the object.

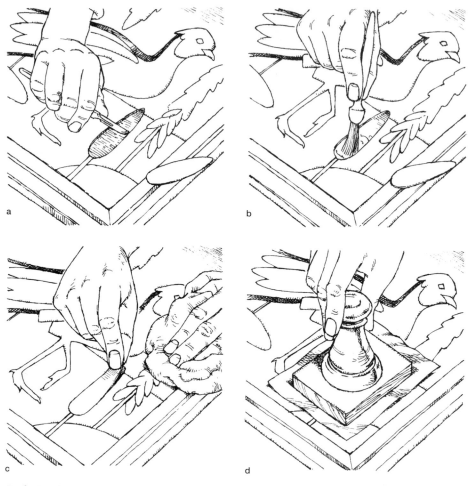

Replacing detached veneer or inlay
(a) *Clean off the old adhesive with a scalpel* (b) *Apply glue* (c) *Insert missing piece, wiping off excess glue* (d) *Secure with polyethylene or silicone release paper and a weighted block.*

Small pieces of veneer, marquetry and inlay often become detached; gluing them back will prevent them from being lost. Clean off the old adhesive from the carcass and the loose piece using a scalpel or chisel. Glue the section in place with a little hot Scotch glue or cold-setting fish glue. Secure it by placing the polyethylene or silicone release paper and blocks on the surface and clamping them in position with a wood clamp or G-clamp. Alternatively, place a **weight** on top of the silicone paper or polyethylene and blocks. Leave the glue to dry for about 24 hours. Use only a small amount of glue; if it oozes out, remove the excess with a damp cloth before clamping. Masking tape can also be used temporarily to hold small sections in place while the glue dries but only where it will not damage the surface when removed. Masking tape should not be used on painted, gilded or lacquered objects, or on any loose or flaking surface.

The veneer or inlay may sometimes be loose but not detached. In these instances, remove any old glue or dirt with a **bamboo stick**, taking care not to damage the veneer, then insert a little Scotch glue, gently push the section down with your fingers and wipe off any excess adhesive with a barely

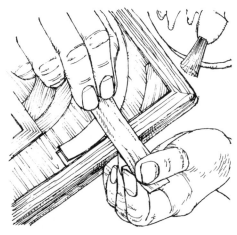

Securing a piece of loose veneer with tape.

damp cloth. Hold it in place with a clamp, weight or tape as described above.

● REPAIRING INLAY
Sometimes a metal inlay will spring up from the wood; where possible, it should be replaced in position so that the problem does not worsen.

Carefully clean out the old adhesive from the channel using a **swab stick**, but do not scratch the surround. Then degrease the underside of the inlay and, if possible, the channel using a small cotton wool swab dampened with a little **acetone** or **alcohol**. Take great care not to get the solvent on the surrounding wood, as it will mark or remove varnish.

Using a bamboo stick, place a very small amount of easily reversible adhesive in the channel. Too much adhesive will squelch all over the surface when you replace the inlay and will damage any varnish. If any is squeezed out, wipe it off with a dry cotton wool bud. Press the inlay in position with your finger and then hold it in position as discussed above until the adhesive dries (about 24 hours). Where the shape of the object prevents you from using a weight, use a clamp or elastic bands to hold the board hard against the surface.

● CONSOLIDATING WEAK WOOD
Where an object is very fragile from insect damage, it can be consolidated, but this is difficult to do without marking the surface and takes some experience to ensure that the consolidant has penetrated sufficiently. Commercially available consolidants and wood strengtheners are not suitable for use on antique wooden objects or good quality antique furniture, as the consolidant is often too strong and hard and may cause discoloration of the wood. They are also difficult to remove if further conservation work has to be carried out.

Small areas of damage can be strengthened by using warm rabbit skin glue (*see* **adhesive**), but you would be advised to ask for conservation help for good quality or rare and precious objects. Make up the rabbit skin glue and, while it is warm, slowly drop it on to the damaged area using a syringe or **pipette** and allow it to soak in. Work in a warm room so that the glue does not cool down too quickly and has time to penetrate the wood. Work carefully so that the glue does not spread over the surface. If by chance it does, wipe it off with a damp cloth as soon as possible. When the glue has soaked into the damaged area, leave it to

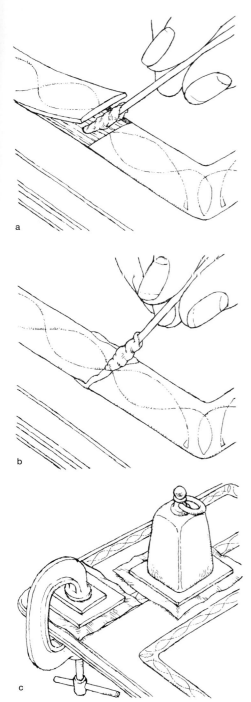

Repairing metal inlay
(a) *Clean out old adhesive with a swab stick*
(b) *Apply fresh adhesive, wiping off any excess with a dry cotton bud* (c) *Secure by pressing with weight or a clamp on polyethylene or silicone release paper.*

dry. Large areas are more difficult to treat in this way as the water in the glue may cause the wood to swell and joints or veneer to loosen. Seek advice from a furniture conservator.

Small pieces or carving, such as petals, leaves and fingers, often become loose or are knocked off. They should be replaced as soon as possible lest they are lost. Use Scotch glue, fish glue or an easily reversible adhesive to stick these pieces in place.

● TREATMENT FOR WOOD-BORING INSECTS

Do not treat old, rare and precious wooden objects, upholstered furniture or objects with special finishes. These should be treated by a conservator or a specialist firm.

See pp.14–15 for the various approaches to killing insects in objects. Simple wooden objects can be treated by all three of the techniques.

If you have one small item with a problem, you may prefer to treat it yourself with liquid **insecticide**. Do not treat painted, lacquered or gilded wood or wood with a varnished surface with an insecticide, as it could be softened or damaged by the solvents mixed with the insecticide.

If possible, take the object to be treated outside or in an outhouse or garage, but if this is not possible, make sure you work in a well-ventilated room that is seldom used and have the windows open wide. Wear goggles, rubber gloves and protective clothing.

Put polyethylene sheet under the object. Take any drawers out of a piece of furniture. Dust and clean objects well, including the inside of drawers.

Use a clear, low-odour liquid insecticide or a **permethrin-based insecticide**. The insecticide can be injected or painted on to the wood and sometimes you need to do both. It is very important that the liquid insecticide does not get on to any finished surfaces; therefore, the insecticide should be injected or painted only on the unfinished sides of the wood.

Although small cans of insecticide come with special nozzles with which to inject the liquid, it is much easier, cleaner and more effective to use a plastic syringe or pipette which will inject the liquid deep into the wood. They can be obtained from chemists or conservation suppliers. Inject the fluid into flight holes at about 5cm (2in) intervals. The tunnels are interconnected and the fluid will run from one to the other. If any liquid gets on a finished surface, wipe it off immediately. The fluid could squirt back at you through other flight holes, therefore always wear goggles. Clean out the syringe when you have finished with the appropriate solvent – it should say which to use on the can of insecticide – or dispose of the syringe safely by wrapping it in paper before placing it in the bin.

When brushing the insecticide on to the unfinished surfaces, it is easier to decant some of the liquid into a smaller glass or metal container; a jar with a screw top is ideal. Apply the insecticide liberally to all the unfinished surfaces with a small, 2cm (¾in) paintbrush. Make sure that no liquid gets on to any finished surfaces, textiles or upholstery.

Allow the object to dry for at least 24 hours or for as long as recommended by the manufacturer on the container. Do not sit or sleep in a room where insecticide has been used or where there are recently treated objects. The flight holes can then be filled in with a soft coloured wax that matches the colour of the wood. This improves the appearance of the piece and also makes it easier to see if further flight holes appear.

Upholstered furniture can be treated against woodworm when the upholstery has been removed. If you intend to have a piece of furniture re-upholstered, that would be a good time to treat the frame. Make sure that you allow the insecticide to dry well before re-upholstering, otherwise it could stain the new fabric.

Polychrome or Painted Wood

Furniture, sculptures and carved ornaments were often painted either as part of an overall decorative scheme or to complete an individual work of art, sometimes to simulate marble, tortoiseshell and exotic woods.

Very often the surface is prepared by applying a ground, frequently white, to the wood before painting. This levels the surface, covers the grain and provides a smooth surface that holds the paint well. The ground layers can be oil paint or a softer material made from whiting (calcium carbonate), slaked plaster of Paris (calcium sulphate) and/or kaolin held with a protein glue such as rabbit skin glue or parchment size.

Paint is made up of powdered pigments held in a **medium**. The medium has to be able to stick to the surface, hold the pigment and not remain sticky. Throughout the world, local natural resins, gums and glues have been used as mediums, in Europe oil paint is common, but you can also find egg tempera, casein, natural resins, gums, complex mixtures of oils and gums, wax, as well as more contemporary

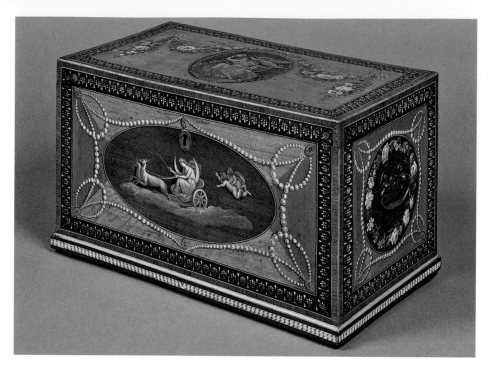

Late eighteenth-century satinwood tea chest, with delicate painted decoration, from Fenton House in Hampstead, London.

mediums such as acrylic resin. The appearance and behaviour of the paint will vary according to the medium and pigment used and its application. The paint may be applied directly to the wood or to the ground and is often applied in layers with detail or colour washes as the final layer. There may also be a layer of varnish on top of the paint. Unbound pigment occurs on some ethnographic items and contemporary art.

Problems

Painted wood is subject to the same problems, including wood-boring insects and mould, as discussed in WOOD.

Wood changes dimension with changes in **relative humidity**, so the paint layer is very vulnerable and is easily lost. The dimensional changes can cause painted surfaces to crack, lift and flake. The medium can also lose its strength, making the paint powdery.

The paint may discolour and the varnish darken from light and/or pollution. Paint is also quite soft, so it is easily marked or chipped. The white ground often shows through where the paint is damaged.

The particular problem of looking after painted objects is that it is easy to damage or remove the top layers of paint while cleaning or caring for a piece. Cleaning and handling should be very gentle. Observe and monitor the paint surface to note any deterioration. Look for loose paint or cracks appearing on the surface. Use a torch

to help, holding it so that the light rakes across the surface and reveals blemishes, lumps and bumps.

Handle, Display and Store as for WOOD.

Housekeeping and Maintenance

Use a soft brush and vacuum cleaner to remove dust (*see* pp.19–20).

Check for insect attack at least once a year in spring as described in WOOD. If the paint is powdery and barely adhered to the wood, do not attempt any kind of cleaning, not even dust removal.

Cleaning

Good quality and rare or precious painted wood should only be cleaned by a conservator, as should polychrome sculpture and other works of art.

Any further cleaning is problematic, as many cleaning agents can harm the paint. You can at the most expect to remove only grime and dirt; if the varnish is discoloured, you will need conservation advice. Where the paint is flaking or damaged, it is safer not to clean the object and to get conservation advice.

To clean painted ornament or decorative wood where the paint is in good condition, first dust and then try a dry **chemical sponge**, which is often effective at removing dirt, but do not rub too vigorously or you will lift or damage the paint.

Before trying any cleaning agent, always test it in a small inconspicuous area on each colour, as the solubility and durability of the colours can vary. Test to see that the method removes dirt but no paint and leaves no mark on the surface. Then, once you start to clean, keep looking at the swab to make sure that it is not picking up paint. If it is, stop and seek advice. Do not rub, but gently roll the swab over the surface to soften and pick up the dirt. The cleaning solutions can soften the ground layers, causing the paint to come off, so work very cautiously and stop if you see the appearance changing. During cleaning, use almost dry swabs. Do not allow the painted surface to become very wet or the liquid could penetrate the paint layer and cause damage to the paint and to the wood.

For small objects, especially sculpture, saliva is a very useful cleaning agent. Dampen a cotton bud with saliva and roll it over the surface gently. Follow this by using a bud dampened with purified water.

Using saliva on a larger object is not very practical and not everyone likes the idea of using it. The other cleaning solutions to try are purified water with a drop of **conservation-grade detergent** or a white spirit:water:detergent mixture (*see* **solvent mixtures**). Try the water first and then try the mixture only if the water has no effect. After cleaning, wipe the surface with clean swabs dampened with clean water and allow it to dry naturally.

Repair

See WOOD. Do not attempt to treat painted wood objects with liquid insecticide. The liquid may stain and soften the paint or cause it to lift off. Seek advice from a conservator if you have an insect infestation in painted wood.

Bamboo

Bamboo is a giant tropical grass or reed with a hollow stem. It was used in the Far East to make simple household furniture that began to be exported to Europe from the end of the eighteenth century. Some bamboo furniture was lacquered and decorated. The term bamboo is also applied incorrectly to late eighteenth- and nineteenth-century furniture made of European woods, carved and usually painted to simulate bamboo. Bamboo is recognisable by the double ridge that appears at fairly regular intervals along its length. In 'fake' bamboo, these knuckles are much more evenly spaced.

Check bamboo furniture to make sure that joints are secure. Check particularly carefully for active wood-boring insects, which can wreak havoc in bamboo in a very short time.

After dusting with a brush, bamboo can be cleaned with warm water containing a few drops of **conservation-grade detergent** or a mild household detergent. If the bamboo is painted, test a small area before you begin cleaning. Dampen a cloth or cotton wool swab with the solution and wipe it over the surface. Rinse with clean swabs dampened with clean water and dry with a soft, clean cloth. If the bamboo looks dull, apply a little **microcrystalline wax** on a brush and buff it with a clean, soft bristle brush or a soft cloth.

Billiard Tables

An English billiard table has eight legs; the table framework is fitted with sections of slate, which are secured so that a perfectly flat surface is achieved. The slate is then covered with superfine green woollen cloth with a strong nap running from the balk end (bottom end), to the black spot end (top end).

In order to keep a good, smooth surface, the table must be lightly brushed and ironed regularly. Brush from the balk end to the black spot end to bring up the nap and to keep the surface dust-free. Check for moths and, if necessary, a modern fabric can be sprayed with a **permethrin** spray, taking care not to get the spray on any wood. Do not use insecticide on historic fabric.

Boulle Furniture

André Charles Boulle was a French cabinetmaker to Louis XIV who perfected the art of brass and tortoiseshell marquetry, which is now known as Boulle or buhl work. Boulle designs are often very elaborate, with flowers, scenes, scrolls and other ornate patterns, and were used on clocks, cabinets and tables. Usually either the tortoiseshell or the gilt brass, which is often embellished with engraving, dominate the design. Copper and tin were also used and later Boulle work was often inlaid with mother-of-pearl, horn and other materials.

The tortoiseshell was generally painted or gilded on the reverse to enhance the colour and a sheet of paper was sometimes applied to the paint to protect it during the construction.

Boulle pieces were frequently made in pairs, known as *première partie* and *contre partie*. The thin sheets of tortoiseshell and gilt brass were glued together and then the design was cut through. Once separated, the cut-outs from one sheet could be placed into the piercing of the other, making one of the pair 'positive' and the other 'negative'.

The brass and tortoiseshell often lift from the base wood because of the dimensional changes in the wood. It is extremely difficult to re-lay the brass inlay and this should be done only by a furniture conservator who specialises in the restoration of Boulle furniture, as should any other repairs.

It is extremely important that Boulle furniture is kept at as constant humidity as possible (around 50–65% RH).

Always dust Boulle furniture with a brush and vacuum cleaner (*see* pp.19–20), not a duster. The brass should not be polished.

Cane and Rush Furniture

The cane used to make seats and backs of furniture is made from split rattan, which is a type of palm. It was first imported into Europe from the Malay Peninsula in the middle of the seventeenth century.

Rush-seated chairs are known to have been made in Europe since the Middle Ages and have been in use in America since the arrival of the Pilgrim Fathers. Rush has also been used to make carpets, mats and baskets.

Cane and rush are long-lasting materials, but they will dry out and become brittle in dry, centrally heated atmospheres. Never stand on a chair with a cane or rush seat.

Check cane and rush seating for woodworm, although it is more likely to be found in the wooden frame.

Wooden chair of the seventeenth or eighteenth century, in the Fettiplace Closet at Chastleton House in Oxfordshire. The cane is in good condition apart from slight sagging of the seat, and has undoubtedly been replaced at some time.

Rushes are prone to damage by gritty dust. Carefully vacuum them regularly with the vacuum cleaner set on *Low*. If the rush or cane is very fragile use netting over the vacuum cleaner (*see* TEXTILES p.144).

Cane and rush work can be cleaned with warm water containing a few drops of a **conservation-grade detergent**. Dip a cloth or cotton swab in the water, wring it out and wipe it over the surface. Wipe the rushes along their length in order not to catch their edges. Rinse with clean water and allow to dry. Do not let the rush become very wet, as it may stain and the rush may be weakened. Rush is very vulnerable to mould, so leave the piece somewhere warm until it is completely dry.

There is now a revival in chair-caning and rushing and there are numerous good and simple books to show you how to do it yourself. Take the object to a conservator if the chair has historic value or is part of a set.

Cupboards and Chests of Drawers

When closing cupboard doors, always make sure that the catches on the first door are fastened before closing the second door. Do not push doors back further than they can go comfortably or let them swing back hard, as this puts a strain on the hinges.

If a cupboard door does not open and close smoothly or does not close properly, it could be either because the hinges are not securely fixed or the frame is out of true because the piece of furniture is not standing level. Check that all the screws in the hinges are present and secure. Try tightening up any loose screws or replace an ill-fitting screw with one of the correct size. It may be necessary to take off the hinge and plug the screw holes before refitting the hinge. If the door still binds on the frame, put a small wedge or pack a piece of cardboard under one or both front legs to make the piece more level and see if that helps.

Open drawers by pulling both handles and close them by pushing evenly on both sides. If a drawer is difficult to pull in and out, check that it is not overloaded. Do not try to force it if it is sticking. If you run a household candle along the runners of the drawer, it will make it run more smoothly.

If the drawer is one of several, for instance in a chest of drawers, and appears to be really jammed, try taking out the drawer that is directly above or below it. Reach in with both arms and, if there is room, hook your fingers round the back of the drawer and, with someone else pulling carefully on both handles, pull gently on the back of the drawer. This may help to get the drawer out, but be careful as it is easy to pinch your fingers.

Glass-fronted Display Cabinets and Bookcases

If the glass is not too dirty, it can be polished with a dry, soft lint-free duster or **microfibre cloth**. Take care not to rub the wooden mouldings around the glass, particularly if they are gilded. Protect the mouldings by holding a piece of card against the edge. A little saliva on a cotton wool bud will help remove flyblow and other marks.

If the glass is very dirty, remove the worst of the dust with a cloth and then, very carefully, wipe the glass with swabs of cotton wool moistened with warm water containing a few drops of a **conservation-grade detergent**. A few drops of **alcohol** in the water will help remove greasy dirt. Use circular movements and do not let the swab touch the edges of the wood, particularly if the wood is polished or gilded. Hold a piece of thin card against the inside edge of the moulding to keep the swabs away. Finally, polish the glass with a dry cotton wool swab or soft, clean lint-free cloth. Do not clean the glass with commercial glass cleaners as they sometimes contain ammonia or vinegar which can change the colour of the wood and strip off a decorative finish. They may also contain silicone which will build up a residue and is difficult to remove.

Some glass panels in furniture have painted decoration on the inside. Never touch the painted surface. *See* GLASS.

Desks

The flaps of drop-fronted desks should never be fully opened without both of the pullout supports in position or the hinges will tear out. Do not put anything too heavy on an open desk.

Garden Furniture

Garden furniture is usually made of teak. If it is left untreated, it will eventually turn an attractive silvery grey colour. If you wish your furniture to remain a uniform brown, bring it in every autumn and, when it has thoroughly dried out, paint teak oil all over the surfaces, including the undersides. The teak oil turns the furniture a rich dark brown and, if the oil is used annually, the furniture should last a long time.

If you are storing garden furniture in a shed, cover it with a tarpaulin or **dustsheet** to keep dirt, dust and particularly bird droppings off it and, if possible, raise it off the ground or stand it on cork or polyethylene sheet to prevent damp from rotting the legs.

Tunbridgeware

Tunbridgeware was developed in Tunbridge Wells in Kent in the late seventeenth century. It is the name given to small wooden objects lavishly decorated with marquetry patterns by using rods of various coloured woods glued together. The rods were about 15cm (6in) long and were glued together and finely sliced transversely to produce about thirty sheets of an identical pattern. The woods used tended to be hardwoods, such as beech, sycamore, holly, cherry, blackthorn and mulberry. The objects made included small boxes, frames, games boards, and sometimes larger objects, such as writing boxes and games tables.

The inlays can be damaged by damp, which causes the marquetry to rise. Clean and care for Tunbridgeware in the same way as STRAW MARQUETRY. If the surface is dull, apply a little **microcrystalline wax** with a soft bristle brush and polish it off with a soft, clean bristle brush. If the surface is raised and can be pushed down flat, repair it as for WOOD.

Japanned and Lacquered Furniture

See JAPANNED AND LACQUERED OBJECTS.

Papier Mâché Furniture

See PAPIER MÂCHÉ.

OBJECTS

Bookshelves in the Night Nursery at Lanhydrock in Cornwall.
Alongside the dolls and teddy bears are much-loved children's books
showing signs of wear, such as lost spines, through use.

Arms, Armour and Weapons

The category of arms, armour and weapons encompasses a vast range of different types of objects and materials. Included in this group are: swords, crossbows, arrows, cannon, pistols, guns, maces, axes, cutlasses, daggers, spears, knives, bows, clubs, armour, helmets, javelins, lances, shields, chain mail and many other items. Almost all of these have one aspect of their structure in common: part of the object will be made of metal and usually at least one other material is included. The other materials can range from wooden butts of guns and pistols, ivory and jade hilts, leather straps

and textile padding of shields and armour, wooden carriages for cannon, beaded handles for ethnographic weapons, and leather and textiles on wooden sword scabbards.

Arms and armour are frequently richly decorated. The decoration can be in many forms, including gold, silver or brass inlay, precious stones inlaid into jade, ivory dagger hilts, and mother-of-pearl and bone inlaid into wooden gun stocks. The surface of the metal is often intricately silvered, browned (sometimes known as russeting), blued or damascened, a form of decoration in which the steel or iron is inlaid with gold or silver beaten into undercut grooves engraved into the surface. Many sword blades are made of patterned or textured steels; most commonly encountered are Javanese krises, Damascus or watered-steel

ABOVE: *The Gun Room at Springhill in County Londonderry. Rifles and pistols displayed on the wall are correctly supported at both ends: padding will help to prevent scratching. The swords too are correctly mounted, though beware of light on leather scabbards. Strict regulations are imposed on ammunition, so the barrel is for display purposes only.*

Indo-Persian sword blades and Japanese swords. Each of these is manufactured in different ways, but the pattern is intentionally developed on the metal surface using special techniques, and can be radically altered or completely lost as a result of even mild cleaning attempts (*see* STEEL, p.84).

The conservation of arms and armour is a very specialist subject. Extensive information is required for each object and

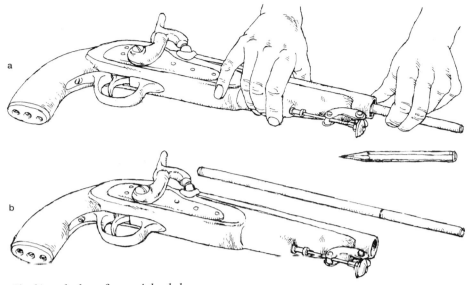

Checking whether a firearm is loaded
(a) *Push a wooden dowel as far as it will go into the barrel, mark the position on the dowel*
(b) *Remove the dowel, place alongside the barrel with the mark by the muzzle. If it reaches the touch-hole/nipple, it is not loaded.*

material, so it is recommended that owners of arms and armour do not attempt to conserve or restore their collection themselves. Only a conservator with a particular interest in this field should treat the objects. The damage that can be done in a very short time is great and irreparable. It is better to leave arms and armour alone than to have them damaged by an inexperienced person.

That said, many people have small collections of weapons that they have acquired over the years, such as muskets and daggers, a sword or two, or simply constructed flintlock or early percussion weapons.

If you acquire an old firearm, it is most important, before you begin any work on it, that you make sure that it is not loaded. Even ancient gunpowder can explode. To find out whether a muzzle-loading firearm is loaded, take a wooden dowel and carefully insert it into the barrel until it will go no further. Mark the position of the end of the muzzle on the dowel with a pencil. Remove the dowel and place it along the outside of the barrel with the pencil mark by the muzzle. If the other end of the dowel does *not* reach the touch-hole or nipple, then the firearm may be loaded. If it does reach the touch-hole or nipple, then the firearm is not loaded. If the gun appears to be loaded, do not attempt to clear it yourself. Take it to a gunsmith.

Problems

The materials used in the construction of firearms are subject to the same processes of deterioration discussed in the appropriate chapters, but the most common problems found in arms, armour and weapons are:
• Wooden stocks of firearms and handles of weapons split, and all wooden parts, such as stocks, shafts and scabbards, can develop active woodworm.
• The blades, barrels and other iron or steel parts of weapons can rust. Patterned blades must be protected from corrosion and kept dry.
• Inlay and other applied decoration may become loose.
• Textiles can be damaged by insects or mould.
• Leather can be dry and cracked or mouldy; it can also be damaged by insects.

Handling

Operating any of the moving parts of an antique firearm can result in serious damage, for instance cocking an antique firearm can break a weak main spring. If it is not your gun, do not do this without first asking the owner's permission and be prepared to be refused. Also, pulling the trigger on a cocked flintlock that has no flint can create enough force to snap the metal.

The salts on your hands will attack the metal surface on arms, armour and firearms, so always wear clean **gloves** when handling a collection. If an object is inadvertently handled without gloves, wipe the surface of the metal with a clean rag moistened with **gun oil** to remove corrosive finger marks. Sometimes cotton gloves can catch on inlay, so vinyl or latex gloves are recommended for such pieces.

Sheathed swords and daggers should be removed from their scabbards carefully while holding them pointing downwards. Scabbards can split and the blade edge may come through, so never hold the scabbard by its edges, as the blade may still be razor sharp. Always hold the scabbard at the top where it meets the hilt.

Arrows and spears in ethnographic collections may retain traces of poison on their tips and must be handled with the utmost care.

Display

There are statutory regulations regarding the security of firearms that can be obtained from your local police station.

Arms and armour need to be kept in conditions that will suit all the materials included in the construction of the object. This means that the **relative humidity** should be as constant as possible and neither too low nor too high (see p.18).

Textured steel blades must be kept dry (below 50% RH), because if they corrode, the pattern may be lost and removing the rust can cause even more damage.

Arms and armour should be protected from dust as much as possible, so avoid displaying them above open fires, radiators or other heat sources (*see* p.18). Outside walls that may be damp can cause corrosion or mould; if you have no other choice, use corks or other spacers to hold the objects away from the wall. Metal fixings used to support arms, armour and firearms should be padded with plastic tubing or **polyethylene foam** so that the object is not in direct contact with the metal to prevent wear, staining and a reaction between the metals. A useful method of displaying guns and spears is to make brackets from wooden dowelling cantilevered into the wall and pointing slightly upwards. Rest the object on two or three brackets, depending on its weight and the strength of the wall. It should be noted that oiled weapons will stain wallpaper and paintwork, so you may want to place some **clear polyester film** between the object and the wall.

Ideally, swords and long firearms should be displayed in a glass-fronted case for security and to help protect them from dust. Stand firearms on their butts on a pad of polyethylene foam with the trigger facing forward. Support the barrels with a rack fixed to the back of the cupboard. The

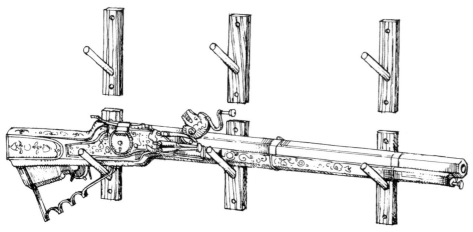

Stand for firearms.

rack can be made from a strip of wood about 2cm (¾in) thick. Cut a line of half moons along the front of the wood. Secure the wood into the cupboard. Cover the edge of the wood strip with chamois leather or polyethylene foam.

Storage

Store arms and armour in a cool, dry, clean, well-ventilated area that is free from pests. Make sure that the conditions are as suitable as possible for all the materials included in the construction of the object.

One way of storing ethnographic weapons is to fix a wooden frame to an inside wall and stretch heavy-duty garden **nylon netting** across it. Attach the weapons horizontally to the net using white cotton tape. Do not use metal wire to attach them as it may corrode. Protect them from dust with a clean **dustsheet**.

Arrows can be kept in shallow drawers. To prevent them from rolling against each other, you can cut two or three strips of **polyethylene foam** about 2cm (¾in) wide

to the width of the drawer. Before placing the strips in the drawer, cut grooves across their width. The distance between the grooves depends on the widest part of each arrow, but there must be enough room to prevent the arrows from touching. Place one strip in the centre of the drawer and the others towards the back and front so that the shaft of the arrow can be supported in three places.

Long firearms, swords and ethnographic weapons can be stored in wooden or steel storage cupboards using wooden racks. A metal cupboard, such as an office stationery cupboard, can be adapted, provided it has adequate ventilation to prevent condensation. The cupboard must stand at least 8cm (3in) away from the wall, particularly an outside wall, to allow the air to circulate round the cupboard. No part of the weapon should touch the metal of the cupboard. The guns can be supported in a rack as described above, using polyethylene foam as padding.

Swords can be supported by their hilts, leaving the blade free. It is advisable not to

store swords in their scabbards, particularly leather scabbards, as they tend to absorb moisture, which will encourage corrosion. Always make sure that a sword and its scabbard are kept together.

Housekeeping and Maintenance

Remove dust with a soft brush, catching the dirt with a vacuum cleaner held in the other hand (*see* pp.19-20). A duster can grind the dust into the surface of the metal and mark it; it may also pull off any inlay or applied decoration.

If there is evidence of active woodworm infestation, this should be treated as for WOOD, but be aware that the solvent in the insecticide may stain or damage textiles and leather.

Oil the lock mechanism of firearms occasionally with a **light machine oil** with rust-inhibiting properties or **gun oil**.

A common method of protecting the iron and steel in arms and armour from rust is by applying a light machine oil or petroleum jelly. The disadvantage of this is that the oil can collect dust and look unsightly. **Microcrystalline wax paste** is now more generally used in museums and historic houses for this purpose, but it is a little more difficult to apply well and to cover the surface completely. Apply the wax evenly with a bristle brush and polish it off with a plate brush or a similar soft brush.

If you prefer to use oil, use a good quality gun oil and apply it very sparingly. Make sure you do not get the oil on the **organic materials**, as it may stain.

Check iron objects at least once a year for corrosion and re-wax or oil as necessary or once a year.

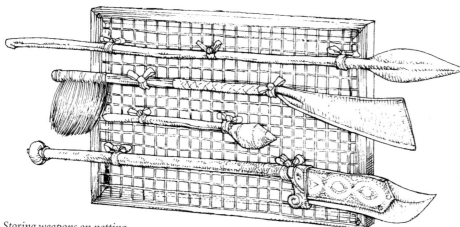

Storing weapons on netting.

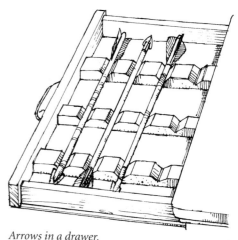

Arrows in a drawer.

ABOVE: *One of a group of Japanese samurai armour collected in the 1940s by Charles Paget Wade, displayed in the Green Room at Snowshill Manor in Gloucestershire. This piece presents a challenge to keep clean, let alone repair, as it contains so many different materials: the antlers are gilded and lacquered, the leather embossed and painted; there are different metals, including brass and copper, and fibres for the moustache. Most vulnerable of all are the textiles, as shown by the fraying tassels.*

Cleaning

Always consult a conservator before attempting any conservation on weapons that may be rare or precious or about which you are unsure.

To clean a firearm thoroughly, it may be necessary to dismantle it. Ideally this should be done by a weapons conservator. The construction of firearms varies, therefore it is not wise to dismantle any weapon unless you are very familiar with the type and know that you will be able to reassemble it. The person who reassembles the weapon must be the person who takes it apart.

When weapons are in bad condition, it is very difficult to recognise the different materials and surface finishes that may have been used in their construction. If you clean in ignorance, you may well lose decoration that is hidden by the corrosion. Therefore, get conservation advice before attempting to clean badly corroded objects.

The pattern on patterned steel blades is easily damaged or lost by inappropriate cleaning and should be cleaned only by an experienced conservator.

Cleaning and treating the individual materials are discussed in the appropriate sections of the book.

Repair

Arms, armour and firearms should not be repaired by an amateur. For fixing small pieces of loose inlay, *see* the relevant section.

Beads

Beads have been made from almost every material, including glass, ceramics, precious and semi-precious stones, seeds, grasses, papier mâché, amber, metals, wood, bone, ivory, pearls, shells, teeth, feathers, porcupine quills, stalactites, marble and plastic. *See* the individual materials for more details on Maintainance, Handling, Cleaning, Display and Storage.

A common problem is that beads often have a sharp edge either around the holes or in the centre of the drill-hole made by drilling through the bead. This eventually cuts through the string. Check the thread regularly to see that it has not frayed.

Do not wash a string of beads by immersing it in water, as the thread will get wet and weaken or possibly shrink. Remove dust with a **brush**. Clean each bead with a cotton bud moistened with saliva or **alcohol**, or a 1:1 mixture of **acetone** and deionised water; *see* the individual material chapters for the appropriate cleaning mixture. Test the cleaning solution to make sure that it does not remove any surface decoration or colour. If it does, try one of the other **solvent mixtures**. Clean about 5cm (2in) of the necklace at a time, then dry it with a soft clean cloth or paper towel, before continuing to clean the next 5cm (2in).

Some beads may be strung on grasses or a similar fibrous material that may not be very strong. Rather than removing the string, which will change the appearance, it can be reinforced or supported by passing nylon thread through the beads. This does not show but will hold the beads if the original string breaks.

Bicycles

Bicycles are made from a mixture of different materials, including metals, wood, rubber and leather. The rubber parts are usually the ones that deteriorate first. This process is difficult to control, but keeping the bicycle out of direct sunlight and in reasonably dry conditions will help. Like all vehicles, it is best to prevent an old or antique bicycle from resting on its tyres. If possible, raise it up using a floor stand, or hang it up by its frame from brackets fixed to the wall or rope suspended from a ceiling. If you have nowhere to suspend it, turn

it upside-down on a sheet of polyethylene or wooden slats and rest it on its handlebars and seat.

If the tyres are rubber, try to keep them inflated. Dust them with talc and keep oil and petrol off them. If the wheels are wooden, check them regularly for woodworm (*see* WOOD). Do not let the wooden wheels stand directly on a brick, concrete or stone floor. Insulate them with cork or wooden slats.

Where the saddle is made of leather, clean it by brushing off as much loose dirt as possible and, if further cleaning is necessary, wipe it gently with a soft cloth moistened with water containing a little **conservation-grade detergent**. Rinse with a soft cloth moistened with clean water. If you feel it needs polishing, apply a little colourless **beeswax polish**. (*See* LEATHER Cleaning.)

Clean the chrome as described in CHROMIUM and lightly wax it with **microcrystalline wax**. Do not get any wax on the rubber tyres as the solvent can damage the rubber.

If the bicycle is very dirty with oily grime, use **white spirit** and a hogshair brush to remove the oil and grit. Take care not to get the solvent on the rubber or leather. Provided the paintwork is in good condition and not flaking off, clean it with a sponge or cloth wrung out in the white spirit:water cleaning mixture (*see* **solvent mixtures**). Again, take care not to let the mixture run on to the rubber. Rinse with clean water. Dry the paintwork with a soft, clean cloth and lightly wax it with microcrystalline wax.

Oil the mechanical parts, including the chain, with **light machine oil**. Regularly check the bicycle for corrosion and clean off any dust with a soft brush. Cover the bicycle with a **dustsheet** when it is in store.

See the appropriate materials section for the care of bicycle accessories such as bells, pumps, baskets and panniers.

Books

The Western-style book, known as the codex book, is comprised of leaves (pages) that have been sewn or glued together and then attached to a cover for protection. The individual leaves or folded sheets that make up the text block can be made of various materials but parchment was

commonly used throughout the Middle Ages. Although paper was available in Europe from the eleventh century, it was not generally used in bound books until the fourteenth century. However, the use of paper became almost universal with the introduction of printing in the mid-fifteenth century, but parchment and, very occasionally exotic materials like silk, remained popular for creating special editions. During the nineteenth century paper-making techniques changed, and rag pulp paper was gradually superseded by less durable paper made from wood pulp with far-reaching consequences for the survival of books produced from this period. The leaves or folded sheets are gathered into sections, sewn together and attached to the boards used to form the protective cover. Not all books are sewn: instead, the pages may be glued together and the cover glued onto the text block. This type of binding is known as a case binding.

The boards used to protect the leaves were originally made from wood but paperboard became a common substitute from the late fifteenth century, and strawboard was introduced in the late nineteenth century for cheaper books. The boards and spine were covered with cloth, parchment or leather. Sheepskin was the cheapest and most common leather but calf and goatskins were also used. Often the spine was covered in one material, usually leather, and another material such as paper or cloth was used on the sides. The leather bindings were decorated in many ways but frequently by blind, silver or gold tooling.

Books from the Far East usually have paper covers. The sheets of paper are often only printed on one side and folded at the fore-edge rather than the spine of the book. Islamic books are usually bound in leather and there is often an additional flap at the fore-edge to protect the text block. The cover is usually flush with the text block.

Problems

Books are vulnerable to the problems caused by inappropriate humidities, temperature, light, insects and chemical deterioration, as discussed in PAPER and LEATHER.

Low humidities below 40% RH cause the materials to become brittle (*see* the appropriate section). High humidities (over about 65%), especially in badly ventilated areas, may lead to mould growth, foxing or insect activity, and speed up the

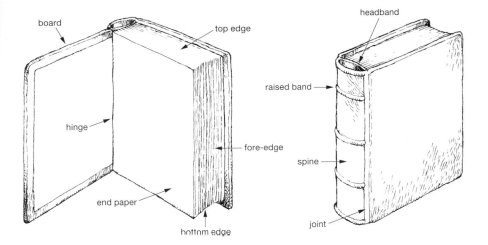

development of acidic compounds, which embrittle the majority of papers dating from the 1860s onwards. As discussed on p.105, the materials from which books are made deteriorate more slowly at lower temperatures.

The damage to books from pests is most commonly caused by:

• Furniture beetle, death-watch beetle and, in tropical countries, termites, which drill through the bindings and pages.
• Carpet beetles and spider beetles, which tend to eat animal glues and bindings made from skin, wool and silk.
• Moth larvae and silverfish, which graze on the surface of materials, such as leather,

bookcloth and paper; silverfish also eat through the pages, leaving them looking lacy and frayed.

Books can also be damaged by rodents, which use the paper for nests; dogs often chew the bindings, cats may use books for scratching posts and snails consume paper.

Light damages binding materials, leaving them bleached, weakened and brittle.

Pollution, generally sulphur and nitrogen compounds in the atmosphere, also weakens and embrittles binding materials, but affects the edges of the text-block as well. This can often be seen as browning around the margin of the pages.

Inappropriate handling can cause damage as the structure of books is surprisingly delicate. Vulnerable areas are corners of boards, which can be torn and delaminate, the spine, which can split along the centre, and the joints. Broken sewing, torn and detached pages, wrongly folded oversize plates and maps, and torn dust-jackets are all common problems. Take care that any loose pages, sections or illustration plates stay with the right book in the correct place.

Structural damage is caused to books where the boards are larger than the text-block, this is the case with the majority of books bound from the fifteenth century onwards, with the exception of modern paperbacks and Islamic books. The text-block sags, causing tremendous strain at the top and bottom of the spine. This distorts the spine and will cause the joints to split so the board will eventually become detached or the text-block will fall out of the case. Albums, folios and thick books are particularly prone to this type of damage and should lie flat rather than stand upright. Conservators can make book-shoes of archival board, which can dramatically reduce the rate of decay (*see* Protection).

Poorly ventilated, warped and overcrowded shelving will cause physical damage.

Dust and dirt, including building dirt, is abrasive and may eventually stain and damage the paper. The top edges of books may become very dusty. Books can also become stained from spillages, greasy hands and ink.

If the binding is made of leather, look out for dry or crumbling leather, which may be caused by wear or red rot (*see* LEATHER).

Leather-bound books in the Library at Dunham Massey in Cheshire. As they bear the cypher of George Booth, 2nd Earl of Warrington, they date from the first half of the eighteenth century. A whole range of problems can arise. The spines are vulnerable to cracking, especially when pulled out of the shelf by fingers (see book on lower, right-hand side). Red rot and insect damage pose constant dangers.

Handling

Remove pens, ink, tea, coffee, flower vases and other potential risks as far away as possible from your books. Ensure that your hands are clean and dry and that you have not used hand cream recently, and remove any rings set with stones. Bindings with matt surfaces, which may include paper, textiles, leather and parchment or vellum, are especially susceptible to staining from dirty hands. If you prefer to wear **gloves**, use tight-fitting vinyl, nitrile or fine rubber latex rather than cotton gloves, which reduce your dexterity and may abrade damaged areas of the bindings. Always wear gloves when handling illuminated vellum or parchment pages or silver bindings. A damaged book should be handled as little as possible.

Do not open a dirty book until the dust and grime have first been removed. *See* Cleaning.

Old, rare, special or large books, or books with damaged bindings should never be opened flat. Support the covers of these books, or those that do not open easily, with blocks or wedges made from **poly-ethylene foam** or another smooth, soft material. If the book is opened near the front, support the front board by placing a block of polyethylene foam underneath it and similarly place a block under the back board if it is opened near the back. Where a book does not open easily, it must not be forced and should be supported on two wedges which will support both the front and the back boards evenly at an angle no greater than 90°.

Books which have folding maps, documents, plates or tables in them need to be handled carefully, as these inserts tear very easily. Open these items as little as possible, and fold them up following the original order and folds.

Never turn down the corner of a page or use low-tack adhesive paper (eg. Post-it Notes) to mark pages; slips of **archival** paper can be used if they are to remain in the book for any length of time.

- **REMOVING A BOOK FROM A SHELF**
Shelves should never be packed so tightly that it is hard to get the books out. If a book is difficult to remove, try not to replace it on the shelf until you can reorganise it so that the books are less tightly packed.

The best way to remove a book from a shelf is to reach to the fore-edge of the book and gently pull the book towards you, provided your hand will fit between the top of the book and the shelf above. If there is no space for your hand, push the books on either side of the book you want further

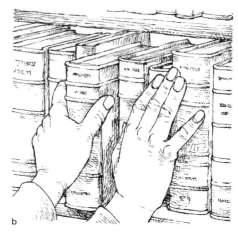

Removing a book from a shelf
(a) *Reach to the fore-edge with one hand, pulling book forwards, while supporting spine with other hand* (b) *If there is little space above the book, push flanking books back, providing a firm grip.*

back into the shelf. This will allow you to get a better grip on the sides of the book you want. Do not pull the book from a shelf by grabbing the top or the sides of the spine, as it will eventually break.

If neither of these methods works, place your fingers 2–3cm (1in) behind the top of the spine, gently press down and draw the book towards you; once there is enough of the spine protruding to hold it safely, change your grip and remove the book.

When removing a large book make sure that you support the weight underneath before you pull the book completely off the shelf.

If the books remaining on the shelf fall over, the boards may be ripped off. Prevent this from happening by placing another book in the gap or by laying a few others flat in a small pile until the removed volumes are replaced. When using a ladder to remove books from high shelves, you will need help from someone to whom you can hand the books and who will steady the ladder.

When replacing a book on a shelf, gently push the books on either side of the gap to the side to make room for it. Take care not to scrape the bottom edge of the book on the shelf by keeping it slightly above the surface.

- **CARRYING BOOKS**
Do not carry too many books at once. Carry them in small piles which will fit within the span of your hand, rather than in a tower held steady by your chin, as the books are likely to fall out from the middle. Try to carry books of the same size together. If you are moving books some distance or up and

down stairs, put them in a box or plastic crate lined with bubble wrap. Lay the books on their side rather than on an edge and do not jam too many into a box at once. Put wedges of **acid-free** tissue paper in to stop the books from sliding about. When packing books in a box, bear in mind their weight. Check that the bottom of the box will not fall out. Plastic crates are stronger and less likely to collapse. Do not put books loose in a car, as a sudden jolt will send them flying.

When carrying large folios, hold the book under your arm with your hands cupping the spine to prevent strain on you and the binding. Some large folios or portfolios may require two people to carry them in safety, particularly if the covering materials or structure have been damaged in any way.

Display

It is important to assess the physical condition of a book before deciding to display it other than on a bookcase, particularly if it is to be shown open. Weaknesses in structure, such as damaged sewing or loose boards, are likely to be exacerbated, which can lead to major damage. If a binding is stiff, do not force it open in order to display a particular page. Books on exhibition should be displayed under the same conditions as paper and leather. The display area must be clean and dry and kept at a steady humidity. The light levels should be as low as possible and ultraviolet filters used where feasible. Keep books away from fan heaters, radiators and electric fires (*see* PAPER and LEATHER).

To display an open book, support the front and back boards on wedges

Display open books under glass to protect them from dust. Use materials that will not be damaging to make the display case (*see* p.19), and ensure it provides adequate ventilation. Consult a conservator for advice.

Support an open book with a cradle made from **archival** board, **polyethylene foam** or **acrylic sheet**. If the book has a tight spine, i.e. the covering material sticks to the back of the pages and flexes with them, the spine as well as the boards should be supported. If the book has a hollow spine – one in which the covering material lifts away from the back of the pages when the book is opened – the book needs to be supported only beneath the boards. Supports are a fraction smaller than the object they are supporting. Only open a book as far as it will open easily and without resistance. This may be only to 90°, or even less.

Whether the book is open or closed, if it is displayed with its spine at an angle to the floor of the display case, text-block supports will be necessary to prevent the pages from sagging.

If an open book is put on display, do not leave it open on one page for more than a few weeks to avoid excessive light exposure, but turn the pages periodically. As the pages are turned, the profile of the book changes and the supports will need to be altered or replaced.

Strap books to their supports using 23 micron tape made from **clear polyester film** or strips of polyethylene 1–5cm (½–2in) wide to ensure that the book is held gently but firmly and that the straps do not cut into the pages. With a neutral pH **adhesive**, stick the straps to themselves in loops around the book, or to the cradle, not to the book itself.

Bookshelves should be strongly constructed and the shelves made from wood or coated metal, with a clean, smooth surface but not necessarily polished. The shelves need to be at least 2cm (¾in) thick and 23cm (9in) deep. They must be deep enough so that books do not stick out beyond the front edge of the shelf. A wooden shelf should not be longer than 76cm (30in) without being supported, otherwise it will sag with the weight of the books. The distance between the shelves depends on the size of the books, but allow for a minimum of 2·5cm (1in) headroom for smaller books, increasing to 10cm (4in) for folios and larger books. If the shelves are adjustable, you can alter the height to suit the books.

The fittings of adjustable shelves may protrude and are frequently the cause of damage to the books on either end of the shelf. If the fittings are not flush with the surface, cut a piece of archival board to the size of the height and depth of the shelf and place it between the end book and the fitting so that the books are not marked or harmed by the metal.

Good ventilation in a bookcase is essential, so leave a gap of 2·5cm (1in) between the back of the shelf and the wall. If the shelf is on an outside wall, this 2·5cm (1in) gap is extremely important. Some permanent shelves are built directly against a wall with no space between them and the wall. In this case, drill holes of 2·5cm (1in) diameter at 10cm (4in) intervals along the back of the shelves for ventilation. Smooth off the cut edges and splinters and remove the debris; you could also consider fixing a thin strip of wood along the shelf in front of the holes to prevent the books from being pushed back, but make sure that the books are not rammed into the strip. Adequate ventilation is particularly important if you keep books in a glass-fronted cabinet.

Built-in shelves often have a backboard. It is important that air can circulate between the wall and the board, particularly on an outside wall.

Although you need enough shelf space so that the books are not too tightly squashed together, the books should not be so loose that they lean over and are unsupported, as this will break the joints. You can always fill any spare space at the end of the shelf with smooth wood blocks or blocks of zero formaldehyde **medium density fibreboard (MDF)**, which provide better support than most book-ends.

Where possible, keep books of the same size together on a shelf. Very large books often have to lie on their side, as they cannot support their own weight, and shelves are often not large enough. Make sure that the whole of the side of the book is supported by the shelf or adjacent volumes, otherwise the book will bend and distort.

Books with metal clasps or bosses must be kept separate from other books, as they will damage them. You can protect these books a little by making a simple folder of **acid-free** card.

Storage

Store books in a clean, dry, well-ventilated and dark area. Do not store books in basements, cellars and outhouses which are damp or in lofts or attics, where the temperature can fluctuate greatly. Steady humidity is preferred for books (40–65% RH). Books with vellum bindings must be kept in very stable conditions (*see* pp.17–18). Help protect the books from insects by keeping the area clean.

Inspect books regularly for mould and mildew, mice and insects (*see* pp.14–16).

Books survive better in bookcases or on shelves than in chests, drawers or boxes. If you have a lot of books to be stored long term, it is worth investing in good shelving.

Books are heavy. If you are storing a large number, ensure that the floor is strong enough to bear their weight.

● **STACKING BOOKS**

If you have to stack books temporarily, keep them flat, not on their fore-edge, as this will damage the spine, the boards and possibly the pages. Keep the piles small and try to keep the same sized books in each pile. If this is not possible, put the smaller books on top of the larger ones. Do not stack books with three-dimensional covers, such as those with studs or metal fixings.

Books from the nineteenth and twentieth centuries often have spines that are thicker than the rest of the book. To make stable stacks of such books, place them alternately spine to fore-edge, allowing the spines to protrude beyond the fore-edges of the books on either side of them. Some early printed books are also wedged-shaped, though in these cases they are usually thicker on the fore-edge than the spine; they, too, should be stacked fore-edge to spine, checking always that the stacks are stable and that books with metal fittings are not stacked. Albums and scrapbooks should never be stacked in piles because of the strain to their bindings and the potential harm that may be done to their contents (*see* PHOTOGRAPH ALBUMS).

Housekeeping and Maintenance

Old, rare, precious and fragile books should be cleaned by a book conservator. However, there is a great deal you can do to keep your books clean and in good condition.

Try to clean books and the bookshelf regularly every year. Take the books off the shelf one at a time. Keep the books closed firmly as you take them off the shelf so that the dust does not get between the pages. When you have removed them all, dust the shelf. Look for silverfish, mould, woodworm and mouse droppings, and rough areas or damage to the shelf, such as splinters.

If the book is not very dusty, gently brush the dust off the top edge and then the other edges with a soft brush, such as a shaving brush, working from spine to fore-edge at the head and tail and keeping it tightly closed. Use a hogshair brush to remove the dust and dirt from near the headband. Some books had scenes painted on the fore-edge that do not show unless the book is slightly fanned out. Make sure you brush these edges gently so as not to cause damage.

Dusting a book.

If the book is very dusty, gently brush the dust into the nozzle of a vacuum cleaner (*see* pp.19–20). Cover the nozzle with a piece of fine **nylon net** to prevent loose pieces of the cover from being sucked up into the cleaner.

Clean the sides of the cover and the spine with a soft brush. If the books are in excellent condition, you may prefer to use a soft, clean duster or a **microfibre cloth**. Take

care not to catch the edges of the book or pull off bits of the binding.

If the pages are slightly cockled, some dust will have penetrated between them. Dust this off with a soft brush page by page and inside the boards, supporting the book on blocks, as described on p.188. Never bang books together to remove the dust.

When cleaning suede bindings, brush them very carefully so that you do not remove any of the suede. Do not use any kind of suede cleaner.

● **LOOSE PIECES**
Spine title labels may fall off or pieces of binding may come off during cleaning. Keep them safe in a good quality envelope, clearly marked with what is inside and from which book it came, until you can get the book to a conservator.

● **DOG-EARS**
Corners of pages are often turned down to mark a page. This harms the paper and lets dirt in. Gently unfold the corner, close the book and leave it closed. There is no need to rub the crease or to press the book. Do not straighten the corner if the paper is very brittle, as the corner could break off; this often applies to books made from the

nineteenth century onwards. If the folded corners seem to indicate the reading habits of an early or famous owner, it may be best to leave them as they are.

Occasionally, the corners were folded down before the edges were trimmed and are now therefore larger than the rest of the leaves. These should never be trimmed, as they show the original size of the sheet the book was printed on; they are left turned in.

● **BOOKMARKS**
Books often have postcards or bookmarks or even pressed flowers in them. These may be part of the book's history and, if so, should be kept with it. If they are making the book too fat and putting extra strain on the binding, put the pieces in a well-marked, good quality white envelope or **clear polyester film** sleeve and keep it somewhere safe. Put a piece of **archival** paper in the book that says where you have put the bits.

● **MOULD**
If a book gets very damp, it may cockle, stain and warp, and mildew and mould are likely to develop. To dry the book, stand it on one end and open it so that the pages are fanned out and separate. Allow the book to

An eighteenth-century book from the Library at Felbrigg Hall in Norfolk, showing the kind of damage that can attack paper: water-staining and holes from insects.

dry in a cool, well-ventilated area. Do not use direct heat, as it will cause even more damage. Once the book has dried, set up a clean table outside on a fine, still day, take the book outside and brush off any powdery mould with a clean hogshair brush or shaving brush. Take care not to spread the mould spores on to other books or objects. Wash and dry the brush after use. Examine all the books that may have been affected. When handling mouldy books, protect yourself from spores with a suitable mask and gloves (*see* p.23).

● INSECTS

If you find insects or evidence of insects in books, take the books outside and carefully brush or vacuum them out. Before returning the books, clean the shelves well and check that there is good air circulation, which will prevent pockets of damp from developing, as insects prefer a damp environment. Improve the air circulation if necessary and eradicate other sources of damp before replacing the books (*see* pp.17–18). If you have a serious infestation in the books you may need to have them treated or frozen (*see* pp.14–15).

Where the shelves have woodworm, remove the books and treat the shelves as described in WOOD. Do not replace the books for at least four weeks.

● POLISHING THE LEATHER

Leather dressing has often been rubbed into leather bindings in the past. This is no longer considered to be good practice, as the dressings can cause considerable harm. Creams or leather preparations should never be used. Books made from vellum or parchment should be cleaned and treated by a book conservator.

Cleaning

If, after dusting, a rare, fragile or valuable book needs further cleaning or repair, it should be done by a book conservator.

Brown spots on the paper from foxing are difficult to remove, so consult a book conservator (*see* PAPER). On no account use domestic bleach or any kind of bleaching agent to remove foxing as is suggested in some books, as they may destroy the ink and paper. Gently brush off any loose dirt or spores.

Coffee, tea, ink, grease, oil and other stains are difficult to remove. It is likely that the stain will be made much worse by attempts to clean it; cleaning may also

weaken the paper or the binding. If the stain really bothers you, take the book to a book conservator.

Pencil marks on the pages and the endpapers inside a book usually add interest and should not necessarily be removed. However, if you want to clean them off, it may be possible, provided that the paper is not coloured and is in good condition. There is a risk of damaging the surface of the pages and, in some instances, of tearing the page. Do not attempt to remove the marks if you have any doubts about the strength of the pages. If there are many marks, seek the advice of a conservator.

Make sure that you have a clean working area and clean hands. If you are going to clean the inside of the book, open the book and place supports under the cover as described on p.188 to prevent any strain on the joints. Use a soft, smooth **pencil eraser** and work gently in circles. If the fibres of the surface of the paper start to lift, stop.

Pencil underlining can sometimes be taken off using an eraser cut into a small point. Work in one direction only and use short, light strokes. Work from the spine towards the edge of the book. Brush out any pieces of eraser. Do not clean over the print; *see* PAPER.

Protection

If the book is fragile, precious, has a limp binding, clasps or ties, or is missing part of its cover, a simple wrapper can be made out of archival **acid-free** card and tied closed with cotton tape.

If the spine and boards of a hardback book are loose, but you do not want to have it conserved for the moment, tie the book

up with two lengths of unbleached cotton tape. Tie the tape in a bow at the fore-edge so that it is easy to undo and does not damage adjacent bindings. Do not hold the book together with rubber bands or string, as they will cause damage. Never tie up a book that has a limp binding or one where the pages protrude beyond the hard covers, because the tapes will cut into them.

Check to see whether the books are beginning to sag (*see* Problems) and if they need a book-shoe. The book-shoe is like a slipcase, without a top and including a text-block support. Consult a book conservator for advice.

Repair

Rare, good quality, old or precious books should be conserved only by a book conservator or binder. Ideally the same applies to all books, as a great deal of damage can be caused by inappropriate repairs and it is all too easy to exacerbate problems unwittingly.

Repairs done at home should only be on books of no value or importance, as it is easy for the process to go wrong without the experience of a book conservator. What must be emphasised is that self-adhesive tape or document repair tape should never be used for minor – or major – repairs, as it is extremely damaging. The adhesive may migrate into the paper and stain it. Instead you will need to make your own adhesive tape, but be aware that repairs may cause staining to the paper, the ink to blur and further physical or chemical damage within the book.

To repair small tears in pages of modern books, use Japanese tissue paper and starch

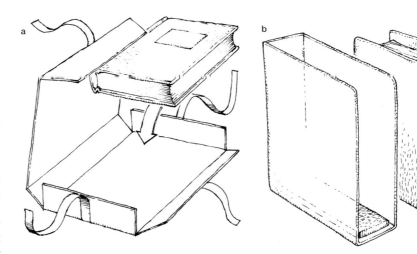

To protect a book, make a wrapper (a) *or a book-shoe* (b).

Some book covers are extremely ornate, such as this binding for a bible now displayed in the Corridor at Killerton in Devon. The cover is made of velvet, decorated with silk, pearls and beads, with a metal clasp and silk marker. Such a piece should be displayed not in a bookshelf, where the binding will be damaged, but ideally in a box. Any conservation work should be undertaken by a trained conservator.

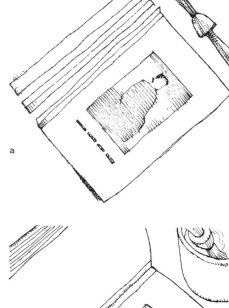

Refixing an illustration
(a) Make a hinge from a narrow strip of tissue, and fold in half (b) Using starch paste, attach hinge to the illustration and to the adjacent page.

paste, as described in PAPER. If you use a thicker paper it will prevent the pages from lying flat. Use wax paper or **silicone paper** underneath the page and on top of the repair to separate it from the other pages. If the book is used a lot, repair both sides of the page. Having repaired the tear, close the book and put another book on top and leave it overnight. When the repair is dry, very carefully peel off the wax or silicone paper; the print should be visible through the remaining tissue.

Sometimes full-page illustrations become loose. They can be replaced in position using a narrow strip of **Japanese tissue paper**. It is important to line the plate up exactly so that it is in the correct position and not protruding from the text-block.

Work on a clean table. To make a hinge, tear a narrow strip of tissue about 1cm (½in) wide and cut it to the same length as the height of the book, i.e. the length of the spine. Fold the strip in half lengthways and put some starch paste on one half of the strip. Lay this half along the inside edge of the plate so that the fold of the hinge will point towards the spine and press down so that it is smooth. Put the plate in position with the inside edge against the hinge. Apply starch paste to the other half of the tissue

and press this on to the adjacent page. Place some folded wax paper the full length of the hinge, close the book and press it for 24 hours with another book or a piece of board with a light weight on top.

Often the plate will stick out slightly further than the other pages. Some books advise you to cut the inside edge of the hinge to make it the right size. If you do this, and then in later years come to have the book rebound, the plate will be too small to be sewn into the book correctly. It will then have to have a piece added. Therefore, it is better not to cut the plate, but the book will need to be handled carefully to prevent the edge of the plate from being damaged.

If any gold lettering or tooling is missing, it should not be replaced with gold paints, as they tarnish very quickly; gold leaf should be used. This is a job best carried out by a bookbinder.

Chandeliers

Chandelier was a French term used to describe candlesticks, wall lights and sconces, as well as a light-fittings suspended from the ceiling. We now mostly use the term for a ceiling-suspended glass light-fitting, although some glass lamps and candlesticks with lustres may have a similar construction. For information on wood, gilded wood, metal and ceramic examples, *see* the appropriate materials sections.

Chandeliers may appear to be made almost entirely of glass, but are, in fact, held together by concealed metal elements. More metal was used in the construction of later chandeliers, but they were dressed with a much larger number of cut-glass lustres – perhaps as many as one thousand.

Eighteenth-century chandeliers were constructed with a central metal rod encased in glass pieces to which the branches of the candle arms were attached at the receiver plate. The dressings or lustres consisted of cut-glass pear drops, buttons and festoons connected by silvered brass pins and hooks to the branches, canopies and pans, the trays beneath the candle holders. Table candelabra were similarly constructed.

Later Regency chandeliers had a hollow, tent-like construction with a circular 'waterfall' of chains of cut-glass buttons and icicle pendants hanging from concentric brass rings, to which metal candle sconces were directly attached. Nineteenth-

ABOVE: *Detail of the rococo carved and gilt chimney mirror in the Drawing Room at Fenton House in Hampstead, London. The early nineteenth-century chandelier of five lights has a brass corona hung with rows of prismatic icicle drops and bands of cut-glass prisms. The pair of candlesticks on the mantelpiece are English, late eighteenth century, of cut glass with bulb-shaped holders over a glass collar and ear-shaped pendants. Also on the mantelpiece is a pair of cut-glass confitures, English, dating from the early nineteenth century.*

century French chandeliers had a more complex and ornate central metal framework with integral candle branches, heavily dressed with large, flat cut-glass pear-shaped drops and circular glass balls.

The metal chain and ceiling fixing may be covered with a textile sleeve and tassels.

Many chandeliers have been converted from candle power or gas to electricity, so there may be an interesting array of wiring, often without adequate insulation or earth connections.

Problems

The main chain, safety hauser and ceiling fixings may become weak or corroded. The electric wiring may be unsafe and need replacing. The hooks holding glass elements may open, and screw fittings can loosen.

Glass elements become chipped, cracked or broken. The glass candle tubes and arms break while light bulbs are being changed. The lustres may be incorrectly arranged or missing. The tiny holes in glass drops or lustres split, and the metal linking pins become weak, corroded, tarnished or broken.

Chandeliers quickly lose their sparkle if they are allowed to become dirty, but they are time-consuming and difficult to keep clean.

Handling

Chandeliers often need to remain hanging for repair and maintenance, so it is advisable to install a rise-and-fall mechanism to facilitate the work. A portable tower scaffold also provides safe access, but requires two people to assemble and move.

When replacing light bulbs or candles, support the pan and branch with one hand underneath to counteract the pressure you are applying to the bulb with the other

Replacing a bulb in a chandelier, support the pan and branch with one hand and insert the bulb with the other.

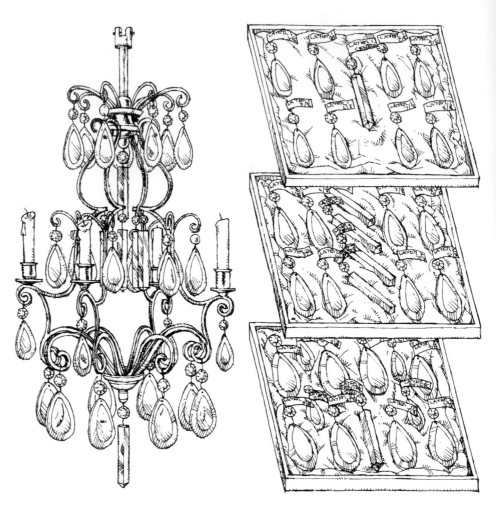

When dismantling a chandelier, label each piece, indicating what belongs to which tier.

hand. Where possible, it is safer to replace bayonet bulb holders with screw fittings as they require less force to insert and remove bulbs.

It is very difficult to dismantle, clean, pack or move large chandeliers, so always call in a specialist firm to do this work. Before dismantling a chandelier, take black-and-white photographs to record the construction and dressings. These usually show glass better than colour photographs.

Turn the power off before starting work on a small chandelier. It takes two people to dismantle a chandelier: one on the scaffold to remove the parts and hand them down to the other on the ground, who labels and packs them. However large or small the chandelier or candelabra, it is a good idea to identify each lustre or chain with a tie-on label written in waterproof ink, so it can be correctly replaced. The manufacturer may have engraved the receiver plate and the branches with letters to help with its assembly. You can devise a simple code with letters and numbers to identify each vertical

tier and each horizontal position around the circumference of the chandelier. Attach some labels to the branches and a few key points, such as the receiver plate, if there are no manufacturers' marks.

Always turn a chandelier from left to right to ensure that the centre stem does not become unscrewed while it is being rotated. The lustres usually unhook very easily. Support each branch while you unhook the drops. Lay them in boxes or shallow plastic trays lined with **acid-free** tissue padding, keeping the parts from each branch together.

Follow a similar procedure if you are moving objects with only a few lustres, such as candlesticks.

Display

Chandeliers are very heavy, so they must be firmly attached to a structure that can take the weight, using special fixings installed above the ceiling. Where possible, install a rise-and-fall mechanism with a limiting

Nineteenth-century chandelier of Venetian glass in the South Gallery at Lacock Abbey in Wiltshire. An area of missing glass can be seen in the top right corner, and one branch has broken. Originally designed for candles, it is now wired for electricity.

device to hold the chandelier about 50cm (1¾ft) above the floor.

Storage

A chandelier hanging in a room that is not being used can be kept clean by covering it with a **Tyvek**, muslin or calico bag, or one made from an old, clean sheet. Disconnect the power to prevent any risk of fire: it may be necessary to have an on/off switch inserted into the leads if there is no other way to disconnect the power.

A small chandelier can be stored hanging from a specially constructed wooden tripod frame.

A large chandelier will need to be dismantled, with all its parts individually labelled and carefully packed together padded with **acid-free** tissue. Include plenty of diagrams and photographs to indicate the method of assembly, which is easily forgotten.

Housekeeping and Maintenance

Every ten years ask a specialist to check the safety of the main chain, safety hauser, fixings and electrical wiring of a chandelier.

Every time the chandelier is cleaned, check the safety of the fixings and electrical wiring. Also inspect the glass elements and metal pins for damage or weakness. Turn off the power at the mains before you begin.

Simple dusting can be carried out from a ladder or a tower scaffold. The scaffold should be erected by a scaffolder or someone trained in the safety of scaffolding. Use a large, soft ponyhair brush to remove the dust. Hold the lustres steady and polish them with a dry or damp **microfibre cloth**. Always rotate the chandelier from left to right to prevent the stem from becoming unscrewed. You may need to secure the chandelier to the scaffolding tower to prevent it from swinging, but make sure that this does not make the scaffolding unsafe.

Cleaning

First remove the light bulbs, candle tubes, lustres and chains as described above, and label them carefully. Wash the lustres in warm water and a few drops of a **conservation-grade detergent** or a mild household detergent. A little isopropanol **alcohol** in the washing mixture may help to revive the sparkle of very dirty glass. Rinse in warm water and drain on a tea-towel or paper towel. Make sure that the lustres are dry,

particularly the hooks, as they corrode easily. If necessary, use a hairdryer on *Cool* to dry the hooks. Polish the lustres with a soft, lint-free cloth.

Clean the structural glass with cotton buds barely moistened with the same cleaning mixture and rinse with clean swabs dampened with clean water. Do not let water run behind the glass on to the metal elements. Dry well.

To clean the structural elements made of other materials, such as metal, *see* the appropriate section.

Repair

There are conservators and specialist firms who are very experienced at cleaning and repairing chandeliers. If you have a rare, valuable or badly damaged chandelier, you should seek professional advice.

Regularly check the condition of the metal hooks and pins, and replace them if necessary. Close open hooks by squeezing the wire gently with fine tapered or needle-nosed pliers. Poorly repaired or corroded hooks should be replaced.

Always use linking pins or silvered wires specially manufactured for the purpose. Soft brass linking pins have sufficient strength to support the lustres and pendants, and yet can be bent easily in different ways, according to the period and style of the chandelier. Consult a specialist restorer, and do not be tempted to use iron wire or common pins that may cause the lustres to split. For long vertical chains of lustres, ask a specialist chandelier restorer to fuse the ends of the pins together so that they do not stretch and open, causing the chains to fall.

Glass is a difficult material to stick together, so if you have broken lustres, consult a glass conservator (*see* GLASS). If a glass branch or other load-bearing part is broken, it may be necessary to have a new piece of glass blown and cut by a specialist firm. Sometimes a cracked glass branch can be strengthened by covering it with a silver-plated metal tube held in place with plaster of Paris; a chandelier restorer can do this for you.

The metal parts of chandeliers were usually lacquered to prevent them from tarnishing. If the lacquer coating is damaged or wears thin, the metal will corrode. Sometimes the lacquer was tinted to make brass or silver resemble gold, so ask a metalwork conservator to reapply the appropriate tinted lacquer.

Clocks and Watches

No one knows when the first mechanical clock was made, but by the end of the thirteenth century, large iron clocks, made by blacksmiths, could be found in monasteries in central Europe. They had no dial or hands, but would strike a small bell at appropriate times to summon the monks to prayer. Domestic versions of clocks were soon developed and portable house clocks appeared with the invention of the mainspring as a driving force in the mid-fifteenth century.

Early mechanical clocks were driven either by a weight or a spring and were poor timekeepers: at the end of a day's running they could be inaccurate by at least 20 minutes. However, when the pendulum was developed as a timekeeping element in 1656, clocks became capable of telling the time to within a few seconds a day. By 1500, mechanisms small enough to be worn round the neck, called watches, were being made in southern Germany and were soon made in centres in France and Flanders and, by 1600, in England.

Clocks were used by astronomers to track the stars and planets, and accurate timekeeping was very essential for the safe navigation of ships. John Harrison's

ABOVE: *Three eight-day musical clocks from Sir Francis Legh's collection displayed in various rooms at Lyme Park in Cheshire. The clock on the left, by John Berry of London, c.1735, can present problems because so many different materials have been used. The centre clock is by John Taylar of London, c.1790, with mahogany case, pagoda top and brass finials. The clock on the right by Nathaniel Barnes of London, c.1760 is in rococo style with tortoiseshell veneered case.*

Owners of clock collections have to decide whether to keep their collections running.

groundbreaking work on precision timekeeping in the mid-eighteenth century saw the beginning of the modern mechanical clock and watch.

Early electric clocks, in which the mechanical movement was driven by electricity instead of weights and springs, began to be made from 1840. Electronic clocks have now superseded mechanical clocks. They are controlled by a vibrating quartz crystal. In the 1970s these were reduced in size to make very small clocks.

The simplest clocks tell the approximate time with only one hand, but more complex clocks give the time in hours, minutes and seconds, as well as the day, season, year, month, phase of the moon and position of the stars and the sun.

The movements of clocks are usually made from brass and steel, but can include wood, silk and other materials. The movement usually has four parts or sections:
• The frame, usually a pair of plates known as the front plate and the back plate, holds the whole mechanism together and is the structure in which the moving parts run.
• There has to be a source of energy to drive the mechanism. This power usually comes from a clock weight hanging on a line or chain, or a coiled-up spring, known as a main-spring.
• The train is the series of wheels which transmits the drive and enables the hands to show the time correctly. The 'going train' tells the time and, in clocks that strike the hour, the 'striking train' enables the hour to be struck on a bell or gong; there may also be a 'chiming train' if the clock chimes the quarters.
• The wheels have to be controlled or regulated so that the hands move evenly and accurately. The escapement and controller perform this task. The escapement allows the train of wheels to 'escape' tooth by tooth and this is regulated by the controller, usually either a swinging pendulum or a balance wheel. The escapement is connected to the pendulum by the crutch. The end of the crutch is either in the form of a fork through which the pendulum rod fits, or a pin that runs in a slot in the pendulum rod. The crutch has to be adjusted to ensure that the clock has an even beat.

A clock case can be made of almost any materials, including wood, marble, glass, alabaster, ceramic, tortoiseshell, metal and plastic, and may be very ornate or merely functional. The purpose of the case is to protect the movement from dust and dirt, but it is also decorative. Cases are generally cared for in the same way as a piece of furniture or an object made from the same material. Refer to the relevant section for information on checking the condition of a clock case.

Watch movements are also made from brass and steel and often include small jewels, such as rubies as bearings. The cases are usually made from metal or metal alloys, particularly silver and silver gilt, although copper and copper alloys or gold are used too. The cases can also be made of enamelled metal, plastic and shagreen.

The mechanisms of watches are very similar to clocks, the main difference being that they must have a movement that will run whichever way up the watch is, so watches are never regulated by a pendulum, always by a balance wheel.

Problems

Mechanical clocks and watches, even large ones, contain sensitive mechanisms that can be easily damaged by neglect or by mishandling.

When an antique clock or watch is used for its original purpose, the mechanism becomes worn and is exposed to deterioration and risk of damage from regular winding, stopping, setting, starting and adjusting. The dismantling and cleaning activities of conservators during the necessary overhauls also cause wear. For this reason, it is sometimes recommended that antique watches, in particular, are not used but enjoyed as static antiquities. Clocks in collections are often not run so that the movement is preserved, but this is not always desirable at home.

Because the mechanisms are complex, there are a large number of potential problems that might be encountered in a clock. Frequently, the problems are not major and can be avoided if the clock is set up properly to ensure reliable and safe operation. Electrical, as well as mechanical failure can cause problems in electric clocks and they require a specialist electric clock conservator's attention.

The movement may be dusty, corroded or have parts missing. Most problems with the movement are due to a breakdown in the lubrication. Keeping the clock in appropriate conditions, where it is not too hot, dusty or damp will prevent early deterioration of the clock's oil (*see* Display).

The clock may no longer run properly or accurately. To be accurate, the clock must run 'in beat', i.e. the tick and the tock should be even. Check that the clock keeps good time and make sure that it strikes properly and at the correct time.

Many nineteenth-century mantel clocks, particularly those made in France, were originally intended to be displayed standing on a gilt or ebonised wooden base under a glass dome. Often the dome is missing and the clock has no protection from dust and handling. French clocks without doors at the back were almost always intended to have such a dome; if it is now missing, it should be replaced. Early electric clocks and skeleton clocks were also frequently protected with a glass dome that should also be replaced if it is missing. Replacements are available from specialist suppliers.

Clock and watch mechanisms are very delicate and easily damaged, so if in doubt, seek the advice of a professional horological conservator.

Handling

Clocks should be moved only when absolutely necessary. The whole mechanism can be disturbed and sometimes never runs as well again. Antique watches are particularly fragile and should be handled with the greatest of care.

It is advisable to wear protective **gloves** when handling or winding clocks and watches to avoid leaving fingerprints on the case of the clock or metal parts.

Clock cases often have handles, but these are more for ornamentation than practical use, so never use them for lifting a clock. Carry the clock by supporting it from underneath.

Where the clock, such as a carriage clock, has a platform escapement with a balance wheel, it can usually be moved safely without special preparation, but carry it carefully.

● **PENDULUM-CONTROLLED CLOCKS**
A pendulum-controlled clock should have the pendulum secured or removed before a major move so that it does not swing when the clock is carried.

When a spring-driven mantel or table clock is being moved a short distance, say, from one side of the room to the other, lift the clock under its base and, with the dial against your front, tilt the clock towards you so that the pendulum rests against the back of the movement. For longer distances, the pendulum must be secured.

Some clocks have pendulums which cannot be removed but have a built-in securing device. Seventeenth- and eighteenth-century English table clocks may have a short 'bob' pendulum, which must

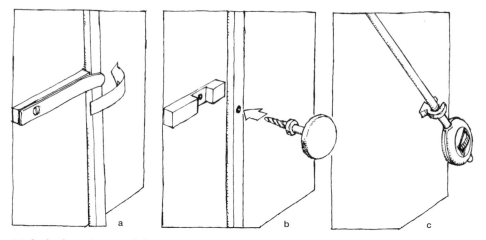

Methods of securing a pendulum
(a) *A clip* (b) *A screw-down knob with back plate* (c) *A hook.*

be gently moved across to one side and placed in a hook provided for the purpose. Later clocks have a clip or screw-down knob to fix the pendulum in place. The latter type has a separate knob which is normally stored in one of the case brackets but can be unscrewed and fixed over the pendulum for safe transporting. If this is missing, then the pendulum must be removed by lifting it up off its support and taking it out backwards. Be very careful to protect the vulnerable suspension spring at the top of the pendulum rod during removal and storage. If possible, tie the pendulum to a wooden splint, at least as long as the pendulum, using cotton tape to keep the rod and suspension spring safe from damage.

French clocks have a different system, in which the pendulum unhooks by lifting the pendulum up and off, but leaving the suspension safely behind in the clock. With most French clocks and some other clocks, you have to remove the bell in the back of the movement before you can get to the pendulum. Unscrew the securing nut that holds the bell in place, taking care not to let the bell or nut drop inside the case, as it can be difficult to rescue. Remove the pendulum and replace the bell and nut on the movement.

The clock may run fast or 'trip' if it is not run down when the pendulum is taken off. This will not do any harm, although it may sound alarming, as a striking clock will strike very often. You can wait for the clock to run down completely or you can wedge the crutch through which the pendulum fits by placing card between the crutch and the backplate to stop the tripping. If you do this, ensure the card is not touching any of the sinks on the backplate which contain oil, as the card may absorb the oil and make the clock run dry when it is set up again.

● **WEIGHT-DRIVEN CLOCKS**
Weight-driven clocks such as longcase, lantern, cuckoo and tavern clocks must have the weights, and where appropriate the pendulum, removed before being moved. Allow these clocks to run down completely before moving them. In the case of longcase clocks, and many wall clocks, the movement must be removed from the case as well.

The movement of a longcase clock and a wall clock is covered with a hood. This is the part of the clock with the glass door in front of the dial. The hood will have to be removed to reach the movement. The hood is usually held on by a swivelling catch or vertical bolt that is found up inside the tank below the bottom of the hood. The hood usually slides forward but, on some very rare early pendulum clocks, it is lifted up.

Next, unhook the weights from their pulleys. If there is more than one weight in the clock, use tie-on labels to identify which line, rope, or chain they come from. Generally the heavier weight is on the striking side, which is usually the left.

Hold the movement steady with one hand or, even better, get someone else to support the dial for you. Carefully lift the pendulum off the suspension block by lifting it up and then gently push the top of the suspension back, towards the wall. Lower the pendulum gently so that the thin suspension spring can slide through the crutch. Make sure you do not damage the delicate suspension spring. Protect the pendulum by tying it to a long wooden splint with cotton tape.

The movement, with its dial, sits on the seat board, which straddles the top of the case and forms the platform for the movement. The movement is held in place by the sheer weight of the pendulum and weights. Once these have been removed, it can easily topple off the seat board and crash to the floor, hence the need for two people to dismantle a clock.

Lift the movement, dial and seat board off the top and carefully feed the lines out of the case and wrap them neatly around the seat board. A 30-hour longcase clock movement is not usually fixed to the seat board, but lifts straight out, leaving the seat board behind. If an eight-day longcase clock has the seat board fixed down, then the lines will have to be cut and for this it will be necessary to call in a conservator.

Many English wall clocks, eg. a hooded wall clock or lantern clock, are like their 30-hour longcase equivalents and can be treated similarly. Tavern clocks are the same, except that once the weight and pendulum have been removed, the movement does not need to be taken out. With English dial ('school-room') clocks, the pendulum has to be taken off by reaching through the access doors on the side and/or bottom of the case, and it is then safe to move.

Place the movement upright in a deep, strong cardboard or wooden box well padded with **acid-free** tissue or **polyethylene foam**. Make sure that the movement is firmly held in the box. Protect the dial with acid-free tissue paper and ensure that the movement does not lean forward on to it. Cover the movement with acid-free tissue to protect it from dust. Keep the weight lines wrapped around the seat board or coiled up so that they do not get tangled with each other or the movement.

Carry the weights and pendulum separately. If you are moving more than one clock, label the weights and pendulum to identify which clock they come from.

Some elaborate clocks have moving figures; wedge these carefully with acid-free tissue so that they will not move.

Once you have taken these precautions, move the case as you would a piece of furniture or other object.

● **SETTING UP CLOCKS**
Weight- and spring-driven clocks are both set up in the same way. This is a job that should be done by two people and is the reverse of the process for dismantling and moving.

Place the clock case so that it is vertical

and not tilting backwards, forwards or to one side. Longcase clocks should be fixed to a wall, preferably using existing holes in the backboard of the case rather than drilling new ones. The clock will be most secure if the fixings are positioned both towards the top and base of the case.

Pass the lines, rope or chains into the trunk or through the hole in the seat board and set the movement in position. Make sure it is centred in the case and that the crutch does not touch the back of the case. Where necessary, re-screw or secure the seat board with its fastenings. While a second person is holding the movement, make sure that the weight line runs properly in the groove in the pulley. Replace the weights on the pulley. Do not worry if the movement trips or runs faster than usual. Carefully replace the pendulum by passing the suspension spring up through the crutch and sliding it forward through the slot in the suspension block. Lower the pendulum until the upper part of the suspension spring sits on the block and the pendulum is secure.

● WATCHES

When packing a collection of watches for moving, wrap them well in acid-free tissue. Label any keys and chains and pack them carefully with the watch. Make a list of what is in each box so that when you unpack them nothing gets left in the wrapping. Do not leave watches packed for long, particularly if you have used bubble wrap for the packing, as the packing can hinder ventilation and cause the steel in the watches to rust.

Display

Place clocks where they are not likely to be moved, as both large and small clocks are delicate and easily damaged or put out of adjustment.

All clocks should be on a stable base that does not move with the floorboards as people walk past. Weight-driven clocks and longcase clocks should be on a firm base and fixed securely to the wall. Spring-driven mantel and table clocks also need a stable support, such as a sideboard, rather than a delicate table. A chimneypiece over a seldom-used fire can provide a firm and secure site.

Clocks and watches should be placed where there are not extreme or frequent changes of temperature and humidity (*see* pp.17–18), and where they will be free from

Longcase clock by Thomas Tompion, 1685, in the Chapel Parlour at The Vyne, Hampshire. The case is showing signs of wear, with light fading the wood on the left-hand side. Clocks on wooden floors can be vulnerable to vibration.

dust. Do not place clocks and watches in direct sunlight, and avoid window sills, radiator shelves, mantelpieces of used open fires and places near heating vents. The wood or other materials of the clock case may need different conditions from the metal of the movement, so compromise by not letting the clock get too damp or too dry.

Watches should always be displayed behind glass to protect them from dust and for security. Display table cases, as long as they are solidly fixed, are a very effective way of exhibiting a collection of watches.

Storage

Store clocks and watches in a cool, clean, dry, dust-free area. Keep the parts wrapped in **acid-free** tissue to keep off dust (*see also* METALS and WOOD).

Any loose parts of clocks, such as weights, pendulums, keys and pieces of moulding should be kept with the clock or, if boxed separately, clearly labelled or bagged to indicate which clock they came from.

Remove batteries from electric clocks before storing them. Keep the batteries in a sealed plastic bag and label them to identify the clock from which they came and the

Housekeeping and Maintenance

Dust can be removed from coins and medals with a soft brush or lint-free cloth. Use a silver **metal polishing cloth** to maintain the polish on silver medals.

Cleaning

The **patina** and the surface of the coin are very important to collectors and the value of a coin or medal can be greatly reduced if it has been badly cleaned. Never try to remove any corrosion and do not clean, polish or use abrasives on coins or medals. Remove any dust with a soft **brush**.

If you are fortunate enough to unearth a few coins in the garden, do not attempt to clean off the corrosion. The coins may appear to be in good condition, but they are probably made only of corrosion products, without any metal left. Once you start to clean them, they may fall apart or the surface detail may be lost and the information can never be retrieved again. Some books recommend dipping coins in acid, lemon juice or vinegar to remove corrosion; you could ruin or lose the whole coin or collection if you do this.

Modern silver medals should be polished as little as possible to prevent the inscription and design from wearing away. Use **Silver Foam** to clean a tarnished medal. Seek advice from a conservator, who should be able to assess the condition of the coins or medals and recommend treatments. Important coins should be cleaned by a conservator.

When a coin is made into jewellery, the value of the coin is reduced. These coins can be polished with the appropriate metal cleaner.

RIGHT: *The kitchen in the Fenman's Cottage at Wicken Fen in Cambridgeshire, furnished as in the 1930s. The domestic equipment shown here is made from a range of materials that influence the way the pieces are conserved. The mangle has wooden rollers, and ironwork that has been oiled and greased or painted to protect it from rust. There is some evidence of rust, but it is a good idea to retain as much of the original paint as possible. The enamel bread bin is chipped, showing rust from the underlying iron. The black cooking pots would have originally been black-leaded.*

Domestic Equipment

Antique domestic equipment such as kitchen utensils, picnic sets, washing equipment, vacuum cleaners, spits, radios, prams and sewing machines can be made from most materials. Glass and ceramics were used for rolling pins, moulds, bowls, bottles, and containers; tinned copper for moulds and pans; wood for spoons, rolling pins and chopping boards; iron and steel for spits, knives, pans and washing equipment; enamelled iron for bread and flour bins and other containers, as well as signs and advertisements; aluminium for pans; plastics and rubber in electrical equipment. Many pieces of equipment were made from more than one material: for example, wood and metal, or wood and ceramics. For instance, a pram might have metal wheels with rubber tyres, a painted wood or metal carcass, and metal fittings with a textile hood and pram lining. A treadle sewing machine might be constructed of metal parts but fitted in a wooden table-top. There may also be surviving paper labels or card packaging.

Problems

Physical damage often occurs from previous use. Some parts, such as electrical wiring, rubber and textile finishes, deteriorate readily, but the metal, ceramics and glass can be quite robust. The common problems are insects in wood, metal corrosion, damaged varnish or paint and deteriorating plastic. *See* the appropriate section on each material.

Handling

Even though some of these objects were originally made for daily use, they should be handled with the same care as other antiques as they are just as vulnerable to damage. Wear **gloves** when handling metal objects or objects with metal parts. Plastic can be as brittle as glass or ceramics, so should be well protected if being moved.

Display

Objects displayed in a kitchen will become dirty quite quickly and very often a film of grease is deposited on the surface. These items must be cleaned regularly to prevent a build-up of dirt that becomes harder to remove in time. Where possible, keep objects away from the cooking area. Plastic and rubber as well as textiles and other **organic materials** are vulnerable to light damage and so should not be placed in a window or in direct sunlight. *See* the appropriate section on each material.

Storage

Protect the objects from dust by covering them with clean **dustsheets** or tissue paper or by storing in boxes. Support soft items such as bags or baskets with **acid-free** tissue so that they can keep their shape. The hoods of prams are best stored up to reduce deterioration along the creases. Check regularly for insect infestation in organic materials such as vacuum cleaner bags or pram interiors, and for corroding metal. Make sure that objects do not lean against each other.

Housekeeping and Maintenance

Remove dust with a soft brush and vacuum cleaner or use a dry **microfibre cloth** on smooth surfaces in good condition.

Lubrication of working parts should be

ABOVE: *Early twentieth-century kitchen equipment at Wightwick Manor, West Midlands, shows a wide range of materials. The coffee roaster, of painted metal, has a ceramic handle. The Pasteur water softener is stoneware. The knife, with a bone handle, is ready to be sharpened in the knife sharpener of wood and cast iron. The glass piece on the right is a cockroach trap, with beer to entice. The wooden roller is constructed to make pie tops. The churn for ice-cream is of wood with a zinc alloy, the moulds are of pewter. The mysterious object on the left is possibly a sausage stuffer. In their day, all these were very ordinary objects, but now highly collectable.*

carried out with care as excess lubricant may attract dust and grit, and lubricant running over a surface can damage paint or varnish. A machine may not run well and parts will wear quickly if inappropriate parts are lubricated. Where possible, get advice from a conservator or knowledgeable collector. Use an appropriate lubricant, such as a light sewing machine oil, rather than spray oils.

Cleaning

Cleaning objects made from a mixture of materials can be difficult as each material may require a different treatment. *See* the appropriate section for information on each material, and make sure that cleaning fluid does not run from one material to another. For example, when polishing a metal fitting on a pram, protect any paint from the metal cleaner. Cleaning fluids should not be allowed to run inside electrical equipment or into the mechanism of a sewing machine or similar.

Repair

See the section on the appropriate material. Repairs to domestic machinery or electrical equipment should be carried out by an experienced person. In order to keep some objects running, it may be necessary to replace some parts; this may change the nature and value of the object, and should only be carried out if you are not concerned about the authenticity of the object.

Fans

The Chinese are thought to have developed the first folding fan. Before then fans were usually paddle-shaped and attached to the end of a stick. This paddle type of fan is still used in many countries.

By the early seventeenth century, folding fans were becoming very popular and developed from being a small arc to a full semi-circle with supporting sticks made of tortoiseshell, ivory or mother-of-pearl, among other materials. The finest fans were made of silk, lace, paper or ostrich feathers and were sometimes encrusted with jewels, gold and silver. They could be painted or embroidered. Simpler fans were made with bamboo, wood, bone or plastic sticks and fairly simple coverings of paper or fabric.

Chinese export fans and some early eighteenth-century French lacquered fans were made from sticks, often ivory or bone, with silk ribbon threaded through the outer edge of the sticks to control the spread.

Problems

The most common problems seen in fans are: cracked or broken sticks; weak ribbon, which, when it disintegrates, will let the fan over-extend; and cracked and split material where it folds. Other problems are associated with the types of material used in the construction of the fan. The spindle, which holds the base of the sticks together, may break or work loose and leave the sticks to hang free.

Handling

The opening and closing of a fan puts a strain on the fabric and wears it out, so fans of any age or value should be opened and closed as little as possible.

The sticks are often very fragile and easy to snap but difficult to mend.

Display

For general conditions for display, refer to the section on the appropriate material.

Fans are usually displayed open, but when a fan is lying open it does not lie flat – one side is higher than the other. The fan should therefore be supported or it will eventually distort as strain is put on the unsupported sticks. **Polyethylene foam** or layers of **acid-free** card can be cut to provide a sloped support.

Ideally, fans should be mounted and displayed in a case or framed to protect them

from dust. This should be done by a textile or paper conservator. As fans are three-dimensional, they will need a box frame which should be made by a frame-maker.

Storage

If you have the space, fans can be stored open as this allows the folds to relax and helps prevent the material splitting. A storage support can be made by padding a piece of **museum board** or **polypropylene twinwall board** with **acid-free** tissue paper, polyester wadding or **polyethylene foam**. If you have more than one fan, they can be stacked on top of each other by sticking some equal-sized polyethylene foam blocks to the corners of each board. Double-sided self-adhesive tape can be used to stick the blocks to the board. These blocks will separate the boards and they can then be stacked in a drawer. However, it is preferable to store each fan in its own archival box to make handling easier and reduce any risk of damage from handling.

If the fan cannot be stored open, wrap it in acid-free tissue paper and store in an acid free box.

Housekeeping and Maintenance

See TEXTILES.

Cleaning

Fans made of textiles are difficult to clean, particularly if they have painted decoration, as the paint may easily be removed. Provided the material is strong enough,

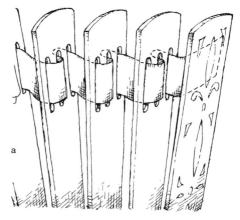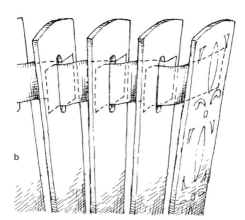

Threading fans
(a) *Where the sticks have three slits, one long piece of ribbon is threaded in and out of each slit*
(b) *Where the sticks have one slit, small lengths of ribbon are required to fix one stick to the next, plus two to fix to the guards.*

loose dust and dirt can be brushed off with a soft brush using a vacuum to catch the dust (*see* pp.19–20). **Compressed air** may also be useful to blow off dirt, but do not use this on a worn or weak textile, as it will blow a hole through the cloth. You could try to remove more tenacious dirt by very gently stroking the surface with a **chemical sponge**, but stop immediately if it is damaging the material. Rare, old and valuable fans should be cleaned only by a conservator.

Refer to the section on the relevant material for advice on cleaning feathers, paper, lace and other materials used to make fans and the guards.

Repair

Old, rare and precious fans should be repaired only by a conservator.

The spread of the top of the sticks of some fans is controlled with a ribbon. If the ribbon is weak or missing, it can be replaced. The ribbon must be made from silk and should be thin and narrow, and fit easily through the slots. Ribbons supplied in haberdashery shops are not suitable for using with fans as they are too thick and often have a thicker edge or selvage which will cause the fan sticks to distort. The correct type of ribbon should be flat from edge to edge and may be obtained from suppliers of dolls' clothes or doll repairers.

There are two different ways of threading fans. The sticks have either one or three slits. Where the sticks have three slits, the ribbon is continuous. Open the fan and measure a piece of ribbon longer than the outside circumference of the fan. The length of the ribbon is taken up by weaving in and out of the slots. It is important to get the length right, so cut it too long rather than too short; you can always cut off the excess.

Glue one end of the ribbon to the inside of the right-hand guard with an easily reversible **adhesive**. The guards are the sticks at either end that form the top and bottom of the fan when it is closed. Snip the other end into a point. On the first stick, thread the ribbon from the front to the back through the first slit, back through the second slit and then back again through the third. Pass the ribbon through the slits in the next stick in the same away, starting from front to back. Make sure that the first stick just overlaps the second stick as you pull the ribbon taut. Continue through all the sticks in the same way. Before sticking the ribbon to the left-hand guard, check that the fan will open and close and that all the sticks are overlapping each other evenly. You may have to adjust the ribbon slightly.

If the sticks have only one slit, rethreading them is slightly more complicated. You will need two more small lengths of ribbon than there are sticks, i.e. if there are eight sticks, you will need ten pieces of ribbon.

ABOVE: *Early eighteenth-century fan from the collection of Geraldine Hervey, wife of the 3rd Marquess of Bristol, now on display on the Museum Landing at Ickworth in Suffolk. The blades are of mother-of-pearl and ivory, the paper is painted with a Bacchanalian procession. Typically, the wear is showing along the paper folds. When fans are open, the folds can relax, but there is a danger from light, and the fan must be well supported.*

Cut the ribbon approximately the same length as the width of two sticks. Fix one end of a piece of ribbon to the back of one of the guards with a small amount of easily reversible adhesive. Fix the second piece of ribbon to the front of the first stick and the third piece of ribbon to the front of the second stick; carry on to the end.

Once the adhesive has dried, return to the right-hand guard. Thread the ribbon attached to the guard and the ribbon fixed to the first stick through the slit in the first stick, from front to back. Position the first stick so that it is slightly overlapped by the guard. Keeping the second piece of ribbon out of the way, fix the first ribbon to the back of the first stick. When the adhesive has dried, trim off any spare ribbon. Carry on to the end. Make sure you wait long enough for the adhesive to dry or all the pieces of ribbon will come unstuck.

If you need help or advice, consult a conservator.

Frames

Frames are usually associated with photographs, paintings and works of art on paper, but other objects, such as textiles, tapestries, ceramic tiles, low relief carvings and plaster casts, are also often enclosed in a frame. The primary purpose of the frame is to protect the object from physical damage and, in the case of glazed pictures, to hold the glass and backboard together. However, frames may also enclose and enhance the image and may be valuable in their own right.

Many materials can be used in the construction of a frame, including aluminium, ceramic, copper, ivory, mirror, papier mâché, silver, other metals and wood. Frames range from the very plain to the extremely elaborate. The majority of larger frames – those that hang on the wall rather than those used on a table-top – are made from wood. They may be made up of a simple moulding and painted, varnished, or gilded, but more elaborate decoration can be produced by carving or by applying decorative elements made from composition, lead or plaster and then gilding the surface (*see* GILDED OBJECTS). Some wood frames are inlaid with metal, bone, ivory and mother-of-pearl or may be decorated with other materials, such as feathers, paper, shells, semi-precious stones, glass or textiles.

Problems

Because of the wide range of materials used to make frames, the type of damage caused and the treatment needed will vary from one material to another. Frames are very prone to physical damage from people inadvertently brushing against them, being knocked, and from manoeuvring the picture or object. Inappropriate cleaning can also damage the surface. Low or fluctuating humidity can cause the joints to open, the gilding or paint to flake and inlay to become loose. Plywood backings of mirrors, pictures and other works are particularly prone to insect attack. See the section on each material for further information.

Handling

Wear **gloves** when handling frames, particularly if they are gilded. Do not manipulate them by grasping delicate decorative elements but take the weight on the more

Seventeenth-century portrait by Thredder of John Bankes, now hanging in the South East Bedroom at Kingston Lacy in Dorset. The frame, of gilded, carved wood, shows a lot of damage. Cracks have exposed the wood and the white ground. In some places the damage has been repainted with bronze paint that is now discolouring. Dust has settled on the surfaces of the frame.

solid parts. It is usually safer to keep the frame vertical and support the weight on the firm parts of the lower edge.

When a framed work is to be moved, assess the route and check that large objects will go through doors and round corners. Prepare the destination with appropriate padding and support. Framed works can be very heavy, particularly if the glass is still in place, so always try to judge the weight before lifting or moving a frame and have enough help and equipment available. At least two people should take down and move framed works; ideally a third person should be on hand to help unhook chains, open doors, etc. (*see* PAINTINGS). Support the weight along the lower edge and place the other hand about two-thirds up the side of the frame to act as a balance.

When laying frames face down, make sure that the full weight is evenly distributed. If necessary, pad some blocks of wood with **polyethylene foam** or a soft, clean padding and place them under the flat areas to support the frame and ensure that no protuberances take the weight. Place the frame face down on a clean soft surface such as a clean blanket.

When removing glass, take care not to damage the site (inner) edge.

Display

Avoid placing framed works, particularly those in elaborate frames, in areas where passing people may knock or brush against them, such as narrow corridors, behind a dining chair, or on narrow staircases. Frames over working fireplaces and radiators will be vulnerable to damage from fluctuating humidity and from dust deposited by the rising hot air.

See the appropriate material section, PAPER, and PAINTINGS.

Storage

Wrap all the corners and any protruding areas with padding such as thin **polyethylene foam** or wedges of **acid-free** tissue before moving or storing a frame.

Empty frames should be hung rather than stacked: they can be hung from two padded brackets, but should not be hung by the corners.

If you need to stack frames, raise them off the floor on a pallet or on timber battens. Stack them front-to-front and back-to-back, and where possible store frames of the same size together. If the sizes vary, place the largest at the back and the smallest at the front and stack them front-to-back with a piece of hardboard, card or polyethylene foam between each frame. Do not lean too many frames against each other – no more than six to ten depending on size; the larger the frames, the smaller the stack should be, due to the weight. If you have a number of frames or framed works to store and you cannot hang them, it would be preferable to construct a stand similar to a large plate rack with pigeon holes that will support the frames.

Housekeeping and Maintenance

Remove dust with a soft brush and vacuum cleaner (*see* pp.19–20). A dry **microfibre cloth** can be used to clean a simple moulded frame with a sound surface. It is advisable to have an assistant to hold the frame steady during cleaning. Wherever possible frames should not be removed for dusting; too much handling exposes them to risk of damage.

Cleaning

Do not use water on gilded or painted frames because it can remove the finish.

A frame in good condition made from plain, varnished wood, ceramic or metal may be lightly cleaned after dust has been brushed off, using cotton buds slightly dampened with de-ionised water containing a drop of **conservation-grade detergent**. Saliva may help remove stubborn spots of dirt from frames. Make sure the buds are only slightly damp, as the cleaning liquid must not run off the frame onto the work, and check that the surface finish is not being removed.

When cleaning the glass in a frame, use a dry or slightly damp **microfibre cloth** and protect the innermost or site edge of the frame by holding some card against it.

If the glass of the painting or mirror is very dirty, clean it with a swab of cotton wool barely dampened with warm water containing a few drops of conservation-grade detergent. A few drops of **alcohol** in the water may help to remove greasy dirt. Rinse the glass with a clean swab moistened with fresh tap water and a few drops of alcohol, then polish with a lint-free cloth. Take care that the liquid does not drip onto gilding or run behind the glass and do not touch the site edge of the frame as the gilding or other finish may come off. Protect the edge of the frame with a piece of card, as above. *See* the appropriate material section for further information.

Repair

When gilded frames are damaged, white from the ground layer or raised decoration may be visible. This can be concealed by carefully retouching the white with a yellow ochre gouache or watercolour (*see* GILDED OBJECTS). Do not retouch or repaint the area with 'gold' paint as this usually discolours and does not look as pleasant as gold leaf. It is very hard to remove at a later date and will make the eventual cleaning and conservation very difficult, and thus expensive. *See* the appropriate material section for further information.

Gilded Objects

Gilding is a metal finish, usually gold, applied to all kinds of different objects and surfaces from ceramic plates to furniture and railings. It is generally used on metal or wood, but may also be found on other materials such as paper, leather, ivory, plaster,

Detail of a gilded side-table ornamented with lion's heads, probably supplied by Banting, France & Co. in 1829 to the Hervey family and now on display in the Dining Room at Ickworth, Suffolk. It is possible to see where the leaves of gold overlap, producing a thicker colour. Some of the gilding has flaked off, exposing the wood and preparation layers of white, red bole and black bole. The diamond and flower pattern is made from composition; regular cracks can develop as the material shrinks. Oil gilding has been used for the diamond and flower pattern, water gilding for the lion's head.

plastic and composition. Gilding creates an opulent appearance and carved furniture and frames would have sparkled and glittered in candlelight. Gilding on metal can also help to protect the underlying metal from tarnish or corrosion.

The best-known form of gilding is where the metal leaf is applied to a prepared surface and held in place by a type of adhesive or 'mordant'. This process is known as water or oil gilding. Gold, silver, copper, tin, aluminium, brass (known as Dutch metal) and alloys of gold, silver or copper are all suitable for gilding. The metals and their alloys provide a range of colours, from the pink of copper and the white of silver and aluminium, to the yellows produced by alloys of gold, which can vary from lemon yellow to rich gold by changing the proportions in the alloy.

Other methods of gilding are:

- Firegilding: an amalgam, generally of gold and mercury, is applied to the surface of ceramic, glass or metal objects. When the object is heated, or fired in a kiln, the mercury evaporates and a thin layer of gold remains.

- Electroplating: a more recent development, where the object is placed in a solution containing a salt of the metal to be applied, usually silver or gold. An electric current is passed through both the solution and the object, causing a thin layer of metal to be deposited on the object's surface. Electroplated objects are usually metal but may also be made of non-conductive materials such as plastic.

- Painting: gold paint was originally made with powdered gold in a **medium** such as gum arabic. However, this is very expensive, and there have been many attempts to simulate the precious metal using gold-coloured paint, made with powdered brass, bronze, aluminium or synthetic materials in a medium. Other metal paints, such as white and silver colours, are used occasionally. These paints are often used on architectural decoration and in the restoration of gilded metal work. They do not have the lustre and appearance of the metal gilding and may change colour in time.

The care of gilded objects varies with the gilding process, so it is important to learn how to identify it. If in doubt, seek advice from a specialist. Distinguishing between firegilding and electroplating is not easy as both processes produce smooth, shiny, even and coherent surfaces (*see* METALS). Gold paint seldom attains the lustre of metal leaf, and when examined closely it is usually possible to see small particles of metal in the paint. In each case, you should refer to the section on the base material – wood, metal, plastic, or ceramic, for instance – for more information.

On objects gilded with metal leaf, the leaf is very thin and is often worn away to reveal a yellow, red or white base underneath. Even when highly burnished, the surface remains very slightly matt and is not completely smooth or even. It may occasionally be possible to see the overlap of the leaves.

This process of gilding involves applying at least one preparation layer before laying the metal leaf on to the smooth surface. Usually there is a coloured layer immediately under the metal leaf: pink, red, brown or yellow under gold; grey under white metal. Next there is sometimes a white ground. An adhesive, known as mordant or size, holds the leaf in place, and there is usually either a drying oil or a water-based glue such as rabbit skin glue. Tinted varnishes may be applied on top of the metal, especially over silver or white metals where the varnish is coloured yellow to give the appearance of gold.

The reflection of the light off the metal can be varied by the degree of burnishing – or lack of it – and by delicate tooling and surface textures in the ground. Subtle changes in colour are produced by varying the underlying colours and by using metal leaf made of different alloys.

From the eighteenth century onwards 'composition' was employed on frames, furniture, fireplaces and decorative schemes. Initially it was used to add decorative elements, but by the nineteenth century whole frames were made of composition.

It is a beige, putty-like material, which can be modelled and moulded when warm. Its development enabled repeated decoration to be made more rapidly than by carving. More flamboyant composition decoration may be modelled around an iron armature. Most composition shrinks over time; it is quite hard, and often develops a series of parallel cracks at regular intervals along the decoration.

Papier mâché, plaster of Paris and wood were also used to make repetitive decoration on gilded objects like frames. Papier mâché looks similar to composition but does not crack in the same way. It may be beige or dark brown and is usually slightly softer and more fibrous than composition. Plaster of Paris is white and quite brittle and may be soft and powdery. Wood is much more fibrous than these, it does not break cleanly and splits or splinters rather than breaks.

The two methods of gilding, water gilding and oil gilding, are quite difficult to distinguish, but water gilding comes off very easily with water or on damp fingers, whereas oil gilding is easily removed by **organic solvents**. Gilding by both methods is frequently found on frames and pieces of furniture, therefore any cleaning, other than light dusting, should be carried out by a conservator. External metalwork and signs are usually oil gilded.

Problems

The problems associated with gilded objects are similar to those of painted surfaces, in that the metal leaf and the preparation layers may separate from the base material giving rise to cracking, lifting and flaking ground or metal leaf (*see* PAINTINGS and PAINTED WOOD). If the base is made from **organic materials**, flaking is usually due to changing **relative humidity** or to the base material drying out over a long period of time; this applies particularly to wood.

Gilding will be affected by the performance of the substrate (underlying material). For example, gilding on iron will be pushed off by iron corrosion, while on wood it will become loose as the wood dries out and shrinks. Iron armatures used to support plaster or composition may rust and split, forcing the gilding off. Gilding does not adhere well to ivory or tortoiseshell. It wears off easily and must be handled with particular care (*see* IVORY and TORTOISESHELL).

Water gilding is easily damaged by moisture which can come from hot hands, flower vases, plant leaves, drips from plant sprayers, rain, condensation on drinking glasses, wet cleaning and flooding. Oil gilding is more resistant to moisture but is easily damaged by **organic solvents**.

Gilded surfaces are particularly prone to physical damage as the metal leaf is very thin and soon wears off with aggressive cleaning or wear from handling and the underlying ground is soft and easily bruised or damaged.

Layers of varnish over the gilding may break up, craze, lift and flake, or darken.

Handling

Always wear **gloves** when handling gilded objects as fingerprints may leave marks and water gilding can come off on your fingers, particularly in warm weather. Where the gilding is flaking, take particular care to hold the object where the surface is sound so as not to break the flakes off. *See also* WOOD, CERAMICS, IVORY or the appropriate section for the base material or substrate of the object.

Display

Avoid placing gilded wood or other gilded organic materials in an area where the humidity changes. Take particular care that water-gilded objects do not get wet or damp; therefore do not display plants or flowers on a gilded surface. Avoid placing gilded objects over radiators or fires as dust will be deposited by the hot air circulating.

Protect gilded objects such as frames and furniture from physical damage. Position them in places where the surface is in no danger of being accidentally brushed against or knocked, to prevent the gilding from wearing off. If possible, raise the feet of gilded furniture up a little by placing 1cm (½in) blocks under them to protect them from damage from vacuum cleaners or floor washing. The blocks can be painted to match the carpet or gilded to blend with the furniture.

See also information on displaying the substrate material, such as WOOD, IRON or IVORY.

Storage

Use pallets or battens to raise gilded objects up off the floor. Where possible hang frames on a wall out of the way or stack them according to size (see FRAMES). Even light cleaning can be time-consuming and wear away the metal layer, so protect stored objects from dust by covering them with **acid-free** tissue, **Tyvek** or clean **dustsheets** and store smaller objects in **archival** boxes. See appropriate sections for information on storing the base material.

Housekeeping and Maintenance

Gilding is easily damaged by inappropriate cleaning. Regularly remove dust using a soft brush and vacuum cleaner (see pp.19–20). A hard brush will remove the metal layer. Do not use a duster or cleaning liquids as the duster may remove flakes of gilding and a liquid may take off the metal leaf.

Commercial glass cleaners can damage gilded frames so where possible use a dry **microfibre cloth** or dry chamois leather to clean the glass and protect the inside edges of the frame by holding a piece of thin card against them. A little saliva or de-ionised water on a cotton bud will help remove fly-blow and other marks from the glass.

Cleaning

If the gilded surface is sound, you could try a dry **chemical sponge** to remove any obvious areas of dirt. If this is not successful do not try alternatives but seek conservation advice. Further cleaning could remove toning – or even the metal leaf.

Repair

Damaged areas of gilding, where the ground or base is showing through, can be very distracting. Retouching them using a little watercolour or gouache paint will make them less obvious; usually the colour yellow ochre, sometimes mixed with raw umber, will be sufficient to disguise the damage. Carefully paint it on to the white damaged area using a small watercolour paintbrush. Do not use oil or alkyd paints and do not be tempted to use gold-coloured paints as most varieties age badly, never look as good as the real metal and make future conservation extremely difficult.

If gilding is in poor condition it can be conserved and restored but this should be done by an experienced conservator or gilder. In the past gilded objects were often 'improved' by gilding over the original surface; some objects may therefore have several layers of gilding. Subsequent layers of gilding do not reflect the original detail or decorative scheme and often the detail of the carving or ornament is lost as the layers build up. A conservator may be able to remove the top layers revealing the original gilding but this is a time-consuming process and may be expensive. However, it is often worthwhile as the earlier gilding can be very subtle and beautiful.

It has been common in the past to strip off worn or damaged gilding and replace it entirely. This is not usually recommended for antique objects. It is preferable to preserve the original gilding, and consolidate or treat the surface of the object to improve the appearance, as you might with a painted surface.

Mirrors

The first mirrors were made of rock crystal or highly polished, reflective metal, usually bronze or silver or a high tin–copper alloy called speculum. They were constructed in the form of a disc fitted with a decorative handle, with a design on one side and the other side polished.

There are French documents recording glass mirrors in the mid-thirteenth century, but they were rare. From the fifteenth century, the Venetians made flat glass backed with metal foil, which was exported to most European countries. By the seventeenth century, Venetian glass mirrors had spread throughout Europe, with the help of migrant Venetian workers, and metal ones went out of fashion. Mirrors were quite small until it became possible to make large, even plate glass, a technique that the French developed in the mid-seventeenth century.

From the sixteenth century, the 'silvering' on glass was achieved by creating an amalgam of tin foil and mercury under pressure, resulting in a dark grey-tinted reflection; the reverse side resembles rough matt grey aluminium paint. The back of such a mirror is usually covered with a layer of paper or wool blanket, and protected by a softwood backboard. Large sheets of glass may be supported on a wooden stretcher. Some mirrors have no wooden frame, but are bordered with smaller shaped pieces of engraved mirror glass, or *verre églomisé*, held in place by screws concealed under decorative glass or silver tops.

From the middle of the nineteenth century, a solution of silver nitrate was used to deposit a thin layer of silver on the glass, creating a brighter yellow-tinted reflection; the reverse is protected from tarnishing by applying a coat of red lead or other paint. Modern mirrors are coated with aluminium, and also protected by a layer of paint.

Mirrors were made in many different shapes and sizes according to function and taste; for example, dressing-table mirrors evolved to match the changing fashions for hairstyles and wigs. In the eighteenth century, tall pier-glasses became essential for illuminating large rooms in grand houses.

Problems

Metal fixings on the frame or wall may corrode or become loose. The chains, wires or cords can become weak or frayed.

The glass is brittle and can be easily scratched or broken. Small cracks, almost invisible to the naked eye, may travel rapidly through the glass and result in breaks as soon as the mirror is handled, moved or transported.

The softwood backing boards and wool blanket are prone to insect attack in a damp environment.

Dust on the surface of the silvering absorbs damp, resulting in corrosion and oxidation of the reflective surface. Unseen gaps in the frame or backboard allow dust to penetrate and these can often be detected from the front of a mirror as spots or lines of corroded amalgam.

The wooden elements give off organic acid vapours that accelerate the corrosion of tin, causing the amalgam to break down and the mercury to flow to the bottom of the frame. This damage may be seen from the front, when the shape of the wooden stretcher becomes visible in the deteriorated surface of the silvering.

In dry conditions, or where candle or electric light has repeatedly heated the surface of the glass, silvering may shrink, craze, flake and peel away from the surface of the glass.

The applied glass and silver decoration or decorative heads on screws and other fittings on all-glass mirrors can become loose or break during cleaning and can be lost if they are not checked regularly.

For additional physical problems affecting the structure, *see* FRAMES.

Handling

The weight of the glass makes mirrors much heavier than framed paintings. Carved frames provide few points where they can be safely handled (*see* PAINTINGS). Large mirrors should always be carried vertically.

Large mirrors often contain multiple sheets of glass that are not securely fixed to the frame, and the frame itself may be insecure and provide inadequate support for the glass. The glass may snap if the frame is twisted during handling.

The greatest risks occur when a mirror is transferred from a vertical to a horizontal position and back again. It is often necessary to attach the framed mirror to another wooden stretcher or backboard to provide greater rigidity and support during handling, and to transfer it face-forward on to a purpose-built vertical easel. Contact both a glass conservator and a frame conservator, as only skilled and experienced personnel should take down large mirrors or put them up.

Always wear **gloves** to protect gilt frames from fingerprints, and to protect your skin from absorbing any loose mercury, which is toxic. Never touch the reverse of mercury–tin amalgam, as fingerprints cause corrosion that will appear on the face of the mirror.

Sometimes mercury collects at the bottom of the mirror structure when the amalgam is breaking down. If mercury is seen, ventilate the room well, and remove any jewellery, watches, and adjacent metalwork objects. Obtain a mercury spillage kit or follow the instructions provided by the health and safety authority, such as in the UK Health and Safety Executive Information Bulletin SIB(88)14. Use a syringe to pick up the droplets and transfer them to a lidded plastic container, clearly labelled, for disposal as toxic waste.

Display

Choose a wall with a solid structure, but make sure that it is not damp. Leave a space for air to circulate behind the backboard to prevent condensation, which could encourage corrosion or insect infestation.

Large mirrors are heavy and require suitably robust fixings. Usually flat mirror plates are screwed to the frame and to the wall at several points on each vertical side, with iron brackets to support the weight from below.

Storage

Keep mirrors in a dry environment.

Store mirrors vertically, mounted on a rigid backboard or stretcher, and raised off the floor to minimise risk of damage.

Before transporting a mirror, ask a frame conservator to construct an open box structure around the top, bottom and sides to protect the frame and the face of the glass. *See* PAINTINGS.

Housekeeping and Maintenance

Check that the wires, chains and fixings on the wall and the frame are strong and firmly attached. Check frame and backboards for pest infestation. Check that carving, gilding and applied decorations are secure.

Commercial glass cleaners should never be used on antique mirrors, as the chemicals they contain may harm the frame and the mirror.

Remove surface dust with a clean soft ponyhair brush, in combination with a vacuum cleaner (*see* pp.19–20). Polish gently with a clean, dry, soft lint-free cloth, a dry **microfibre cloth** or chamois leather. Protect the edges of the frame from abrasion by holding a piece of thin card against it while you work. A little saliva on a cotton wool bud will help remove flyblow and other marks.

Cleaning

Small mirrors can be taken off the wall for cleaning, but large mirrors should be cleaned *in situ* as the risk of damage is greatest while they are being handled and moved. If the mirror is suspended on wire or chains, ask someone to hold the frame steady while you clean the glass.

Do not clean damaged or repaired glass, as dirt will be drawn into the cracks.

If the mirror is very dirty, wipe it with a swab of cotton wool dampened with warm water containing a few drops of **conservation-grade detergent**. A few drops of **alcohol** in the water may help to remove greasy dirt. Rinse with a clean swab moistened with clean water, then polish with a lint-free cloth or soft chamois leather.

Take great care not to allow any cleaning fluid to run behind the glass, or to touch the frame, as it will damage or remove the gilding, paint or varnish. Hold a piece of **clear polyester film** against the edge of the frame as a barrier against wet cotton wool swabs. Never use a spray.

If the mirror remains smeared, wipe it with a 1:1 mixture of water and alcohol, and then polish (*see* **solvent mixtures**).

Repair

Repairing mirror glass is extremely difficult, and requires the skills and experience of a glass conservator. It is almost impossible to eliminate all signs of a break or crack. However, it may be possible to consolidate cracked glass, bond breaks, cast missing areas in resin and fill chips, but this may be appropriate only for small areas of rare, precious or historically important mirror glass.

As a preventive conservation measure, the glass should be backed with conservation-grade materials, and the frame and backboard made secure and lined to prevent the ingress of dust and dirt. This should be done by a conservator.

To repair a mirror with missing glass elements, a glass conservator may be able to cut complex glass shapes, hand-bevel the edges and match the reflective tint of old amalgam using a polyester film with a metallic finish. This can be inserted behind the glass to create a reflective surface where the amalgam is missing.

The deterioration of mercury–tin amalgam is not reversible. Although it is possible to re-silver glass, replacement with a reproduction can significantly reduce the value of a mirror. The colour of modern aluminium coatings differs from original mercury–tin amalgam and later silvering, and attempts to reproduce the appearance of deteriorated amalgam may prove unsatisfactory. Where a mirror is broken or the amalgam severely deteriorated, it may be possible to purchase old mirror glass in sale-rooms or antique shops to replace it. If a mirror is no longer needed as a looking glass, a slightly reflective surface can be created using silver leaf, which may be more attractive than modern aluminium coatings.

LEFT: *Mirror with painting by Boldini c.1700, in the Old Dining Room at Cotehele in Cornwall. This is a rare piece, but shows the problem common to old mirrors, where the silvering on the back has become detached from the glass so that the tapestry behind is now visible.*

Models

Models can be made of many materials, often in combination. Most commonly, materials such as wood, ivory and bone were used, but cork, matchsticks, quills, paper, metal, string, textiles, mother-of-pearl, mica and lead or even glass have been used. The surface may be painted and/or varnished and the detail may be very intricate. There may also be a mechanism included to move elements within the model. Models are often protected with a glass or clear plastic cover.

Problems

Models are difficult to clean, repair and preserve because of their complicated structure. They are often made of very thin, delicate materials that react rapidly to changes in the environmental conditions. The juxtaposition of materials can be detrimental, because the different properties of each material and differences in their response to the environment can cause splitting, distortion, colour change, corrosion and other forms of deterioration.

The dimensions of the **organic materials** in the model will change with the **relative humidity**. These materials and paint are light-sensitive and prone to mould growth or insect attack (*see* pp.14–16). Glues and adhesives may fail in high or low humidities and high temperatures. Metals included in the model are prone to tarnish and corrosion, particularly where other components produce corrosion-inducing vapours. Paper can be damaged by the acids produced from the wood it is stuck to. All materials can suffer physical damage, but brittle materials such as glass are particularly vulnerable (*see* the appropriate sections). Models become dusty and can be difficult to clean.

Handling

See p.12.

Display

Protect models from dust and physical damage by covering them with a suitable cover of glass or clear **acrylic sheet**.

Protect them from light, particularly sunlight, and take care that artificial lighting does not increase the temperature (*see* pp.16–17).

A model ship in the Court Room of the Treasurer's House in York. It was made by French prisoners-of-war, c.1800, from animal bones and baleen (whale bone). The rigging and sails are remarkably intact for a model of this age, probably due to the fact that it has been kept in a glass case, protected from dust. Nevertheless, it shows a problem common with sails, which ruckle up and become distorted.

Storage

Store models in a cool, dark, dry area where the temperature and relative humidity fluctuate as little as possible. Protect them from dust with clean **dustsheets** or **Tyvek** or with **acid-free** tissue paper if the weight of the cloth is likely to damage the objects. Alternatively, make a framework to protect a model from the weight of the dustsheet.

Housekeeping and Maintenance

Remove dust using a small soft paintbrush and vacuum cleaner (*see* pp.19–20). Place **nylon net** over the nozzle, as described for TEXTILES, to prevent small parts of the model from being dislodged and sucked into the vacuum cleaner.

Further cleaning should be undertaken with great care and gentleness. Use methods suitable for each material, and test first to ensure that the object will not be damaged (*see* the appropriate section).

Repair

Repairing a damaged model is very difficult because of its complex structure and, frequently, the small scale of the model's elements. Seek advice from a conservator for the repair of an old, fragile or significant model. *See* the section on the appropriate material for further information.

Mosaic

Mosaics are made from small pieces of glazed or unglazed ceramic, glass or stone, set into lime or cement mortar. They have been produced from very early times and are thought to have developed from embedding coloured pebbles. The pieces, or tesserae, are often placed so that they form a design or picture. Mosaics are frequently found on floors, but walls and ceilings can also be decorated with them, and fragments of a mosaic can be hung like a picture.

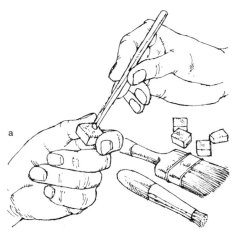
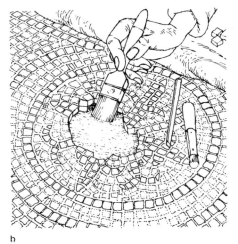

Cleaning and repairing mosaic
(a) *Clean the back of the detached tessera using a soft bristle or stencil brush*
(b) *Clean the holes in the mosaic with a soft brush, removing any old mortar.*

Micro-mosaics are made up of tiny glass tesserae, usually set in pitch or resin mixtures and held in a metal tray. They were popular in nineteenth-century Italy, but earlier examples are also known. Micromosaics are usually framed and hung in a similar manner to paintings. Micromosaics are also found in jewellery and other decorative items.

Problems

See TILES. Mosaics on the floor or wall may suffer from problems of soluble salts and damp. The cause of the damp problems must be resolved before work can be undertaken on the mosaic. The mortar may fail, and tesserae may work loose.

Display

Historically, mosaics were backed and mounted on a wall, but this is no longer considered appropriate except for mosaics designed for this purpose.

Housekeeping and Maintenance

Dust the mosaic with a soft brush and a vacuum cleaner to catch the dust (*see* pp.19–20).

Cleaning

Before cleaning, check that the tesserae are all securely fixed. If any are loose, remove them from the mosaic, record the position of the tesserae, and keep them until they can be replaced.

Clean a mosaic in good condition in the same way as described for Wall and Floor Tiles. It may be more effective to use a soft bristle brush or a stencil brush rather than a soft cloth to clean the mosaic. The surface of a mosaic is often uneven and the edges of the tesserae can hook on to the cloth.

The grouting around the tesserae of micro-mosaics is often painted, so never clean them with **organic solvents**. Remove dust with a soft brush. Use a dry **chemical sponge** or a mixture of water and **conservation-grade detergent** on a **cotton bud** for further cleaning, but check that the paint is not being pulled off. If it is, seek conservation advice.

Repair

Any repairs should be carried out using lime mortars or tile adhesive. Do not use other adhesives as they may cause problems in the mosaic and can make future conservation difficult (*see* TILES). Ancient and valuable mosaics should be conserved by a conservator. Clean the back of the tesserae and the holes from which they come to remove any old mortar and refix them in position with a tile adhesive, as for TILES.

Musical Boxes

The tune of a musical box is usually played on the teeth of a hardened steel comb; these are plucked by tiny pins fixed into a revolving cylinder. In elaborate musical boxes, there are also bells, which are struck by small, often butterfly-shaped, hammers. Antique musical boxes usually have a choice of tunes.

The mechanism of a musical box is very similar to a clock movement, except that musical boxes are often more highly stressed and can 'self-destruct' if mishandled. The mechanism is generally housed in a wooden box, although the box can also be made of glass, ceramic, leather, tortoiseshell, metal and other materials. Some boxes have moving or dancing figures. These figures are often made of, or dressed with, textiles, leather or paper; *see* the appropriate section.

Gilt musical box decorated with a conductor monkey and a harp, from the Sultana Room at Attingham Park in Shropshire. This piece is in very good condition, apart from a little corrosion on the iron strings of the harp.

Problems

Musical boxes need the same care and treatment as CLOCKS. The case must be checked for the problems associated with wood, such as woodworm, cracks and raised inlay (*see* WOOD).

There may be lists of the tunes that the musical box plays written or printed on paper. This is likely to be on the inside of the lid. This paper is often torn or foxed (*see* PAPER).

If the musical box does not play the tune evenly, or it makes other odd noises, it could be that the mechanism is worn or dirty, or that some of the teeth or pins are missing. Do not play a musical box if it is in this condition. Do not attempt to clean, repair or treat the mechanism yourself.

Handling

Do not play a musical box unless you are sure it is in good condition. The handling of musical boxes is similar to CLOCKS.

Never stop musical boxes in mid-tune; you must always allow them to run on to the end, otherwise the pins on the cylinder will engage with the teeth of the comb. If the musical box is then moved or jolted, the teeth and the pins could break off. A musical box should be run down as much as possible before moving it but, again, make sure that you stop it at the end of a tune.

When the musical box is played, the speed of running is controlled by a governor, which incorporates thin blades of metal that whirl round like a fan. To prevent the movement from starting while the box is being moved, fold some **acid-free** tissue and place it in the fan blades of the governor, taking the greatest care not to damage the spindle or its tiny bearings.

If the paper list of tunes has been torn off the lid, do not fix it back with drawing pins or self-adhesive tape. Put the torn pieces in a clear polyester envelope and fix this to the lid using appropriate dome-headed pins and the original holes.

Display

See CLOCKS and the section on relevant material for the case. Make sure that an antique musical box does not get hot or the shellac cement in the cylinder will melt.

Storage

Keep musical boxes in a cool, dry, clean room, but make sure that the area does not become too dry. Store musical boxes with the mainspring run down and the play stopped at the end of the tune. *See* CLOCKS and the section on the relevant material for the case.

Housekeeping and Maintenance

Dust the case with a lint-free cloth or **microfibre cloth** or brush and vacuum cleaner, depending on the material used to make the case. Brush dust out of the interior using a ponyhair brush and vacuum cleaner but do not brush the mechanism itself, and take care not to hit anything with the handle of the brush or nozzle of the cleaner. Do not oil or spray the mechanism with a spray oil. To oil it properly, the mechanism

has to be taken to pieces; this should be done only by a musical box conservator.

Cleaning

Do not clean or touch the mechanism of an antique musical box, as the movement is very complicated and can easily be damaged or even completely ruined. *See* the appropriate section for information on cleaning and caring for the case.

Repair

Musical boxes should be cleaned and repaired by a musical box conservator. Some clock conservators also restore musical boxes, but it is better to find a conservator who specialises in musical boxes. For the repair of the case, *see* the appropriate material.

Automata

Although there are earlier examples of automata, they appear to have reached their peak in the sixteenth century when very elaborate ones were being made in Europe, primarily in southern Germany. They have been universally popular since the nineteenth century.

The mechanism of an automaton is usually hand-cranked or spring-driven. The latter is normally wound with a key, and is sometimes started by putting a coin in a slot. The mechanism is normally made up of wheels, springs and metal armatures, often with pieces of leather or rubber as washers and connections. The cases were frequently made from rough sawn wood covered with paper or textiles, but they can also be made from a large range of other materials, from painted metal sheet to plastic. The figures were often made from fur, feathers or leather, or textiles stuffed with newspaper. Very often automata were made from materials that were not designed to last, which makes their preservation difficult.

Automata should be cared for according to the materials of which they are made. If they are kept too damp, iron will rust, and other metals, such as brass, will corrode; mould will grow on materials such as leather, paper or wood. If automata are kept too dry, some materials will become brittle or shrink. If the temperature and humidity fluctuate too much, paint will flake off and many materials will deteriorate very rapidly.

Avoid placing automata in direct sunlight and keep them as dust-free as possible. If the mechanism is spring-driven, allow it to run down before moving or storing the object.

Remove any dust with a soft brush and vacuum cleaner. Clean automata according to the different materials included in their construction. Make sure that the cleaning fluids from one material do not run on to another.

Do not attempt to take apart and clean the mechanism of an antique automaton. *See* CLOCKS and SCIENTIFIC INSTRUMENTS for the care of the moving parts.

These objects are difficult to conserve and restore and should be dealt with by a conservator specialising in this field. *See also* SCIENTIFIC INSTRUMENTS.

Musical Instruments

The care and maintenance of musical instruments is a wide and specialist field and it is beyond the scope of this book to give it sufficient coverage. Conservators specialising in musical instruments are the most suitable people to repair and conserve them and to advise on their care.

Because of the complexity of the construction of musical instruments, the range of information needed is so extensive that

RIGHT: *The Entrance Hall at Erddig in Clwyd was traditionally used by the Yorke family as their music room: it holds a chamber organ, 1865 by Bevington & Sons of London; a harp lute, c.1810, with black lacquered body and gilt decoration by Edward Light of London; a brass euphonium, late nineteenth century by J. Higham. The table also contains a group of mechanical musical players, including an automaton of an old lady playing an upright piano, French, c.1900, and a cylindrical musical box. The 'Polygon' musical box with metal discs and the 'Ariston' pneumatic musical player with cardboard discs were both made at the turn of the twentieth century. The Edison Standard Phonograph with sound horn from New Jersey, played cylindrical vinyl records in cardboard tubes.*

The instruments are in good condition, apart from the strings on the harp lute, which are loose and frayed, and a bit of wear on the euphonium.

people who own or collect musical instruments are unwise to attempt to conserve or restore their collection themselves. The damage that can be done in a very short time is great and irreparable, so it is preferable to leave musical instruments alone. In particular, if your instruments are in the Stradivarius league, you must discuss them with a musical instrument conservator.

That being said, many people have small collections of musical instruments that they have acquired over the years or brought back from their travels. These instruments need caring for as much as any others.

Musical instruments are made from a wide variety of materials, such as silver, brass, ivory, felt, wood, gourds, leather, earthenware, shells, beads, iron, textile, paper, skin and hair, and are frequently made from a combination of different materials. A piano can have an iron framework, wooden casework, ivory and wood keys and felt-covered hammers. An African drum may combine an earthenware body and a skin membrane with shell or bead decoration.

Problems

A large number of instruments are made from **organic materials**, such as wood or leather. These materials are very susceptible to changes in temperature and **relative humidity**, as well as insect and mould attack (*see* pp.14–18).

The wood used for violins, guitars, lutes, harpsichords and other instruments can be very thin, about 2mm (¹⁄₁₆in) thick. Not only are these instruments delicate and likely to break if mishandled, but they will also split if they are exposed to low humidity and distort if they are too damp.

Each material responds differently to changes in the environment. This can make them distort, split or separate; for instance, the ivory on piano keys may curl up or inlay on a guitar may fall out. The fact that the various components require different conditions makes caring for instruments very difficult.

Ethnographic instruments may also contain vegetable fibres that can be weak and brittle and very often any paint may be powdery or flaking. Some instruments include rubber or early plastic (eg. ebonite) components. These may break down or become sticky.

Stringed instruments, particularly pianos, can be under a lot of tension from the tautness of the strings. Sometimes this tension causes or increases distortion.

Instruments should be checked for metal corrosion, mould, dry and brittle skin, splits, flaking paint and distortion. Examine musical instruments regularly for woodworm or moth infestation (*see* WOOD and TEXTILES). If you have an instrument that has suffered woodworm attack, seek professional advice, as some woodworm treatments can change the tone of the instrument.

Refer to the relevant sections for further information on the materials used for the construction of musical instruments.

Handling

Rare or valuable instruments should be played as little as possible to reduce the risk of damage and wear and tear. However, instruments were made to make music and many old and rare instruments are played. It is always advisable to seek advice from a musical instrument specialist who is able to assess the risk of playing a particular instrument.

When moving larger instruments, take the precautions discussed in the Introduction (*see* p.12). Grand pianos are very heavy because of their iron framework and are best moved by professional piano movers.

Pianos and other instruments on legs should be lifted and carried rather than dragged across a floor. If possible, use a dolly or trolley. The legs on pianos are not designed to take the moving weight of the instrument, so they may well break or come loose; the castors were often added for effect rather than for use. Lift a piano by the main body and not by its mouldings. Attach foam plastic or a clean blanket to the corners of a large instrument before moving it. Before you set off, check that a piano or other instrument will go through doorways and corridors, downstairs and around corners. When moving harpsichords, virginals and spinets, two people will be needed to move the stand and two or three to carry the instrument itself.

Carry smaller instruments, such as violins or flutes, one at a time. Do not carry a stringed instrument by its neck. For protection against knocks, place your hands on the outside of an instrument when you carry it.

If the musical instrument has a carrying case, check it occasionally to see that the handle and the locks are still securely attached, and that the internal padding is free from mould and pests.

Make sure that bits do not fall off instruments as you move them about. Protect drum skins from keys in doorways and other sharp objects. Some ethnographical instruments are flimsily constructed and the materials may be dry and brittle, so examine them carefully before you move them.

Unless stringed instruments are being used regularly, they should not be left with the strings at playing tension.

Display

Display instruments away from direct sunlight in a clean, dust-free room. Do not place them near radiators or open fires. Make sure that instruments are not placed where they might be physically damaged by handling or accidental kicking.

Do not allow musical instruments to get too damp or too dry. It is important that the **relative humidity** remains as steady as possible (*see* pp.17–18).

Ideally, delicate instruments should be displayed in a display case with buffering material to maintain a steady and appropriate relative humidity. If instruments are displayed on a wall, make sure that their mounts provide adequate support so that the instrument will not distort.

Take care when watering plants on a piano that water does not get on the polished surface or into the mechanism. Ideally, plants should be placed elsewhere.

Storage

Store musical instruments in a cool dry, well-ventilated room away from direct sunlight with as constant a temperature and **relative humidity** as possible. Keep musical instruments away from outside walls or windows, as there may be damp or condensation, and protect them from dust.

Slacken the tension of the strings on stringed instruments. The various mechanisms of the harpsichord and early pianos should not be left engaged.

Do not hang a stringed instrument only by its neck. The weight should be supported from underneath the main body of the instrument.

Stand instruments on wooden slats, cork or other material to raise them off the floor.

Moths will attack felt and baize used in instruments unless they are kept clean. *See* pp.14–15 for insect control.

Housekeeping and Maintenance

Instruments which have cases are generally kept in them and should not need dusting or cleaning, but a ponyhair brush can be used for removing any dust if necessary.

The exterior of keyboard instruments can be dusted in the same way as furniture (*see* WOOD). As the internal construction is so delicate, its cleaning is best left to a conservator or musical instrument specialist, particularly if it is painted.

Remove the dust from stringed instruments with a soft brush. Take care not to damage the rose or sound hole of a lute or guitar.

Carefully dust the surface of woodwind instruments with a soft, lint-free cloth or **microfibre cloth**. If you need to clean under the key levers, use a strip of the same cloth or a soft brush. Do not lubricate the mechanical parts of woodwind instruments if they are used only for display.

Modern brass musical instruments are often lacquered. These should be dusted and wiped with a soft, clean cloth dampened with warm water containing a few drops of **conservation-grade detergent**.

Metal instruments that are purely on display are best allowed to develop a natural **patina**. If the finish is marred by patches of tarnish or finger marks, the metal may be lightly cleaned and protected with a coat of **microcrystalline wax** thinly applied and well polished off.

Clean drumheads with **powdered eraser** granules as described in LEATHER. Do not clean painted drumheads in this way, as the paint may come off. Lightly dust them with a soft brush.

Cleaning

Piano and organ keys are usually faced with ivory or bone, and pianos and organs made after 1880 often have celluloid-faced keys (*see* PLASTICS AND RUBBER). They can be cleaned by wiping the surface with a swab of cotton wool barely moistened with warm water containing a few drops of **conservation-grade detergent**. Rinse with a clean swab moistened with clean water. A few spots of dirt can be removed using saliva on a cotton bud. Do not try to bleach piano or organ keys of any type. A certain amount of exposure to natural light – though never to direct sunlight – will help prevent their yellowing.

Older brass band instruments may on very rare occasions require polishing, but always check for the presence of original lacquer, which should not be removed. Polish the metal using a **fine abrasive paste** and cotton wool (*see* BRASS). Once clean, a light rub with a long-term silver or brass **metal polishing cloth** should be sufficient. Too much polishing can make the metal thin and remove the maker's name, engraving and decorative designs, and cause silver plate to wear off. Gilded metal instruments should not be polished. Do not polish the brass fittings on woodwind and other musical instruments (*see* METALS).

Repair

Do not attempt to repair an instrument yourself. It should be repaired either by a musical instrument conservator or an instrument-maker who has experience of repair and restoration.

Do not try to play a damaged instrument; it could cause further damage.

Natural History

Natural history specimens include preserved small and large mammals, birds, butterflies, moths and other insects, eggs, shells, fish, reptiles and amphibia, as well as plant material, fossils and other geological samples.

During the nineteenth and early twentieth centuries there was a general interest in the natural sciences and many amateur collections were formed. Some of these and earlier collections have formed the base of major museum holdings. Specimens and hunting trophies were also brought into houses from postings and travels abroad.

Today there is legislation covering the collection of wildlife, including plants and geological specimens, so if you are hoping to build up your own collection, check the law. Information is available from local museums, natural history organisations and public libraries.

The long-term preservation of mammals, birds, insects, fish and plants depends on the thoroughness and care taken during the preparation and preservation process.

Problems

Natural history collections are prone to deterioration from insect attack, light, dirt, inappropriate or excessive handling and **relative humidity** (*see* pp.17–18). The colour of most animals, birds and insects fades very rapidly but, if protected, it can last for many years, depending on the intensity of light and other environmental conditions. Light also causes skin, feathers and fur to break down.

High humidity can cause mould to grow on skin, fur, feathers, pinned insect bodies, and dried plants, and may also cause rusting of the internal wire supports or armatures of mounted specimens that give the animal its shape, leading to the collapse of the specimen and rust stains appearing. The pins holding insects can become corroded, causing the growth of green crystals which can colour the specimen and even destroy it. Geology specimens are also affected by high humidity, leading to pyrite decay (see FOSSILS, ROCKS AND MINERALS). If the humidity is too low, skin will dry out, causing it to tear, flake and sewn seams to split open.

Insect attack is one of the greatest problems for these collections. The main enemies are the larvae of clothes moths, carpet beetles and booklice. Booklice graze on the surface of cellulose-containing materials such as paper or plants, while moth and carpet beetle larvae eat fur, feathers or flesh. In the past, specimens were treated with poisonous chemicals to protect them from insect attack.

Moth damage on a bird of paradise. The moths have eaten the feathers, and exposed the core of the specimen.

Many animals, insects and birds are kept in glass cases. These must be well sealed so that insects and dirt are kept out. They should be examined at least once a year, preferably in the spring, for insect attack. Inspect any new specimens for insects. The signs to look for are:

- falling hair or feathers – check for other signs of insect attack such as frass, but do not touch the affected areas, as hair or feathers may come away in quantity.
- bald patches – check around the heads, napes of necks and rumps of mammals and birds, and under the wings of birds.
- larval cases on the base or attached to the fur or feathers.
- small holes in legs, feet, bills and between the rays of fish fins.
- frass on the base of the object or nearby (frass is debris made by insects, which can range in texture from fine powder to tiny pellets).

If the animal or bird is losing its fur or feathers, but there is no sign of insect attack, it could be that it has been badly stuffed. Check for greasy spots on skins, known as fat burn. If this is the case, the specimen will soon become bald, so consult a taxidermist or specialist conservator.

If insects appear to be attacking the specimens, you will need to get some help from a taxidermist or conservator, as your collection can be destroyed in a very short time. *See* pp.14-15 for information on insect control. Good housekeeping, regular cleaning and spring-cleaning will help control insect attack.

Recently inhabited birds' nests are a breeding ground for fleas, carpet beetles and other insects that attack mounted (stuffed) animals, so if you are making up a new case with birds and mammals, do not use birds' nests unless they have been deep frozen, fumigated or otherwise treated against insects (*see* pp.14-15).

Shells and birds' eggs kept in boxes or cabinets that produce organic acid vapours, such as cardboard, oak and chestnut, can develop Byne's disease, which is an efflorescence of salt crystals forming on the surface of the shell. If severe, this will weaken and destroy the shells. Marine shells that retain some residual sea salt are more prone to suffer from this type of deterioration, (*see* SHELL).

Handling

All specimens and cases should be handled as little as possible and with great care. The specimens can break very easily. Never pick up an animal or bird by its head, neck, limbs or tail. Carry the animal with two hands, supporting the weight from the main part of the body. If the animal is mounted and on a base, pick it up and carry it by the base, but, where necessary, prevent the animal from swaying and breaking at vulnerable points such as the ankles by holding it steady with one hand. Never carry more than one small specimen in each hand. Do not try to move a large animal on your own. Ears, limbs and tails are very fragile and break easily with careless handling. Eggs should always be handled with the utmost care. Avoid carrying taxidermy specimens outside on windy and/or damp days.

The processes of preserving animals, plants and birds has involved toxic chemicals such as salts of mercury or arsenic or DDT. If you are handling old specimens, protect yourself by wearing gloves, a particle filter mask, goggles and an overall, as the dust that comes off these specimens will be toxic. It is a good idea to keep a record of chemically treated specimens for future reference.

Display

Natural history specimens should preferably be displayed under the cover of glass domes, or in glass cases. This makes handling easier and reduces the need for cleaning. Larger animals are usually free-standing.

All specimens should be displayed away from direct sunlight and under as low a light level as possible. Ultraviolet absorbing filters on lights and cases or windows will provide additional protection. Specimens should also be displayed in a room where the **relative humidity** is steady and is not too high or low (45-65% RH).

Free-standing animals and mounted heads should be placed away from open fires, radiators or other heat sources to protect them from dirt and changes in temperature and humidity. Place them where they cannot easily be touched, as fur is easily abraded with handling.

Use stainless steel and **acid-free** material for the display. Where possible use acid-free material to make up the cases and supports, particularly when displaying eggs and shells, which can be attacked by acids. Avoid using materials such as cardboard, oak, blockboard or chipboard and **MDF**, which give off acid vapours, and cotton wool, which can adhere to the surface and holds moisture.

Storage

Store natural history specimens in a cool, dry, dark, dust-free area. The store should be kept clean to discourage insects and checked regularly.

Store specimens so that they are not overcrowded, otherwise protruding tails, crests and wings can easily be bent or broken. Make sure that the specimens do not touch each other and cover them with a clean **dustsheet, calico** or **Tyvek**. Avoid using polyethylene, as it attracts dust and reduces the necessary ventilation. Do not stand specimens directly on a stone, brick or concrete floor; raise them up on wooden slats, **polyethylene foam** or a similar material to protect them from damp and physical damage.

Store smaller specimens wrapped lightly in **acid-free** tissue. Place insect repellent or insecticidal dust in the cupboard but be aware of the health and safety implications of the materials used. **Insect traps** can also be used to monitor for insects. Check the store at least once or twice each year in the spring and autumn for insect damage.

If the animals are not mounted but need support, make some pads from acid-free tissue to support them. Do not use cotton wool as padding for eggs, shells or small creatures, as the fibres cling and cotton wool attracts damp and mould. Use crumpled acid-free tissue or polyethylene foam overlaid with tissue. Pinned insects are often stored in wooden drawers; check these at least twice a year – in spring and summer – for signs of insect attack.

Housekeeping and Maintenance

Cleaning natural history specimens is difficult and can be damaging, so protecting them from dirt is vital. Specimens in cases should need very little cleaning; this can usually be done while checking for insect attack. Free-standing specimens may need more cleaning – at least twice a year. Very dirty animals or birds should be cleaned by a taxidermist or conservator.

Cleaning should be carried out away from other specimens to prevent spreading insects and dirt from one specimen to another. If possible, clean specimens outside on a warm, still, dry day.

Do not clean a specimen that is losing fur or feathers. If it is stable, brush the specimen with a soft brush and catch the dust with a vacuum cleaner on a low setting (*see* pp.19–20). Cover the end of the nozzle with a piece of **nylon net** to prevent fur or feathers being drawn into the nozzle (*see* TEXTILES). Always use a brush, and do not directly suck the dust off or you may take the fur and feathers with it. In some cases, a photographer's puffer brush or **compressed air** can help to remove dust. Rearrange the fur with a wide-toothed comb and gently stroke it with your hand, but do not flatten the fur. Carefully tease bird feathers lightly between your finger and thumb to preen the bird (*see below*). Do not add oil or grease to produce a lustre.

Eyes, teeth and hooves can be cleaned with a cotton wool bud dampened with isopropyl **alcohol**. Take care not to get any alcohol on the skin, as it is a strong dehydrating agent. Clean fragile ears very carefully with a soft brush. Use an artist's hogshair brush to dust noses and antlers.

Elephants, rhinos, giraffes and other large animals can be cleaned by brushing off the dust with a 5cm (2in) paintbrush while holding the nozzle of a vacuum cleaner in the other hand to catch the dust. Take care not to touch the animal with the cleaner.

A lion's mane may be preened with a soft brush, but be careful not to strike the brush against its ears, which may be very brittle.

● BIRDS

Remove dust from feathers by brushing them with a clean feather or soft brush or a photographer's puffer brush in the direction of the lay of the feathers. Use a **bamboo stick** or your fingers and thumb gently to re-lay the feathers.

Sometimes grease marks appear on the birds' feathers, legs and feet. This may mean that the bird has not been prepared correctly, in which case it should be isolated, as it may attract insects. A taxidermist or conservator may be able to remove the grease and correct the situation. Grease will cause dirt to adhere.

Dust birds' eggs with an artist's soft brush. Do not try to wash them.

● SHELLS

Remove any dust with a hogshair brush. If they show signs of Byne's disease, brush off the crystals with a soft brush (*see* SHELL). Provided the shells are not showing signs of having been weakened (splitting or flaking), they can be carefully washed in de-ionised water. If in doubt, move them to drier conditions and seek conservation advice (*see* p.126).

● OSTEOLOGY MATERIAL

Osteology material includes loose bones and teeth, as well as skeletons which are difficult to clean if they get very dirty. Brush off the dust with a soft brush. Wash osteology material with warm water containing a few drops of **conservation-grade detergent**. Rinse with clean water and remove the excess with a paper towel or soft cloth and let them dry naturally. Very dirty or greasy material can be cleaned with cotton buds dampened with **acetone**.

● BUTTERFLIES, MOTHS AND INSECTS

These specimens are very fragile and should not be touched. If the base of the drawer or case in which the collection is kept is dirty, very carefully dust it with a soft brush or a hogshair brush, taking care not to touch the specimens. When you clean the glass, ensure it is completely dry before replacing it on the drawer.

If individual entomological specimens have to be moved, always use angled forceps with serrated grips. Keep two pairs of forceps handy so that you do not have to put the specimen down during this process. Grip under the specimen to ease the pinpoint gently from the cork or foam lining the container; any jerking movement will cause the insect's body parts to become detached. Then hold the pin from the top as normal.

The pins may corrode; once this happens, they are difficult to remove without destroying the specimen; seek conservation advice. To avoid this, use stainless steel pins on new specimens and keep insects reasonably dry and in an **acid-free** environment. The traditional wood cabinets are very attractive, but some, particularly oak, can unfortunately produce high concentrations of acid vapours within the drawers (*see* FOSSILS, ROCKS AND MINERALS).

● GLASS CASES

Many specimens are displayed in wooden-framed glass cases. Glass domes are both

The Harpur Crewe family of Calke Abbey in Derbyshire were fervent collectors of natural history specimens, and nineteenth-century glass cases with mounted animals and birds are to be found throughout the house. Many of the cases contain carefully arranged groups against painted backgrounds. The problems that are encountered with this type of display are insect damage and fading through exposure to light.

expensive to replace and very fragile. Wear **gloves** when handling the dome in case it breaks. Glass domes that are not very dirty need only be wiped over with a **microfibre cloth**. *See* GLASS. Before removing a dome, check it for stress cracks, and use self-adhesive tape to secure these. Cracks can be strengthened by using a UV curing cyano-acrylate **adhesive**. Place a dot of adhesive on the crack and allow it to penetrate the fracture. When it has cured, remove any excess adhesive with a sharp blade. The dome can then be washed in a plastic bowl with warm water and mild detergent. Rinse in clean water and dry with a soft cloth or paper towel. Make sure that the dome is well sealed when you replace it.

Commercial glass cleaners can contain chemicals that may be detrimental to the specimens or the case if used frequently or if sealed inside. It is therefore better not to use them. Instead, wipe the glass with a microfibre or damp cloth. If it is very dirty, add a little isopropyl alcohol to the water. Rinse using a clean cloth and clean water. Polish with a soft, clean cloth.

Make sure all cases, frames and boxes are well sealed so that insects and dust cannot penetrate. Rubber and leather seals are used in some boxes, but others are often sealed with gummed paper tape. Do not use self-adhesive tape to replace missing tape, as it will start to peel off and will leave a residue that is difficult to remove; always use gummed paper tape and paint it black when it has dried.

Cleaning

Do not try to clean very dirty birds, as dust embrittles feathers. This should be done by a taxidermist or conservator. The dust in the feathers of white birds is removable, but the grey stain left behind can be reduced only slightly by very careful cleaning, which should be carried out by a conservator experienced in this work. Total exclusion of dust from the specimen is the best way of preventing this problem.

Most shells can be washed provided they are in good condition with no sign of Byne's disease, and that they do not contain dried remains, which will decompose and smell if they get wet. Sound shells can be washed in warm water containing a few drops of **conservation-grade detergent**. Rinse them in clean water; dry them carefully first with a paper towel or soft cloth and finally with a hairdryer set on *Cool*.

Repair

Apart from very minor repairs, any damage to natural history specimens should be dealt with by a taxidermist or specialist conservator. Loose teeth can be stuck back into place using an easily reversible **adhesive** or neutral pH emulsion adhesive. The material used for modelling lips and gums sometimes shrinks, cracks and detaches itself from the skin and bone. Hairline cracks can be filled with wax and painted; anything larger should be repaired by a specialist.

If the skin splits because it is too dry or grease appears from bad preparation, get help from a specialist. Not all taxidermists are trained or experienced in remedial work on old specimens.

Botanical Collections

Plants, like other natural history specimens, are protected by law, so if you are developing your own collection, you should take care to include only the permitted plants. Contact your local natural history society, public library or museum for information.

Dried plants are very brittle and should be handled with care. Until recently, most plant specimens were treated with heavy metal preservatives such as mercuric chloride, and so be particularly vigilant about health and safety precautions (*see* p.23). Check for insect and mould attack. Nineteenth- and twentieth-century collections may be mounted on paper that has a high acid content. This can sometimes be replaced, but where there are annotations on the paper this may be undesirable. If the problem is very severe and the specimens are at risk, the annotations may be cut out and kept with the mounted specimen in envelopes made of **clear polyester film**. The specimens are usually mounted on the paper by gluing, sewing or strapping with glued strips of paper, or with a specific fabric adhesive cloth. If the specimen becomes loose or detached, the safest method of securing it would be to tie it carefully to the paper using cotton or linen thread. Do not pierce the specimen, but hold it in place by passing the thread though the paper on either side of the stem.

A large stack of plant material can cause the specimens to break so they are usually placed in **archival quality** folders and then in archival **Solander boxes**. Check regularly for insect attack as some plants are particularly vulnerable to this (*see* above and pp.14–15).

Fish, Amphibians and Reptiles

Fish, amphibians and reptiles are mounted by traditional taxidermy techniques, but it is difficult to retain the colour, translucency and shape of fish and amphibians, so these are often cast in resin or plaster of Paris and painted. If this is expertly done, the results are excellent and often more accurate than the traditional skinning and mounting techniques. Traditionally-mounted fish and amphibians are likely to be very fragile. Thicker-skinned fish and amphibians are mounted with a wire armature and **wood wool** filler. Reptiles were also cast, but most were mounted in the traditional way, as their skins are generally tougher.

Traditionally-mounted specimens are fragile and vulnerable to careless handling. Feet and claws in particular break off easily. Any fat left inside fish, amphibian or reptile specimens breaks down and oozes into the skin, drastically discolouring it to a dark brown or black and eventually destroying it. The stickiness of this condition also causes dust to adhere and can encourage insect infestation. The specimen will need degreasing and repainting by a taxidermist or conservator. Insects are attracted to the head, tail and fins in particular. *See* NATURAL HISTORY for information on Handling, Display, and Storage.

Plaster of Paris casts chip easily if they are handled roughly. Do not get a plaster cast wet or it will deteriorate. Modern casts are usually quite robust but any thin or delicate areas may break off if handled carelessly. (*See* PLASTER OF PARIS.)

Fossils, Rocks and Minerals

Fossils, rocks and minerals are collected from all parts of the world for their decorative appearance as well as for scientific study. As for other natural history specimens, there are statutory controls over the collection of these materials. Contact your local natural history or geological society, public library or museum for information.

Detail of geological specimens collected in the nineteenth century by the pioneer of photography, William Henry Fox Talbot, and by his son Charles, in the Brown Gallery at Lacock Abbey in Wiltshire. The red background shows dramatically the effects of light. The Fox Talbots have carefully annotated their collection with little pieces of paper. If you acquire an old collection such as this, keep these captions for historical interest, and for your own information.

Problems

Minerals can be damaged or chemically changed by high humidity, light and pollution, while some fossils, sub-fossil bone and stones, such as shale, may crack and split in low humidity. Some semi-precious stones, such as topaz, sodalite and fluorite, change colour if exposed to strong sunlight, although some revert to their original colour in the dark. There are other minerals, particularly silver salts, which undergo extreme changes on exposure to air and light and must be stored in light-proof boxes made from **acid-free** materials.

Many rocks contain pyrite, an iron sulphide, which will oxidise if the **relative humidity** is too high. This is known as pyrite decay or fossil disease, which has a characteristic sulphur smell, and can cause specimens to develop orange, then white, then yellow crystals. The specimens may even crack and break up into powder. The mineral form of pyrite is sometimes known as fool's gold because of its colour. Rocks and fossils containing pyrite should be kept at between 45-55% RH. Marcasite, which is similar to pyrite, can develop a white feathery encrustation if it is kept in damp conditions. If the relative humidity within rock, fossil and mineral collections is not controlled, other problems may occur, such as deliquescence (dissolving in water taken from the air), hydrolysis (decomposition by chemical attack from water in the air), efflorescence (becoming covered in salt crystals which may lead to disintegration), hydration, shrinkage and distortion.

Handling

The physical strength of samples varies enormously. Some minerals are very brittle, so they should not be exposed to sudden jarring or vibrations. Carry the specimens carefully. If you are carrying more than one at a time, use a tray or box and make sure that they do not jostle each other. If you are transporting specimens in a vehicle, make sure that there is enough padding provided by **polyethylene foam** or bubble wrap to absorb the vibrations from the car. Most minerals can be picked up with bare hands, but a few are tarnished by the acids and grease left from fingers so it is advisable to wear latex, vinyl or similar **gloves**. Do not expose specimens to sudden changes in temperature.

As a safety precaution, always check that no minerals are radioactive. Lists of radioactive minerals are available from the Natural History Museum, London or your local natural history museum. Radioactive and radon-emitting specimens should be labelled and screened to protect people and the surrounding environment. Specialist storage and handling equipment will be required.

Display

Collections should be protected from dust and are normally displayed in glass cases or glass-fronted cabinets out of direct sunlight. Do not display samples over a fireplace, radiator or other heat source. Do not use cotton wool as padding, because it absorbs moisture, and the fibres can catch on specimens. Make sure that samples are displayed on enough shock-absorbing material, such as pads of **acid-free** tissue or **polyethylene foam**. Cases made from wood may buffer vibrations and humidity changes, but do not use oak or other materials which give off acidic fumes (*see* COINS AND MEDALS). Avoid displaying specimens near continuous noise or vibrations, for instance from air-conditioning and ventilation plants, major roads, railways and building works.

Storage

Store minerals and fossils in a clean, dry, dark area, free from vibrations and changes in **relative humidity**. Traditional wooden cabinets used for storing specimens are attractive but not ideal, as acidic vapours produced by some woods can damage the minerals; therefore, metal cabinets are preferable. **Acid-free** card boxes and padding can help to buffer vibrations and changes in humidity. Specimens that are likely to be damaged by vibrations should be placed on **polyethylene foam**. Do not use cotton wool as padding.

Although a traditional wood storage cabinet may not be ideal from the conservation point of view, it might have historical importance or you may want to continue to use it because of its appearance. It is possible to take some precautions against acid vapours damaging the more sensitive samples. For example, the interior of the cabinet and drawers can be sealed with a special varnish and 'scavengers', such as activated **charcoal cloth**, can be placed in the drawers to help absorb the acid vapours. A conservator familiar with protecting collections should be able to advise on the appropriate action.

Housekeeping and Maintenance

Brush off dust with a ponyhair brush or hogshair brush. Washing can harm fossils and minerals, so do not attempt any further cleaning. Seek conservation advice.

Repair

In the past, fragile minerals or fossils were consolidated with wax or resin or coated with lacquer. This has been found to be harmful to the specimens. If you have any specimens disintegrating or in need of consolidation, consult a geological conservator for help and advice. Minor repairs can be carried out using an easily reversible **adhesive**.

Wet Collections

Zoological and botanical specimens are sometimes stored in fluid in sealed Kilner or ground-glass jars. The preserving fluid is often 80 per cent **alcohol** (IMS) (*see* p.244) or 4 per cent aqueous formaldehyde. Jars need to be topped up to prevent the specimens from drying out. If they have already dried out, keep them in this state until specialist rehydration work can be done. Bear in mind that formaldehyde, even at 4 per cent, is toxic, causes dermatitis and its vapours aggravate mucous membranes and cause toxic headaches. IMS is a strong dehydrating agent and removes the skin's natural oils. This type of work should be carried out by an experienced person.

Office Equipment

Office equipment includes typewriters, telephones, die-stamps, punches, tills and other equipment associated with offices. They are usually made from a mixture of materials, such as metal, plastic, wood, textiles and rubber.

Remove any dust from the object with a soft **brush**. If the object is very dusty, and particularly if the dust is greasy, loosen it with a hogshair brush and catch it with a vacuum cleaner held in the other hand (*see* pp.19–20).

A soft **pencil eraser** or a dry **chemical sponge** should remove most surface dirt and grime. If you feel that further cleaning is necessary, you can try a cotton wool swab dampened with water containing a few drops of a **conservation-grade detergent** or a mild household detergent. Before cleaning, test an inconspicuous spot to make sure that the paint, varnish, gilding or lettering are not affected by the cleaning solution. Do not get the object very wet.

The Steward's Room at Lanhydrock in Cornwall, furnished as it was in the early twentieth century. The mixture of materials presents conservation problems: many of the objects are sensitive to light, while the typewriter should be protected from dust, likewise the telephone which is of Bakelite (see page 123) and therefore scratches easily.

Rinse with clean swabs dampened with water. Make sure that the object has dried thoroughly by wiping it with a soft cloth followed by drying it with a hairdryer set on *Cool*, or leaving it for a few hours in a warm place. Stubborn dirt may come off more easily with saliva on a cotton wool bud.

Oily or greasy dirt that is not removed by water and detergent may be cleaned with a cotton wool swab or bud dampened with **white spirit. Organic solvents** such as white spirit should not be used on rubber or plastic so take care not to get the solvent on these parts and always check that the white spirit does not remove any paint, etc. **Alcohol** may also help to clean it, but use it with the same precautions. Always test the solvent on an inconspicuous spot to make sure it does not remove paint, gilding or a surface coating.

Congealed oil from machines such as typewriters can usually be removed with paraffin if white spirit is not successful; take care not to get paraffin on plastic or rubber and use it in a well-ventilated room, or preferably outside. Relubricate the mechanism with a **light machine oil** or sewing machine oil. Apply the oil very sparingly and do not leave oil on painted, plastic or rubber surfaces.

If the paint is damaged, it is not recommended that you repaint the object, as these pieces are of more historic interest with their original paintwork.

A thin layer of **microcrystalline wax** applied with a soft brush helps to protect the metal, wood and painted surface and improves the appearance. Do not let the wax get on to rubber, textiles or plastic and first test the paint in a small, hidden area to check that the solvent does not remove or damage it.

See the individual materials for more information on Handling, Cleaning, Display and Storage.

Paintings

Paintings are made up of a number of different supports, including stretched canvas, wooden panels, copper or other metal sheet, hardboard, glass, leather, vellum, silk and stone.

Paintings on canvas are the most common. The canvas is tacked to a wooden frame known as a stretcher. Wooden wedges

Garrick's Sister, Sire Shakespeare, one of a famous herd of Staffordshire longhorns championed by Viscount Anson at Shugborough Hall, Staffordshire. This portrait, oil on canvas, was painted in the mid-nineteenth century by John Boultbee. It is in very good condition, apart from some areas of missing paint that expose the white ground.

fit into the joints of the stretcher and these can be used to adjust the canvas tension, which should be quite tight in order to keep the canvas in plane. Some canvases are tacked to strainers, which are rigid frames with fixed joints that cannot be expanded.

Many types of wood have been used for painting support, such as oak, poplar and pine. The wooden panel may be a single piece of wood or many pieces joined

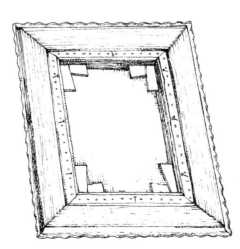

Structure of a painting, showing the stretcher and wooden wedges driven into the joints to maintain tension.

together. Sometimes the reverse is strengthened with battens or a cradle.

The support is prepared with a ground to provide a suitable surface for the artist to paint on. It is made using the same range of binding media and pigments used in the preparation of the paint, but usually with the addition of inert materials, such as chalk or gypsum (calcium sulphate), to add bulk.

The paint is made up of coloured pigments in a binding **medium**. The binding medium is often a drying oil, such as linseed oil. Before oil painting was introduced, egg yolk, wax and animal or fish glue were used, and more recently synthetic acrylic media have been introduced. The proportion of medium to pigment, and the nature of the components, determines the viscosity of the paint, which can be applied as a thin glaze or in thick layers that form a surface texture, known as impasto.

A layer of varnish is usually applied on top of the paint to protect it and to enhance the appearance of the painting.

Paintings are usually framed; the painting fits into a rebate and is held there with suitable framing fixings. Most oil paintings are not glazed, but those with delicate surfaces should be protected with glass or **acrylic sheets** mounted in the frame.

Problems

Canvases are delicate and are easily split or dented. Anything resting on the front or back of the canvas can leave an impression. The outline of patches or labels stuck on the reverse can show on the front. The tacks holding the canvas to the stretcher or strainer sometimes rust and weaken the canvas around them. The stretcher or strainer may be infested with wood-boring insects.

Changes in **relative humidity** cause the canvas to expand and contract (stretch and shrink) and this movement can result in paint cracking, lifting and flaking off. If the paint is lifting, the painting should be taken to a conservator as soon as possible. It is far easier for a conservator to fix back lifting paint than successfully to reposition and attach a flake that has fallen off.

The continuous expansion and contraction from changes in relative humidity cause canvases to become bigger, as they expand more than they contract. The tension becomes looser, and eventually the canvas may bulge on the stretcher. A conservator should be asked to adjust the tension to put the canvas in plane again. The tension of canvases on strainers cannot be adjusted and a conservator may need to replace the strainer with a stretcher.

Paintings on wooden panels are particularly sensitive to changes in relative humidity and can easily split and crack. The panel may warp, usually with a convex warp if you are looking at the panel from the painted side. Panel paintings should be inspected regularly to check that the amount and direction of the warp has not changed. Provided that the degree of curve remains the same, the warp is quite acceptable. It is not desirable to try to flatten a panel painting, as this can damage the paint.

If the degree of curve changes, and particularly if it begins to curve in the opposite direction (concave), then a conservator should be consulted as soon as possible. Do not remove the painting from the room where it has been, as a sudden change of conditions could make the situation worse. It is also important to check if the paint is cracking, lifting or flaking; if it is, consult a conservator.

Wood panels may be infested with wood-boring insects such as the furniture beetle. If any new exit holes are seen on the front or back of the painting, then a conservator should be asked to treat the infestation. It is not advisable to carry out treatment with insecticides yourself, as the solvents may affect the paint layers.

Paintings on metal sheets are fragile, as they can be bent and dented very easily. If the metal is bent, it is virtually impossible to straighten it without damaging the paint layers. Paintings on metal are prone to corrosion (*see* COPPER). They may be affected by extreme temperature changes, which cause the metal to expand and contract and the paint to fall off. However, the flaking of paintings on metal is more often caused by poor adhesion between paint and metal.

Oil paintings may not be as light-sensitive as watercolours or textiles, but they can still suffer dramatic colour change when exposed to excessive light. Varnishes become yellow and pigments can also change. Furthermore, light is often associated with heat, and beams of sunlight, spotlights, picture lights and table lamps placed under paintings can cause damaging levels of

Detail of the painted frieze in the Long Gallery at Blickling Hall in Norfolk. The paintings in gouache on wooden boards were made by J. H. Pollen, who began work in 1858 and took five years to complete the task. This detail shows birds from Africa and Asia with trees and flowers interlaced with white vine. Splits in the wood can be seen, as well as missing paint that has exposed the white preparation ground. There is some evidence of restoration.

low relative humidity on the paint surface. Of these, exposure to sunlight is the most important to avoid. A whitish bloom on the surface of the varnish may indicate that the air is too damp. The varnish also collects dirt and grime. The true colours of the painting can only be recovered by having the varnish removed by a conservator (*see* Cleaning).

Frames are often gilded and are vulnerable to physical damage (*see* FRAMES and GILDED OBJECTS). Any pieces that become detached should be saved and placed in a labelled envelope for a conservator to reattach.

The fixings that are used to hang paintings may deteriorate and should be checked at regular intervals. Chains, wires and other metal fixings may corrode, both on the reverse of the painting and in the wall. Cord may fray and lose strength where it is near a corroding metal fixing.

Handling

Ask advice from a conservator before moving a painting with any structural problems, such as a torn canvas or flaking paint. When moving a painting from one room to another, the **relative humidity** in the new room should be similar to that in the previous room. If a painting has to be taken down, for example, when work such as rewiring or decoration is being carried out or if the painting is to be moved elsewhere, there are a few precautions that can be taken to lessen the risk of damage.

When paintings are displayed in rows on a wall, take down the lower ones first. Remove any furniture that is in the way. If the painting hangs on chain, it is a good idea to mark the link that the hook fits into with a piece of string or a paper clip so that it can be rehung on the same link. Framed paintings are heavy, so at least two people are needed to lift them safely; for paintings that are larger than a half-length portrait (75 × 62cm/30 × 25in), four or more people may be needed. When taking the painting down, be careful that the chain or hook does not fall on to the painting and damage its surface. Keep the painting upright as it is lowered to the floor and bend your knees as you lower the painting so that your back remains straight. Rest the frame on **polyethylene foam** or on cushions made of clean blankets or bubble wrap. Tip it back slightly against the wall, so that its weight is taken on the back edge of the frame behind the carved moulding.

Carry a painting vertically with the longest side horizontal (landscape format) to lower its centre of gravity and to reduce the chance of it hitting door lintels, light-fittings and other obstacles. Paintings should be carried by their frames and never by their stretchers. Check the route before moving the painting, looking out for obstructions such as doorknobs and electric leads. Pay particular attention when going up or down stairs. Damage is less likely to occur if one person watches the back of the painting and the other the front. Before setting off, prepare a place with suitable cushioning on which to rest the painting, both at the final destination and along the way if the painting is particularly heavy or needs to be moved some distance.

Ideally, paintings should be moved in vans in which they can be transported vertically in the direction of movement of the vehicle (i.e. parallel to the sides of the van); this is essential for large paintings and long journeys. A small painting may be transported by car for short journeys, after wrapping it in a well-sealed polythene parcel, and placing it face up on padding, such as a blanket, in the back of the car. The padding will cushion the painting from bumps and jars and will reduce vibration. Prevent the painting from moving by padding all the way round it with cushioning material. If the painting is glazed, stick **low-tack tape** to the glass in parallel strips from top to bottom and side to side, so that if the glass breaks the damage caused by the fragments will be limited. Make sure that the tape does not stick to the frame.

Display

The position in which paintings are hung is important and the **relative humidity** should be as constant as possible. Do not hang paintings near or over radiators or over fireplaces that are in use, heating vents, pipes carrying hot water or on a wall with internal flues or hot pipes running through it. These heat sources cause dust to rise, which can be deposited on the paintings and frames, and pockets of low relative humidity. Avoid hanging paintings over a sideboard in a dining-room where steam or splashes of food may affect them. Some air circulation around the painting is beneficial, particularly if it is hanging on a cold and damp outside wall, but avoid draughts. Fix spacers, such as corks, to the bottom corners of frames on paintings on outside

Cork spacers attached to the lower corner of a picture to improve ventilation.

walls to isolate the frame from the wall and to encourage air to circulate behind.

To protect against physical damage, place pieces of furniture under a hanging painting so that it cannot be reached easily. Ideally, paintings should not be hung where they may be knocked by passing people, such as in narrow corridors or on staircases; where they have to be hung in these locations, they should be glazed for protection.

Take care that the lighting is not too strong and does not heat up the area around the painting. If a painting can be reached by beams of sunlight, appropriate light reduction methods, such as blinds or curtains should be used at the windows (*see* pp.16-17). Some lights produced for illuminating paintings can give off a lot of heat, so should be avoided or replaced. These lights may also emit UV rays, so UV-absorbing filters should be fitted over them.

Cord, wire or chain is used to hang a painting from a picture rail. If the fixing method is meant to be invisible, hang the painting from two strong hooks fixed to the side members of the frame by two short lengths of chain attached to the wall using screws, washers and rawlplugs. The degree at which the painting leans forward depends on how low or high the hooks are positioned on the back of the frame and the length of the chain. Paintings that are quite high up on a wall may need to lean forward more than usual to make them more visible from the ground. This can be achieved by positioning the hooks close to the centre of the frame.

Heavy frames need to have additional support from underneath to prevent too much strain on the joins of the frame and

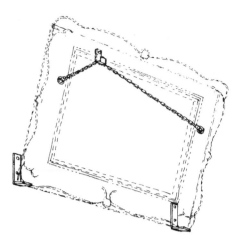

Corner brackets provide additional support for heavy frames.

to reduce the risk of the chain breaking or the fixings coming out of the wall. Fix one or more brackets to the wall on which the base of the frame can rest. Check that the picture wire or chain is taut, otherwise it may come off the wall fixing; if necessary, tie the wire or chain to the fixing.

Do not hang a painting on freshly plastered walls for several months until the plaster has completely dried out, or on freshly painted walls until the smell of paint has gone.

Some paintings are fixed in architectural frames, which are part of the decorative scheme. The area behind the painting may not be plastered to leave a gap for air circulation. The wall surrounding the painting should not be painted with modern synthetic resin-based paint, because it is non-porous and will prevent moisture from passing through. Therefore any damp in the wall will come through the unpainted area behind the painting and may cause a damp environment to build up there. If possible, use limewash or a porous paint for painting around these architectural frames. If you are concerned about the wall or the painting, the reverse of these paintings can be backed with a moisture barrier such as polyethylene to isolate the painting from the wall and to ensure that it is exposed to the room air rather than to any damp air from the wall behind.

FRAMING

Frames should have a rebate that is deep enough to take the stretcher or wooden panel. Metal sheets are thinner so the rebate is narrower. Line the rebate with velvet ribbon or felt strips to protect the varnish and painting at the edge from being abraded by the rough surface of the rebate. Position the

stretcher in the frame using balsa strips, corks or strips of **polyethylene foam** pinned or glued into place within the rebate. These strips should hold the painting firmly so that it cannot slip within the frame, but not so tightly that it is difficult to put the painting in or take it out of the frame. Secure the stretcher using brass framing plates or mirror plates that are screwed into the frame and overlap the painting. These plates are less damaging than the nails that were used in the past, which had to be hammered into the frame, causing vibrations that sometimes detached moulding and gilding from the frame.

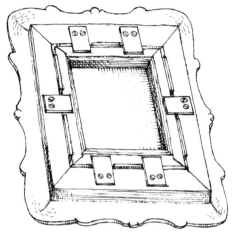

Securing the stretcher in frame with mirror plates.

Framing panel paintings is more difficult than framing canvas paintings, as the framing plates must be positioned so as not to cause any strain on the panel when relative humidity fluctuations cause it to move within the frame. It is advisable to ask a conservator to frame panel paintings. Paintings on metal should also be framed

by a conservator, because of the fragility of the metal sheets.

Back paintings with hardboard, **museum board**, foam boards or clear plastic sheets such as **clear polyester film** to help buffer paintings from changes in relative humidity as well as to keep them clean.

Paintings may be glazed with glass, **acrylic sheet** or polycarbonate to protect against dirt and physical damage. The glazing should be spaced within the frame so that it does not touch the surface of the painting and should be sealed with gummed paper tape or **gummed linen tape** so that dust cannot enter from the front.

Storage

Store paintings in rooms with as constant **relative humidity** as possible – that is, neither too damp nor too dry. The room should be cool and should not be vulnerable to water infiltration (*see* pp.12 and 18). Cellars and basements are unsuitable, because they are often damp; attics are also unsuitable because they experience fluctuating extremes of temperature. Avoid areas that are locally heated or draughty. The room should be as dark as possible and curtains or shutters should be kept closed, not only to reduce light levels but also to reduce changes in the temperature and relative humidity.

Where there is room, hang stored paintings on the wall to 'keep them out of harm's way'. The same precautions should be taken as when hanging paintings on display.

If there is no room to hang paintings, then a construction like a large plate rack can be made. The inside of the rack should be padded with **polyethylene foam** or bubble wrap and the paintings slotted in;

A rack for storing paintings, with sections to provide good support.

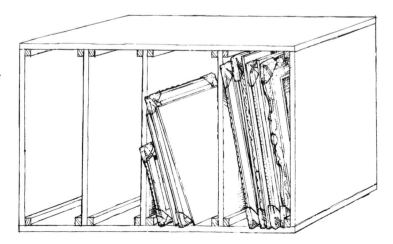

When temporarily resting a frame against a wall, make sure that the back edge is taking the weight, and provide some padding.

provide additional cushioning for ornate frames.

Making a rack is costly and is only likely to be considered for paintings in long-term storage. An alternative is to stack paintings against the wall, but precautions need to be taken to protect the stacks from people, vacuum cleaners and other damage. Choose a section of wall that is free from radiators or heating pipes and that is not under a window. Place wooden battens, polyethylene foam or an equivalent material on the floor, at right angles to the wall to raise the pictures off the floor.

Remove picture lights, brackets, wires and other projections to prevent damage to adjacent paintings and frames. The stacks should be made of no more than six similarly sized framed paintings. Place the largest and heaviest at the back of the pile and arrange the paintings so that they are face out from the wall and their weight is taken by the back edge of the frame to protect the moulding on the front. If the moulding is ornate, lift it clear of the floor using polyethylene foam blocks or rolls of polyethylene foam sheet or bubble wrap. A painting with a very ornate frame should be placed on the front of a stack or on its own. Separate the paintings with cushioning of an appropriate thickness. For plain frames, this might consist of sheets of hardboard; for more ornate frames, it might be polyethylene foam or bubble wrap. Place a **weight** or piece of furniture at the front of the stack to prevent the stack from sliding out from the wall. Cover the stack with a clean **dustsheet** or **Tyvek** to protect it from dust.

Stack unframed pictures separately from framed ones. The canvases should face the wall with only the top front edge of the painting touching the wall or the back of the painting in front. Stack paintings of similar size together with the largest closest to the wall. Take care that the surface of the painting does not touch anything.

Housekeeping and Maintenance

The cleaning of paintings is best carried out by a properly qualified painting conservator, who has been trained in the safe removal of surface dirt, discoloured varnish and overpaint. Irreparable damage can be caused by unskilled or inexperienced people attempting to clean paintings. The only cleaning that is safe to do at home is the removal of surface dust, but even this should only be attempted after a very careful inspection of the paint surface to ensure that there is no lifting, flaking or blistering paint. Also check frames for any signs of flaking gilding before cleaning them.

Place the painting face up with padding such a **polyethylene foam** blocks or rolls of bubble wrap under the frame. Use a vacuum cleaner and clean soft ponyhair or large cosmetic **brushes** (*see* pp.19–20). Use separate brushes for the surface of the painting, its reverse and the frame so that the surface is not scratched by any bits of grit. Collect the dust and any other debris on the back of the frame in the nozzle of a cylinder vacuum cleaner using a brush to direct the dirt. Never let the nozzle of the vacuum cleaner touch the painting or frame. It may be advisable to pad the nozzle by wrapping a piece of polyethylene foam around it, secured with a rubber band, to protect against accidental impact. Then clean the reverse of the painting very gently using another brush in the same way; be particularly careful not to apply pressure to the reverse of canvas paintings.

Turn the painting and frame over and repeat the process on the front. First, carefully dust the frame using the brush and vacuum cleaner. Then dust the surface of the painting with a clean, soft brush.

If the painting has been kept in damp conditions, it may have mould on it. After it has dried out at **relative humidity** levels below 65%, remove the mould by brushing if off, but take care to do this in a well-ventilated space, preferably outside, and wear suitable protection, such as a dust mask with filters that will prevent you from breathing in the mould spores.

Cleaning

Further cleaning of a painting should be carried out by a painting conservator.

Repair

A damaged painting should be inspected by a conservator, who can advise you on what treatment is needed. The conservator should also look at the frame in case that has also been damaged.

If the painting has got wet or if a canvas is torn and there is loose paint around the tear, remove the painting from the wall and place it face up on blocks of polyethylene foam or rolls of polyethylene foam sheet or bubble wrap until the conservator arrives. Do this very carefully to avoid the loss of paint flakes and leave the painting on the wall if you think you will cause more damage by handling it. Allow wet paintings to dry slowly with plenty of air circulation, particularly underneath. The varnish may develop a white bloom, which is usually removable, but more serious flaking is likely to develop as the painting dries out. Consult a conservator as soon as possible.

Miniatures

A miniature is a small, highly finished painting or drawing, often a portrait, painted in watercolour or gouache, on a variety of supports, including ivory, vellum, paper, card, wood veneer, silver or copper. Before the eighteenth century, egg tempera and other media were used. Miniatures are also made in enamel. Miniatures are round, oval or occasionally rectangular and are often presented in silver, gold or silver-gilt frames with convex or flat glass. Miniatures were particularly popular in the seventeenth and eighteenth centuries. The term miniature is also used to describe detailed illuminations from texts (*see also* PAPER).

Problems

Miniatures are particularly sensitive to changes in relative humidity and to light. Because the support is very thin, it responds to the slightest change in relative humidity by contracting and expanding and will easily warp or crack. This movement causes the paint to crack, lift and flake. Ivory miniatures are especially vulnerable, as the oils in ivory prevent the paint from adhering strongly when first applied.

Occasionally, the support can warp sufficiently for it to touch the glass. The paint may then become attached to the glass. Under these circumstances do not try to open the miniature yourself, but discuss the problem with a conservator experienced in working with miniatures.

Strong light or long exposures (*see* pp.16–17) will cause changes to the colour of the pigments. But light is also damaging because of the heat generated (*see* p.18), so the type of lighting used to illuminate miniatures is very important.

When kept in a damp environment or one with poor air circulation, mould may grow on the paint medium and/or the support.

The glass in the miniature can deteriorate and 'weep' (*see* GLASS). The alkaline liquid produced by the glass during this process is detrimental to the paint. Discuss the problem with a conservator experienced in working with miniatures, as you will need to decide whether it is appropriate or necessary to change the glass.

Metal frames may tarnish (*see* METALS).

Handling

Do not remove miniatures from their frames to inspect them, as they are very vulnerable when unframed; if this is absolutely necessary, seek advice from a conservator.

ABOVE: *Portrait miniatures collected by Mrs Ronald Greville and now on display in the Study at Polesden Lacey in Surrey. They are British School, eighteenth and nineteenth century, painted on ivory, with a variety of frames, including two with pearls and two with gems. On the whole, they are in good condition, although there is some evidence of glass deterioration. They are displayed on silk in a case; a curtain is drawn across to protect them from light.*

Metal frames will tarnish quickly if handled without **gloves**, therefore, wherever possible, wear latex or vinyl gloves. There is a danger that a miniature will slip from your hands if you wear cotton gloves.

Elizabeth I, from the collection of portrait miniatures in enamel on copper by the early nineteenth-century artist Henry Bone now on display in the Drawing Room at Kingston Lacy in Dorset. For his depiction of the Queen, Bone has copied the large 'Ditchley' portrait by Marcus Gheeraerts, c.1592, that now hangs in the National Portrait Gallery in London. It is a tribute to his skill that he could reproduce the detail in a miniature measuring only 33·75 × 22·5 cm (13½ × 9 in).

Because of their size, miniatures are easily lost when moving. Pack them yourself in plenty of **acid-free** tissue paper and mark on the box the number of miniatures inside so that you can check that they have all been unpacked.

If a miniature is moved from one location to another, the **relative humidity** must be the same in both locations and a steady relative humidity must be maintained during the journey. Pack the miniatures with plenty of buffering acid-free tissue in a **sealed plastic box**. Wait for 24 hours after they have arrived in their new location before unpacking miniatures, but do not leave them in the plastic box for any longer than that. A conservator would be able to help you with this process.

Display

Display miniatures in low light. If possible, keep them in drawers or cabinets that can be closed or hang curtains that can be drawn when the miniatures are not being looked at. Use blinds or sun curtains on the windows to reduce daylight and to prevent sunlight from falling on the miniatures (*see* PAINTINGS).

Display miniatures away from heat sources or draughts and do not place them on an outside wall. (*See* PAINTINGS and PAPER.)

Storage

Wrap miniatures in acid-free tissue paper and store them in a cool, dry, clean, dark area in **archival quality** boxes. Boxes or cabinets can be adapted to hold miniatures in 'cells', as with COINS AND MEDALS. Do not wrap them in sealed polyethylene or cling film, as condensation could form inside, and do not wrap them in cotton wool, as it will absorb moisture and the fibres may stick to the object.

Housekeeping and Maintenance

Dust the outside of the glass and frame with a soft, clean lint-free cloth or **microfibre cloth**. A little saliva on a cotton wool bud will help to remove flyblow and other marks. Do not use commercial glass cleaners. Silver frames can be polished gently with a silver **metal polishing cloth**, but do not use silver polish, as it may get on to the miniature and be very damaging. A soft **pencil eraser** may remove stubborn tarnish on silver. Handle the miniature very gently when cleaning the frame and lay it flat on a table as you polish it.

Cleaning

Do not attempt to clean or restore miniatures. A great deal of damage can be caused by inappropriate cleaning or repairs. If you are concerned about the condition of a miniature, consult a conservator.

Repair

Do not attempt to conserve, repair or repaint a miniature, or to take it out of its frame. This should be done only by a conservator experienced in working with miniatures.

Wall Paintings

Wall paintings are executed directly on to walls or ceilings. The term 'fresco' is often inaccurately used to refer to all types of wall painting. A true fresco is painted while the wall plaster is still wet; the pigment soaks into the plaster and becomes incorporated with it during the setting of the plaster. Once the plaster is dry, the pigment is securely held in place. Sometimes details are painted on top of the fresco once it is dry. Unless the wall or plaster is damaged, frescoes are fairly resilient.

Other types of wall paintings, known as 'secco' painting, are executed on to dry plaster. The medium used to bind the pigment and fix it to the plaster can be egg, animal glue, casein, drying oils, natural resin mixtures, acrylic resins or many other materials. Secco paintings are often made up of complex layers of ground, paint, glaze and varnish.

The plaster is applied to a prepared wall or ceiling made of masonry or studwork covered with laths. It can be a lime plaster, which is a plaster mix made from lime (calcium hydroxide) and aggregate, such as sand and/or hair, or a gypsum plaster (calcium sulphate hemihydrate), also with an aggregate. Wall plaster may also be a mixture of lime plaster with some gypsum plaster to help the setting. Lime plaster sets very slowly, whereas gypsum plaster sets rapidly. Gypsum plaster is not generally used on exterior walls, as it is slightly soluble, but is more often found on interior walls.

True frescos are painted on to lime plaster, while secco paintings can be painted on to any dry plaster. It is not always easy to differentiate between a true fresco and a well-executed secco painting, particularly if the fresco has been restored. However, if you look closely, the colouring of a fresco appears to sink into the plaster and to be part of the plaster, and the colour is not built up on the surface. Secco painting usually has a surface sheen that can be quite glossy, while the surface of a fresco is matt unless it has been restored or coated. Secco painting or a mixed fresco/secco technique is the most common type of painting found in Britain.

Early or significant wall paintings in the United Kingdom may be Listed, in which case no work can be undertaken to the painting without the agreement of English Heritage or the local conservation officer. Similarly, work cannot be undertaken on a wall painting in a church in the UK without agreement from English Heritage and the appropriate ecclesiastical authorities.

Problems

The durability of a wall painting very much depends on how well it was made, the paint medium, the condition of the wall and building, the use of the room and the standard of maintenance of the building.

The plaster may soften or disintegrate, usually caused by damp in the wall. Damp can transport soluble salts into the plaster, or activate soluble salts already there, and cause considerable disintegration (*see* STONE). Cracks can occur from movement within the building. The adhesion of the plaster may not be sustained and the plaster will eventually fall off the wall. There may be gaps between the plaster and the wall which sound hollow when the surface is tapped gently.

If the wall appears unusually damp, you will need to establish the cause of the damp and have it corrected immediately. Likely causes include missing tiles, cracked or blocked guttering, no damp-course, a bridged damp-course, leaking pipes, plants such as ivy growing up or against the exterior and wood, such as a pile of logs, stacked against the outside of the wall. At certain times of the year, condensation can occur when warm air meets a cold wall. The condensation can be on the surface or inside the wall, and may not always be visible.

On secco paintings the paint layer may crack, lift and flake, and light can cause the colour of the pigment and varnish to change.

Occasionally, a wall painting is exposed during building work. It may have been painted or plastered over. Wall paintings are very vulnerable to damage under these circumstances and you should seek conservation advice as soon as possible. Removing overpaint from the surface of a wall painting is very skilled work and should be undertaken only by a conservator of wall paintings.

Display

Ensure that the building is well maintained.

A wall painting must be protected from physical damage caused by passing people, the backs of chairs and vacuum cleaners. Keep plants and flowers away from wall paintings in case of accidents. If necessary, rope off the area or attach a sheet of **acrylic sheet** (Perspex or Plexiglas) in front of the painting. Fix the sheet to an unpainted part of the wall. Make sure that there is plenty of space, at least 2·5cm (1in), between the wall and the acrylic sheet for air circulation.

Some pigments and varnishes on secco paintings are light-sensitive, so avoid using bright directional lights that are on all the time. If possible, light the painting only when it is being viewed.

Do not paint around wall paintings with modern plastic-based paints. They do not permit the wall to breathe, therefore any damp in the wall will be forced to come through the wall painting. Use lime wash or porous paints.

Housekeeping and Maintenance

The best way to look after a wall painting is to ensure that the building on which it is painted is well maintained, particularly the roof, drains and rainwater goods. If you are worried about the state of a wall painting, discuss its care with a conservator. Do not attempt any kind of conservation or restoration yourself. If the wall painting is deteriorating, even very slowly, you should get advice from a conservator as soon as

Wall painting in the Pompeian Room at Ickworth. This nymph is part of a scheme designed by J. D. Crace in 1879, based on Roman wall paintings uncovered a century earlier at the Villa Negroni on the Esquiline Hill. It is made in the secco technique, and is in good condition, though the paint is shrinking and beginning to lift off the plaster, creating large craquelure.

possible. If paint is deteriorating or peeling off or the plaster is disintegrating, it will be much easier and cheaper to solve the underlying problem before it becomes too severe.

The cleaning of wall paintings is best left to a properly qualified wall painting conservator, who has been trained in the safe removal of surface dirt, discoloured varnish and overpaint. Irreparable damage can be caused by unskilled or inexperienced people attempting to clean wall paintings. The only cleaning of a wall painting that is safe to carry out is the removal of surface dust, but even this should be attempted only after a very careful inspection of the paint surface to ensure that there is no lifting, flaking or blistering paint or loose or deteriorating plaster.

To clean a wall painting in sound condition, remove any dust with a clean, dry, soft brush to direct the dust into a vacuum cleaner (*see* pp.19–20). Take care not to let the nozzle of the vacuum cleaner touch the paint.

Cleaning

If after dusting further cleaning is necessary on a modern wall painting that is in excellent condition, try gently wiping the surface with pieces of a dry **chemical sponge**. Test it first: if the paint is being pulled off by the sponge, do not continue. Similarly, if the sponge polishes the surface undesirably, discontinue its use.

Repair

Wall paintings should be conserved only by a wall painting conservator who will be able to indentify the underlying causes of deterioration. If these problems are not addressed, damage will recur and treatment will have been unsuccessful.

Photographs

A photograph is a visual image produced by the action of light on a sensitised material. Most of us tend to think of a photograph only in terms of prints on paper and strips of film, but photographs can be produced on any material that can carry the chemicals necessary to make the surface sensitive to light, such as glass or metal plate.

The South Gallery at Lacock Abbey in Wiltshire photographed by William Henry Fox Talbot. Fox Talbot began to experiment with paper sensitised with silver chloride in 1834, patenting the process as 'calotypy' seven years later. He took several photographs of Lacock, his family home, and this is one of the earliest known photographs of an interior.

Traditional photographs are produced as either negative or positive images. A positive photograph records tonal values as we read them naturally, whereas a negative shows the tones in reverse. For instance, a negative photograph of a newspaper would show the printing ink in white and the paper in black. The first colour was added to black-and-white photographs by hand; this was done even on daguerreotypes and lantern slides. Some colour processing was carried out as early as 1907, but was not widely available until the mid-1930s.

Photographs have a complicated, multi-layered structure. Most are made up of:

- a base or support: usually paper, metal, glass or plastic.
- a binder, known as the colloid or emulsion layer, which is the viscous medium in which the image material is suspended. The most common ones are albumen, gelatine and collodion.
- an image-forming component held within the binder, which is a light-sensitive material, most commonly silver salts.

Some types of photograph have more layers than others. Photographs are very sensitive because the combination of layers can lead to inherently unstable material. Moreover, each component has its own characteristics and will therefore degrade accordingly.

In the developing process, the image darkens automatically on exposure to light. Further processing in the darkroom is needed to make the image visible, using chemicals to 'fix' the image to make it permanent. If the image is not fixed, the image-forming component would continue to darken on exposure to light and the image would be lost. The exception to this is silver printing-out papers, which required no chemical development and were common in the nineteenth century.

- **PAPER BASE**
Paper has been widely used since William Henry Fox Talbot experimented with his Photogenic Drawing process in the 1830s. In 1841 Fox Talbot patented his invention of the negative-positive calotype process – the forerunner of modern photographic processes.

- **METAL BASE**
In 1839 Louis Jacques Mandé Daguerre announced his invention of the daguerreotype. It was made from a sheet of highly

Late nineteenth-century photograph of a wedding group from the photo album of Rosalie Chichester at Arlington Court, Devon. The print shows typical wear and tear.

polished, silver-plated copper. The image has a mirror-like surface and can appear to be either negative or positive depending on the angle at which the plate is held and how the light strikes the surface. An image from a daguerreotype may only be reproduced by re-photographing and printing it. The daguerreotype was usually produced in standard sizes and in a glass and leather case. Daguerreotypes are rare, but may turn up amongst family possessions. If you find a daguerreotype, treat it with care and ask for professional help sooner rather than later.

The tintype or ferrotype was used a little later than the ambrotype (*see* below) but was produced until the 1930s. It is a direct, positive image on a thin, sensitised iron plate. The image is dull grey and often varnished. The reverse is painted black or dark brown. Tintypes were produced in many sizes and often without a case, although they are sometimes found in daguerreotype or ambrotype cases. Tintypes were cheaper to produce than daguerreotypes and were therefore more common. Rust spots can help to identify a tintype.

● GLASS BASE

Glass was a popular support for photographs throughout the latter half of the nineteenth century for ambrotypes, lantern slides and glass negatives.

The ambrotype (or wet collodion positive) was produced from about 1854. The image was produced on glass in the same sizes as the daguerreotype and the same type of leather case. The ambrotype is actually a negative but appears as a positive image because a black layer of paper, varnish or textile is placed behind it. Unlike daguerreotypes, ambrotypes will always appear as positives unless the black backing is damaged.

Lantern slides are a positive image on a transparent base. They are usually 8 × 10 cm (3 × 4 in) in size and can be both black and white or coloured. The image is on a plate of glass and is protected by a cover glass. The two plates are bound together at the edges with black tape. Lantern slides should not be confused with glass negatives, which vary in size and have a negative image.

Glass negatives include the wet collodion negative dating from about 1851, which has a hand-coated appearance and warm, milky-coloured highlights. The later gelatine dry-plate negative is more commonly found and has neutral black-and-white tones. It also has sharp edges to the image area where the emulsion has been applied by machine. Usually the emulsion on a negative is not protected by a cover glass, so make sure that you do not touch the image.

● PLASTIC BASE

Plastic was first used as an alternative to glass as a transparent support for photographs in the late 1880s. The three main types of plastic supports are cellulose nitrate, cellulose acetate and polyester.

Cellulose nitrate film was used for film and cinematographic or movie film from the 1890s to 1951. Cellulose nitrate is considered a hazardous material and you must seek advice if you suspect you own any. It is extremely flammable and, under conditions of high temperature and inadequate ventilation, it has been known to self-ignite. This is a particular risk with movie film stored in its original metal canisters. The cellulose nitrate deteriorates, giving off acid which accelerates the decomposition of the film. The signs of deterioration are a faded image with brownish or amber yellow discoloration. Bubbles may form on the surface and the film becomes sticky and gradually softens, the negatives weld together and eventually they disintegrate into a brownish powder that has the acrid smell of nitric acid. Be aware that the fumes from deteriorating nitrate film are extremely toxic. Some nitrate film has 'NITRATE' embossed on the side. A photographic conservator, or some professional photographers, should be able to help you identify nitrate film and advise on its storage or disposal.

Safety-based film, which was first made from cellulose acetate, began to replace cellulose nitrate film from the early 1930s, but for some years both were used. Modern acetate film is a great deal more stable than nitrate film and is still used today, but early acetate is prone to severe deterioration. The film base will bubble and give off a smell of vinegar. Acetate film sometimes has 'SAFETY' embossed on the edge of the film. It is flammable but not to the degree of nitrate film.

Polyester-based film was introduced for movie film and still negatives in the 1960s. Sound-track is also made from polyester. It usually has 'ESTAR' printed on the edge of the film. It is long-lasting, but the emulsion does not always bind firmly to the polyester base.

● IMAGE-FORMING COMPONENTS

There are photographs which use metals other than silver as the image-forming component, such as iron in cyanotypes, distinguished by their striking blue colour, or platinum in platinotypes, identified by an unfaded image and exceptionally neutral black and white tones. Some photographs have no metal compounds; for example, gum bichromate prints, which have a pigment image in a gum arabic emulsion.

Problems

The most common image-forming component is silver, which is easily affected by chemicals in the air. Staining, yellowing and fading can all occur. As a result, photographs are very susceptible to deterioration from atmospheric pollution and gases produced by cleaning, storage and display materials such as mounts, adhesives or storage envelopes (see pp.19 and 104).

Light causes photographic images to fade, albumen emulsion to yellow and paper to become brittle. Organic dyes used to tone nineteenth-century black-and-white prints and the dyes in twentieth-century colour photographs are exceptionally light-sensitive.

Heat will increase the rate of deterioration (see p.19) and is particularly damaging for deteriorating acetate or nitrate film and colour photographs. Heat causes photographs to fade even in the absence of light.

Low **relative humidity** leads to the drying and embrittlement of some supports and emulsion layers. High relative humidity can cause worse damage, as it may promote mould and insect activity and swell the gelatine emulsions which can stick to other surfaces. Metal supports may corrode, paper will weaken and glass is more susceptible to deterioration (see GLASS). Albumen emulsions have a strong tendency to yellow and their surface to fissure and crack. The image will fade. If the humidity fluctuates from damp to dry, the emulsion will crack and flake.

If the chemicals from the processing are not completely washed off, they too will eventually affect the image.

Fingerprints leave a residue of grease and

acid on the surface of the negative or photograph which eventually will harm the image. Harmful acids can be in the paper used as a base as well as in the card and board used for mounting a photograph. The acid causes the paper and the image to deteriorate. The alkali present in some paper-based storage enclosures is harmful to acid-stabilised photographs such as cyanotypes and so should be avoided. Use lignin-free or **silver-safe paper**.

It is imperative to prevent moisture from coming into contact with the emulsion side of any photograph. This causes enormous damage.

● PAPER BASE

The paper used for photographs is subject to deterioration by light, acidity and pollution, insects, mould, foxing and physical damage, as discussed in PAPER.

● METAL BASE

Daguerreotypes are quite robust when the case is intact, but the metal will corrode or tarnish if they are kept in damp conditions. The glass can also deteriorate (see GLASS). Daguerreotypes should be handled with care to ensure that the glass covering does not crack. If this happens, the image will tarnish. Never touch the metal surface.

As tintypes were not always protected by a case, they are often bent and have flaking emulsion. The iron is prone to rusting in damp conditions. Keep tintypes dry to prevent rust from forming. Do not touch the image.

● GLASS BASE

All types of photograph which use a glass support are susceptible to damage from breaking and cracking and should be handled carefully. Lantern slides and glass negatives are usually quite stable so, if handled carefully, they are quite durable. Glass disease is sometimes seen, particularly on the cover glasses of daguerreotypes (see GLASS).

● PLASTIC BASE

Nitrate and acetate film deteriorates as described above. When film is kept in very dry conditions, the emulsion may crack, shrink and flake. In very humid conditions, mould may develop, the plasticiser which is incorporated in the plastic base to keep if flexible may crystallise and the image may distort. If the temperature fluctuates, the emulsion will become detached from the base. Cellulose acetate and nitrate film can discolour.

The mantelpiece in the Dining Room at Shaw's Corner, Ayot St Lawrence in Hertfordshire. The photographs lined up on the shelf on either side of the Bakelite clock reflect G.B. Shaw's extraordinary life – Gandhi, Dzershinsky (a Bolshevik and leader of the KGB), Lenin, Stalin, the dramatist Granville-Barker, Shaw's birthplace in Dublin, and Ibsen. On the wall hang prints of Dublin. Keeping photographs in frames has helped to preserve them, especially when displayed over a fire.

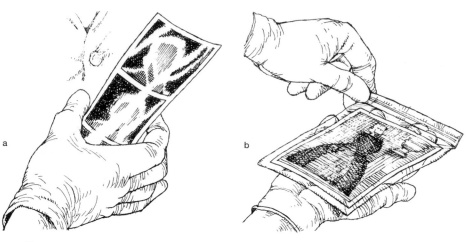

Handling negatives
(a) *Keep the matt emulsion side towards the body* (b) *Handle the edge only, and support the photograph with the other hand.*

Handling

Handle photographs as little as possible and always wear **gloves**, as the oils and acidity from our fingers deposited on photographic emulsions will lead eventually to irreversible staining.

Never touch the surface of the image on the print or the negative. Handle negatives, including modern ones, by an edge and the shiny, non-emulsion side. Keep the matt emulsion side towards you to ensure that it is not damaged. If the photograph is to be handled a lot, mount it on **acid-free** card or put it in a transparent polyester envelope or enclosure made from **clear polyester film**. (*See* Storage.)

Avoid lifting a photograph by one corner; support it from behind with the flat of your hand or a tray. If you want to remove a photograph from its enclosure, or envelope, place it flat on the table. Hold the photograph in one hand and gently ease the envelope away, i.e. remove the enclosure from the object rather than the other way round. If there is any resistance, stop immediately, examine the photograph carefully and if it appears to be stuck to the enclosure, seek help from a photographic conservator, who should be able to release it without causing any damage.

When moving photographs from one location to another, carry them on a tray with a lip and do not move them from a cold to warm location, as condensation may form on the surface. Do not underestimate the weight of the material, particularly boxes of glass plates, as you move them.

Avoid looking at photographs while there is food and drink or other liquids nearby.

If you need to make notes on the reverse of a photograph, use a soft pencil. Sharp, hard pencils or pens will leave permanent indentation marks on the image. Ink will stain the image and cannot be removed, if it accidentally gets onto the photograph.

If you try to flatten a rolled-up photograph, there is a risk that the emulsion will split and peel off. Seek conservation advice.

Never use self-adhesive tape on photographs, *see* Repair.

See PAPER for more information on Handling.

Display

Where possible, display a copy of an original photograph rather than the original itself, because the image is likely to fade. If you want to make prints from a negative, it is advisable to have the negative copied and to use the new negative for prints. If you do not have the original negative, it is still possible to have the photograph copied. A reputable photographer should be able to help.

Similarly, if you want to use lantern slides or 35mm transparencies regularly, it is a good idea to have them copied, because of the risk of damage from handling and from the intense heat and light of a projector. Try to limit exposure to a short duration and, where possible, use a hand-held viewer.

When displaying an original photograph, choose a cooler (below 20°C/68°F), drier room, internal walls and areas where direct light will not fall on it. If possible, keep photographs in the dark or cover them when you are away or they not being viewed. Avoid heat sources (*see* PAPER and

pp.17–18). Damp locations should also be avoided.

Where possible, have original photographs mounted and framed for display by a photographic materials conservator. Frame a photograph as discussed in PAPER. Use the original mount, a new overmount or fillets to keep the photograph from touching the glass. The mount card and mounting materials must be **archival quality**, lignin-free and **silver-safe**. **Museum board** or certain **acid-free** boards may contain some alkali, which could damage acid-stabilised photographic processes, so they should not be used.

It is not advisable to dry-mount original photographs nor to use open-sided ready-made frames which clip together for long-term framing, as they are open to dust, insects and air pollution.

See PAPER for more information on Display.

Storage

Photographic material, particularly colour material, deteriorates more slowly in cool conditions. Therefore, the temperature of a storage area should be below 20°C/68°F, but it is also important, particularly for film and metal plates, that it is not damp. Avoid locally produced pollution as discussed in the Introduction (*see* p.19). The area should be clean and well-ventilated. Open drawers and boxes occasionally, at least once a year, to ventilate them and inspect for pests or mould.

Ideally, photographs should be stored in individual enclosures or envelopes, in appropriate boxes and then in cupboards, drawers or on shelves to protect them from light, dust pollution and unsuitable humidity.

The enclosures should contain the whole object with no part protruding. Prints are often stored in **clear polyester film** enclosures so that there is no need to handle them directly once they have been protected in this way. Do not store more than one photograph in an enclosure. Make sure that the enclosures are not made from polyvinyl chloride (PVC), which is also transparent but gives off vapours which are harmful to the film. Glassine paper, a translucent, off-white crisp paper often traditionally used for this purpose, is not suitable for storage, as it too produces acid vapours. Film should be stored in **silver-safe** paper. Clear polyester film is not recommended for storing film, and particularly not for cellulose acetate or nitrate film, as it reduces ventilation. If you are unable to purchase the enclosures, lay the photographs flat in the box and interleave the photographs with smooth **acid-free** tissue. If you write any form of identification on the enclosure, do it before the negative or print is placed inside.

Ideally, the boxes should be bought from a specialist conservation supplier and made from **archival quality**, acid-free, silver-safe materials. If you are unable to purchase specialist storage boxes, a clean, sturdy cardboard box may be a suitable alternative, as it is better than having the photographs loose in a drawer. Line the box with acid-free tissue and interleave the photographs with more tissue paper. This helps to buffer the harmful effects of the cardboard. Store the box horizontally.

If you suspect you have pre-1930s film, or there is obvious deterioration, consult a conservator who will be able to tell whether you have cellulose nitrate and advise on suitable treatment. The film should be kept in very cool, well-ventilated conditions away from other photographs.

Cased images (daguerreotypes, ambrotypes and tintypes) can be carefully wrapped in acid-free tissue and placed inside a box.

Loose glass plates are best kept in sturdy, purpose-made archival boxes that store them in the upright plane. If you have the original wooden boxes, these too provide good physical protection and a buffer against changing environmental conditions. Dust the boxes out thoroughly after removing the plates. Ideally, the plates should also have individual wrappers made from silver-safe paper.

Housekeeping and Maintenance

Inspect your collection at least once a year, in the spring, for pests and mould.

Remove the dust from photographs in their frames using a soft, clean duster, a **microfibre cloth** or a soft brush. Do not allow the dust to penetrate inside frames.

Cleaning

Before storing photographs in new enclosures, they may need dusting. Prints, glass plates, including lantern slides, tintypes, roll and sheet film may all be dusted, but only if they are in good condition. If the photographs are torn, broken, mouldy, curled or have a flaking emulsion layer, it is essential to leave the cleaning to a specialist conservator.

Work in a clean area on a clear surface, such as a clean sheet of blotting paper. Use a very soft brush, made from squirrel or ponyhair, and use the brush for this purpose alone. Gently brush both surfaces, working from the centre outwards. Place the dusted photograph in its new enclosure immediately after cleaning.

Do not attempt to remove a cased photograph, such as a daguerreotype or ambrotype, from its casing for dusting, and do not use any fluids or other methods to remove dirt or stains. These problems must be taken to a conservator. Dust the outside of the case with a soft, clean duster or **microfibre cloth**.

Repair

There are no repairs to original photographs that a non-specialist can carry out safely. Self-adhesive tape and incorrect adhesive can cause irreversible damage to the emulsion layer of the photograph. A conservator can repair a torn print.

The good news is that if you have a damaged photograph, the image may still be recoverable if you have it copied. There are ways of retouching a copy photograph, which means that you can enjoy a complete image while not continuing to harm your original. Directly retouching an original photograph for the purposes of display or copying is not recommended, as it has the potential to cause irreversible damage.

Broken glass plates should not be repaired. Place them on paper towels in a box, emulsion side up, until you can take them to a photographic conservator.

See PAPER for Framing.

● **WATER-DAMAGED PHOTOGRAPHS**
If a small spillage occurs, soak up the liquid by holding a piece of paper towel vertically at the edge of the spill and allow the moisture to soak upwards. Do not touch the surface of the print directly, as the emulsion layer is easily disturbed. Gelatine emulsions and aged emulsions soften in water and will come off readily.

In the case of more serious water damage, you should seek specialist advice as soon as possible. Do not leave wet photographs where they will not be able to dry or sitting on a non-absorbent surface, as it does not take long for mould to develop and this could lead to irreversible staining.

Let most types of photograph air dry face up, separated from their enclosures, on blotting paper or paper towel.

Cased photographs should be opened, but not disassembled, and should be allowed to air dry.

Soak up spillage by holding paper towel vertically, avoiding touching the surface of the photograph.

Photograph Albums

Protect photograph albums against dust with a cover made from clean cotton or linen sheeting or **Tyvek**. Additional physical protection can be provided by an **acid-free** box, such as the boxes made for books. Unless the albums are very large, they can be placed in a vertical position to avoid unnecessary pressure on the fragile emulsion surface of the prints inside. However, if there are loose prints inside, it is preferable to store the albums flat. The shelf on which it is stored must be as wide or wider than the album.

The outside of photograph albums may be cleaned in the same way as BOOKS. However, great care must be taken not to allow dust to penetrate inside an album while dusting it. This may be difficult if the pages of the album are warped. In this case, it may be preferable to vacuum off the dust as much as possible before using the brush. Do not touch the block of pages with the vacuum cleaner; hold the nozzle a little way from the album.

Remove loose dirt from inside the album with a clean cotton wool pad; dust the endpapers and spaces between the photographs, working from the centre outwards, away from the photographs. Prevent the dust from falling on to the photographs by using a clean sheet of paper as a mask. Dust the prints with a soft, clean brush.

Albums are not recommended for storing historical photographs unless they are original, but if you prefer to keep your photographs in this way, use acid-free and **silver-safe** materials. Hold the photographs in place with corner hinges. Do not stick the photographs on to the pages of an album or use albums with transparent self-adhesive pages. Choose an album that is bound in such a way that it will close when the photographs are on the pages. A system of polyester pages with pockets that fit in to an acid-free file type box (available from conservation suppliers) makes a very good alternative to an album.

Records, Discs and Cylinders

The first phonographs used cylinders for reproducing sounds and music. They were originally made from wax and then from an early synthetic thermosetting material (*see* PLASTICS AND RUBBER; *see* WAX for wax cylinders). Discs or records took over from cylinders as a method of reproducing music at the end of the nineteenth century (*see also* MUSICAL BOXES and AUTOMATA). Early records were made from shellac and a filler, because shellac accepts the visible traces of sound in very fine detail (*see* PLASTICS AND RUBBER). They were black and brittle, and are often referred to as 78s, as they turned at 78 revolutions per minute on the turntable. 78s were superseded in their turn by extended-play (EP) and long-playing (LP) records, revolving at 45 and 33 rpm respectively, made from much tougher and more flexible vinyl plastic.

Handling

Handle 78s with great care, as they are very brittle. They also scratch very easily, so always keep them free of dust and, when they are not being played, in their card or paper sleeves. If a record sleeve is missing, make one up from **acid-free** card; alternatively, **archival quality** sleeves can be purchased from conservation suppliers. Avoid touching the playing part of the record, as the oil left from your fingers will collect dust.

Do not hold the record at the edge with one hand, as a piece could snap out of the edge. Hold it with two hands and, where

Boxes of pianola rolls in the Drawing Room at Sunnycroft in Wellington, Shropshire. These boxes are just as important to preserve as the rolls themselves, as they not only provide protection, but identification too.

possible, support the weight of the record on the palm of one hand, while holding it securely with the other. Alternatively, support the weight of the record with the fingers under the central label and the edge resting on the balls of the thumbs. Always handle records individually and never carry many at the same time.

If you are looking through records that are stored like index cards (i.e. on their edges in a box), take care that edges do not snap off the lower half of the records as you flip through them. When removing or replacing a record on a shelf, there is a danger that the outside edge will chip.

Keep records cool, as shellac and vinyl warp very easily at fairly low temperatures. When 78 rpm records were in production they were often turned into flowerpots by dipping them in hot water and moulding them around a pot. The plastic of EPs and LPs will also distort at higher temperatures.

The more records are played, the faster they will wear out, particularly if they are dirty and the needle is blunt. Ensure that you use the correct stylus, cartridge type and weight to play each particular type of record; a specialist shop will be able to advise. Always clean a record before you begin playing it. It is advisable to make recordings of your early records and listen to your copies.

Display and Storage

Keep records out of direct sunlight and away from radiators or fires, as the shellac will warp easily. Ideally, records should be kept in their dust sleeves and stored vertically like books; new dust sleeves can be obtained from conservation suppliers. It is important that the records should not be squashed too close together nor be too loose. Divide the shelf with vertical dividers like pigeonholes so that each section holds about ten records. This will prevent too much pressure or weight being on one record. The records should not be allowed to lean; they must be kept vertical or they might crack. Use a block of wood or a book-end to keep the records upright. The shelf must be as wide or wider than the records. Use a thin sheet of **polyethylene foam** to pad the floor of the shelf. If you keep your records in boxes, again divide them into sections so that not more than about ten records are in each section. The dividers must be fixed vertically into the box so that they do not lean over with the records. If the records have to be stored flat in boxes, make sure the boxes are rigid, and put only a very few records in each. Alternatively, records can be stored in **Solander boxes** which have a side that drops down when the box end is removed to ease access to the records.

Keep cylinders in their protective sleeves. If the sleeve is missing, make a new one from **acid-free** card or wrap it in acid-free tissue. The cylinders can be stacked on their side, but do not pile them up or the bottom ones will be crushed. They are very brittle and break easily.

Keep records and cylinders in a cool, dry, clean area. Do not store them in the attic, which can be very hot or cold, nor in a damp basement. Keep the temperature and **relative humidity** as steady as possible.

Housekeeping and Maintenance

To remove dust from 78s, first use a soft brush, then gently wipe the playing surfaces with a soft sponge dipped in warm water containing a few drops of **conservation-grade detergent** or a mild household detergent. Wipe in the direction of the grooves; do not scrub the surface and do not wet the label. Rinse the sponge in clean water and squeeze it out well before wiping the record again. Gently use a paper towel to pat moisture from the surface before leaving the record to dry naturally. Never use artificial heat to dry records, and always remember how easily they break.

EPs and LPs can be washed in the same way, but water must not be used on wax cylinders. They can be brushed clean with a soft ponyhair brush, but do not try to clean them further as they are brittle and easily damaged.

Clean and store plastic cylinders as recommended for Records and PLASTICS AND RUBBER.

Repair

Do not attempt to repair broken records. It may be possible to have a recording made from a broken record by a specialist.

Scientific Instruments

Microscopes, telescopes, theodolites, compasses and many other items are generally classified as scientific instruments. These objects are usually made from metal combined with other materials such as leather, wood, glass, ceramic, paper, textiles, plastic and shagreen. The metals used include brass and other copper alloys, iron or steel, or silver or nickel alloys. Scientific instruments are often stored in purpose-made wooden or leather cases. They were, and in some cases still are, used for many purposes, including navigation, surveying, scientific examination, medicine and astronomy.

Problems

The problems associated with this group of objects are metal corrosion, loss of parts, broken lenses and deterioration of the **organic materials** caused by mould, woodworm and red-rot of leather. The brass used in scientific instruments was frequently coated with a red- or yellow-tinted translucent varnish. This should not be removed. For more information on each type of material, *see* the appropriate section.

Handling

Wear **gloves** before handling antique scientific instruments, as sweat from fingers is very corrosive.

Before lifting or moving an instrument, any moving parts should be removed or tied down or carefully wedged into place with **acid-free** tissue. Do not pick up these objects by holding on to fragile projections. For instance, hold a microscope by the main arm, not the actual microscope piece. Support the weight from underneath with your other hand. Take care not to drop the instrument, as a sharp blow can dislodge lenses and mirrors and upset springs, etc.

Do not force tight or locked screw threads nor apply oil or penetrating fluids to the surface of rusted movements. It is difficult to control the flow of fluids, and they may damage other parts of the object.

Use antique instruments as little as possible. The more they are used, the more damage is caused from wear.

Do not open a compass if it is filled with liquid. If the liquid has leaked and some air is in the reservoir, it should be properly filled by a chandler or compass manufacturer, as it is very difficult to expel the air completely.

Display and Storage

Display and store scientific instruments in a cool, clean, dry, dust-free area. The area should not be too dry, otherwise the **organic materials** will become brittle or crack, nor so damp that the metal will corrode. There should be good ventilation around the objects to prevent the metal from tarnishing and mould from growing on the organic materials. Do not store scientific instruments in an attic or loft where the temperature fluctuates greatly nor in a damp basement. Keep scientific instruments away from direct sunlight. Delicate instruments can be displayed under glass domes available from some clock-makers' suppliers.

The best method of protecting scientific instruments from dust while they are stored is to make fine linen, **Tyvek** or washed calico bags to cover them. Alternatively, you can lightly wrap them in **acid-free** tissue or cover with a plastic bottle, having cut off the top. Use only **archival quality** cardboard boxes.

Any loose or broken pieces should be kept with the object. Do not attach them with self-adhesive tape or rubber bands: use good quality string or cotton tape. If the pieces are very small, place them in a good quality white envelope and label it clearly.

Housekeeping and Maintenance

Remove dust using a soft brush and vacuum cleaner (*see* pp.19–20). **Compressed air** may also help to dislodge dust from crevices.

Cleaning

Where dirt remains on the surface after dusting, a dry **chemical sponge** or a cotton bud dampened with saliva might remove it. Use a clean **microfibre cloth** for cleaning lenses and mirrors. Do not allow liquid to penetrate inside the instrument.

Scientific instruments are complex and delicate, and inexperienced handling can cause a lot of damage. Further cleaning should be carried out by a conservator experienced in working with these objects.

Make sure that you do not remove any of the original lacquer left on metal parts, particularly on brass. Avoid using commercial glass cleaners, as they often contain products such as vinegar or ammonia that cause the metal to tarnish.

It may be necessary to take an object apart so that each piece can be thoroughly cleaned. If any pieces are stiff or jammed, do not force them. This is best done by a conservator working with scientific instruments, but if you do this yourself, carefully record how the pieces go together and label each one to avoid the risk of problems during reassembly.

It is not often possible to find replacement gaskets for any that have perished. You may be able to make them from leather off-cuts or black **polyethylene foam** using the original as a pattern.

Check wooden cases for woodworm. Clean and treat them as described in WOOD.

Repair

Scientific instruments are very delicate and should be repaired only by someone qualified and knowledgeable in treating instruments.

ABOVE: *Charles Paget Wade was a collector supremo, filling his home, Snowshill Manor in Gloucestershire, with all manner of collections. 'Admiral' houses his extensive collection of nautical and scientific objects. This photograph shows a model of a Norwegian Nordland boat, a planetarium, a Culpeper-type microscope in its original box, c.1750, various compasses and other navigational and surveying instruments, and ship's logs. All these pieces should be protected from the light. The metal parts of the microscope are precision-made and need protection from corrosion, so they cannot be moved.*

Barometers

Barometers are instruments for measuring changes in atmospheric pressure and are used to forecast the weather. Barometer cases are often decorated with ivory, mother-of-pearl, marquetry or metal inlay. The mechanism of most barometers is very delicate; it can include a long glass tube containing mercury and often a fine hair-thin piece of paper or chamois leather if a hygrometer is included. A hygrometer measures the humidity of the air.

Aneroid barometers do not have a column of liquid mercury and comprise a vacuum box with gear-train amplification. Mercury barometers contain a glass mercury tube.

Check for the problems usually associated with wood, such as woodworm, missing or rising veneer, missing or loose inlay and cracking (*see* WOOD). The hair-spring mechanism of an aneroid barometer may be broken; in which case, the needle will not move or may just be pointing downwards.

Handling

The mechanism within barometers is very delicate and is easily damaged with incorrect handling. Before moving a barometer, you will need to know if it is a mercury or an aneroid barometer. If in doubt, seek advice; very often clock dealers or conservators are able to help with barometers.

Ship's barometers can be moved vertically, but other mercury barometers should be turned very gently to an angle of 45° before moving them. If the barometer has a closing screw, turn the screw completely, then you can lay it horizontally. Avoid sudden jolts and jars.

Display

Barometers are usually designed to hang on a wall. Make sure that the fixing is strong enough and the wall is solid and in good condition. If the barometer is to be hung on a partition wall, use fixings designed specifically for hollow walls; this will prevent the barometer from pulling itself off. Avoid hanging a barometer on an outside wall, as these are often damp. If this is the only available space, ensure air can circulate behind the barometer by placing spacers, such as pieces of cork, behind the instrument.

Hang the barometer in a position where it will not get knocked or hit by people passing by. Do not display barometers in direct sunlight, or over a radiator, near an open fire or over a heating vent (*see* p.18).

Storage

Store a barometer upright in a clean, dry room. It must be secured so it does not fall over. If possible, hang it on a dry wall out of harm's way.

To protect a barometer from dust, wrap it lightly in **acid-free** tissue, **Tyvek**, washed calico or an old clean sheet. Do not leave it wrapped up tightly in a lot of padding, as this may absorb damp and could affect the mechanism of the barometer. Do not wrap a barometer in sealed polyethylene.

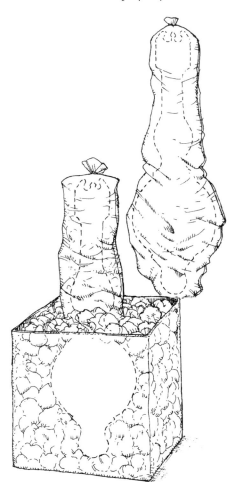

Wrapping a barometer lightly to avoid absorbing damp and storing it upright.

Housekeeping and Maintenance

Clean the wood as described in WOOD. Do not get cleaning materials into the mechanism.

Do not clean the glass with commercial glass cleaner, as the chemicals in the cleaner will harm the metal and the wood. Use a dry **microfibre cloth**. If necessary, saliva on a swab will help remove stubborn spots. Take great care not to get the glass wet. Do not attempt to clean the dial.

Repair

See WOOD for repairs to the case. Do not attempt to repair the mechanism yourself. There are conservators who specialise in barometers and some clock- or furniture-makers also handle barometers.

Cameras

Cameras are similar to scientific instruments in that they are composed of a combination of materials, including glass, leather, wood, brass, steel, textiles, rubber and plastics.

Clean the camera as described above, but never take it apart.

Cameras often contain a certain amount of varnished wood. Clean the wood as described in WOOD, taking care not to remove the lacquer. Do not attempt to clean or treat the inside of the camera.

Even the earliest cameras were very sophisticated, so do not try to repair or restore the mechanism. This should be done by someone experienced in this field. If any part of the mechanism is stuck, do not force it; seek expert help.

Tools

Carpenters' planes, gardeners' scythes, butter moulds, silversmiths' tools and other tools are now very collectable. They are usually made from wood and ferrous metal with brass fittings. Certain tools may include rubber, silver, leather, glass, string and other materials.

Problems

The wood is vulnerable to insect attack and the metals corrode in a damp environment.

Many tools have developed a **patina** from use. On historic tools this is considered an interesting part of the tool as it indicates how it was used. Therefore, tools are not usually so thoroughly cleaned that they

dilute solution of **conservation-grade detergent** and water. Check that you are not removing a varnish or **patina**. Wipe the surface with a clean, damp swab. If you want to apply a finish to the handle, apply a little colourless **beeswax polish** and buff with a soft cloth.

The brass components of the tools can be polished in the same way as furniture fittings (*see* BRASS). Remove light rust with cotton wool and a **fine abrasive paste** (*see* IRON AND STEEL). Heavier corrosion can be removed with fine wire wool (grade 0000) and fine abrasive paste (*see* IRON AND STEEL).

Toys and Games

This group of objects can include rocking horses, teddy bears, and dolls as well as board games, playing cards, train sets, bagatelle and footballs. They are often made from printed card and paper but also from wood, textiles and a wide range of materials. The heads of dolls, for example, can be made from plastic, wax, ceramic or painted wood; there may be a mechanism in the body, which can be made from wood, plastic or a soft filling bound in a textile. The doll may be dressed in cotton and wool clothes with leather shoes.

Problems

Toys and games are often damaged from previous use. Soft toys, dolls' costumes and wood are vulnerable to insect attack. Card and paper used to make games may contain materials that decompose to form acids and become discoloured and eventually brittle, particularly when exposed to light (*see* PAPER). Light will also fade inks, paints and dyes and will damage textiles. Metal parts may corrode. See the appropriate material sections for further information.

Handling

Even if these objects are used, they should still be handled with care and protected from physical damage. *See* appropriate material sections.

Display

See the appropriate material sections.

look 'as good as new'. However, tools do require some maintenance and occasional cleaning to keep them in good condition.

Handling, Display and Storage

See pp.12–14 and the appropriate material. If the tools are stored in an outhouse, make sure it is dry and inspect the tools regularly for woodworm and rust.

Housekeeping and Maintenance

See pp.14–15 for treatment against insect attack. Remove dust with a brush and vacuum cleaner (*see* pp.19–20).

ABOVE: *George Bernard Shaw was a practical man, as revealed in this neat collection of tools now on display in the study at Shaw's Corner, Ayot St Lawrence in Hertfordshire. Tools must be protected from corrosion, especially mild steel.*

Protect the iron with a thin film of a **microcrystalline wax** or **light machine oil** with rust-inhibiting properties. Oil or wax the metal regularly, once a year or as needed. Use microcrystalline wax to protect the brass.

Cleaning

Further cleaning of wood can be done with cotton swabs or buds dampened with a

Storage

Store toys and games in clean and dry conditions. Protect them from dust and dirt by covering them with clean **dustsheets** or **acid-free** tissue or put them in **archival quality** boxes. Pack games with loose parts such as counters, cards or dice, so that the parts are kept with the game and not separated. Label with the name of the game to avoid confusion in the future. Check in the spring and summer for signs of insect attack and metal corrosion.

Housekeeping and Maintenance

Remove dust with a soft brush and vacuum cleaner (*see* pp.19-20) or use a dry **micro-fibre cloth** on smooth surfaces in good condition. Lightly vacuum soft toys, as described in TEXTILES.

Cleaning

See the appropriate material sections for information on Cleaning. Where an object is made from more than one material, care must be taken to prevent the cleaning fluid from one running on to the other.

Repair

See appropriate material sections. Self-adhesive tape can stain and pull the paper off the surface if it is used to repair boards and boxes; use **Japanese paper** and starch paste or a conservation-grade gummed **brown paper tape** as described in PAPER.

ABOVE RIGHT: *The early twentieth-century Nursery at Wightwick Manor, West Midlands. The little dog on the right, of painted wood with a wooden base, has been well-used and shows signs of flaking and cracking. On the walls are songs and rhyme sheets of paper stuck on card: these show signs of staining and of discolouring through deterioration. The books have retained their original paper dustcovers.*

RIGHT: *Nineteenth-century wooden rocking horse bought for William Henry Fox Talbot's children, in the Stone Gallery at Lacock Abbey in Wiltshire. The paintwork is lifting, and there are areas that are missing. The wood is beginning to crack where sections are coming apart. The base shows the most wear, with chipping and evidence of repainting. These battle scars are well worth keeping as they show use by generations of children.*

GLOSSARY

Trade names have been given as a guide, but other suitable products are available.

Acetone
Also known as propanone. An **organic solvent** used for removing grease, some adhesives and some paints (*see* **solvent mixtures**). Acetone can damage paints, lacquer, varnish and plastics, and should always be used with care. It can remove the oils from skin so wear neoprene gloves (*see* **gloves**) when using acetone, and follow the health and safety instructions provided with the solvent.

Acid-free or archival quality
These terms refer to materials that are recommended for use when displaying and storing objects. Acid-free and archival quality materials do not give off damaging acids or other harmful compounds.

There are two categories of archival paper: those that are acid-free (usually made from cotton rag or chemical pulp containing neither lignin nor other acidic components such as alum-rosin size), and those that contain an alkaline buffer, usually calcium carbonate. The latter should not be used with photographs. Special papers (eg. Silversafe™) are produced for use with photographic materials.

Some plastics, such as PVC, may evolve acids and should not be used to store antiques; **clear polyester film** is usually used where transparent storage or display material is required.

Acrylic sheet, blocks, rods
Trade names: Perspex; Plexiglas
Clear acrylic sheet, rods or blocks used for framing and displaying objects. It is acid-free and stable but scratches easily and has high static attraction, so accumulates dust. Acrylic sheet should not be used for glazing charcoal and pastel drawings, or very deteriorated textiles.

Adhesives
A wide range of adhesives is available but only a few are used in conservation. Adhesives vary in their durability, strength, colour and flexibility. Conservation adhesives are chosen so that they hold the object safely but do not cause long-term problems from being too strong or rigid, or by producing products that can be harmful to the object. Generally they remain soluble so that they can be removed if necessary.

The following groups of adhesives are referred to in the book:

Cyanoacrylate adhesive
Trade names: Loctite; Superglue
These very strong adhesives are seldom used in conservation as they are extremely difficult to remove or reverse successfully. However, they are sometimes used for glass conservation as glass does not bond easily. If possible, choose an adhesive that is made especially for glass and also one that cures with daylight or ultraviolet light as this will give you time to ensure that the join is precise.

Easily reversible adhesive
The term 'easily reversible' refers to adhesives that are known to be stable and can be removed using a solvent. HMG Paraloid B72, made of an acrylic resin, is widely used by conservators, but it is too soft for very hot climates. Under these circumstances, HMG cellulose nitrate is recommended; however, it is used less by conservators because it can turn yellow or brown in time. UHU All Purpose Clear Adhesive, made of a polyvinyl acetate resin, is widely available and is an acceptable alternative. Other commercially available adhesives are less predictable because manufacturers change their ingredients; they may include materials that can cause the adhesive to discolour or change nature, or the adhesive may be too strong or otherwise damaging to the object. *See also* **Neutral pH emulsion adhesive**.

Epoxy resin
Trade names: Araldite; Devcon
Two-part resin used as an adhesive and for other purposes. It is also used as a casting material, a gap filler and in the manufacture of a wide range of items. Although epoxy resins are strong, they are not recommended for use with most antiques as they are hard, discolour, and are difficult to remove, so can cause much damage. However, there are occasions when their use is justified. Read the manufacturer's health and safety guidelines carefully when using these adhesives.

Fish glue; Isinglass
Isinglass is produced from the swim-bladder of the sturgeon. It is a protein-based glue, as are gelatine, rabbit skin glue and Scotch glue, but unlike those glues, it does not gel before setting. It is weaker than Scotch glue but is useful for small repairs on wood and gilded surfaces. Cover a small quantity of isinglass strands with de-ionised water and allow to soak overnight. Warm the mixture in a double boiler until the strands are fully softened. The glue may be cloudy when ready for use. It can be stored in a covered container for a few days in the fridge.

Isinglass can be obtained from specialist conservation suppliers and some art shops.

Gelatine
Like Scotch and rabbit skin glue, gelatine is extracted from cattle and sheep hides and/or bones. It gels when cold, so use it warm. In conservation it is occasionally used as a paint consolidant and an adhesive. Most widely known as a constituent in cooking, gelatine is also used in photographic emulsions. Swell the gelatine in cold water and then dissolve by warming in a double boiler.

Neutral pH emulsion adhesive
Trade names: Lineco; Evacon Conservation Adhesive
These are vinyl acetate polymer emulsions which are neutral pH and water-soluble. Used widely in conservation, particularly for **organic materials**, as they are more stable than commercial PVAC emulsion adhesives (*see* below) and do not emit harmful acid vapours.

Polyester resin
A two-part resin used in car body filler and sometimes as an adhesive. Polyester resins set hard and are difficult to remove, so are not recommended for use with antiques. However, polyester film is used for storage (*see* **clear polyester film**).

PVAC (Polyvinyl acetate) emulsion adhesive
Trade names: Evostick Resin W; Elmo's glue
A white liquid with the consistency of single cream, which is almost clear when set, but remains quite soft and flexible. It is often sold commercially as an adhesive for wood. The adhesive can be thinned with water and, before it is set, can be wiped off with a damp cloth. Once set, the adhesive can be dissolved with difficulty using **acetone**. PVAC emulsion adhesives may emit organic acid vapours and may become insoluble in time. **Neutral pH emulsion adhesives** are preferred in conservation as they are more easily reversed, and do not produce acid vapours.

Rabbit skin glue
Rabbit skin glue is a protein glue similar to gelatine used for gilding and in some other areas of conservation. It forms a gel when cool, so is used warm.

Add 10 parts of de-ionised water to 1 part of rabbit skin glue in a glass or ceramic container and leave to soak overnight. Gently heat in a double boiler until all the glue has dissolved. The glue can be stored in a covered container for a few days in the fridge, but then must be warmed in the double boiler for use.

Rabbit skin glue is supplied by art shops, gilding suppliers, furniture restoration suppliers and some conservation suppliers.

Scotch glue
Also known as animal glue or pearl glue. A protein glue stronger than gelatine and rabbit skin glue, commonly used in furniture manufacture and conservation. Place a small handful of beads in a ceramic or glass bowl, cover with de-ionised or purified water and allow to soak overnight. Warm the mixture gently in a double boiler until all the beads have dissolved. The glue has to be used warm as it gels when cool. It can be stored in a covered container fridge for a few days; warm it in a double boiler before use. Apply the glue to both surfaces of a join when warm and clamp together while the glue cools and dries.

Scotch glue is obtainable from some art shops, gilding, furniture restoration and conservation suppliers.

Alcohol
Generally the alcohol used in conservation is ethanol (ethyl alcohol) but in some countries such as the UK the sale of ethanol is restricted, therefore near equivalents are used. Purple methylated spirit (meths) is easy to find but is not recommended as it contains an oil and a denaturant in addition to colouring material, all of which may be damaging to objects. You can buy isopropanol or propan-2-ol (two names for the same thing), which is almost as good as ethanol for cleaning, from pharmacists or chemists. Conservators usually have a government licence to buy industrial methylated spirit (IMS), which is mainly ethanol and is slightly more effective than isopropanol. *See* **solvent mixtures**.

Ammonia
Ammonia is a gas usually used dissolved in water as a liquid (colloquially known as ammonia, but actually ammonium hydroxide solution). It has an overpowering smell and is very alkaline. The most concentrated solution of ammonia has a specific gravity of 0·880 and is commonly called '880' ammonia.

Ammonia is sometimes recommended for cleaning, but care must be taken as it can damage or discolour many materials, including paint and metals, and can be highly damaging to brass. If ammonia is used, it must be diluted with water and stored in a lidded glass container.

Ammonia is obtainable from pharmacies and chemists.

Anti-creep tape
Tape or mat, available from carpet suppliers and some hardware shops, that helps to prevent carpets and rugs from slipping. Some brands have an adhesive on one side so that they may be attached to the carpet; others have no adhesive but lie between the floor and carpet. Both types prevent slippage by friction. The non-adhesive type is preferable as adhering tape to the carpet should be avoided. The tapes deteriorate over time and should be replaced as necessary.

Archaeological objects
These are objects that have been dug up or excavated after being buried for many years. When an object is buried it often reaches a state of equilibrium within the burial environment and is quite stable. Once it is excavated, deterioration can take place very rapidly. Often the corrosion products or other material closely associated with the object contain information about the object or its burial condition which can be lost by inappropriate cleaning. Looking after archaeological objects requires specialist skill, so they should be cleaned and conserved by a conservator specialising in archaeological work.

Archival quality
See **acid-free**.

Area Museum Council (AMC)
Area Museum Councils are regional bodies in the United Kingdom that promote the interests of museums and galleries in their regions and provide advice. The regions are: Council of Museums in Wales/Cyngor Amgueddfcydd yng Nghymru; East Midlands Museums Service; North East Museums; North West Museums Service; Northern Ireland Museums Council; Scottish Museums Council; South Eastern Museums Service; South West Museums Council; West Midlands Regional Museums Council; Yorkshire & Humberside Museums Council.

Bamboo sticks
Bamboo sticks are sold as satay or kebab sticks in many supermarkets or oriental food stores. They are very useful for making **cotton buds** as the bamboo is strong and so is more durable than wooden cocktail sticks or toothpicks. Bamboo sticks may also be used for scraping dirt off some surfaces such as ceramics and metal. They are less likely to damage a surface than a metal blade or pin, but bamboo contains silica phytoliths, which can scratch silver, paint and soft surfaces quite badly, so they must be used with care; keep checking that there are not scratches. Where this may be a problem, **softwood sticks** should be used.

Beeswax polish
Trade names: Antiquax; National Trust Wax
Wax polish containing beeswax. Solid paste waxes are preferred to liquid or cream waxes as they are easier to control during application, and are less likely to run on to other materials. Do not use polishes containing silicone on antique furniture.

Biological washing powder
Trade names: Ariel; Biotex and others
Contains enzymes that help to remove organic stains on some materials.

Black lead
Trade name: Zebrite
A paste containing graphite used to blacken cast iron.

Blotting paper
Trade name: Multisorb
Heavy-duty blotting paper used for pressing and drying during the conservation of some materials.

Bocage
Modelled leaves and flowers often found around ceramic figures or groups.

Borax
Occasionally used for cleaning some ceramics. It is sold as an antiseptic, for laundry cleaning and many other uses. May be harmful if it is inhaled, ingested, or absorbed by the skin, and can irritate the eyes and skin. Read the manufacturer's health and safety information, and wear protective clothing such as a respirator, gloves, and safety goggles when using borax.

Available from pharmacists, supermarkets and hardware shops.

Bovid
An animal of the cattle group, including buffalo and bison.

Brown paper tape
Gummed brown paper tape has an adhesive on the reverse that must be dampened to make it sticky. Gummed white paper tape is also available, but is less common. These tapes are used in conservation as they can easily be removed when dampened and are more durable and less damaging than self-adhesive tapes. They are particularly useful for sealing picture frames.

Brushes
Brushes are used in place of dusters for cleaning objects (see Introduction). If the bristles are too soft they are not effective for dust removal, while if they are too hard they will scratch delicate surfaces.

Soft brushes, such as ponyhair, large cosmetic and artist's soft paintbrushes are used on delicate surfaces such as lacquer, parchment and silver. Hogshair brushes are stiffer and suitable for removing dust from objects such as bronze sculpture.

Carat/karat
A unit of weight for gemstones (equivalent to 200mg), and a unit of purity of gold (pure gold is 24 carats). The amount of pure gold in an alloy is given as parts of 24; thus 18 carat gold is 18 parts pure gold and 6 parts of another metal. In American English the term karat is used as the unit of purity for gold.

Carbon-fibre clamps
Small clamps, available in model shops and from some conservation suppliers, for holding parts of an object in position. They are softer and easier to control than metal clamps but can still mark or damage an object if too much pressure is applied.

Charcoal cloth
Activated charcoal in a textile form that removes organic vapours such as acids emitted by wood and wood products. It is sometimes used in display cases or storage to help to retard metal tarnishing, and deterioration of paintings, paper and textiles.

Chemical sponge
Trade names: Smoke Sponge; Wishab Sponge
A sponge-like material used dry for cleaning. Dirt is absorbed into the sponge, or removed by light abrasion.

Clear polyester film
Trade names: Melinex manufactured by Dupont; Mylar manufactured by ICI
Used for protecting objects, including some paper, and used extensively for packing and display. Available in different gauges by the roll, metre or as ready-made enclosures. Made from a polyester known to be stable and containing no plasticizers, surface coatings or UV inhibitors. It is dimensionally stable and resistant to most chemicals, moisture and abrasion. This product is supposed to have low static attraction but even so, charcoal, chalk, pastel drawings should not be placed in polyester enclosures. Polyester film cannot be heat-sealed without special equipment.

Composition
A mixture of rosin, linseed oil, Scotch glue and whitening used to make ornaments on frames, fireplaces, etc., often referred to as 'compo'. It is a beige putty-like material that is soft when warm, but cools to a hard, brittle material. It is hand-modelled or pressed into wooden moulds when warm. In time it frequently shrinks, producing characteristic regular cracks. Other materials, such as papier mâché and wax/resin mixtures, were also used for similar purposes.

Compressed air or pressurised dusting products
Trade name: Dust Off
Tins of pressurised difluoroethane or tetrafluoroethane are available from art shops and photographic or conservation suppliers for removing dust from equipment. A variable trigger is essential to allow control of the pressure. A rubber bulb, also sold by photographic suppliers, can be used to puff dust away. Some vacuum cleaners may be adjusted to blow out rather than suck. A compressor can also be used to supply a flow of air for cleaning but should not be used unless the pressure can be adjusted to a low level.

Conservation-grade detergent
The detergents used in conservation are undergoing reassessment in the UK and other countries due to environmental considerations and a government directive. Suppliers of conservation materials and equipment will be able to advise which detergents are available as new recommendations are made. Before 2000, when it became the subject of a voluntary ban in the UK, the detergent widely used in conservation was Synperonic N, which is a nonylphenol ethoxylate and is non-ionic. It is available elsewhere but its use is likely to cease.

A detergent for conservation use must be free of colour, perfume, optical brighteners, enzymes and bleach. It should be predominantly made up of a non-ionic detergent and have a neutral pH. Some manufacturers produce liquid detergents for sensitive skins that can be used if a conservation-grade detergent is not available, provided they are free of perfume and the other ingredients mentioned above. However, wherever possible use a detergent sold for conservation purposes.

Proprietary detergents which can be used if necessary include Boots' Concentrated Sensitive Skin Washing Up Liquid (available from Boots the Chemist Plc, UK), and Surcare Washing Up Liquid (manufactured by Robert McBride Ltd, UK, and available from some supermarkets; telephone 0161 653 9037 for stockists).

Corrosion-inhibiting bags
Trade names: Corrosion Intercept, Tarnpruf
Bags made from a material that reduces the amount of tarnish-producing sulphur compounds, such as hydrogen sulphide, in an object's environment. In some cases the material changes colour when the corrosion protection wanes.

Cotton bud
Ready-made cotton buds can be purchased from pharmacies and large supermarkets. Conservators usually make their own using bamboo sticks and cotton wool so that they can control the size of the bud. Hold the stick in your writing hand and some cotton wool in the other hand, slightly moisten the tip of a bamboo stick, pick up a few strands of cotton wool on the tip and wrap them around the point, by rolling the stick until the bud is the size you want.

Dental tape
A flat tape sometimes used to tie together sections of a damaged object, particularly basketry. It is used in preference to dental floss, which is narrower and therefore may cut or mark soft surfaces.

Desiccated insect powders
Trade names: Bendiocarb; Permethrin; silica aerogel
An inert siliceous powder, used in dead spaces, that absorbs part of the insect's outer coating, causing dehydration and death.

Dichloromethane-based paint remover
Trade names: Nitromors; Strypit
Some commercial paint removers contain the organic solvent dichloromethane (also called methylene chloride) and are useful for removing paint and adhesives from some materials. Dichloromethane can destroy plastics, paint and varnishes, and must be used with care. Many brands come in two forms: water washable and solvent washable.

The water washable form is the most useful. Apply the paint remover gel to a small area using a hogshair brush or cotton bud. Leave for about two minutes and wipe off with a clean cotton wool swab. Repeat if necessary. Rinse off all traces of paint remover with cold water or **white spirit**. Do not let paint remover dry on the object as it is very difficult to remove. Never heat paint remover, do not use hot water for rinsing, and refrain from smoking when using these products. Work in a well-ventilated area, wear gloves and eye protection and follow the manufacturer's health and safety instructions carefully.

Dustsheets, calico, or Tyvek
Clean dustsheets can be used for covering objects in store, or when work is taking place in a room, to protect them from dust and dirt. Calico is used for the same purpose but should be washed before use. Tyvek, a white, water-repellent, micro-porous, non-woven, spun polyester fabric, sometimes used to make disposable overalls, may be used for the same purpose. One of its advantages over dustsheets and calico is that Tyvek does not produce dust. They are all washable.

Egyptian faience
Egyptian faience is a sintered silica that was shaped by hand or moulded and fired until the silica particles were partially fused together. The body was usually coated with a blue or green glaze coloured by copper, although other colours are found. Egyptian faience, correctly termed glazed siliceous ware, was used by the ancient Egyptians to produce *ushabti* figures and amulets. It is not to be confused with **faience**. *See also* **frit**.

Eraser
See **pencil eraser**.

Faience
Tin-glazed earthenware, named after Faenza. *See also* **Egyptian faience**.

Fine abrasive paste
Trade names: Prelim; Rubin-Brite Polish; Preen; Solvol Autosol
Fine abrasive pastes are sometimes used for cleaning hard, polished surfaces. The abrasive paste should not contain reagents, such as **ammonia**, or **organic solvents**. Prelim is most commonly used by conservators, but other pastes may be suitable. The paste is polished off with a soft cloth and excess paste is removed with **white spirit** before it has dried. Some of the pastes are sold as chrome cleaners and are coarser than Prelim.

Frit
In antiquity glazes were often made by combining and heating the raw materials; the resulting glass was pulverised and known as frit. It was subsequently applied to pottery and fired to produce a glaze.

Furniture cups
Often made from glass or plastic, these are placed under the legs of furniture to protect carpets.

Gloves
Fingers leave small deposits of oils and salts on the surface of objects. Sometimes this can be damaging, for example it encourages metal corrosion, the deterioration of *urushi* lacquer, and some gilding can be lifted off the surface by damp fingers. The deposits from our fingers also attract dirt, so a surface that is frequently touched, such as the side of a door, can become dirty very quickly. For these reasons, you are advised to wear gloves when handling objects at all times, except when there is a greater risk of other damage. Ceramics and glass may slip through gloved hands and works of art on paper can be physically damaged. If gloves are not worn, your hands must be clean.

Gloves are usually cotton, vinyl or latex. Cotton gloves are generally the most comfortable but reduce your dexterity and can become very dirty themselves. When the weather is very hot, they can act as a wick to leave sweat and oils on the object's surface. Some cotton gloves have little plastic dots on the fingers and palms that improve the grip. The dots can leave marks on the surface but they are used quite widely by object handlers. Do not wear these gloves when handling precious metals as they may leave a deposit that encourages tarnishing.

Vinyl gloves are cheap and disposable but seldom fit well. Disposable latex gloves usually fit well and are fine enough not to inhibit dexterity much but they are not always popular as they can be rather sweaty; one solution is to wear cotton gloves underneath them.

Gloves should also be worn to protect your hands when carrying out some conservation work. Solvents and detergents remove oils from skin and can cause dermatitis to develop. Most domestic rubber gloves will soften in solvents other than alcohol, so when using any quantity of solvents use gloves that are resistant to solvents: neoprene gloves for acetone and nitrile gloves for white spirit and dichloromethane.

Gloves are available from conservation suppliers, protective clothing and safety wear suppliers.

Graphite paste
Trade name: Xebo & Zebrite
Paste in which one of the constituents is graphite. Used to blacken and protect stoves and cast iron.

Gummed linen tape
Trade name: Lineco
Linen tape with a neutral water-activated adhesive used for repairing leather and some other materials. Moisten with de-ionised or distilled water applied with a sponge. Lighter weight tapes are also available.

Gun oil
Used for protecting arms and some other iron or steel objects from corrosion. Available in some sports and gun shops.

Hook and loop fastener
Trade name: Velcro
A soft fastener made from two strips of synthetic material; one strip is made up of tiny hooks, and the other strip has loops for the hooks to catch. Used in conservation for hanging textiles and to hold textile coverings in place.

Hydrogen peroxide
Hydrogen peroxide is an oxidising agent and bleach. Wear gloves and protective clothing, such as an overall, when using it. It is purchased from chemists or pharmacists and is sold according to its strength. The most concentrated form commonly available is 100 volumes, but 20 volumes is the strength required for treatments described in this book.

Impregnated wadding
Trade name: Duraglit
Soft wadding containing metal polish, sometimes used for cleaning severely tarnished metals such as brass, copper and silver. Wadding is produced for copper and copper alloys as well as for silver: do not use the copper wadding on silver. The polish is quite harsh and abrasive and may leave polish in the depths of decoration, so is not recommended for general cleaning.

Indian ink
Ink made from carbon black pigment, used for drawing. Traditional Indian ink contains gelatine as the medium. Some 'waterproof' products contain shellac.

Insect traps
Insect traps detect the presence of insects rather than act as a means of controlling them. They are three-dimensional structures made of card with a sticky patch on the bottom which catches insects. Traps need to be examined periodically to see which insects are present. Sometimes

pheromones are used on traps to attract particular insects, such as the clothes moth or cockroach. Insects can be identified by an entomologist or a specialist in pest management for historic collections.

Insecticide for wood
Low-odour or **permethrin-based insecticides** are recommended for wood. They should not be applied to a finished surface and take care to ensure that the product does not run on to varnish or paint. Be aware that these insecticides remain in the wood and therefore can be picked up on your hands when touching the object, so wear latex or vinyl gloves when handling an object after it has been treated.

Integrated pest management
A system of monitoring, preventing and treating pest infestations in museums and historic houses (*see* Reading List).

Iridescence
The rainbow-like colours on a surface that change according to the angle of view or the angle of the source of illumination. Sometimes seen on glazes or glass when the glass surface has deteriorated. The effect is caused by the interference of light through several layers that have air between them.

Japanese paper
Hand-made paper, traditionally produced from bast fibres of the paper mulberry plant. The process of manufacture varies from European paper. The paper is made from long fibres and is flexible, strong, absorbent and translucent.

Japanned
A method of decorating a substrate, usually wood, developed in Europe to imitate *urushi* or lacquer from the Far East. The process involves the application of layers of a natural resin and colour, often over a coloured or white ground.

Lacquer for brass, copper and silver
Trade names: Covolac; Incralac; Ercalene; Frigilene
Air-drying lacquer for use with brass, polished copper and copper alloys, and silver to protect from tarnishing. Covolac can be used on most polished metals: it is a vinyl resin and corrosion inhibitor in solution with organic solvents (xylene and butyl acetate) and should be used according to the health and safety recommendations. Incralac contains a corrosion inhibitor designed for use with copper and

copper alloys. Cellulose nitrate lacquers (Ercalene and Frigilene) are still used to protect silver, but Covolac is easier to apply successfully. These lacquers can all be removed with an **organic solvent**.

Lacquers that polymerise, such as polyurethane or epoxy resins, are not recommended as they cannot be easily removed.

Laminated surface
Trade names: Formica; Contiboard
Often used in kitchens to provide an easily-cleaned flat surface.

Leather dressing
Leather dressings are traditionally liquids made from oils, fats and waxes, and were applied to leather for protection. It has been found that these dressings can cause considerable damage to the leather, and are no longer recommended for use (*see* Leather).

Light machine oil
Trade name: Three-in-one
Commercially available light oils for lubricating bicycles, gardening equipment and household machinery. Some have rust-inhibiting properties and are described by the manufacturers as being able to lubricate, clean and prevent rust.

Low-tack tape
Self-adhesive tape with a low-tack adhesive, such as masking tape.

Magnification
A hand-held magnifier can help you to examine an object. Magnifiers on an extending base or arm, or that can be worn as headbands or spectacles, will allow you to keep your hands free. Different strengths of magnification are available: ×2 is useful for general examination. Conservators frequently work with a binocular-stand microscope with ×10 or higher magnification.

Medium
A paint medium is the binder that holds together the pigments in the paint and adheres the paint to the surface. Gums, resins, waxes and oils are most commonly used. The medium in oil paint is a drying oil such as linseed oil; gum arabic is used for watercolours; egg is in egg tempera and an acrylic resin is the medium for acrylic paint.

Medium Density Fibreboard (MDF)
Trade name: Medite
MDF is used widely to make mounts and shelving for objects. It contains various substances that

may produce acid vapour and so is not recommended for long-term display and storage. However, Medite is free of formaldehyde and may be used in most circumstances.

Mercury gilding
Also known as firegilding or amalgam gilding. A method of gilding on metal, usually silver or copper alloy, in which the gold is applied to the metal surface in the form of an amalgam with mercury. It is then heated to drive off the mercury, leaving a surface layer of gold. Mercury gilding is now seldom carried out for health and safety reasons, and only under special circumstances.

Metal cloth, metal polishing cloths
Impregnated cloths for maintaining the polish of certain polished metals. Cloths are produced for silver, gold, copper and brass, and should only be used on the metal specified, i.e. do not use the copper cloth on silver. These cloths are used dry and are lightly rubbed over the surface to remove light tarnish and fingerprints; they help to keep the metal clean without abrading the surface. Metal polishing cloths are not to be confused with cloths containing polish that are dampened and used to remove tarnish and corrosion.

Microcrystalline wax paste
Trade name: Renaissance Wax
A paste made up of microcrystalline wax and polyethylene wax to produce a hard wax with a high gloss that can be used to protect many materials, especially metal.

Microfibre cloth
Cloths made for removing dust and for cleaning spectacles and lenses; lens cloths are finer than those produced for domestic cleaning. They are usually used dry, without chemical cleaners.

Museum board
Thick conservation-grade card or acid-free foam board used for mounting textiles and some other lightweight objects. Available from conservation suppliers.

Nylon net
Available from fabric shops and haberdashers. White is preferred as it is the most visible, and avoids the danger of colour transfer. Fine net (nylon tulle) can be used to protect delicate textiles while vacuuming, but more open net may also be suitable, depending on the condition of the object.

Organic and inorganic materials
Organic materials are products of plants or animals, and include paper, leather, ivory, wood, bone, tortoiseshell and natural fibres. This differs slightly from the chemical definition of an organic compound – a material whose molecules are constructed of chains of carbon atoms and also contains other elements such as hydrogen, oxygen and/or nitrogen. Adhesives and modern synthetic resins are usually organic compounds.

Organic materials all remain sensitive to moisture and so take in or give up water vapour from the surrounding environment. This usually results in a slight change in dimension; they may expand when the air is moist, or shrink when it is dry. Organic materials are also prone to insect attack as they may provide a food source for insects.

Inorganic materials derive from minerals; they include stone, glass, ceramics and metals. Their natures vary, and they have few characteristics in common.

Organic solvents
Organic solvents are chemical compounds, in our case liquids, where the molecules are constructed on a chain of carbon atoms. Common organic solvents include acetone, alcohol, white spirit and turpentine.

Patina
The term patina is generally associated with bronzes, and refers to the surface colour, usually green or brown, which may either have developed over time, or been deliberately formed or applied. It is also used to describe the surface colour and texture of old furniture, silver and stone. In this case the patina has usually developed gradually with use, polish and handling, but occasionally has been deliberately applied.

Pencil eraser
Trade name: Artgum Eraser
Soft, non-abrasive pencil eraser for cleaning many surfaces including well-adhered paint and lightly tarnished silver.

Permethrin-based insecticide
Trade name: Constran
Insecticides based on the chemical permethrin, related to pyrethrum which is obtained from plants (*see also* **insecticide for wood**).

Pipette
A glass or plastic tube, with a soft bulb at one end, used for transferring small quantities of liquids like a glass dropper.

Polyethylene foam

Trade names: Plastazote; Ethafoam
Sheet foam used as packing and padding for objects. It is used in preference to polystyrene foam because it is softer, less likely to scratch, inert, resistant to most organic solvents and easier to cut and shape. It is black or white, and can be purchased in various thicknesses and densities. Jiffy foam, sold as packing and for laying under wooden floors, is a similar material and is very useful for wrapping objects in place of bubble wrap.

Polypropylene twinwall board

Trade names: Correx; Coroplast
A lightweight equivalent to corrugated cardboard made from polypropylene. Used for making storage boxes and protecting floors.

Powdered eraser

Trade name: Draft Clean
Powdered eraser sold by conservation suppliers or commercial art suppliers. Use by rubbing gently with the fingertips or make a small muslin bag and lightly rub this over the surface. Vacuum up the powder or brush it off with a soft brush.

Pressurised dusting products

See compressed air.

Relative humidity

Relative humidity is the ratio of the amount of water vapour in a given volume of air to the maximum amount of water vapour that the volume of air can hold at that temperature, and is expressed as a percentage. 100% RH usually indicates precipitation, i.e. when droplets of water are formed. The RH in temperate climates is usually between 30% and 70% (*see* pp.17-18).

Sachets for insect control

Sachets of plant material, mostly lavender and cedarwood oil, are sold in some stores as insect repellents. There is some scientific evidence that lavender will discourage insects but, as yet, there is no scientific evidence to support the use of other plant material. There is, however, a long tradition of using cedar shavings and some other plant materials as insect repellents which have been found to be effective. The right species of cedar is effective.

Sealed plastic boxes

Trade name: Stewart
Lidded boxes made from polypropylene, frequently sold for food storage, can be used for storing objects if conditioned **silica gel** is included. The silica gel should be checked every two months. Do not use plastic boxes without silica gel for long-term storage as condensation may occur inside them if they are subjected to fluctuating temperatures (the silica gel should prevent this).

Silica gel

Conditioned silica gel is used in storage boxes or display cases to dry air and/or to act as a buffering agent to maintain the relative humidity at a constant level. Some silica gel is self-indicating; this means that it is treated to indicate by colour change when it is no longer acting as a desiccant. Silica gel needs reconditioning from time to time. Advice on the amount of silica gel needed and on conditioning it can be obtained from a conservator or the supplier (*see also* Reading List).

Silicone (release) paper

A non-stick paper treated with silicone (*not* traditional greaseproof paper) sold for baking and by conservation suppliers.

Silver Dip

A commercially available liquid used for removing tarnish from silver. It is not abrasive but can cause silver to tarnish rapidly if it is not thoroughly removed.

Silver Foam

A commercially available cleaning product made from a fine abrasive that is applied to a silver surface with a damp sponge. It can be washed off with water.

Silver protection cloth

Trade names: Tarnpruf; Pacific Silvercloth
Soft cloth impregnated with a chemical that helps prevent silver from tarnishing. It is available in ready-made bags, pouches, jewellery and cutlery rolls for storing silver. Bags can be made to order.

Silver-safe archival materials

See acid-free or archival materials

Sodium hexametaphosphate

See water softener

Softwood sticks

See bamboo sticks

Solander box

A box that will open flat at the spine for easy removal of the contents. These boxes, or boxes of similar construction, are used for storing paper, archives, books and works of art, and are made from archival quality materials.

Solvents

A solvent is a liquid that will dissolve a solid, or that will mix with another liquid; water is a solvent for sugar or salt; amyl acetate and acetone are solvents for nail varnish.

Solvent mixtures

Mixtures of water and organic solvents are recommended for cleaning some materials.

Acetone or alcohol:water mixture
Useful for cleaning many materials, including ceramics, glass and stone. Mix 2 parts purified water with 1 part of either acetone or alcohol. A small drop of conservation-grade detergent may also be added to both solutions to help remove grease and dirt.

White spirit:water cleaning mixture
A very useful solution for cleaning painted surfaces, stone and some other materials, sometimes known as the V&A mixture. Put 300ml/10fl oz of purified water with 300ml/10fl oz of white spirit and a small teaspoon of conservation-grade detergent in a screw-top glass jar. Close the jar and shake the mixture. A white emulsion will form. The mixture will gradually separate out leaving the white emulsion on top and clear liquid below. Use the white emulsion for cleaning. The mixture can be kept in a screw-top glass jar to be used when necessary. Do not use a metal container. Wipe off with clean water or white spirit.

Solvent resistant gloves

See gloves

Spray oil

Trade name: WD40
A mixture of oils and solvent.

Starch

Trade name: Robin
Old-fashioned starch was usually made from rice starch and is easy to wash out. Modern spray starches are much more complex and should not be used on antique textiles as they are harder to remove.

Swab sticks

See bamboo sticks

Thermal expansion

Most materials expand and contract when heated and cooled. The coefficient of linear expansion is the increase in length per unit length caused by the rise in temperature. Fractures can appear between materials with different coefficients of expansion during temperature increase/decrease cycles.

Tyvek

See dustsheets

Velcro

See hook and loop fastener

Water

Water is used for cleaning objects but must only be used in small quantities as directed. Tap water contains various chemicals that are either naturally dissolved in the water or added during the purification process. De-ionised, purified or distilled water is treated to remove chemicals. These purified waters are recommended for use with antiques as they do not leave a deposit on the surface (*see* **water softener**).

Water softener

Trade name: Calgon
Chemical water softeners are sometimes used to prevent soap and detergent from forming a scum in hard water. Water softeners consisting of sodium hexametaphosphate are recommended. Chemically softened water is *not* the same as purified water but is used occasionally for washing textiles. Purified, de-ionised or distilled water is usually used for most cleaning (*see* p.23).

Weights

Trade name: Benchmark weight bags
Weights are used for pressing surfaces flat while they dry. Small cloth bags of glass beads make useful weights for flat and curved surfaces.

White spirit

An **organic solvent** that does not mix with water. It is often used as a paint thinner and is available from DIY stores. Follow the manufacturer's health and safety instructions and use in a well-ventilated area away from sources of heat. *See* **solvent mixtures**.

Wood wool

Fine wood shavings used for stuffing toys and some natural history specimens as well as for packing and transporting goods. It is susceptible to insect attack and mould.

READING LIST

GENERAL

Caring for objects and collections

Canadian Conservation Institute Notes and Technical Bulletins Available from:
Canadian Conservation Institute, 1030 Innes Road, Ottawa, Ontario K1A 0M5. Fax: (613) 998 4721.
NOTES:
5. Ceramics and Glass; 6. Ethnographic Materials; 8. Leather, Skin and Fur; 9. Metals; 10. Paintings and Polychrome Sculptures; 11. Paper and Books; 12. Stone and Plaster; 13. Textile and Fibres; 15. Other Materials; 16. Care of Photographic Materials.
TECHNICAL BULLETINS:
8. The Care of Wooden Objects; 10. Silica Gel; 11. Dry Methods for Surface Cleaning of Paper; 16. Care and Preservation of Fire Arms.

Conservation Forum, *Guidelines for the Commissioning and Undertaking of Conversation Work*, (Conservation Forum, London, 1998).

Ours for Keeps?: A Resource Pack for Raising Awareness of Conservation and Collections Care (Museums and Galleries Commission, 1998).

BACHMANN, Konstanze (ed.), *Conservation Concerns: A Guide for Collectors and Curators* (Smithsonian Institute Press, 1992).

DORGE, Valerie and JONES, Sharon, *Building an Emergency Plan: A Guide for Museums and Other Cultural Institutions* (Getty Conservation Institute, 1999).

FISHER, Charles E. (ed.) et al., *Caring for Your Historic House* (Harry N. Abrams, Heritage Preservation and National Park Service, 1998).

KNELL, Simon J. (ed.), *Care of Collections* (Routledge, 1994).

NELSON, Carl L., *Protecting the Past from Natural Disasters* (Preservation Press, 1989).

PRICE, Nicholas Stanley, TALLEY, Jr., M. Kirby and VACCARO, Alessandra Melucco, *Historical and Philosophical Issues in the Conservation of Cultural Heritage* (Getty Conservation Institute, 1996).

PYE, Elizabeth, *Caring for the Past: Issues in Conservation for Archaeology and Museums* (James & James, 2000).

SANDWITH, Hermione and STAINTON, Sheila, *The National Trust Manual of Housekeeping* (The National Trust, 2000).

SCHULZ, Arthur W. (ed.), *Caring for Your Collections: Preserving and Protecting Your Art and Other Collectibles* (Harry N. Abrams and National Institute for the Conservation of Cultural Property, 1992).

WATKINSON, David (ed.), *First Aid for Finds*, 2nd edn (Rescue, The British Archaeological Trust, 1987).

Environmental effect, monitoring and control

CASSAR, May, *Environmental Management: Guidelines for Museums and Galleries* (Routledge and Museums and Galleries Commission, 1995).

PINNIGER, David, *Insect Pests in Museums*, 2nd edn (Archetype Publications, 1994).

PINNIGER, David and WINSOR, Peter, *Integrated Pest Management: Practical, Safe and Cost-Effective Advice on the Prevention and Control of Pests in Museums* (Museums and Galleries Commission, 1998).

THOMSON, Garry, *The Museum Environment*, 2nd edn (Butterworth-Heinemann and the International Institute for Conservation of Historic and Artistic Works, 1994).

Theory of conservation

Science for Conservators, Vols 1–3 (Routledge and Museums and Galleries Commission, 1992).

CRONYN, J.M., *The Elements of Archaeological Conservation*, (Routledge, 1990).

HORIE, C.V., *Materials for Conservation: Organic Consolidants, Adhesives and Coatings* (Butterworths, 1987).

TORRACA, Giorgio, *Solubility and Solvents for Conservation Problems*, 4th edn (ICCROM, 1990).

Health and safety

CLYDESDALE, Amanda, *Chemicals in Conservation: A Guide to Possible Hazards and Safe Use*, 2nd edn, (Scottish Society for Conservation and Restoration, 1990).

SCOTT, Ronald M., *Chemical Hazards in the Workplace* (Lewis Publishers, 1989).

Books, Paper and Photographs

Standards in the Museum Care of Photographic Collections (Museums and Galleries Commission, 1996).

CLARKE, Susie (ed.), *Care of Photographic, Moving Image and Sound Recordings* (Institute of Paper Conservation, 1999).

FEATHER, John, *Preservation and the Management of Library Collections*, 2nd edn (Library Association Publishing, 1996).

PICKFORD, Christopher, RHYS-LEWIS, Jonathan and WEBER, Jerry, *Preservation and Conservation: A Guide to Policy and Practices in the Preservation of Archives* (Society of Archivists, 1997).

Ceramics and Glass

BUYS, Susan and OAKLEY, Victoria, *The Conservation and Restoration of Ceramics* (Butterworth-Heinemann, 1993).

NEWTON, Roy and DAVISON, Sandra, *Conservation of Glass* (Butterworths, 1989).

TENNENT, Norman H. (ed.), *Conservation of Glass and Ceramics: Research, Practice and Training* (James & James, 1999).

TEUTONICO, Jeanne Marie (ed.), *Architectural Ceramics: Their History, Manufacture and Conservation: A joint symposium of English Heritage and the United Kingdom Institute for Conservation* (James & James, 1996).

Clocks, Watches and Scientific Instruments

WILLS, Peter B. (ed.), *Conservation of Clocks and Watches* (British Horological Institute, 1995).

Decorative Arts

HORIE, Velson (ed.), *The Conservation of Decorative Arts* (Archetype Publications and United Kingdom Institute for Conservation, 1999).

Ethnography

WRIGHT, Margot M. (ed.), *Ethnographic Beadwork: Aspects of Manufacture, Use and Conservation* (Archetype Publications and Conservators of Ethnographic Artefacts, 2001).

Fibres

FLORIAN, Mary-Lou E., KRONKRIGHT, Dale Paul and NORTON, Ruth E., *The Conservation of Artifacts Made from Plant Materials* (Getty Conservation Institute, 1990).

Frames and Framing

BELL, Nancy (ed.), *Historic Framing and Presentation of Watercolours, Drawing and Prints* (Institute of Paper Conservation, 1997).

KISTLER, Vivian, *The Library of Professional Picture Framing*: Vol. 1: *Picture Framing*; Vol. 4: *Conservation Framing*; Vol. 6: *Framing Photographs* (Columbia Publishing Co., 1994, 1997, 1996).

PENNY, Nicholas, *National Gallery Pocket Guides: Frames* (National Gallery Publications, 1997).

SIMON, Jacob, *The Art of the Picture Frame: Artists, Patrons and the Framing of Portraits in Britain* (National Portrait Gallery, 1996).

Furniture

EASTOP, Dinah and GILL, Kathryn, *Upholstery Conservation: Principles and Practice* (Butterworth-Heinemann, 2000).

Leather

CALNAN, Christopher (ed.), *Conservation of Leather in Transport Collections* (United Kingdom Institute for Conservation, 1991).

Metals

ASHURST, John and ASHURST, Nicola, *Practical Building Conservation*, Vol. 4: *Metals* (Gower Technical Press and English Heritage, 1988).

DRAYMAN-WEISSER, Terry (ed.), *Dialogue/89: The Conservation of Bronze Sculpture in the Outdoor Environment: A dialogue among conservators, curators, environmental scientists, and corrosion engineers* (National Association of Corrosion Engineers, 1992).

DRAYMAN-WEISSER, Terry (ed.), *Gilded Metals: History, Technology and Conservation* (Archetype Publications, 2000).

GAYLE, Margot and LOOK, David W. and WAITE, John G., *Metals in America's Historic Buildings: Uses and Preservation Treatments* (National Park Service, 1992).

SCOTT, David A., PODANY, Jerry and CONSIDINE, Brian B. (eds), *Ancient and Historic Metals: Conservation and Scientific Research* (Getty Conservation Institute, 1994).

Modern Materials

GRATTAN, David W., *Saving the Twentieth Century: The Conservation of Modern Materials* (Canadian Conservation Institute, 1993).

MORGAN, John, *Conservation of Plastics* (Plastics Historical Society and Museums and Galleries Commission, 1991).

MOSSMAN, S.T.I. and MORRIS, P.J.T. (eds), *The Development of Plastics: An Introduction to Their History, Manufacture, Deterioration, Identification and Care* (Royal Society of Chemistry, 1994).

QUYE, Anita and WILLIAMSON, Colin (eds), *Plastics – Collecting and Conserving* (National Museums of Scotland Publishing, 1999).

Musical Instruments

Standards in the Museum Care of Musical Instruments (Museums and Galleries Commission, 1995).

BARCLAY, R.L. (ed.), *The Care of Historical Musical Instruments* (Museums and Galleries Commission, 1998).

Natural History

CARTER, David and WALKER, Annette K., *Care and Conservation of Natural History Collections* (Butterworth-Heinemann and Natural History Museum, 1998).

CHILD, R.E. (ed.), *Conservation of Geological Collections* (Archetype Publications, 1994).

CHILD, R.E. (ed.), *Conservation and the Herbarium* (Institute of Paper Conservation, 1994).

HOWIE, Frank M.P., *Care and Conservation of Geological Material: Minerals, Rocks, Meteorites and Lunar Finds* (Butterworth-Heinemann, 1992).

Paintings

BOMFORD, David, *National Gallery Pocket Guides: Conservation of Paintings* (National Gallery Publications, 1997).

BOMFORD, David et al., *Art in the Making: Rembrandt* (National Gallery Publications, 1988).

BOMFORD, David et al., *Art in the Making: Italian Painting before 1400* (National Gallery Company, 1989).

BOMFORD, David et al., *Art in the Making: Impressionism* (National Gallery Publications and Yale University Press, 1990).

Sculpture

NAUDÉ, Virginia N. and WHARTON, Glenn, *A Guide to the Maintenance of Outdoor Sculpture* (American Institute for Conservation of Historic and Artistic Works, 1993).

Textiles

Standards in the Museum Care of Costume and Textile Collections (Museums and Galleries Commission, 1998).

MAILAND, Harold F. and ALIG, Dorothy S., *Preserving Textiles: A Guide for the Nonspecialist* (Indianapolis Museum of Art, 1999).

MARKO, Ksynia (ed.), *Textiles in Trust* (Archetype Publications and The National Trust, 1997).

ROBINSON, Jane and PARDOE, Tuula, *An Illustrated Guide to the Care of Costume and Textile Collections* (Museums and Galleries Commission, 2000).

Wood

BIGELOW, Deborah (ed.) et al., *Gilded Wood, Conservation and History* (Sound View Press and the Foundation of the American Institute for Conservation, 1991).

DORGE, Valerie and HOWLETT, F. Carey (eds), *Painted Wood: History and Conservation* (Getty Conservation Institute, 1998).

LARSON, John and KERR, Rose, *Guanyin: A Masterpiece Revealed* (Victoria and Albert Museum, 1985).

SHIVERS, Natalie, *Walls and Molding: How to Care for Old and Historic Wood and Plaster* (Wiley and National Trust for Historic Preservation, 1995).

WEBB, Marianne, *Lacquer: Technology and Conservation* (Butterworth-Heinemann, 2000).

Commissioning Conservation Work

Working with Independent Conservators: Guidelines for Good Practice (Museums and Galleries Commission, 2000).

INFORMATION SOURCES AND SUPPLIERS

Many of the materials mentioned in the book can be purchased from high street stores such as pharmacies, hardware or DIY stores, art suppliers and stationery shops. Health and safety equipment suppliers usually stock a range of protective clothing including gloves. Most organic solvents can be ordered through pharmacies. Telephone directories, such as yellow pages, include local suppliers. There are specialist conservation suppliers, but they are not very plentiful and cater mainly to professional conservators. Some of the major specialist suppliers or general art suppliers are listed below. Your local museum or organisations given here may be able to provide you with a list of local suppliers and help you to find a conservator either to give advice or to carry out conservation. Some of the professional bodies, such as UKIC and AIC, maintain a register of accredited conservators. To find museums in your area, consult one of the websites listed below or a museum guide for your country, such as *The Museums and Galleries Yearbook* published by the Museums Association in the UK.

Addresses and numbers at time of going to press.

INFORMATION SOURCES

Websites

CoOL (Conservation OnLine)
http://palimpsest.stanford.edu

VLmp (Virtual Library museums pages)
http://icom.museum/vlmp

International Organisations

ICOM (The International Council of Museums)
Maison de l'UNESCO
1, rue Miollis
75732 Paris cedex 15
France
Tel: +33 (0)1 47 34 05 00
Fax: +33 (0)1 43 06 78 62
www.icom.org

ICOMOS (International Council on Monuments and Sites)
49-51 rue de la Fédération
75015 Paris
France
Tel: +33 (0)1 45 67 67 70
Fax: +33 (0)1 45 66 06 22
www.icomos.org

ICCROM (International Centre for the Study of the Preservation and Restoration of Cultural Property)
Via di San Michele 13
I-00153 Rome, Italy
Tel: +39 (0)6 585531
www.iccrom.org

IIC (International Institute for Conservation of Historic and Artistic Works)
6 Buckingham Street
London
WC2N 6BA
England
Tel: +44 (0)20 7839 5975
Fax: +44 (0)20 7976 1564
www.iiconservation.org

United Kingdom

UKIC (United Kingdom Institute for Conservation of Historic and Artistic Works)
109 The Chandlery
50 Westminster Bridge Road
London
SE1 7QY
Tel: +44 (0)20 7721 8721
Fax: +44 (0)20 7721 8722
www.ukic.org.uk

The National Trust
36 Queen Anne's Gate
London
SW1H 9AS
Tel: +44 (0)20 7222 9251
Fax: +44 (0)20 7222 5097
www.nationaltrust.org.uk

The National Trust for Scotland
Wemyss House
28 Charlotte Square
Edinburgh EH2 4ET
Tel: +44 (0)131 243 9300
Fax: +44 (0)131 243 9301
www.nts.org.uk

The Scottish Conservation Bureau and Historic Scotland's Conservation Centre
Historic Scotland
Longmore House
Salisbury Place
Edinburgh EH9 1SH
Tel: +44 (0)131 668 8600
Fax: +44 (0)131 668 8669
www.historic-scotland.gov.uk

BAPCR (British Association of Paintings Conservator-Restorers), formerly known as the Association of British Picture Restorers (ABPR)
Station Avenue
Kew
Surrey TW9 3QA
Tel: +44 (0)20 8948 5644
Fax: +44 (0)20 8948 5644
www.abpr.co.uk

IPC (The Institute of Paper Conservation)
Leigh Lodge
Leigh
Worcester WR6 5LB
Tel: +44 (0)1886 832323
Fax: +44 (0)1886 833688
www.ipc.org.uk

BAFRA (British Antique Furniture Restorers' Association)
The Old Rectory
Warmwell
Dorchester
Dorset DT2 8HQ
Tel: +44 (0)1305 854822
Fax: +44 (0)1305 854822
www.bafra.org.uk

MA (Museums Association)
24 Calvin Street
London E1 6NW
Tel: +44 (0)20 7426 6970
Fax: +44 (0)20 7426 6961
www.museumsassociation.org

Resource: The Council for
Museums, Archives and
Libraries
16 Queen Anne's Gate
London SW1H 9AA
Tel: +44 (0)20 7273 1444
Fax: +44 (0)20 7273 1404
www.resource.gov.uk

SSCR (The Scottish Society for
Conservation and Restoration)
Chantstoun, Tartraven
Bathgate Hills
West Lothian EH48 4NP
Tel: +44 (0)1506 811 777
Fax: +44 (0)1506 811 888
www.sscr.demon.co.uk

Scottish Museums Council
20–22 Torphichen Street
Edinburgh EH3 8JB
Tel: +44 (0)131 229 7465
Fax: +44 (0)131 229 2728
Information service:
+44 (0)131 538 7435
www.scottishmuseums.org.uk

Council of Museums in Wales
The Courtyard, Letty Street
Cardiff CF24 4EL
Tel: +44 (0)29 2022 5432
Fax: +44 (0)29 2066 8516
www.cmw.org.uk

IPCRA (Irish Professional
Conservators' and Restorers'
Association)
The Secretary
c/o Ulster Museum
Department of Paper Conservation
Botanic Gardens
Belfast BT5 9AB
Tel: +44 (0)28 90 383000
Fax: +44 (0)28 90 383003
www.ipcra.org

Northern Ireland Museums
Council
66 Donegall Pass
Belfast BT7 1BU
Tel: +44 (0)28 90 550215
Fax: +44 (0)28 90 550216
www.nimc.co.uk

Eire

Department of Arts, Heritage,
Gaeltacht and the Islands
Dún Aimhirgin
43–49 Mespil Road
Dublin 4
Tel: +353 (0)1 647 3000
Fax: +353 (0)1 667 0826
www.ealga.ie

The Heritage Council
Kilkenny
Tel: +353 (0)56 70777
Fax: +353 (0)56 70788
www.heritagecouncil.ie

IPCRA (Irish Professional
Conservators' and
Restorers' Association)
The Secretary
c/o National Gallery of Ireland
Paper Conservation Department
Merrion Square West
Dublin 2
Fax: +353 (0)1 662 6942
www.ipcra.org

ICHAWI (Institute for the
Conservation of Historic and
Artistic Works in Ireland)
73 Merrion Square
Dublin 2
Tel: +353 (0)1 663 3585
www.conservation-ireland.org

Irish Museums Association
The Secretary
c/o National Print Museum
Beggars Bush
Haddington Road
Dublin 4
Tel: +353 (0)1 660 3770
Fax: +353 (0)1 667 3545

United States of America

AIC (American Institute for
Conservation of Historic and
Artistic Works)
1717 K Street, NW
Suite 200
Washington, DC 20006
Tel: +1 202 452 9545
Fax: +1 202 452 9328
http://aic.stanford.edu

The Getty Conservation
Institute
1200 Getty Center Drive
Suite 700
Los Angeles, CA 90049-1684
Tel: +1 310 440 7325
Fax: +1 310 440 7702
www.getty.edu/conservation/institute

National Trust for Historic
Preservation
1785 Massachusetts Ave, NW
Washington, DC 20036
Tel: +1 202 588 6000
Fax: +1 202 588 6038
www.nthp.org

US National Park Service,
Department of Conservation
Harpers Ferry Center
PO Box 50
Harpers Ferry, WV 25425-0050
Tel: +1 304 535 6139
Fax: +1 304 535 6055
www.nps.gov/hfc/conservation

AAM (American Association
of Museums)
1575 Eye Street, NW
Suite 400
Washington, DC 20005
Tel: +1 202 289 1818
Fax: +1 202 289 6578
www.aam-us.org

Canada

Canadian Conservation
Institute
1030 Innes Road
Ottawa, Ontario K1A 0M5
Tel: +1 613 993 3721
Fax: +1 613 998 4721
www.cci-icc.gc.ca

CMA (Canadian Museums
Association)/Canadian
Association for Conservation
280 Metcalfe Street
Suite 400
Ottawa, Ontario K2P 1R7
Tel: +1 613 567 0099
Fax: +1 613 233 5438
www.museums.ca
To engage the services of a conservator:
www.cac-accr.ca/eselect.html

Australia

AICCM (Australian Institute
for the Conservation of Cultural
Material Inc.)
GPO Box 1638
Canberra, ACT 2601
www.aiccm.org.au

Museums Australia
PO Box 266
Civic Square, ACT 2608
Tel: +61 (0)2 6208 5044
Fax: +61 (0)2 6208 5015
www.museumsaustralia.org.au

National Trust of Australia
www.nationaltrust.org.au

New Zealand

Museums Association of Aotearoa
New Zealand
Level 12, 105 The Terrace
PO Box 10 928
Wellington
Tel: +64 (0)4 499 1313
Fax: +64 (0)4 499 6313
www.museums-aotearoa.org.nz

National Library of New Zealand
PO Box 1467
Wellington
Tel: +64 (0)4 474 3000
Fax: +64 (0)4 474 3035
www.natlib.govt.nz

New Zealand Professional
Conservators Group
www.conservators.org.nz

Directory of Museums
www.nzmuseums.co.nz

Singapore

National Heritage Board
#03-02 MITA Building
140 Hill Street
Singapore 179369
Tel: +65 62 70 79 88
Fax: +65 68 37 94 80
www.nhb.gov.sg

Hong Kong

Leisure and Cultural Services
Department, Central
Conservation Section
Room 417
Hong Kong Museum of Art
10 Salisbury Road
Tsim Sha Tsui
Kowloon
Tel: +852 2734 2106
Fax: +852 2301 3610
www.lcsd.gov.hk/indexe.html

Antiquities and Monuments
Office
136 Nathan Road
Tsim Sha Tsui
Kowloon
Tel: +852 2721 2326
Fax: +852 2721 6216
www.lcsd.gov.hk/CE/Museum/
    Monument/index.html

Public Records Office
Conservation Unit
5/F Hong Kong Public Records
Building
13 Tsui Ping Road
Kwun Tong
Kowloon
Tel: +852 2195 7700
Fax: +852 2804 6413
www.info.gov.hk/pro

India

INTACH (The Indian
National Trust for Art and
Cultural Heritage)
71 Lodhi Estate
New Delhi 110003
Tel: +91 (0)11 4645482
Fax: +91 (0)11 4611290
www.intach.net

INTACH Indian Conservation
Institute
B-42 Nirala Nagar
Lucknow 226020
Tel: +91 (0)522 787159
Fax: +91 (0)522 787159

INTACH Art Conservation Centre
71 Lodhi Estate
New Delhi 110003
Tel: +91 (0)11 4641304
Fax: +91 (0)11 4611290

INTACH Chitrakala Parishath Art
Conservation Centre (ICKPAC)
Kumar Krupa Road
Bangalore 560001
Tel: +91 (0)80 2250418
Fax: +91 (0)80 2263424

ICI Orissa Art Conservation Centre
State Museum Premises
Bhubaneswar 751014 Orissa
Tel: +91 (0)674 432638
Fax: +91 (0)674 409209

ICI Art Conservation Centre
Rampur Raza Library
Rampur 244901 UP
Tel: +91 (0)595 325045
Fax: +91 (0)595 340548

ICI Mehrangarh Art
Conservation Centre
Mehrangarh Fort
Jodhpur 342001
Tel: +91 (0)291 548790
Fax: +91 (0)291 548992

NRLC (National Research
Laboratory for Conservation
of Cultural Property)
Sector E/3, Aliganj
Lucknow 226024
Tel: +91 (0)522 328930 (conservation)
Fax: +91 (0)522 372378
www.nrlccp.org

Sri Lanka

Department of National Museums
PO Box 584
Sir Marcus Fernando
Mawatha, Colombo 07
Tel: +94 1 692092
Fax: +94 1 695366
www.mca.gov.lk/N_museum/
    national_museums.htm

Central Cultural Fund
212/1, Bauddhaloka
Mawatha, Colombo 07
Tel: +94 1 508960
Fax: +94 1 500731
www.mca.gov.lk/C_fund/
    cultural_fund.htm

Archaeological Department
Sir Marcus Fernando
Mawatha, Colombo 07
Tel: +94 1 695255
Fax: +94 1 696250
www.mca.gov.lk/D_archeo/
    dept_archeo.htm

South Africa

SAMA (South African Museums
Association)
National Office
PO Box 699
Grahamstown 6140
Tel: +27 (0)46 636 1340
Fax: +27 (0)46 622 2962
http://sama.museums.org.za

Directory of Museums
www.museums.org.za

Malta

MCR (Malta Centre for
Restoration)
Bighi, Kalkara CSP 12
Tel: +356 21 823290
Fax: +356 21 674457
www.mcr.edu.mt

SUPPLIERS

United Kingdom

Preservation Equipment Limited
Vinces Road, Diss
Norfolk IP22 4HQ
Tel: +44 (0)1379 647400
Fax: +44 (0)1379 650582
www.preservationequipment.com

Conservation Resources (UK)
Limited
Unit 1, Pony Road
Horsepath Industrial Estate
Cowley
Oxfordshire OX4 2RD
Tel: +44 (0)1865 747755
Fax: +44 (0)1865 747035
www.conservationresources.com

Conservation by Design
Limited
Timecare Works
5 Singer Way
Woburn Road Industrial Estate
Kempston
Bedford MK42 7AW
Tel: +44 (0)1234 853 555
Fax: +44 (0)1234 852 334
www.conservation-by-design.co.uk

United States of America

Archival Products
PO Box 1413
Des Moines, IA 50305-1413
Tel: +1 800 526 5640
Fax: +1 888 220 2397
www.archival.com

Conservator's Products
Company
PO Box 601
Flanders, NJ 07836
Tel: +1 973 927 4855
Fax: +1 973 927 4855
www.conservators-products.com

Conservation Resources
International, LLC
8000-H Forbes Place Springfield,
VA 22151
Tel: +1 800 634 6932
Fax: +1 703 321 0629
www.conservationresources.com

University Products, Inc.
517 Main Street
PO Box 101
Holyoke, MA 01041-0101
Tel: +1 413 532 3372
Fax: +1 413 532 9281
www.universityproducts.com

Canada

Carr McLean
Conservation Material Supplier
461 Horner Avenue
Toronto, ON M8W 4X2
Tel: +1 800 268 2123
Fax: +1 800 871 2397
www.carrmclean.ca

University Products of Canada
6535 Millcreek Drive, Unit 8
Mississauga, ON L5N 2M2
Tel: +1 800 667 2632
Fax: +1 905 858 8586
www.universityproducts.com

Australia

Artlab Australia
70 Kintore Avenue, Adelaide SA 5000
Tel: +61 (0)8 8207 7520
Fax: +61 (0)8 8207 7529
www.artlab.sa.gov.au

Conservation Resources
International (Australia)
Gate 1, 167 Hyde Road,
Yeronga, QLD 4104
AND
PO Box 6184
Fairfield Gardens, QLD 4103
Tel: +61 1300 132570
Fax: +61-73-848-5503
www.conservationresources.au.com

New Zealand

The Frame Place
932 Heretaunga Street, West Hastings
Tel: +64 (0)6 878 7505
Fax: +64 (0)6 878 7505
www.frameplace.co.nz

ArtZone
57 Hanover Street, Dunedin
Tel: +64 (0)3 477 0211
Fax: +64 (0)3 477 0211
www.art-zone.co.nz

Singapore

Singapore Art (Directory of
Art Suppliers)
www.singaporeart.org

South Africa

Art Board Creative National cc
Johannesburg
Tel: +27 (0)11 450 2418
Fax: +27 (0)11 450 2439
www.artboardcreative.co.za

INDEX

Numbers in *italics* refer to captions of the line drawings and photographs.